WEALTH MANAGEMENT

The Financial Advisor's Guide to Investing and Managing Client Assets

HAROLD EVENSKY, CFP

The Irwin/IAFP Series in Financial Planning

McGraw-Hill
New York   San Francisco   Washington, D.C.   Auckland   Bogotá
Caracas   Lisbon   London   Madrid   Mexico City   Milan
Montreal   New Delhi   San Juan   Singapore
Sydney   Tokyo   Toronto

McGraw-Hill

A Division of The McGraw·Hill Companies

Library of Congress Cataloging-in-Publication Data
Evensky, Harold
  Wealth Management: the financial advisor's guide to investing and managing client assets / Harold Evensky.
   p. cm. —(The Irwin/IAFP series in financial planning)
  Includes bibliographical references and index.
  ISBN 0-7863-0478-2
  1. Portfolio management — Handbooks, manuals, etc. 2. Financial planners. I. Title. II. Series.
HG4925.9.F94. 1997
332.6 — dc20   96-32590

Printed in the United States of America
  6789.DOC/DOC902109

CONTENTS

Chapter 9

Optimization   235

Chapter 10

Policy   281

Chapter 11

Manager Selection and Evaluation—Basics   301

Chapter 16

Philosophy   443

ACKNOWLEDGMENTS

This book began during the 1994 IAFP National Convention, in the very classy bar of the Boston Ritz-Carlton over glasses of very proper sherry. Amy Gaber and my partner Deena Katz persuaded me that I "had a book in me." I naively agreed. If I'd known in advance what I know now, I'd never have agreed. Writing a book is HARD! Luckily for me, I didn't know. The preparation of *Wealth Management* has provided me an opportunity to read, study, and, most important, think about the many 100s of books and articles I've accumulated over the years. It has been an intellectually exciting experience. To Amy and Deena, my everlasting appreciation for the push.

Now that I am an author, I understand the frustration writers must face in attempting to pen thank you's. So many people deserve credit for the reality of this publication. Without our clients (and friends) there would be no point to this book, so my first nod of thanks is to our clients. At my publisher, Irwin, in addition to Amy Gaber, I thank Amy Ost, my editor, for guiding me through the strange world of book publishing. To the extent the content is cogent, I give thanks to my many reviewers for their insightful comments—Diana Kahn, Jack Firestone, Matt McGrath, and Deena Katz each read and improved the manuscript many times. My other partners, Peter Brown and Robert Levitt, and my Alpha friends provided valuable suggestions in many areas. To the extent the content fails to please, the responsibility is solely mine.

Many thanks are due to my friends at Evensky, Brown & Katz. Bridget Nanette Moore not only successfully interpreted my hieroglyphics and typed the manuscript innumerable times but also offered insightful suggestions on both content and format. Also, without the EB&K family supporting (and coddling) me continuously, I would still be on page 1. So, a special thanks to Mena Bielow, Scott Wells, Lane Jones, Peggy Daley, and my own "Della Street," Tammi Wells.

Although much of the book reflects my own biases and opinions, I have included innumerable items of research, conclusions, recommendations, tables, and graphs that are the intellectual creation of others—ones I consider the best and brightest. Included in this list are the writings of my personal favorites—Charles Ellis, Peter Bernstein, and Mark Kritzman. I have taken great effort to credit everyone for his or her work and thoughts, for without their having shared with all of us, we could not grow as a profession. In addition, my personal thanks to all these professionals for so willingly sharing their knowledge with the rest of us.

Finally, a few very personal notes. To my parents, Herbert and Sylvia Evensky, thank you for being you and guiding me to be me. I have been one lucky kid to have y'all as parents. Thanks also to Peter Brown, ostensibly my partner, but in reality, much, much more. The closest I've ever come to describing how I feel about Peter is to think of him as my fairy godfather but that understates Peter's importance to me. And finally, thanks to Deena Katz, my partner, my wife, my best friend, and best of all, my bersherta.

HAROLD EVENSKY, CFP

> Short-term clients look for gurus. Long-term
> clients want sages. There are no gurus.
>
> —*Harold Evensky*

Welcome to *Wealth Management*. What you are about to read is a blend of a textbook, an investment process road map, a marketing story, lessons, opinions (lots of them), and recommendations based on the experience of a practitioner.

It is easy for a professional interested in portfolio or asset management to find and accumulate a library appropriate to the subject (references to the best sources will be provided throughout this book). There is a continuing stream of books published on the evaluation, selection, and management of individual stocks and bonds. However, for the holistic practitioner, responsible for orchestrating a portfolio of multiple managers, no books have yet been published. The only guidance has been to attend professional conferences and network with like-minded professionals. *Wealth Management* has been written to fill this need.

Perhaps a brief profile of the practitioners targeted by this book will help you determine if this book is for you.

- Those whose clients are individuals, pensions, or trusts with significant investable assets whose primary goal is to earn reasonable returns for the risks they are prepared to take.
- Those who advise clients on the development and/or implementation of an investment policy.
- Those who assist clients in the selection of multiple managers and/or mutual funds.
- Those who monitor and manage multiple asset class investments for client portfolios.
- Those who call themselves financial planners.
- Those who provide financial planning services.

Even if your primary profession is as a comprehensive financial planner, accountant, insurance specialist, investment advisor, securities broker, trustee, or lawyer, if you are involved in advising clients about investing and/or managing multiasset class portfolios, this book has been written for you.

FINANCIAL PLANNING AND WEALTH MANAGEMENT

One of the most confusing issues for the public (and many professionals) is distinguishing between the profession of money management, the pseudoprofession of asset management (also referred to as portfolio management), and the profession of wealth management. In order to proceed without further semantic confusion, I will define these terms as they will be used in this book.

MONEY MANAGERS

Money managers are professionals responsible for making decisions regarding the selection of individual bonds and/or stocks for a portfolio. The money manager offers the client an expertise, a philosophy, and a style of management.

How then does the customization required of the wealth manager differ from that of the money manager? The difference relates not to the resources or the demographics of the clients but to rather the differences in their goals. As already discussed, wealth management clients' goals vary over a wide spectrum; money manager clients' do not. If money managers present themselves to the market as experts in the investment of large-cap domestic equities, they may well define their goal as providing a risk-adjusted return superior to the S&P 500. Hence, all investors selecting that money manager should have, by definition, the same goal.

The money manager informs the public of his expertise and philosophy and invites investors to trust him with investment dollars. It is the investor's responsibility to determine how much of his portfolio to allocate to a particular asset class (e.g., intermediate corporate bonds) and the money manager's responsibility to do a competent job of managing the funds in that class.

For example, the manager might have expertise in intermediate corporate bond management and a philosophy that value can be added by his unique analytical ability to discover value through the analysis of underlying but unappreciated credit qualities. The money manager's focus is on the asset class of his expertise. His efforts are devoted to the process of successfully implementing his philosophy. In the case of the corporate bond manager described above, it may be through a detailed study of bond indentures, corporate earnings statements, and corporate earnings prospects.

The practice of a money manager is focused and institutional. He is focused on the implementation of his philosophy. His goal is to maximize return. He is an "institution" in that he expects to be measured against other institutional managers in his asset class.

Much of the confusion in separating these two professions results from the fact that many practitioners perform both roles. Nevertheless, each profession entails separate responsibilities and requires different areas and levels of expertise.

ASSET MANAGERS/PORTFOLIO MANAGERS

These are new marketing titles that have emerged as a result of the media hype associated with the popularization of the research of Brinson, Hood, and Beebower[1] and others regarding the importance of asset class diversification. Along with the proliferation of inexpensive optimizers and packaged model portfolios, the marketing appeal of becoming an asset manager has been overwhelming for many practitioners. In theory, an asset manager differs from a money manager in that the former is focused on multiple asset class portfolios whereas the latter concentrates on individual securities in a single asset class.

Unfortunately, in reality many self-proclaimed asset managers are neither competent to implement recommendations based on optimizers nor trained to intelligently evaluate and select from the multitude of predesigned models offered to practitioners by the "middle man" packagers. Finally, many self-proclaimed asset managers are not professionally educated to adequately integrate the unique needs of the client with the portfolio design. The title *asset manager* suggests a pseudoprofessional. A typical ad reads "Complete Turnkey System Allows Your Brokers to Be Totally Dedicated to Marketing and Sales!" A practitioner falling into this classification should either read further and strive to become a wealth manager or return to the field of his primary expertise.

WEALTH MANAGER—A NEW PROFESSION

Generally, most professionals whose practices have evolved into wealth management are experienced financial planners. Having been involved for years with financial planning organizations, I have little doubt that wealth management is a specialty of financial planning. However, there continues to be an ongoing debate as to who is a financial planner. In order to avoid arguing the issue, I've elected to call this new profession (or financial planning specialty) *wealth management.*

As is the case with any professional financial planner, the wealth manager's focus is the client. His efforts are devoted to helping clients achieve life goals through the proper management of their financial resources. Whereas the money manager may not necessarily know if his client is male or female, single or married, a doctor, lawyer or candlestick maker, the wealth manager will know all of this, as well as the client's dreams, goals, and fears. As a financial planning specialist, the wealth manager designs a client-specific plan. In doing so, he is concerned with data gathering, goal setting, identification of financial (and nonfinancial) issues, preparation of alternatives, recommendations, and implementation of and periodic reviews and revisions of the client's plan.

The practice of the wealth manager is holistic and individually customized. It is holistic because there is very little about the client's global fiscal life that is not important information. He is a customizer because success is measured not by performance relative to other managers (he does not try to maximize returns) but rather by the client's success in meeting life goals.

INVESTMENT PLANNING TODAY

Clients' unique needs come in an almost endless array of combinations. There is no generic client for the wealth manager. Much of the popular literature offers two forms of modeling guidance for investors—multiple choice and life cycle investing. Both are carried over from the institutional concept of a model portfolio.

A major function of the wealth manager is to advise clients on the allocation of their investments across different asset classes. In order to place the contents of this book in perspective, consider the simplistic advice that is currently proffered to the investing public.

MULTIPLE CHOICE INVESTING

One form of asset allocation advice is based on scoring the results of a simple investor questionnaire. The process may be so basic that the investor simply has to select, from among a series of descriptions, the single phrase that most closely represents his goal. The following is an example:

- My objective is to have minimal downside risk.
- My objective is long-term growth of capital and an income stream.

Other simple questionnaires may have from 5 to 25 questions. The following two questions are taken from a 9-question quiz offered by a mutual fund company:

- I have funds equal to at least six months of my pay that I can draw upon in case of an emergency. Yes scores 1 point; No scores 0.
- Does the following statement accurately describe one of your views about investing?
  The only way to get ahead is to take some risks.
  Yes scores 1 point; No scores 0.

LIFE CYCLE INVESTING

An increasingly popular offering is to relate the portfolio allocation decision to the client's stage of life; hence, *life cycle* investing. As I will frequently remind the reader, this is a useful concept for a sociologist but dangerous if applied to the unique needs of individual clients. The life cycle concept tends to institutionalize the belief that age is the paramount, if not the sole, criterion to be considered when designing an investment portfolio.

One of the most popular formulas, designed to provide a stage of life allocation, is:

Investment in stocks = 100 – current age of investor
Investment in bonds   = Balance of investor's assets

The following are examples of this technique:

Age	Stock	Bonds
40	60%	40%
55	45	55
80	20	80

In fact, this is such an easy rule of thumb that it has become one of the most often-quoted suggestions in the popular media and has helped institutionalize the concept of life cycle investing.

Unfortunately, the popular press is not the only supporter of age as the simplistic default solution. The examples below, from a college investment text, reflect a similar academic institutionalization of age as the major portfolio allocation criterion. Although the text refers to investors as "preferring" and "favoring" or being "principally concerned with" certain goals, the conclusion drawn by most readers is likely to be that an investor's age should be the primary determinant of portfolio allocations:

> The middle-age client (middle 40s), is seen as transitioning his portfolio to higher-quality securities, including, 'Low-risk growth and income, preferred stocks, convertibles, high-grade bonds, and mutual funds.'
>
> Investors moving into their retirement age are described as having portfolios that are '*highly conservative* [their emphasis], consisting of low-risk income stock, high-yielding government bonds, quality corporate bonds, bank certificates of deposit (CDs), and other money market investments.'

I will reserve for later a discussion about the wealth manager's concepts of "higher quality," "low risk," and "conservative." They differ significantly from the usage here. Suffice it to say that these canned approaches for planning the financial welfare of our clients are woefully inadequate.

WEALTH MANAGEMENT VERSUS MULTIPLE CHOICE AND LIFE CYCLE INVESTING—AN EXAMPLE

The premise of this book is that there is a professional solution for the investment planning needs of our clients—namely, *wealth management.* Today, much of the advice offered the investing public fails to meet the standards of wealth management.

The following example of two demographically and sociologically similar families will set the stage for the balance of the book and place in perspective the positive difference professional guidance can make for our clients.

The Browns and the Boones

Data

The Browns live in Denver and are working professionals. Both husband and wife are 57 years old, both are in good health, and they expect to retire together when they reach age 62. Our other couple, the Boones, also live in Denver and are working professionals. Both husband and wife are also 57 years old, both are in good health, and they, too, expect to retire together when they reach age 62. Both couples consider themselves moderately conservative. Neither the Browns nor the Boones have any desire to leave an estate.

It takes little imagination to envision personal circumstances that would lead a wealth manager to recommend radically different allocations for the Browns and Boones. For example, through comprehensive data gathering, a wealth manager might learn the following:

Client Wealth and Retirement Goals

	Current Investments	Preretirement Savings (Per Year)	After Tax Standard of Living	Social Security
Browns	$ 800,000	$20,000	$57,000	$12,000
Boones	1,000,000	0	73,000	12,000

Wealth Manager's Assumptions

Based on discussions with his clients and his own research, the wealth manager would also bring to the process his assumptions regarding future inflation and other related issues.

Inflation	4.0%
Social security COLA	3.0%
Life expectancy (Joint)	90
Bonds—expected after tax returns	5.8%
Stock—expected after tax returns	8.8%

Recommendations

With this information about the demographically twin couples, let's see how successfully multiple choice and life cycle solutions would serve the Browns and Boones compared to the recommendations of a wealth manager.

Allocations

First, we must determine the recommended investment allocations. For this example, I have used the published recommendations of a large investment advisory firm, an accounting firm, a major trust company and the recommendation determined by the "100" formula for clients meeting the profile of the Browns and Boones. Also included are the recommendations a wealth manager might make after completing a capital needs analysis. Table I–1 is a summary of these recommendations:

T A B L E   I-1

Asset Allocation Recommendations for the Browns' and Boones'
Multiple Choice and Life Cycle Models

	Stock	Bonds
Investment advisory firm	30%	70%
Accounting firm	80	20
Trust company	50	50
100 – age	43	57

Note that the recommendations above are the same for the Browns and the Boones. Clearly, the demands the Boones will make upon their retirement portfolio are significantly greater than the Browns'. The fact that their ages, risk tolerance, employment, home, health, and planned retirement dates are similar is irrelevant. Based on the data of these simplified cases, the wealth manager's recommendations will differ significantly for each couple.

Wealth Manager Recommendations

	Stock	Bonds
Browns	35%	65%
Boones	65%	35%

Expected Outcome

With the additional information gathered by the wealth manager, we can complete a capital needs analysis for each of the recommended allocations, and determine the likely success of the recommendations. Table I–2 summarizes these results. The column labeled Overfunded/Underfunded is the estimated excess or shortfall in the clients' portfolio at age 90. This is a measure of the success or failure of the recommendations.

T A B L E   I–2

Brown and Boone: Capital Needs Analysis of Various Portfolio Recommendations

	Stock	Bonds	Overfunded/Underfunded	
			Browns	Boones
Wealth Manager				
Browns	35%	65%	0%	
Boones	65	35		0%
Investment co.	30	70	$ 60,000	$1,500,000
Accounting firm	80	20	2,600,000	1,000,000
Trust company	50	50	800,000	700,000
100 – Age	43	57	500,000	1,000,000

Obviously, the wealth manager's recommended allocations not only differ significantly for each couple; they differ from the multiple choice and the life cycle models. These canned solutions fail miserably to provide useful guidance for the Browns and Boones. Multiple choice solutions are simplistic and unprofessional. They are a poor way to plan for a client's future. As noted earlier, life cycle planning, as a concept, may work well for a sociologist dealing with large populations. However, translated to the micro level of individual clients, it results in families consisting of 2.3 children and 1.8 parents.

The differences in the recommendations above can be explained by the fact that in spite of similar demographics and similarities in superficial investment beliefs and constraints, the Browns and Boones have significantly different resources and goals. Although this example may seem trivial, it demonstrates the dangers of simplistic solutions for investment planning and the financial planning basis of proper wealth management.

Whatever a wealth manager calls himself, a competent professional must in fact be following the financial planning process.

WHAT COMES NEXT

The balance of *Wealth Management* will discuss issues of importance to the wealth manager. The depth and nature of coverage of these issues will vary significantly.

Some areas assume an existing familiarity with the subject and only highlight specific issues (e.g., client goals and constraints). Other discussions assume a familiarity but also assume that a review may be helpful (e.g., the mathematics of investing). When there are existing references readily available on the subject, *Wealth Management* provides an overview and will guide you to them (e.g., development of an investment policy). Some issues are well covered by other texts; however, there are particular aspects that deserve special attention. In these instances, in addition to referencing the other work, *Wealth Management* will focus on these special issues (e.g., asset allocation and sensitivity analysis). For issues that are not covered by traditional texts, this book will cover the subject in more depth (e.g., heuristics). In all areas, I have extensively referenced the discussion so that you may read further on a subject you find of interest.

I have attended innumerable professional meetings and have read uncounted articles and books on subjects related to my practice. All too often I've been left with the thought, That's nice, now what do I do with it? If there has been one overriding goal in the preparation of this book, it has been to avoid leaving you the reader with that thought. *Wealth Management* provides immediate and practical assistance for the practitioner. It includes far more than theory and philosophy. At the practice management level, it includes detailed examples of risk tolerance questionnaires, data gathering guides, client reports, and recommendations regarding hardware and software. For use in investment implementation and management, I have included examples of manager questionnaires and specific recommendations for fund selection criteria and asset class rebalancing criteria. Throughout are examples and vignettes that practitioners should find helpful in client presentations and meetings. At a professional level, *Wealth Management* includes many recommendations regarding what I consider investment myths (e.g., tax management, "income" portfolios, and intuitive optimization). My conclusions may contradict the strong convictions of many readers. The purpose is not to pick a fight. You may take my recommendations for what they are worth to you. The purpose is to assist readers in developing a clear philosophy and process that will work for them in their practices.

As you can see, *Wealth Management* is eclectic. It is neither an academic textbook nor a comprehensive practitioner manual. It is some of both and more. It most closely resembles a series of essays on the most important issues for a wealth manager. These essays are integrated, by general subject matter, into a series of chapters. The chapters generally follow the wealth management process. My goal is to assist the reader in becoming a better and more profitable (emotionally and financially) wealth manager. So, make the book work for you. Skip, jump, or plow straight on through. There are no rules—only what works for you.

WEALTH MANAGEMENT PROCESS

The flow chart on the following page is a pictorial representation of the wealth manager's contribution to the financial planning process, and it will serve as a road map for the balance of this book. Reflected in this road map is the primary characteristic of wealth management—it is client driven.

ENDNOTES

1. G. L. Brinson, R. Hood , and G. L. Beebower, "Determinants of Portfolio Performance," *Financial Analysts Journal,* July/August 1986, pp. 39–44.

The Process of Wealth Management

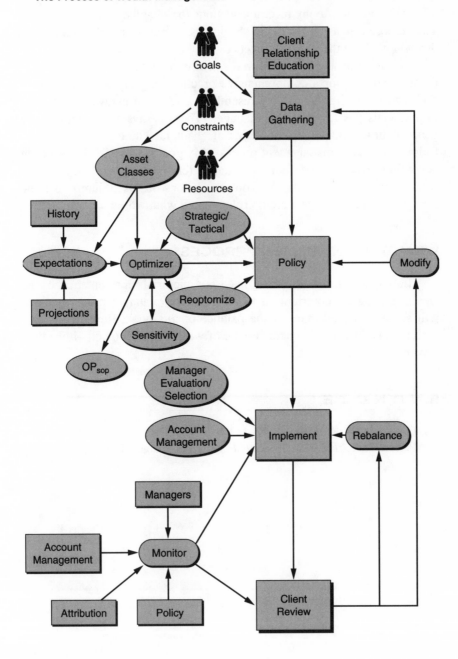

CHAPTER 1

Client Goals and Constraints

Change is the investor's only certainty.

—*T. Rowe Price, Jr.*

As discussed in the Introduction, everything is client driven. The process begins with the formal establishment of the client relationship. Even at this early stage, the wealth manager must customize the process to reflect the client's personal experiences. This would include not only obvious factors such as his* investment experience, but significant personal circumstances such as marital status and motivation (e.g., recent divorce, impending retirement, fiduciary considerations).

GOAL SETTING

Individuals, if they think about goals at all, tend to think of goals as very generalized. For example, a typical client, when asked about his goals, might respond as follows: Well, I really would like to be able to pay for my children's education, retire, and enjoy my retirement.

This rather simplistic response misses all the major attributes necessary for an advisor to begin the planning process—namely, the attributes of specificity and priority. Goals must be time and dollar specific and prioritized. The first step in the process of wealth management is for the client to

---

*The choice of the masculine gender is used as an expedient. Please read it to mean hers/her/she or his/him/he.

1

define his goals with specificity. It is the responsibility of the wealth manager to educate the client in this process.

Goal setting is an integral part of the wealth management process. It is, in fact, the foundation on which all subsequent work depends. The following discussion will address in great detail the issues involved, examples of various types of goals, problems related to recognizing and quantifying goals, and suggestions for assisting clients in resolving these issues.

HIDDEN GOALS

When asked about their goals, clients not only fail to provide specificity; they frequently neglect to include many critical issues—goals I will refer to as *hidden goals*. In particular, issues related to risk management seem so obvious that they are rarely consciously considered as explicit goals. Certainly, if anyone were asked directly, they would agree that they have the goal of avoiding financial devastation as a result of having been found at fault in an auto accident. By the same token, most would agree that, without having to devastate their investment portfolio, they would like to replace their home should it burn down in a fire.

Obviously, although not stated, it is a primary goal of all individuals to cover those risks that might overnight destroy their fiscal lives. As such, it is necessary to address these issues at the beginning of the investment planning process. Wealth management requires that these hidden goals be clearly defined and quantified in order to assure that adequate reserves are available to pay the cost of risk management. Although it may not be the wealth manager's responsibility to determine the total extent and cost of risk management, it is his responsibility to refer clients to other appropriate professionals. Only after adequate reserves have been set aside to cover the client's risk management needs will the wealth manager be able to determine what resources are available for long-term investment.

> *Five Year Rule*—One of the fundamental beliefs of our practice is that no investments should be considered unless the time horizon for the funds in question is at least five years (i.e., roughly an economic cycle). We have captured this in a mantra that we repeatedly drum into our clients' subconscious: "Five years, five years, five years." This constraint should overlay all investment decisions.

The second category of hidden goals is the "rainy day" reserve. Once a determination has been made as to the extent and cost of formal risk management—i.e., cost of insurance—there is still an exposure to uninsured risks and unexpected emergencies or opportunities.

Perhaps the most obvious of these would be the funds required to maintain a family's standard of living in the event of the incapacity of a primary breadwinner until such time as the more formalized risk management (i.e., disability insurance) begins to provide a supplemental income stream for the family. Other less depressing examples would include funds to help a child take advantage of a new business opportunity or to supplement the tuition cost for a son or daughter unexpectedly accepted by a prestigious medical school.

For the purposes of the wealth manager, the hidden goals are first priority. The resources needed to fund appropriate insurance coverage and emergency reserves must be quantified and set aside in appropriate liquid investments.

INTERMEDIATE GOALS

Only after determining and quantifying the cost of the hidden goals can the wealth manager assist the client in moving to the next category, the intermediate goals.

A client's intermediate goals are those that are consciously anticipated, are finite in time, and, generally, will be completed before retirement. These would include college education, weddings, second homes, yachts, and trips around the world.

These are goals that a client can typically describe (e.g., the statement in the example above, I'd like to pay for my child's education). However, the descriptions usually lack three cardinal criteria necessary for goal setting and wealth management—namely, time specificity, dollar specificity, and priority.

For example, to plan for funding the cost of a college education, it is necessary to determine the number of years before the beginning of funding, the length of the funding, and the amount of the funding. The funds required for a college education goal may vary by orders of magnitude depending on any one of these specific attributes.

LIFETIME (RETIREMENT) GOAL

The last of the three major goal categories is generic for all investors: the lifetime goal of financial independence. Retirement planning is unique in its lack of uniqueness. Clients have different hidden goals. Some clients may need 3 months cash flow reserves; others 12 months. Some clients may need disability insurance; others may not. Some may need life insurance; others may not. Intermediate goals are also unique to each client. Most individuals, however, wish to reach financial independence. At that point, their investment portfolio should provide the income needed to maintain their standard of living. The commonness of the goal does not eliminate the need for time and dollar specificity and prioritization. The client who says, I want to retire and keep on enjoying the quality of my life after retirement, has at least elucidated the retirement goal. Still, the wealth manager remains in a quagmire of uncertainty as to how long that retiree may need funds and what *quality of life* means to him. Quantification of time for the retirement goal includes not only the age that an individual wishes to retire but, for a married couple, if both were working, retirement age of each, as well as each of their life expectancies. Quantifying a retirement goal in numbers is far more complex than simply stating, I need $40,000 a year to live. The following is a discussion of some of the major factors.

Living Expense Classes

The dollar amount of living expenses must be separated into four possible, different classes. The following breakdown is based on the National Endowment for Financial Education's (NEFE) excellent advanced studies program on retirement.

Ongoing Increasing Expenses (Basic Living Expenses)

These living expenses are expected to increase annually with inflation. In some cases it may be appropriate for the wealth manager to break this class down into subclasses; for example, subclasses representing those expenses expected to increase in parallel with the Consumer Price Index (CPI), a subclass for those expenses expected to increase at a much higher rate (e.g., medical costs) and a subclass for those expected to increase less than the CPI.

Limited Duration Level Expenses (Fixed and Terminal)

This includes that component of retirement living expenses that does not inflate with inflation, and, in fact, terminates before the client's expected mortality. The most obvious example is a home mortgage. One of the most dangerous errors made in retirement planning is the application of a simple, single inflation factor to a client's projected required retirement living expenses. This is a simplifying assumption endemic to most retail retirement planning software and much of the professional software.

Consider a client whose preinflation retirement goal is $60,000 per year. Using an inflation assumption of 4 percent, a future value calculation shows that this individual would need almost $90,000 to maintain the same standard of living after 10 years. Would the conclusion be different if the $60,000 requirement were composed of $40,000 inflatable living expenses and $20,000 for three more years of home mortgage (principal and interest) payments? Of course it would; in fact, in 10 years, the client would only require $60,000 to maintain the same standard of living. Obviously, the consequences of "simplifying" assumptions can lead to worthless conclusions.

Ongoing Level Expenses (Permanent/ Noninflatable) and Limited Duration Increasing Expenses (Terminal/Inflatable)

These two last categories of expenses, although encountered less often, still arise. When they do, they need to be treated appropriately. The first class includes expenses that are likely to be permanent but will not be subject to inflation. An example is a principal and interest payment on a mortgage that is likely to extend beyond the client's life span. The last class includes expenses that are expected to terminate before expected mortality but will inflate before their termination. Examples include adjustable rate mortgages, college tuition, parent care, travel, and even weddings.

Mortality

I once had a client who balked at extending his fixed income maturities to five years. His excuse was, "I'll never live that long." As a professional wealth manager, I've perfected my response to clients who threaten me with dying early. My answer is: "Go ahead, make my day!" The purpose of this answer, in addition to trying to make light of a difficult subject, is to emphasize that my client's real risk is not dying, but living "too long." I explain that my clients become like family and the thought of losing any of them is painful; however, what keeps me awake at night is the fear that they will outlive our planning. This may seem like a silly conversation, but I frequently find that it serves as one of those rare "Aha!" times, when the client's eyes light up.

Long-term planning for my 70- or 80-year-old client now makes sense to him or her.

Because of the importance of incorporating a time frame into the planning process, the last item of specificity necessary is an estimation of mortality. Bruce Temkin, a highly respected consulting actuary, has made a minicrusade out of educating advisors on the importance of considering heredity in the retirement planning process. As he has so frequently and eloquently pointed out, the use of a standard actuarial table is a poor way of setting specificity for a client's expected mortality. The dominant factor is the client's unique gene pool. To address this aspect of estimating a client's mortality, it is important to query the client regarding the mortality of his closest blood relatives.

The silliness of the approach many advisors take on this issue was best pointed out by a story told by Lynn Hopewell, a respected and well-known wealth manager. It seems Lynn had worked long and hard in the preparation of a plan for a client. This client was an engineer. Lynn anticipated that the engineer would be both interested in and capable of evaluating the details of the plan itself. As Lynn, too, was trained as an engineer, he felt quite comfortable with the detailed mathematics involved in completing his work. Indeed, he was quite proud of the product and looked forward to making a presentation to his client. During the presentation, Lynn felt pleased with the client's questions and his own ability to answer those questions with confidence. The engineer clearly appreciated the quality and mathematical rigor of the plan that Lynn had prepared. Once Lynn had completed his full presentation, he and his client sat back for a wrap-up discussion. Lynn was looking forward to the praise he believed was well deserved for a job well done.

Indeed, the client did begin by complimenting Lynn on his work and the quality and depth of the calculations and presentation. He then added that he did have one little question that was disturbing him. Lynn invited the engineer to ask his question. The client said, "I think I understand this. If I do, it seems to me that this plan is designed to assure that I have adequate funds for the balance of my life." Lynn answered, "Yes, that's true." The client then said, "And if I understand how you arrived at how long I'll need those funds, you used a mortality table." Lynn said, "Yes, that's true. In fact I used the most widely respected and most current of all mortality tables." The client then said, "I appreciate that, and if I understand the way those mortality tables work, they are based on the general population. The age you chose indicates that I am likely to have died by then." Lynn said, "That's absolutely right." The client then said, "And what the mortality table means is that on the average, a man my age will have died by the chart's mortality age." Lynn said, "Absolutely correct." The client then said, "What confuses me is that it seems that you've designed a plan that I have a 50 percent chance of outliving."

Lynn was absolutely floored, but in keeping with the honest and professional person that he is, he answered, "That's right."

The point of the story is certainly not to pick on Lynn Hopewell, who is undeniably one of the finest wealth managers in the country. In fact, it is primarily due to Lynn's personal efforts that advisors today (including our firm) no longer make that mistake. The point to be made is that setting retirement goals with specificity requires the most thoughtful efforts of both the advisor and the client. In terms of mortality, it is well to consider that not only will using a standard mortality figure lead to a 50 percent probability of the client outliving the plan but, in addition, most individuals who have the resources to pay for the advice of a wealth manager also have the resources to pay for better health care and nutrition than the population used to develop the mortality tables. Table 1–1 is the mortality table currently used in our practice.

In most cases, the wealth manager will be peripherally involved in the determination and resolution of the hidden goals. They may or may not be involved in the determination and resolution of the interim goals. In most cases, however, the retirement goal will be the primary guide in the wealth management process. For this reason, a major component of a wealth manager's analytical toolbox needs to be a detailed and competent knowledge of capital needs analysis as well as appropriate analytical software. Because of the importance of the capital needs analysis, it will be discussed in greater detail in Chapter 4, Data Gathering.

GOAL PRIORITY

Once the client, with the advisor's assistance, has determined time and dollar specificity for his hidden, intermediate, and retirement goals, it then becomes necessary to prioritize those goals. Frequently, the client's list of goals includes funding for college education and paying for a child's wedding. These are in addition to the goals of risk management and retirement. Although it might seem reasonable to assume that clients would prioritize the hidden goals first, the intermediate goals second, and retirement third, advisors do not deal with "average" clients. They deal with unique individuals (who are

T A B L E   1-1

Mortality Table
Retirement Planning Mortality Projections

			Probability			
Current Age	**Sex**	**IRS Unisex**	**70%**	**80%**	**90%**	**95%**
50	M	83	88	91	95	98
	F	83	92	95	98	101
55	M	84	89	92	96	99
	F	84	92	95	98	101
65	M	85.5	89	92	96	99
	F	85.5	93	95	99	101
70	M	86	90	93	96	99
	F	86	93	95	99	101
75	M	87.5	91	93	97	100
	F	87.5	93	96	99	101
80	M	89.5	92	95	98	100
	F	90.5	94	97	100	102
85	M	91.9	94	95	99	102
	F	91.9	95	98	101	103

frequently anything but "average" or "reasonable") and they also deal with clients who lack an understanding of the entire process of goal setting, risk management, and retirement planning.

For example, simply due to a lack of knowledge, many clients misprioritize their risk management. They carefully provide for adequate life insurance and ignore their need for disability coverage. Others will attempt the frequently impossible task of funding independently for a multitude of goals without having any reason to believe that they will have the resources to fully fund all of those goals. In some cases, clients will misprioritize their goal planning as a result of a lack of understanding of the rules and regulations of investments and their related tax consequences.

Misprioritizing—An Example: A simple but common error found with younger investors is confusion between the prioritization of their college funding goal and their retirement goal. Consider a young couple with their first new child, desirous of planning for college funding. Further assume that although both parents are working, the most that they can save on a yearly basis is $4,000. Both the husband and the wife qualify for fully deductible IRAs.

It is likely that in this scenario, the family would begin saving funds for their child's education either in their own name or in a uniform transfer to minor's account for their child. If an advisor were to suggest that they consider making contributions to their IRA account, it is likely that they would respond that they can't do that because they plan on using the funds for their child's education. If asked why they could not utilize their IRA account to fund their child's education, they are likely to respond that it is a retirement account and can't be used for education. Even if they are aware that the funds are available to them but subject to a 10 percent tax penalty, they are unlikely to have considered that the possible deferred compounding for 18 years might well offset the tax penalty.

So far, the example has focused on the possible tax efficiency of using an IRA for college funding accumulations. Still to be addressed is the question of the prioritization of the goals. Suppose that with the assistance of the wealth manager, it is determined that the couple will be unable to fully fund both their college education and the retirement goals. The unconscious default assumption is usually that the college funding should be accomplished first and the retirement funding second. Certainly, an argument can be made for this prioritization. The number of years between college funding and retirement is frequently of such length that it is difficult to make reasonable projections. Thus, there is a significant likelihood that during the period, savings could be increased. If the decision is made early to reduce funding of the college education in order to fully fund retirement, later it may be too late to reverse that decision.

In spite of the compelling logic of prioritizing college before retirement funding, it is important to keep in mind that clients are unique. There are clients who believe that it is appropriate for their children to take responsibility for their college costs. These parents would rather err on the side of overfunding their retirement goal.

Prioritization is the client's responsibility. It is the wealth manager's responsibility to assist the client in understanding the consequences of his choices.

CONSTRAINTS

Having completed the education of the client relative to the time and dollar specificity of goals as well as their prioritization, the wealth manager can then begin the education process of the client with respect to his unique constraints.

For each of the goals, the constraints include the client's time horizons, the goal's liquidity and marketability requirements, the client's personal tax environment, his risk tolerance, and existing resources. The balance of this chapter will discuss time horizon, liquidity, and marketability. The next two constraints—risks and taxes—are so complex that they have been allotted their own chapters. As information regarding a client's current resources is captured through the data gathering process, a discussion of this constraint is deferred to Chapter 4, Data Gathering.

TIME HORIZON

The time horizons will have been established by the goal setting process. Having educated the client on the necessity of determining time specificity for each of his goals, including the mortality determination for retirement planning, the client will have not only an understanding but an ownership in the time horizon for each of his goals.

Later, we will revisit the issue of time. First, as time horizon is so integrally related to the issue of risk management, it is also discussed in Chapter 4's section on Risk Evaluation Questionnaire. Second, Chapter 7, Investment Theory, will address the debate over the risk reduction by time diversification.

LIQUIDITY AND MARKETABILITY

Once the client has completed the process of defining his goals with time and dollar specificity, he can then intelligently determine the levels of liquidity and marketability necessary for each of those goals. For example, the goal of an adequate emergency reserve certainly requires the attribute of liquidity. An investor should not place his emergency reserves in the equity market or an intermediate term bond fund. Their moderate liquidity is an inappropriate attribute for the time horizon of an emergency reserve.

The descriptions of liquidity and marketability are often used interchangeably. The concepts described by the terms *liquidity* and *marketability* are all too frequently confused by investors, media, and advisors. In order to avoid semantic confusion, for purposes of this discussion, they will be defined to describe very specific attributes of investments. The descriptions used here were originally developed by NEFE (at the time, the

College for Financial Planning) during the early stage of their education programs for certified financial planner candidates.

Liquidity is an attribute of an investment that measures the ability of an investor to readily convert that investment to cash, independent of any changes in the economy, without risk of principal loss. Liquid investments would include money market funds, T-bills, cash (by definition), and most fixed annuities.

Marketability is an attribute that measures an investor's ability to readily convert an investment to cash. Note that marketability does not come with the qualification, "without risk of principal loss." Marketable investments would include high-quality stocks and bonds and open-end mutual funds. They may be readily converted to cash, but with no assurance of returning the client's investment.

The experience of many years as a host of a call-in investment radio program in Miami taught me, all too clearly, the dangers of misunderstanding the attributes of liquidity and marketability, as defined above.[1] During periods of falling interest rates, I frequently had conversations like the following:

"Hello, Mr. Talk Show Host, I just bought a Ginnie Mae. What is it?" The caller, we'll name her Ms. Wells, was a widow living on Miami Beach and had recently received the proceeds of a maturing jumbo CD (i.e., $100,000). She was very unhappy when quoted the new, lower, CD renewal rate. As a result, she had responded to one of the many brokerage firm ads that tend to crop up during periods of low interest rates (i.e., one advertising safe investments with much higher returns).

Once in the salesman's office, Ms. Wells was presented with a recommendation to purchase a Ginnie Mae (derived from GNMA, which stands for Government National Mortgage Association). The marketing material and the salesman's pitch addressed all of her concerns. She was assured that not only was the interest rate being paid on the Ginnie Mae much higher than the current rate on CDs, but also, like the CD, was government guaranteed. For a conservative investor, there is nothing so musical to the ear as the phrase *government-guaranteed*.

Lest a potential client miss the point, the marketing material typically had a full-color American flag on one side, a picture of apple pie on the other side, and the phrase *government-guaranteed* printed in 80-point type. Generally, the sale was consummated at this point. If Ms. Wells had asked the question, "What happens if I want to sell?" the salesman would employ the "arm around the shoulder" close. This requires him to get up from behind his desk, walk over, put his arm comfortingly around the client and say, "Don't worry, Ms. Wells, if you ever want to sell, just give me a call and we will sell it that very instant." If she had not been convinced before, she is convinced now.

A few days later, while listening to a call-in investment talk show on her radio, Ms. Wells, realizing she really doesn't know what a Ginnie Mae is, calls a total stranger (me), and asks me what she just bought with her $100,000. I proceed to explain the nature of a Ginnie Mae: Although it is, indeed, guaranteed, the investment is subject to interest rate risk. I further explain that this means that if interest rates rise over the next few years and should she wish to sell, she might receive less than her original investment. At this point, Ms. Wells very confidently informs me and 250,000 other listeners that although it might be true of other people's Ginnie Mae, it is not true of hers. Upon asking her why, she patiently explains to me that the salesman said she could "sell whenever she wanted to." Ms. Wells heard "liquid"; the salesman meant "marketable." The sequel to that story (and many, many similar calls) is that interest rates subsequently rose significantly. As a result, there were many Ginnie Mae investors who were unpleasantly surprised at the precipitous drop in value of their government-guaranteed investment.

The emotional trauma suffered by these investors was a direct result of not understanding the difference between liquidity and marketability. The statement of the salesman describing the investment—namely, that it was guaranteed and that the client could sell whenever she wished—was quite true. However, for the average investor, it was very misleading. Most individuals equate the ability to sell when they want with the ability to get their original investment back. Although this is true of a liquid investment, it is not true of a marketable investment.

Another example, familiar to advisors who have been in business for many years, is the case of the retiree, a Mr. Trujillo, who sat down with me and asked what to do with the funds from a maturing CD. It seems he had been rolling over his one-year CDs, and as rates had continued to drop, his income had also continued to drop. He made it quite clear to me that he was extremely concerned about risk. I suggested that he might want to consider a five-year CD. Mr. Trujillo turned so pale that I was concerned for his health, and he told me quite seriously, "Sonny, at my age, long term is a green banana." I explained that if his comfort level for an investment horizon was only one year, there was really no good alternative to the one-year CD that he currently owned. He then gave me a look that suggested that I had no idea what I was talking about. It seems his neighbor had just recently purchased a preferred utility stock, paying almost twice what his one-year CD was paying. He had expected me to make a similar recommendation. I started explaining that if he was uncomfortable with a 5-year maturity, he might be significantly less comfortable with a 5-million-year maturity. I thought my use of the 5-million-year maturity, in lieu of trying to explain an infinite maturity on a preferred stock, was an effective way of emphasizing the point. I was wrong. Mr. Trujillo was not persuaded. He responded that I really did not seem to understand the investment market. Everyone knew that the company issuing the preferred stock that he wished to buy was a big, well-known utility. Their shares traded every day on the New York Stock Exchange. He could sell whenever he wished. Once again, a tragic confusion of the concepts of liquidity and marketability.

The final confusion that relates to the attributes of liquidity and marketability is the investor's common practice of assigning moral judgment to the attributes themselves.

The thought process is that marketable investments are "good"; illiquid investments are "bad." It is common to hear these moral adjectives applied to the spectrum of investments. It is imperative, as part of the education process, for the wealth manager to clarify, for his client, that liquidity and marketability are different attributes of investments. They carry no moral connotation. The wealth manager must guide his clients to evaluate investment attributes in terms of "appropriate" and "inappropriate" instead of "good" or "bad."

Once a client has a solid understanding of the constraints of liquidity and marketability, he will be an infinitely better investor as well as an infinitely better client.

INCOME PORTFOLIOS: THE MYTH OF DIVIDENDS AND INTEREST

The myth of the income portfolio is so closely related to the concepts of liquidity and marketability that a short divergence at this stage seems useful. One of the most insidious and erroneous paradigms adversely affecting portfolios of individual and institutional investors is that of the income portfolio (the *myth*). The term *myth* is used here and in later discussions to describe what I believe to be an unfounded and false belief. The *myth*, rooted in a historical heritage dating back to 12th-century England's land rents, is that investors must construct portfolios that generate dividends and interest (i.e., not touch principal) in order to receive cash flow.

The *myth* is also frequently exacerbated by the myth that retirees are on a fixed income. Wealth managers should disabuse clients of this notion. To the extent that the retiree depends on Social Security, these payments are adjusted annually for inflation, they are not fixed. To the extent that the retiree's income is dependent upon his investment portfolio, he is at risk if he buys into the *myth* and constructs an income portfolio. The problem is that the *myth* is wrong! An income portfolio is "fixed" by design—inappropriate design. An income policy enforces an inappropriate constraint on portfolio design that, in almost all cases, will result in an inferior portfolio. In many instances, it will lead to the design of a portfolio that is not only inefficient but one that will not allow the client to accomplish his goals.

Consider a very simple world in which there are only three investment alternatives—money market, bonds, and stock. These investments have the following expected returns:

Investment	Interest	Dividends	Capital Gains	Total Return
Money Market	5%	0%	0%	5%
Bonds	7	0	0	7
Stock	0	3	10	13

In this world, as in our world, there are likely to be investors with many different cash flow requirements.

Consider Ms. Kahn who has no cash reserve requirement but who needs a 5 percent cash flow per year. What are her investment choices if she is constrained by the myth?

As reflected in Table 1–2, if Ms. Kahn's cash flow has to be generated solely from dividends and interest, the maximum allocation to stock that will accomplish that goal is 50 percent. Any allocation to stock in excess of 50 percent will result in a cash flow of less than her 5 percent requirement.

Table 1–3 considers a number of possible constraints that might face a client such as Ms. Kahn. For example, Scenario #1 corresponds to the need reflected in Table 1–2. Scenario #4 assumes a need for a 5 percent cash flow but also a need for a 15 percent cash reserve. The column labeled "Maximum Equity Allocation" is the maximum percentage that

T A B L E   1–2

Allocation Alternatives for Ms. Kahn

Bond Allocation	Cash Flow From Bonds	Stock Allocation	Cash Flow From Stock	Total Cash Flow
100%	7.0%	0%	0%	7.0%
90	6.3	10	0.3	6.8
80	5.6	20	0.6	6.2
70	4.9	30	0.9	5.8
60	4.2	40	1.2	5.4
50	3.5	50	1.5	5.0
40	2.8	60	1.8	4.6

T A B L E   1–3

Allocations According to the *Myth*

Scenario	Cash Reserve Requirements	Cash Flow Required by Ms. Kahn	Maximum Equity Allocation	Wealth Manager's Equity Allocation
Ms. Kahn #1*	0%	5%	50%	60%
Ms. Kahn #2	0	6	25	60
Ms. Kahn #3	0	7	0	60
Ms. Kahn #4	15	5	43	60
Ms. Kahn #5	15	6	18	60
Ms. Kahn #6	15	7	0	60

*This corresponds to Ms. Kahn's needs as reflected in Table 1–2. It is one of the six scenarios.

could be invested in equities and still result in the portfolio dividend and interest payments meeting the client's needs. The last column is the wealth manager's recommendation for equity allocation based not just on Ms. Kahn's cash flow and reserve but also on her long-term goals.

This table dramatically demonstrates the fallacy of constraining a portfolio to meet the requirements of the *myth*. For all of the scenarios, the wealth manager has determined that taking into consideration the client's need for cash reserves, current income, *and* long-term goals, the portfolio should be 40 percent bonds and 60 percent stocks. A client, heeding the advice of the person designing the portfolio to meet the cash flow requirement by matching it to dividends and interest, would always have a significantly lower allocation to equities. Of course, the consequence of ignoring the recommendations of the wealth manager is likely to be that the investor will run out of financial resources long before she runs out of the need for those resources. In other words, myopically following the *myth* is likely to render the investor destitute long before her death.

Step away from the paradigm of dividends and interest. Focus instead on total return. Without the constraint of the *myth,* it becomes much easier to balance the need for current cash flow with the need for long-term growth. First design the portfolio for the required total return. Then design a strategy to provide for the necessary cash flow from the portfolio's dividends, interest, *and capital gains.* A simple solution is to intermittently sell a portion of the portfolio equal to the amount necessary to meet cash flow needs. In the case above, the investor would follow the wealth manager's advice and invest in a portfolio of 40 percent bonds and 60 percent stocks. Her portfolio would have an expected total return of approximately 8.1 percent. As necessary, she would liquidate adequate resources to provide herself with a cash flow of 5 percent per year. In addition to meeting her cash flow requirements, the remaining 3.1 percent of portfolio growth will meet her long-term needs.

EXAMPLES

Yield Sacrifices Total Return

This simple example was presented by Roger Gibson at the 1992 IAFP Advanced Planners Conference. It may be useful in introducing your clients to the conflict between yield and real returns:

	Portfolio Mix		
	#1	#2	#3
Vanguard Bond Market Fund	100.0%	50.0%	0.0%
Vanguard Index Trust 500	0.0	50.0	100.0
Portfolio Yield	7.3	5.1	2.9
Portfolio Appreciation	0.0	4.0	8.1
Portfolio Total Return	7.3	9.1	11.0
Anticipated Inflation	4.0	4.0	4.0
Sustainable Real Withdrawal Rate	3.3	5.1	7.0

Historical Real World Example

The following is based on actual historical returns for two investors, Mr. Jones and Ms. Bielow. This example may be used to vividly demonstrate the unfortunate consequences of ignoring total return in their cash flow planning.

On December 31, 1984, Mr. Jones decided to invest $100,000. His current cash flow need, after tax, was $5,400. Following the advice of friends, Mr. Jones was told that to get the cash flow he needed, he should look for a good bond fund, as stock fund dividends were too low. After some investigation, he selected Fidelity Intermediate Bond fund. It had a good record and seemed conservative. He invested $100,000 and requested that the interest be paid out and the capital gains be reinvested.

At the same time, Ms. Bielow also decided to invest $100,000. She also needed $5,400 current cash flow, after tax. Ms. Bielow consulted with a wealth manager and, after discussing her needs, she agreed that she needed the cash flow to keep up with inflation. She and her wealth manager discussed her risk tolerance and finally decided on a balanced portfolio. The investment was split—$50,000 to Fidelity Intermediate Bond fund and $50,000 to the Vanguard Index 500. She requested that dividends, interest, and capital gains be reinvested. She would obtain her cash flow by annually liquidating shares to pay the taxes due on the funds' earnings and $5,400 (adjusted for inflation).

Figure 1–1, Relative Cash Flow, plots the excess or shortfall between the cash flow received by the investors and the cash flow required to pay taxes and maintain a real return of $5,400 (in 1984 dollars). It shows that Ms. Bielow annually received her desired cash flow. Mr. Jones, however, did not fare as well. His cash flow was quite volatile. In the first two years, the income from the fund was less than he required. For the next three years it generated an excess (which he placed in money market and drew down to supplement future fund shortfalls), and for the last five years, once again it paid less than he needed.

Figure 1–2, Portfolio Value, shows the growth of the two portfolios. In addition to having provided a consistent cash flow, exactly meeting her needs, Ms. Bielow's portfolio grew in value. This provided her with the security that she would very likely be able to maintain the inflation-adjusted cash flow she needs in the future. Mr. Jones' portfolio grew very little. He faces the future very vulnerable to further inflation erosion of his cash flow. In fact, at the end of 1994, in order to meet his cash flow needs, he had to liquidate $2,974 of the fund.

Relative Cash Flow

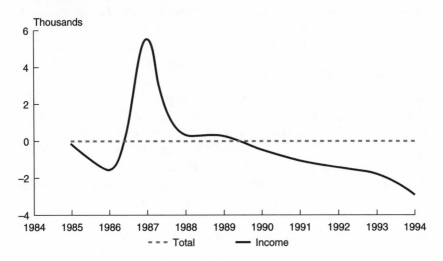

Portfolio Value

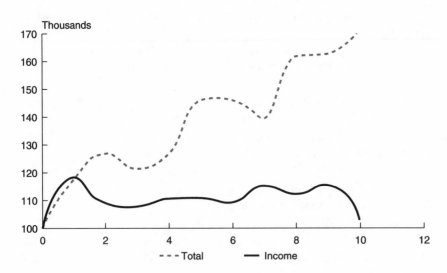

The two major arguments against moving from an income port-folio to a total return portfolio are that the income portfolio is more tax efficient and that the total return portfolio is subject to market volatility. These arguments do not hold up under any historically rea-sonable scenario.

Regarding taxes, there are strategies that can reduce unnecessary trading (an example of one follows). Perhaps more important, an income portfolio is an inherently tax-inefficient strategy for generating cash flow. Cash flow from dividends and interest is subject to the ordinary income tax rate.[2] Cash flow from capital gains is taxed at the lower capital gains rate. The bigger the difference between these two rates, the bigger the rel-ative tax drag on the income portfolio.

Market volatility is a serious concern when designing a strategy to obtain cash flow from a total return portfolio. The real risk is more psychological than financial. There is a real likelihood that the client will at some point be "dipping into principal." Psychologically, this can be a disturbing event. It is, unfortunately, a reality of investing. Part of the solution is client education. In addition, there are strategies that may minimize the client's concern. One used at our firm is dis-cussed below. The financial risk is temporary. Over the planning hori-zon, if the cash flow demand is reasonable relative to the targeted total return, the portfolio value will recover and continue to grow. In fact, Figure 1–2 demonstrates, it is the income portfolio that has real vul-nerability to market volatility.

EB&K CASH FLOW STRATEGY

As the balancing of cash flow and growth is a common problem, we have developed the following strategy.

I discussed earlier our firm's five-year mantra; it serves as the basis for this strategy. Namely, we want to have a significant time window (preferably five years) before having to sell a potentially volatile invest-ment. If we simply sold investments quarterly or annually to meet our cli-ents' cash flow needs, there would be little flexibility. We might be forced to liquidate positions when their value was down. In addition, in order to keep the portfolio in balance, we would have to sell very small percent-ages of many investments.

Our solution is to set up, for our clients, a second account that we title the "cash flow reserve account." We do not charge a fee for this account. It is funded with two years' worth of the client's anticipated cash flow need. For example, if we were to open an investment account for a client requiring a 5 percent annual cash flow from a $1,000,000 investment account, we would open two accounts:

Cash Flow Reserve Account	$100,000
Investment Account	$900,000

This accomplishes a number of goals:

- The client is comforted that we have accounted for his cash flow needs.

- The client has total control over the timing of the withdrawal of the funds from the cash flow fund.*

- We are not accepting funds for management that we know we may have to return in just a few years.

- The client is not paying us a management fee for funds that we would soon be returning to him. After all, we tell him that he is paying us a fee for long-term management. Naturally, the client particularly appreciates this part of the strategy.

- Our clients are not affected by the following problems typically associated with the paradigm of interest and dividends:
  Myth investors are psychologically locked into an artificial cash flow straitjacket. They let the volatility of the markets determine their standard of living. They are likely to constrain their current standard of living rather than "dip into capital," even during periods of exceptional market growth. They spend all of the cash flow during periods of high interest rates and find it extraordinarily difficult to adjust their standard of living downward when rates cycle down.

- Clients invested in income portfolios are likely to be disturbed by a reduction in their monthly cash flow, when market changes result in lower interest rates, or when fund managers adjust their portfolios to reduce dividends or interest.

---

*Our experience is that most clients significantly overestimate their regular cash flow needs. It seems that if they are going to "give up control" of their portfolio to a wealth manager, there is a comfort factor in receiving a cash flow return. A big lump sum cash flow reserve (i.e., $100,000 in this case) is an even bigger comfort factor. The result is that the "two-year" reserve typically lasts much longer than two years.

- Marketing hype often seduces the investor into products offering high current returns at the expense of total returns (e.g., high current payments generated by premium bonds) and into products offering high returns generated either by aggressive investing (e.g., high-yield bonds, emerging market debt) or aggressive strategies (e.g., a heavy concentration in volatile derivatives).

Having set aside a cash flow reserve, we discuss with our clients the likely timing of their draw-down needs and we design a simple investment plan for the cash flow account. In cases where the client is very unsure of his needs, we may recommend starting with 100 percent in money market. For most clients the funds will be laddered using money market and T-bills and/or short- and limited-term, high-quality, low-volatility bond funds (e.g., Solon, Compass Capital, Vanguard, Federated, DFA). We structure this account and monitor the balance; however, as noted earlier, we do not bill the account. This cash flow management is part of our "value added."

We formally review our investment accounts quarterly. At that time we also review the status of the client's cash flow account. If, in the normal course of events, we find a need to trade in the investment account, we use this opportunity to transfer funds from the investment account to the cash flow account, bringing the cash flow account back up to the two-year reserve. If we see no need to adjust the investment account and the cash flow account has at least six months' worth of reserves, we will generally not make any transfers. In our experience, in the normal course of rebalancing, changing managers, adding asset classes, adjusting for new client funds, and so on, there has never been a problem in maintaining the client's cash flow reserve between six months and two years.

We are pleased that our strategy has been successful for many years, but our standard is the 1973–1974 bear market. Although we do not project such a market, we believe it represents a historical reality that few investors and probably none of our clients remember. In order to account for this possibility, in addition to the two-year reserve, our investment portfolio design builds in a second tier of emergency liquidity. This is the short end of our fixed-income ladder.

With the exception of our maximum growth portfolios, we typically allocate between 10 and 15 percent to maturities of under five years. Thus, even during an extended bear market, we could provide for many years of additional cash flow without being forced to sell a position at a significant loss. We, not the market, remain in control.

Our cash flow clients sleep well, they do not press us to chase after unrealistic cash flow products, they do not monitor interest rate changes on an hourly basis, and they take market volatility in stride. Their mental security comes from being able to see, on their statements and in our reports, many years of available cash flow, reserved for that purpose and invested in liquid securities that are effectively immune to the short-term ravages of stock or bond market volatility.

Although we believe that the effort is worth the results, the strategy we employ obviously adds time and cost to our handling of the client's account. A far simpler implementation strategy would be to simply set up an automatic percentage payment from the funds to the client. Although less tax efficient, it is still a superior solution to that of the *myth*.

MY OPINION

The wealth manager should discard the concept of equating the need for cash flow with a need for dividends and interest. He should eschew the concept of the income portfolio. In its place, the wealth manager should design a portfolio's asset allocation for total return. After the allocations have been made, he can then determine the most efficient strategy for generating the necessary cash flow.

The next two chapters continue the discussion of the client's constraints, with a detailed focus on special issues related to risk and taxes.

ENDNOTES

1. My partner at the time, Jeff Kassower, was the show host. He invited me to join him and thus provided me the opportunity to spend many years "attending" the best school for learning about client psychology that exists— talk radio.
2. Obviously, municipal bonds will generally provide tax-free returns, however the income will be lower.

CHAPTER 2

Risk Is a Four-Letter Word

Security is mostly a superstition, it doesn't exist in nature.

—Helen Keller

Risk drives returns.

—Charles Ellis

Fear of risk is probably the client's most restrictive investment constraint. One of the unique contributions of the wealth manager is the ability to assist his clients to effectively grapple with the frightening specter of risk. It is the one constraint that most often prevents him from achieving his life's goals. This chapter will provide the wealth manager with information and insights that will assist him in better communicating with and educating his client about risk.

Any serious discussion of risk is likely to be reminiscent of the story of the Tar Baby. Once you touch it, it gets awfully sticky. Unfortunately, the issue of risk in all its complex, inconsistent, and disagreeable manifestations is perhaps the single most important concept in the universe of wealth managers. Fortunately, it's an interesting story.

Before the development of probability theory, the issue of "investment" risk was moot. After all, the gods either did or did not provide rain for the crops. The concept of risk implies an ability to assume or avoid risk. For our ancestors, things (e.g., rain) either happened or did not happen. With the development of the concept of probability came the modern concept of risk.

For the modern wealth manager the seminal event was the 1952 revelation of Harry Markowitz. "I was struck with the notion that you should be interested in risk as well as return." In hindsight, this seems a fairly obvious observation, but Dr. Markowitz was awarded the Nobel Prize in 1990 for his work that evolved from this simple notion. If you accept that risk is largely an issue of psychology, an even earlier observer, Benjamin Graham, the father of fundamental investment theory, alluded to the importance of risk management when he said, "Investment decisions are 25 percent intelligence and 75 percent psychology."[1]

Charles Ellis, one of my personal investment idols, admonishes that risk management is the responsibility of the advisor, and Peter Bernstein, another personal idol, provides the sobering reminder that risk is in the "eyes of the beholder and the eyes may be myopic."

Clearly, if risk is such an important concept and its management is the responsibility of the wealth manager but its meaning varies for our clients, it is imperative that a wealth manager understand the psychology of risk. This chapter provides a framework for communicating with clients regarding risks and evaluating client's risk tolerance. Chapter 4, Data Gathering, will discuss the application of client risk tolerance evaluation, including a description of EB&K's distillation of this information in terms of our firm's risk tolerance questionnaire.

PSYCHOLOGY OF RISK

People are strange. There is no more apparent example than the psychology of risk. People, in general, and clients, in particular, have difficulty distinguishing between knowledge-based risk and foolhardy speculation. Usually they grossly overestimate their knowledge. Even when provided with good data, they are poor mathematicians of probability.

Clients have difficulty estimating the risks of future events. They are much more comfortable with short-term events where they have more intuitive confidence in their knowledge. This results in a tendency to overstate their own personal risk-taking propensity.

Cognitive psychology tells us that individuals have difficulty processing large amounts of information. A technique they use to reach conclusions is setting bounds and designing a framework for decision making. Nobel laureate Herbert Simon describes the bounds as:

- Knowledge
- Rational thinking

- Values
- Emotions

HEURISTICS AND OTHER MENTAL SHORTCUTS

The client's unique bounds form the psychological structure within which his decision making emanates. Even within this decision-making framework individuals have very limited ability to process large amounts of information. In order to manage quantity and complexity of information, the technique employed in decision making is the use of heuristics. In the language of cognitive psychology, heuristics are cognitive rules of thumb that simplify the decision-making process. More simply, they are mental shortcuts.

As the reader will learn from the following, many common heuristics are modified to become investing heuristics that guide the client's perception of investment risk. By understanding the nature of heuristics, a wealth manager will be able to better understand the underlying issues influencing a client's risk tolerance (e.g., confusion about certainty and safety). Also, the wealth manager will be more effective in assisting the client to modify misleading heuristics, as well as a better educator and guide for his clients in the useful application of these mental shortcuts.

Clients frequently misuse heuristics. For example, the quantity, quality, speed, and immediacy of information provided by regular financial reporting sources such as *The Wall Street Journal* and *Wall Street Week,* overwhelm other information in memory and result in an unwarranted extrapolation of the immediate information into the future.

While heuristics are often valuable and frequently enable an individual to make quick and sound decisions, they can be dangerously misleading. In a sense, heuristics are analogous to mathematical optimizers in that they may maximize error. We tend to overemphasize information that is minimally relevant while minimizing important information. We overestimate our skill and knowledge, we overestimate predictability, and we believe we use far more data to make our decisions than we really do. By using shortcuts in the decision-making process, we magnify the impact of these errors.

As you read the following, consider how you can use the information to revise the tools you currently use to educate your clients (e.g., new graphics), to gather information (e.g., reframe questions in your risk tolerance questionnaire), and to confirm or modify your own personal investment philosophy (e.g., passive investing). For a reader interested in a more in-depth discussion, the most important work in this area is by Daniel Kahneman, Paul Slovic, and Amos Tversky[2] and the proceedings of the AIMR Continuing Education Conference "Behavioral Finance and Decision Making Theory in Investment Management," edited by Arnold S. Wood.*

Representativeness

Estimated Future Probability = f (similarity to past events)

This is an easily recognized and easily applied shortcut. It assumes that the probability of a future event is directly related to its similarity to past events (i.e., predicting the future from the past).

The risks of blindly following representativeness include:

▪ Similarities are often superficial and do not successfully extrapolate over time. Assuming it won't rain tomorrow because it didn't rain last week is a good way to get soaked.[3] Assuming a hot stock won't go down tomorrow because it did not go down last week is also a good way to get soaked.

▪ Similarities may be significant but short term. This can lead to confusing short-term trends within long-term cycles. Hot stocks may be hot, but not profitable.

A related risk is known as the *gambler's fallacy*. This is the belief that in a fair toss a coin landing on heads is more likely after a long run of tails. Representativeness is poor protection against the laws of chance. In spite of these problems, our clients, without our guidance, will use representativeness as an investment guide.

Examples include buying only Morningstar 5-Star Funds, abandoning an asset class (e.g., emerging markets) after it has sustained a loss, or following the advice of the currently successful gurus.

The following are examples and strategies that the wealth manager may find useful in educating clients regarding the danger of a naive dependence on the representative heuristic.

▪ Given the following series of coin flips, which is the more likely?

Series A: HHTHTTTHTH
Series B: HHHHHTTTTT

---

*AIMR is an invaluable source of information for the wealth manager. A catalog of its publications can be ordered from AIMR, c/o PBD, Inc., 1650 Blue Grass Lakes Pkwy, Alpharetta, GA 30201, or through internet @ http://www.aimr.com/aimr/pub/cat/form.html.

In this case, your client is likely to feel very sophisticated in his decision-making process. He knows a coin toss is a random event. Therefore, his heuristic is that randomness will continue; hence Series A is more likely. In fact, they are equally likely because each of the 10 tosses has a probability of 50 percent heads and 50 percent tails.*

▪ Sylvia, 31, single, outspoken, and bright, majored in philosophy. As a student she was concerned about issues of social justice and frequently participated in protest demonstrations. Which is more likely?[4]

A. Sylvia is a bank teller.

B. Sylvia is a bank teller and active in the feminist movement.

If your client is like the majority of respondents in a psychological study using a similar question, he will choose *B*. His shortcut will tell him that the similarity of Sylvia's background to the qualification in *B* is so strong that it most clearly describes her current status. Mathematically, however, choice *B* is a subset of A and cannot be more probable.

The examples above highlight the tendency to emphasize case data over base data. Base data are the underlying reality (i.e., the statistical data of the universe under consideration) and case data are the overlaying story. Many psychologists believe that our information processing system is more attuned to vivid and emotional case data than cold, statistical base data; hence, we tend to overemphasize case data.

▪ A panel of psychologists interviewed a sample of 30 engineers and 70 lawyers. They summarized their impressions in short notes about each of these individuals. The following description was selected at random from the sample:

"Herbert is 39 years old. He is married with no children. His father and grandfather were practicing engineers and his hobby is building miniature villages." Is he more likely to be an attorney or engineer?

Psychologically, once again, the most persuasive information is the case data. It certainly suggests that he must be an engineer. However, the controlling factor is the base data. Seventy percent of a total sample of 100 are lawyers; therefore, there is a much greater probability that Herbert is an attorney.

---

*The result of each toss is independent of the previous toss. There is no memory. For the 10 events in each series above, there are 1024 unique, specific outcomes and the probability of any specific outcome is 1/1024. Thus, not only are the two series above equally likely; a series of HHHHHHHHHH or TTTTTTTTTT would be equally probable. Obviously, using common sense as represented by the use of the representative heuristic may get an investor in trouble.

▪ Consider how investors relate to new stock issues.

A nightly business show anchor reports that the new issue of Techno Industries is highly recommended for purchase by a number of brokerage firms (case data).

A research study reports that 70 percent of new technology issues are lower in price 12 months after their first issue (base data).

Guess which report is likely to be more impressive to the average investor. The belief that they will profit from the purchase of a new issue is driven by the story (case data), not the reality or relative success of new issues (base data). Emphasizing case data over base data typically results in buying high and selling low.

Investment professionals such as Warren Buffett have certainly learned to avoid this trap. High-technology companies are visibly successful and garner much media spread, especially compared to insurance companies. Guess which one Buffett buys.

Availability

Estimated Future Probability = f (information in memory)

This mental shortcut is based on using what comes to mind. It is obviously much easier and faster to make a decision based on what we know now, as opposed to taking the time to research and analyze the history we may not accurately remember. As a result, there is a tendency to overemphasize recent information. The good story of the case data also plays a role in availability. After all, everyone remembers a good story (e.g., technology) far longer than a boring story (e.g., insurance).

A classic example, useful for client education, follows:[5]

▪ Ask your client to picture a word that includes the letter k in its spelling. Then ask if the letter k is likely to be the first letter in the word or the third?

Few of your clients will pass this test. The letter k is three times as likely to be the third letter. Most people searching their memory will find it easier to think of words like *know* and *king* than *acknowledge, make,* and *like.*

MENTAL ACCOUNTING

This can be thought of as mathematics for the brain. Like the math we learned in school, mental accounting has its own form of adding, subtracting, and estimating. It makes a maze look logical. A wealth manager must be adept at its intricacies in order to provide guidance to his client.

Adding and Subtracting

Subtracting costs more than adding. Investors place higher psychological value on losses than gains. This results in a reluctance to *cut losses* (i.e., realize losses). Such an action requires an emotionally charged negative entry into the mental account. It also tends to focus the investor on the individual security and away from the total portfolio.

Techniques for dealing with this include:

▪ For a client still holding a loss position, reframe the question in terms of what would he do with the cash? The obvious question is, Would you buy the stock? Often the answer is, No, it's a dog. With that acknowledgment, the client may have a new and more flexible perspective.

▪ For a client who has agreed to sell, albeit reluctantly, focus the client on the benefits of the trade and the value of the asset purchased with the sale proceeds. The tax savings generated by a bond 'swap' is a classic example of this strategy.

Estimation

The less likely the long-term payoff, the more likely mental accounting will overestimate its probability. Mentally we tend to construct our future estimates on the basis of a series of shorter-term estimates. It seems safer and more accurate to evaluate the probability of individual events than an entire series.

The following example demonstrates the conflict between this form of mental accounting and probability theory.

▪ Hot Tech, a company your client is considering investing in, has a new product under review. If they can get government approval they will develop a prototype. Your client thinks approval is a no-brainer and assigns it a 90 percent probability of success.

Once they start to build the prototype, he estimates the probability of success to be 90 percent. They then propose to build a plant to test the market regionally. He estimates a 90 percent chance of success for the regional test. Once successfully marketed regionally, Hot Tech plans on rolling it out nationally. Your client remains optimistic and once again estimates a 90 percent chance of success.

In order to make an investment in Hot Tech, your client needs to feel confident that the company has a good chance of a successful national launch of its new product (i.e., at least a 75 percent chance). Does he invest? The client's mental arithmetic results in his concluding that the investment has a 90 percent chance of success. He would not only invest but would brag to all his friends about his astute analysis.

Assuming the client's estimates of success for each step in the process are correct, the actual estimate of success is:

$$0.9 \times 0.9 \times 0.9 \times 0.9 = 65.5\%!$$

If there are only three more steps in the chain, each with a 90 percent probability of success, the overall probability of success falls to *less than 50 percent!* Detail in the analysis may make the chance of ultimate success seem real, but it is not reality.

Multiple Accounts

A final interesting twist to mental accounting is the creation of multiple independent accounts. Examples would include classifications based on how the client obtained the funds (e.g., savings account or inheritance) or the nature of the account (e.g., IRA).

Unless there are legal restrictions relative to ownership interest (e.g., Uniform Transfer to Minor Accounts or irrevocable trusts) this form of mental accounting places arbitrary and potentially counterproductive restrictions on the development of an investment policy. Your client should be educated regarding the importance of viewing *all* his investable assets as a part of his *total portfolio.*

Small versus Large Samples

Investors tend to place significant but inappropriate faith in small samples. For example, the success one friend has investing in convertibles may lead to an assumption that convertibles are the place to be. Extrapolating continued success from a short run of extraordinary performance is the same math that results in an investor's moving funds to the "hot manager of the week."

Try the following test to assist your client to understand the danger of small sample math:

Coin #1 was tossed 10 times and landed on heads 8 times.
Coin #2 was tossed 100 times and landed on heads 75 times.

Which coin is likely to be more "honest"?

Coin #1—Although it landed on heads, as a percent of tosses, more times than coin #2, the sample was so small that the results are not statistically meaningful.
Coin #2, however, was tossed enough times to suggest that the probability of its being an "honest" coin is remote.

A POTPOURRI OF OTHER HEURISTICS
AND MENTAL SHORTCUTS

Contagious Enthusiasm

This is the twin brother of bandwagon jumping and the first cousin to the greater fool. When an investment story is hot, the simplest mental shortcut is to follow the crowd. Success at this stage depends on simple luck. When the froth gets so crazy as to become a mania, luck is no longer adequate. Future profits depend on finding a greater fool to sell to when you want out.

The role of the wealth manager is to protect his client from making decisions based on these guides. In this case, in addition to general education, there are a few effective techniques.

- Framing the consequences in a personal way.

1. If you are right, you will make a handsome profit.

2. If you are wrong, you will have to work an extra three years.

- Contrarian exercises entail developing scenarios that would lead to other outcomes. A special case is a scenario that leads to the opposite outcome known as the *reality check*. This is a variation of a technique attributed to Louis Rukeyser. It is another form of framing. It takes the focus off the blind acceptance of the positive by asking the simple question, What could go wrong?

Usually, a client's investing is based on contagious enthusiasm and he has not stopped long enough to consider what can go wrong. Frequently this question is all one needs to bring him back to reality.

Confirmation Bias

The trouble with managing money is that
everyone once made a successful investment.

—Gary Helms

This is a set of blinders an investor may wear after making an investment. It assures him that he will only see information confirming his original judgment. The wealth manager has two responsibilities regarding this bias. First, assume the responsibility of removing the client's blinders. Second, and even more important, the wealth manager must assiduously guard against wearing his own blinders.

Regret, Pride, and Shame

Investors frequently endow their investments with personal characteristics and empower their investment decisions with social commentary.

The mental imperatives of good and bad are frequently applied to investments. It may be as global as, I don't invest in stock, it's risky (i.e., bad), or, more specifically, I don't want to buy that stock, it's a dog!

The result is an avoidance of investments that in the broad sense of a total, diversified portfolio are appropriate. Instead, the investor ends up with an inappropriate concentration of "good" investments (e.g., insured municipals).

Investment decisions are empowered with social commentary when investors avoid actions in order to avoid looking dumb. Consider the investor who buys a "dog" stock (possibly a well-priced value stock) while his friend buys a hot and highly touted growth stock (an overpriced "story"). If they both lose money, the investor thinks he is stupid and his friend unlucky.

Anticipatory Regret

A related symptom is anticipatory regret. If an important decision can have a negative consequence (e.g., losing money), then to avoid the pain and shame of loss, the best solution may seem to be to do nothing.

This aspect of a client's investment psychology is often the most difficult with which to deal. It reflects an individual's core beliefs about his own personality. There are no simple solutions. During the ongoing education process from first meeting to last meeting, the wealth manager needs to help the client to continually air these issues.

Risk Tolerance = ƒ (Memory)

This is the infamous relationship, formally stated as: When risk becomes a reality, memory becomes short term. For the typical client, the formula for this relationship is:

Current Risk Tolerance = Normal State Risk Tolerance × Memory.
Memory = a number between "0" and "2."
Normal State Risk Tolerance = 50 (i.e., a balanced portfolio of 50% fixed income and 50% equities).

When equity market returns are high, memory becomes long term, approaching "2."

When market returns turn negative, memory becomes short, approaching "0."

Thus the normal client has a tolerance for 100 percent equities when the markets are up and 0 percent equities when market returns are negative!

The wise wealth manager discusses this important relationship with his client before investing.

MANIFESTATIONS OF RISK

It would seem that having to consider so many different aspects of the psychology would be an adequate foundation to begin the construction of a risk tolerance questionnaire, but it is not. The wealth manager must also consider the multiple manifestations of risk.

Perceived versus Actual

A classic example is improper tax management resulting from confusion of tax reduction and after tax maximization. The perceived risk is paying excess taxes. The real risk is the failure to maximize after tax returns.

Loss of Principal versus Loss of Lifestyle

This relates to the public's ongoing confusion regarding the need for inflation-adjusted returns versus the need for principal guarantees.

Nick Murray* cautions that risk is not implicit in the market but in the client and his emotions. This point is best made in one of Nick's many vignettes:

> When a client balks at making a risky investment in the stock market, Nick asks, "Whose side are you going to be on in the next Civil War?" The client is obviously confused by what seems to be such an insane question, but Nick explains that since it happened once it certainly can happen again, and since it's been so long already without repeating, it's likely to happen soon.
>
> When the client responds that Nick is talking nonsense, he says, "Of course and so are you." He then launches into his discussion of the "Great Anomaly."
>
> Most investors who fear the market and idolize the safety of guaranteed returns (e.g., treasuries and CDs) are driven by the great anomaly. This is more commonly known as Great Depression Mentality. There are two components of this paradigm.
>
> First, the religious belief that certainty is the equivalent of safety. As Nick points out, certainty of the return of principal is a measure of investment safety in only one economic environment—deflation. In any other economic scenario, the risk of investing is the erosion of purchasing power.
>
> The second is the expectation that, indeed, another Great Depression is just around the corner. Help your client view this expectation with historical reality.
>
> We have almost all the 100 years of the 20th century to look back on. Ask your client how many of these years had deflation greater than 1 percent. The answer is three. Then ask your client, what were those three years? The answer is 1930, 1931, and 1932. It was not just a period of deflation, it was *compounded* deflation. The bad news was that at the end of the three years, everyone was poor. It didn't matter what their store of value was—stock, home, chickens—all lost value. The good news is that it hadn't happened before, it's never happened since, and there is no reason to believe it will ever happen again.
>
> The wealth manager must clarify the importance of loss of lifestyle over loss of principal. The recommendation to buy equities is not for higher return but because they are one of an investor's *safest* assets.

Relative versus Absolute

This is a kissing cousin to the dangerous misuse of statistics. A few good examples to use with your clients are:[6]

> You are participating in a game of chance and are offered the following choices:

---

*Nick Murray is the profession's preeminent writer/speaker on practical client psychology.

A. Do not roll the dice and win $1,000.

B. Roll the dice and win $1,000 per spot on a rolled pair of dice.

If we use standard deviation as our relative measure of risk, choice *A* is clearly less risky. After all, choice *A* has a standard deviation of zero. If we are a little less myopic and look at absolute risk, *B* is clearly superior. If we roll the dice there is no likelihood of underperforming *A*.

Suppose the choice is:

A. Do not roll the dice and win $3,000.

B. Roll the dice and win $1,000 per spot on a rolled pair of dice.

We've now added an element of uncertainty regarding *B* superiority. However, the probability of *B* being the best choice is still 97 percent.

If those examples don't clinch your client's understanding, ask if crossing the street twice in one day instead of once really doubled his risk.

Relative versus Relative

Obviously a member of the same family as "Relative versus Absolute," this is the basis for the controversy between proponents of mean variance and semivariance.*

Mean variance is the traditional financial model for estimating risk, and standard deviation is the most common measure. Semivariance proponents argue that it is nonsense to worry about good variance (e.g., doing better than you expect). All the client and wealth manager should be concerned about is doing worse. Further, if the distribution of an investment return is not normal (as discussed in Chapter 7, Investment Theory), the recommendations arrived at based on downside loss (e.g., semivariance) will differ from those based on total variance (e.g., normal standard deviation).

Even if we resolve this dispute in favor of semivariance, there are additional questions to consider. What are we going to select as the criteria for loss: negative return, not keeping up with inflation, or not meeting a benchmark return? We will revisit this problem again in the discussion in Chapter 9, Optimization.

---

*If this is unfamiliar territory, you may want to skip ahead to the section on semivariance in Chapter 6, Mathematics of Investing. After you've read that entry, you can drop back to this discussion.

Risk Aversion versus Loss Aversion

One of the most effective questions we use in our practice is derived from the research of Tversky and Kahneman.[7]

Which of the two choices would you prefer?

A. You win $80,000.

B. You have an 80 percent chance of winning $100,000.

We then follow up with two additional choices:

A. You lose $80,000.

B. You have an 80 percent chance of losing $100,000.

Although theoretically less accurate than the psychologists' earlier work, we find this an amazingly powerful tool.

Almost without exception, our clients select *A* for series #1 and *B* for series #2. They clearly demonstrate that they do not wish to take risks to get rich, but they will take risks in order to avoid getting poor. We call this series of questions our "Aha," as frequently a conservative client's face lights up with understanding and he says, Aha! I understand! He understands that we might recommend the same percentage allocation of his portfolio to stocks as a broker, but for totally different reasons. A broker will usually recommend the purchase of stock "so we will make money!" while we are recommending stock so our client will not lose his standard of living to inflation. This simple question has converted many long-time CD enthusiasts into very patient and successful long-term investors. You will see this again in Chapter 4, Data Gathering, when we discuss the EB&K risk tolerance questionnaire.

ENDNOTES

1. Stanley Zarowin, "Investing Psychology Winners and Losers," *Sylvia Porter's Personal Finance* (July–August 1987), 50–55.
2. Daniel Kahneman, Paul Slovic, and Amos Tversky, editors, *Judgment under Uncertainty* (New York: Cambridge University Press), 1982.
3. Zarowin, 50–55.
4. Kahneman, Slovic, and Tversky, *Judgment under Uncertainty,* 1982.
5. *The AAII Journal:* 1983, ed. Maria Crawford Scott, Vol. 5 (Chicago: American Association of Individual Investing).
6. Kahneman, Slovic, and Tversky, *Judgment under Uncertainty,* 1982.
7. Kahneman, Slovic, and Tversky, *Judgment under Uncertainty,* 1982.

CHAPTER 3

Taxes

Pay tax on what you take, not what you make.

—Warren Buffett

As much as I would enjoy skipping the subject of taxes, I know that ignoring it would not make taxes go away. Although only the IRS and accountants truly appreciate the wonder and grandeur of taxes, the wealth manager must accept and deal with their reality. In considering what to include about taxes, I realized that not only are there volumes of books about personal tax planning, but whole libraries. Therefore, it would be absurd to attempt to provide comprehensive coverage in this book. My decision was to address, in no particular order, investment-tax myths, tax-related products, and strategies.

A number of myths concerning taxes and investments are endemic to modern investment planning. If the wealth manager is to provide competent guidance for his client he must eliminate myth-based planning from his repertoire. The most highly touted myths include reducing taxes, favoring gains over income, managing excise tax, favoring unsystematic risk over capital gains, including bonds in IRAs, and increasing risk with equities.* My favorite myth, active portfolio tax management, is saved for last. The myths are followed by a discussion of the most popular tax-related product—the variable annuity. The chapter concludes with a review of a number of popular tax strategies available under current tax law. Because of the

---

*You will have to keep reading to see what this has to do with taxes.

controversial nature of many of my conclusions, I have included a significant amount of reference material.

TAX REDUCTION

There are a number of issues important to a client's understanding regarding his personal tax constraints but none is more commonly misunder-
stood or a source of more bad advice than the myth of tax reduction. From
my experience, the single most common piece of investment advice provided to clients by noninvestment professionals is that they should reduce
their taxes. Not only is this among the most common advice, it competes
for the dumbest advice. For a wealth manager, clearly the issue is to maximize the after-tax income, not to reduce the taxes. Unfortunately, the
misunderstanding is rampant.*

Because investors generally feel that tax payments are lost dollars, there
is naturally an instinctive desire not to pay taxes. This is understandable, but
myopic vision results in inefficient investing. I find, in practice, that the most
effective way to clarify this issue is through a very simple example.

I present to my client a simple scenario similar to the following:

	Tax Free Investment A	Taxable Investment B
Return	$10,000	$14,000
Taxes	—0—	3,900

I then ask the client to look at the two investment alternatives that I
proposed and to choose the one that they might wish for themselves. In-
variably, in this simple scenario, the clients choose the taxable investment. When I point out to them that they are choosing an investment that
requires them to pay a tax of $3,900 and have rejected the investment that
is tax free, they answer that they will have more money left over from the
taxable investment after they pay taxes. This is obviously the correct response. Unfortunately, in circumstances any more complex than this, it

---

*Many years ago my wise dad told me, "Don't worry about taxes, they are easy to avoid. Just don't
   make any money."

becomes much more difficult to see the advantage of paying taxes. The wealth manager must keep his clients focused on after-tax returns.

GAINS VERSUS INCOME

Frequently a wealth manager must decide between high-dividend and capital-gains-oriented equity investments. The tax significance of this issue was best highlighted by a study in Sanford Bernstein's superb publication *Taxes and the Private Investor.*[1] The study demonstrates that a naive focus on tax efficiency would favor low-yielding stock simply because the tax rate on dividends is traditionally higher than the tax on capital gains. The naive solution is wrong. The error is the assumption of equal total returns for low- and high-yield equities.

Based on a 23-year history, Bernstein found that high-yield portfolios had an annualized total return of 14.3 percent (versus S&P of 11.3 percent) and low-yield portfolios had a return of 9.6 percent. In any bracket, the excess return of the high-yield portfolio overwhelmed the tax drag of the higher marginal rate on dividends.*

EXCISE TAX

For clients with significant pensions or profit-sharing accumulations, the impact of excise taxes becomes a major concern. As there are many factors that need to be considered in the selection of the most efficient strategy, simple rules of thumb often lead to erroneous conclusions. The common error is to accept that ancient piece of advice, "minimize the taxes paid." As mentioned earlier, at EB&K we have a risk tolerance mantra for investing: "five years, five years, five years." For tax planning our mantra is "maximize after-tax returns, maximize after-tax returns." The wealth manager concentrates on maximizing the after-tax return. He reserves talking about tax payments for political discussion where he can complain about the inept way in which the government is spending our money. Don't confuse the two discussions.

---

*This example is not to suggest that high-yield portfolios will always have a better after-tax
   performance; it does suggest that the wealth manager consider that all returns are not
   necessarily equivalent.

Peggy Ruhlin, a respected financial planner in Columbus, Ohio, presented an excellent example of a retirement plan excise tax analysis to a meeting of the Alpha Group.* Her hypothetical, but realistic case, follows.

RETIREMENT PLAN EXCISE TAX ANALYSIS– AN EXAMPLE

Background:

Dr. David Samuel's attorney asked me to help her advise her client. Dr. Samuel's accountant had advised him to discontinue all contributions to his corporate retirement plans, and to begin taking maximum distributions from his plans as soon as he reached age 59½, in order to minimize the potential excise taxes.

On December 22, 1994, Dr. Samuel had approximately $2.6 million in his retirement plans, of which $1,134,000 was subject to a grandfather election.

Table 3–1:

This scenario assumes that Dr. Samuel stops all contributions to his retirement plans now, but does not begin taking distributions from the plans until the Required Beginning Date (after reaching age 70½).

Table 3–2:

This scenario assumes that Dr. Samuel stops all contributions to his retirement plans now, *and* begins taking distributions equal to the excise tax limit at age 59½.

Table 3–3:

This scenario assumes that Dr. Samuel continues to fund his retirement plans in the maximum amount allowable each year, until his retirement at age 65. He then waits to withdraw anything from the plans until his Required Beginning Date (age 70½). This would be the worst possible option if both Dr. Samuel and his wife die within seven years. If either one of them lives beyond seven years, this is the best option available.

---

*Described in Chapter 15, Business

Observations:

Take a look at Table 3–4 on page 48. If the criteria for recommending a solution were based on the myth of minimizing tax payments, the clear choice would be Table 3–2. If, however, the criteria applied were to maximize the client's after-tax returns, then:

- Table 3–1 is the best choice *only if both* the client and his wife *die within four years.*

- Table 3–2 is the best choice *only if both* client and wife *die* after beginning distributions and *before the client's 66th birthday.* If either Dr. Samuel or his wife live past those ages, this is the worst possible option.

- Table 3–3, *the alternative resulting in the highest total tax payments,* is the best choice if *either* the client or his wife *lives beyond seven years.*

Based on standard actuarial tables, the probability of a joint life expectancy beyond seven years is overwhelming. Clearly, Table 3–3 is the correct recommendation. Ruhlin explains the reason for this in her summary.

Ruhlin's Summary and Conclusions

What most advisors forget in trying to plan around the excise tax is that in the case of a married couple where the spouse is the beneficiary of the entire retirement plan, no excise tax will be due until the second death. They scare clients into ceasing their retirement plan funding (and probably buying life insurance instead), by showing projections of the huge amount of excise, income, and estate taxes that would be due if the client died at some given (usually premature) age.

In all cases we have analyzed, if just one of the spouses lives to a normal life expectancy, the tax-deferred compounding available within the retirement plan overcomes the excise tax penalty. This does not take into account the additional deferral that might be available utilizing the "inherited IRA" concept.

UNSYSTEMATIC RISK VERSUS
CAPITAL GAINS TAXES

This is popularly known as the *low-basis dilemma.* A client comes to you with a large position in a single stock with a low basis. Do you recommend

T A B L E   3-1

Excise Tax Exposure and Net Distribution Summary

Name								Dr. David Samuel
Assumptions								
Accrued Benefit or Account Balance:								$2,600,000
Undistributed Grandfathered Amt:								$1,134,000
Participant's Date of Birth:								17-Sep-38
Beneficiary's Date of Birth:								07-Feb-39
Investment Rate of Return:								10.00%
Rate of Inflation:								4.00%
120% of Mid-Term AFR (rounded to nearest .2%):								8.20%

Year	Age	Life Expect.	Beginning Balance	Required Distrib.	Discretionary (Contribs.)/ Withdrawals	Earnings	Ending Balance	Amt. Grand-fathered
1994	56	33.9	2,600,000	0	0	260,000	2,860,000	0
1995	57	33.0	2,860,000	0	0	286,000	3,146,000	0
1996	58	32.0	3,146,000	0	0	314,600	3,460,600	0
1997	59	31.1	3,460,600	0	0	346,060	3,806,660	0
1998	60	30.0	3,806,660	0	0	380,666	4,187,326	0
1999	61	29.2	4,187,326	0	0	418,733	4,606,059	0
2000	62	28.3	4,606,059	0	0	460,606	5,066,664	0
2001	63	27.3	5,066,664	0	0	506,666	5,573,331	0
2002	64	26.4	5,573,331	0	0	557,333	6,130,664	0
2003	65	25.5	6,130,664	0	0	613,066	6,743,730	0
2004	66	24.6	6,743,730	0	0	674,373	7,418,103	0
2005	67	23.7	7,418,103	0	0	741,810	8,159,914	0
2006	68	22.8	8,159,914	0	0	815,991	8,975,905	0
2007	69	21.9	8,975,905	0	0	897,591	9,873,496	0
2008	70	21.1	9,873,496	0	0	987,350	10,860,845	0
2009	71	20.2	10,860,845	537,666	0	1,086,085	11,409,264	537,666
2010	72	18.9	11,409,264	603,665	0	1,140,926	11,946,326	596,334
2011	73	18.1	11,946,526	660,029	0	1,194,653	12,481,149	0
2012	74	16.9	12,481,149	738,530	0	1,248,115	12,990,735	0
2013	75	16.1	12,990,735	806,878	0	1,299,073	13,482,930	0
2014	76	15.0	13,482,930	898,862	0	1,348,293	13,932,361	0
2015	77	14.3	13,932,361	974,291	0	1,393,236	14,351,306	0
2016	78	13.2	14,351,306	1,087,220	0	1,435,131	14,699,217	0
2017	79	12.3	14,699,217	1,195,058	0	1,469,922	14,974,080	0
2018	80	11.4	14,974,080	1,313,516	0	1,497,408	15,157,972	0
2019	81	10.4	15,157,972	1,457,497	0	1,515,797	15,216,272	0
2020	82	9.6	15,216,272	1,585,028	0	1,521,627	15,152,871	0
2021	83	8.7	15,152,871	1,741,709	0	1,515,287	14,926,449	0
2022	84	8.0	14,926,449	1,865,806	0	1,492,645	14,553,288	0
2023	85	7.4	14,553,288	1,966,661	0	1,455,329	14,041,956	0
2024	86	7.0	14,041,956	2,005,994	0	1,404,196	13,440,158	0
2025	87	6.6	13,440,158	2,036,388	0	1,344,016	12,747,786	0
2026	88	6.3	12,747,786	2,023,458	0	1,274,779	11,999,107	0
2027	89	6.0	11,999,107	1,999,851	0	1,199,911	11,199,166	0
2028	90	5.7	11,199,166	1,964,766	0	1,119,917	10,354,317	0
				27,462,872	0	35,217,189		1,134,000

(continued)

T A B L E   3-1

Excise Tax Exposure and Net Distribution Summary—*Concluded*

Grandfather Election in Effect?	Yes
Recovery Method Elected?	One Hundred Percent
Single or Joint Life Expectancy?	Joint
Recalculate Life Expectancy?	Yes
Participant, Spouse, Both?	Participant
Federal/State Income Tax Rate:	44.13%
Discount Rate for Present Value:	5.59%
	(Investment Rate of Return Less Taxes)

Excise Limit	Excise Tax on Distrib.	Income Taxes on Dist./(cont.)	Excise Limit at Death	Additional Estate Tax at Death	Income Taxes at Death	Accumulated P.V. of Net Withdraws	Year
148,500	0	0	1,393,401	219,990	1,165,036	1,474,974	1994
154,440	0	0	1,428,250	257,663	1,274,623	1,528,327	1995
160,618	0	0	1,462,913	299,653	1,394,926	1,584,072	1996
167,042	0	0	1,497,331	346,399	1,527,013	1,642,314	1997
173,724	0	0	1,531,483	398,376	1,672,063	1,703,161	1998
180,673	0	0	1,565,333	456,109	1,831,373	1,766,726	1999
187,900	0	0	1,598,799	520,180	2,006,364	1,833,123	2000
195,416	0	0	1,631,842	591,223	2,198,604	1,902,473	2001
203,233	0	0	1,664,251	669,962	2,409,808	1,974,893	2002
211,362	0	0	1,695,818	757,187	2,641,862	2,050,505	2003
219,816	0	0	1,726,255	853,777	2,896,837	2,129,435	2004
228,6p9	0	0	1,755,354	960,684	3,177,020	2,211,820	2005
237,753	0	0	1,782,918	1,078,948	3,484,927	2,297,804	2006
247,263	0	0	1,809,003	1,209,674	3,823,345	2,387,549	2007
257,154	0	0	1,833,539	1,354,096	4,195,328	2,481,215	2008
267,440	0	237,272	2,856,556	1,432,906	4,402,567	2,598,908	2009
278,138	1,100	266,397	1,877,837	1,510,303	4,605,505	2,716,939	2010
289,263	55,615	291,271	1,897,214	1,587,590	4,807,328	2,813,331	2011
300,834	65,654	325,913	1,914,220	1,661,477	4,999,601	2,907,425	2012
312,867	74,102	356,075	1,928,368	1,733,184	5,185,163	2,999,259	2013
325,382	86,022	396,668	1,939,315	1,798,957	5,354,471	3,088,179	2014
338,397	95,384	429,955	1,946,897	1,860,661	5,512,122	3,174,323	2015
351,933	110,293	479,790	1,951,039	1,912,227	5,642,899	3,256,820	2016
366,010	124,357	527,379	1,952,040	1,953,306	5,746,068	3,335,519	2017
380,651	139,930	579,655	1,950,278	1,981,154	5,814,930	3,410,022	2018
395,877	159,243	643,194	1,946,313	1,990,494	5,836,536	3,479,665	2019
411,712	175,997	699,473	1,940,518	1,981,853	5,812,370	3,544,411	2020
428,180	197,029	768,616	1,933,182	1,948,990	5,726,953	3,603,581	2021
445,307	213,075	823,380	1,924,217	1,894,361	5,586,385	3,657,331	2022
463,120	225,531	867,887	1,913,193	1,819,314	5,393,852	3,705,766	2023
481,645	228,652	885,245	1,900,969	1,730,878	5,167,305	3,749,564	2024
500,910	230,322	898,658	1,888,737	1,628,857	4,906,783	3,788,881	2025
520,947	225,377	892,952	1,876,171	1,518,440	4,625,118	3,824,252	2026
541,785	218,710	882,534	1,861,823	1,400,601	4,324,107	3,855,908	2027
563,456	210,197	867,051	1,844,769	1,276,432	4,006,070	3,884,100	2028
	2,836,590	12,119,365					

T A B L E   3-2

Excise Tax Exposure and Net Distribution Summary

Name	Dr. David Samuel
Assumptions	
Accrued Benefit or Account Balance:	$2,600,000
Undistributed Grandfathered Amt:	$1,134,000
Participant's Date of Birth:	17-Sep-38
Beneficiary's Date of Birth:	07-Feb-39
Investment Rate of Return:	10.00%
Rate of Inflation:	4.00%
120% of Mid-Term AFR (rounded to nearest .2%):	8.20%

Year	Age	Life Expect.	Beginning Balance	Required Distrib.	Discretionary (Contribs.)/ Withdrawals	Earnings	Ending Balance	Amt. Grand-fathered
1994	56	33.9	2,600,000	0	0	260,000	2,860,000	0
1995	57	33.0	2,860,000	0	0	286,000	3,146,000	0
1996	58	32.0	3,146,000	0	0	314,600	3,460,600	0
1997	59	31.1	3,460,600	0	0	346,060	3,806,660	0
1998	60	30.0	3,806,660	0	173,724	380,666	4,013,602	173,724
1999	61	29.2	4,013,602	0	180,673	401,360	4,234,289	180,673
2000	62	28.3	4,234,289	0	187,900	423,429	4,469,818	187,900
2001	63	27.3	4,469,818	0	195,416	446,982	4,721,384	195,416
2002	64	26.4	4,721,384	0	203,233	472,138	4,990,290	203,233
2003	65	25.5	4,990,290	0	211,362	499,029	5,277,957	193,055
2004	66	24.6	5,277,957	0	219,816	527,796	5,585,937	0
2005	67	23.7	5,585,937	0	228,609	558,594	5,915,922	0
2006	68	22.8	5,915,922	0	237,753	591,592	6,269,760	0
2007	69	21.9	6,269,760	0	247,263	626,976	6,649,473	0
2008	70	21.1	6,649,473	0	257,154	664,947	7,057,266	0
2009	71	20.2	7,057,266	349,370	0	705,727	7,413,624	0
2010	72	18.9	7,413,624	392,255	0	741,362	7,762,731	0
2011	73	18.1	7,762,731	428,880	0	776,273	8,110,124	0
2012	74	16.9	8,110,124	479,889	0	811,012	8,441,247	0
2013	75	16.1	8,441,247	524,301	0	844,125	8,761,071	0
2014	76	15.0	8,761,071	584,071	0	876,107	9,053,106	0
2015	77	14.3	9,053,106	633,084	0	905,311	9,325,333	0
2016	78	13.2	9,325,333	706,465	0	932,533	9,551,401	0
2017	79	12.3	9,551,401	776,537	0	955,140	9,730,005	0
2018	80	11.4	9,730,005	853,509	0	973,000	9,849,496	0
2019	81	10.4	9,849,496	947,067	0	984,950	9,887,379	0
2020	82	9.6	9,887,379	1,029,935	0	988,738	9,846,181	0
2021	83	8.7	9,846,181	1,131,745	0	984,618	9,699,054	0
2022	84	8.0	9,699,054	1,212,382	0	969,905	9,456,578	0
2023	85	7.4	9,456,578	1,277,916	0	945,658	9,124,320	0
2024	86	7.0	9,124,320	1,303,474	0	912,432	8,733,278	0
2025	87	6.6	8,733,278	2,323,224	0	873,328	8,283,381	0
2026	88	6.3	8,283,381	2,314,822	0	828,338	7,796,897	0
2027	89	6.0	7,796,897	1,299,483	0	779,690	7,277,104	0
2028	90	5.7	7,277,104	1,276,685	0	727,710	6,728,129	0
				17,845,094	2,342,903	24,316,127		1,134,000

(continued)

T A B L E   3–2

Excise Tax Exposure and Net Distribution Summary—*Concluded*

Grandfather Election in Effect?	Yes
Recovery Method Elected?	One Hundred Percent
Single or Joint Life Expectancy?	Joint
Recalculate Life Expectancy?	Yes
Participant, Spouse, Both?	Participant
Federal/State Income Tax Rate:	44.13%
Discount Rate for Present Value:	5.59%
	(Investment Rate of Return Less Taxes)

Excise Limit	Excise Tax on Distrib.	Income Taxes on Dist./(cont.)	Excise Limit at Death	Additional Estate Tax at Death	Income Taxes at Death	Accumulated P.V. of Net Withdraws	Year
148,500	0	0	1,393,401	219,990	1,165,036	1,474,974	1994
154,440	0	0	1,428,250	257,663	1,274,623	1,528,327	1995
160,618	0	0	1,462,913	299,653	1,394,926	1,584,072	1996
167,042	0	0	1,497,331	346,399	1,527,013	1,642,314	1997
173,724	0	76,664	1,531,483	372,381	1,606,899	1,714,874	1998
180,673	0	79,731	1,565,333	400,343	1,691,920	1,787,203	1999
187,900	0	82,920	1,598,799	430,653	1,782,484	1,859,342	2000
195,416	0	86,237	1,631,842	463,431	1,879,035	1,931,336	2001
203,233	0	89,687	1,664,251	498,906	1,982,048	2,003,223	2002
211,362	0	93,274	1,695,818	537,321	2,092,043	2,075,042	2003
219,816	0	97,005	1,726,255	578,952	2,209,582	2,146,833	2004
228,609	0	100,885	1,755,354	624,085	2,335,287	2,218,639	2005
237,753	0	104,921	1,782,918	673,026	2,469,839	2,290,508	2006
247,263	0	109,117	1,809,003	726,070	2,613,998	2,362,500	2007
257,154	0	113,482	1,833,539	783,559	2,768,587	2,434,670	2008
267,440	12,289	154,177	1,856,556	833,560	2,903,782	2,504,677	2009
278,138	17,118	173,102	1,877,837	882,734	3,036,142	2,573,486	2010
289,263	20,943	189,265	1,897,214	931,936	3,167,734	2,641,154	2011
300,834	26,858	211,775	1,914,220	979,054	3,293,066	2,707,253	2012
312,867	31,715	231,374	1,928,360	1,024,905	3,413,970	2,771,807	2013
325,382	38,803	257,751	1,939,315	1,067,069	3,524,238	2,834,391	2014
338,397	44,203	279,380	1,946,897	1,106,765	3,626,854	2,895,098	2015
351,933	53,180	311,763	1,951,039	1,140,054	3,711,927	2,953,366	2016
366,010	61,579	342,686	1,952,040	1,166,695	3,778,989	3,009,102	2017
380,651	70,829	376,654	1,950,278	1,184,883	3,823,694	3,062,055	2018
395,877	82,679	417,941	1,946,313	1,191,160	3,837,641	3,111,799	2019
411,712	92,734	454,510	1,940,518	1,185,849	3,821,804	3,158,314	2020
428,180	105,535	499,439	1,933,182	1,164,881	3,766,131	3,201,163	2021
445,307	115,061	535,024	1,924,217	1,129,854	3,674,583	3,240,444	2022
463,120	122,219	563,944	1,913,193	1,081,669	3,549,222	3,276,226	2023
481,645	123,274	575,223	1,900,969	1,024,846	3,401,731	3,308,954	2024
500,910	123,347	583,939	1,888,737	959,197	3,232,163	3,338,735	2025
520,947	119,081	580,231	1,876,171	888,109	3,048,848	3,365,916	2026
541,785	113,655	573,462	1,861,823	812,292	2,852,921	3,390,636	2027
563,456	106,984	563,401	1,844,769	732,504	2,645,869	3,413,057	2028
	1,482,186	8,908,964					

T A B L E   3–3

Excise Tax Exposure and Net Distribution Summary

Name	Dr. David Samuel
Assumptions	
Accrued Benefit or Account Balance:	$2,600,000
Undistributed Grandfathered Amt:	$1,134,000
Participant's Date of Birth:	17-Sep-38
Beneficiary's Date of Birth:	07-Feb-39
Investment Rate of Return:	10.00%
Rate of Inflation:	4.00%
120% of Mid-Term AFR (rounded to nearest .2%):	8.20%

Year	Age	Life Expect.	Beginning Balance	Required Distrib.	Discretionary (Contribs.)/ Withdrawals	Earnings	Ending Balance	Amt. Grand- fathered
1994	56	33.9	2,600,000	0	(30,000)	260,000	2,890,000	0
1995	57	33.0	2,890,000	0	(30,000)	289,000	3,209,000	0
1996	58	32.0	3,209,000	0	(30,000)	320,900	3,559,900	0
1997	59	31.1	3,559,900	0	(30,000)	355,990	3,945,890	0
1998	60	30.0	3,945,890	0	(30,000)	394,589	4,370,479	0
1999	61	29.2	4,370,479	0	(30,000)	437,048	4,837,527	0
2000	62	28.3	4,837,527	0	(30,000)	483,733	5,351,280	0
2001	63	27.3	5,351,280	0	(30,000)	535,128	5,916,408	0
2002	64	26.4	5,916,408	0	(30,000)	391,641	6,538,048	0
2003	65	25.5	6,538,048	0	(30,000)	653,805	7,221,853	0
2004	66	24.6	7,221,853	0	0	722,185	7,944,038	0
2005	67	23.7	7,944,038	0	0	794,404	8,738,442	0
2006	68	22.8	8,738,442	0	0	873,844	9,612,287	0
2007	69	21.9	9,612,287	0	0	961,229	10,573,515	0
2008	70	21.1	10,573,515	0	0	1,057,352	11,630,867	0
2009	71	20.2	11,630,867	575,785	0	1,163,087	12,218,168	575,785
2010	72	18.9	12,218,168	646,464	0	1,221,817	12,793,521	558,215
2011	73	18.1	12,793,521	706,824	0	1,279,352	13,366,048	0
2012	74	16.9	13,366,048	790,890	0	1,336,605	13,911,763	0
2013	75	16.1	13,911,763	864,085	0	1,391,176	14,438,855	0
2014	76	15.0	14,438,855	962,590	0	1,443,885	14,920,150	0
2015	77	14.3	14,920,150	1,043,367	0	1,492,015	15,368,798	0
2016	78	13.2	15,368,798	1,164,303	0	1,536,880	15,741,374	0
2017	79	12.3	15,741,374	1,279,787	0	1,574,137	16,035,725	0
2018	80	11.4	16,035,725	1,406,643	0	1,603,573	16,232,655	0
2019	81	10.4	16,232,655	1,560,832	0	1,623,266	16,295,089	0
2020	82	9.6	16,295,089	1,697,405	0	1,629,5-9	16,227,192	0
2021	83	8.7	16,227,192	1,865,195	0	1,622,719	15,984,717	0
2022	84	8.0	15,984,717	1,998,090	0	1,598,472	15,585,099	0
2023	85	7.4	15,585,099	2,106,094	0	1,558,510	15,037,515	0
2024	86	7.0	15,037,515	2,148,216	0	1,503,751	14,393,050	0
2025	87	6.6	14,393,050	2,180,765	0	1,439,305	13,651,590	0
2026	88	6.3	13,651,590	2,166,919	0	1,365,159	12,849,830	0
2027	89	6.0	12,849,830	2,141,638	0	1,284,983	11,993,174	0
2028	90	5.7	11,993,174	2,104,066	0	1,199,317	11,088,426	0
				29,409,959	(300,000)	37,598,385		1,134,000

(continued)

T A B L E   3-3

Excise Tax Exposure and Net Distribution Summary—*Concluded*

Grandfather Election in Effect?	Yes
Recovery Method Elected?	One Hundred Percent
Single or Joint Life Expectancy?	Joint
Recalculate Life Expectancy?	Yes
Participant, Spouse, Both?	Participant
Federal/State Income Tax Rate:	44.13%
Discount Rate for Present Value:	5.59%
	(Investment Rate of Return Less Taxes)

Excise Limit	Excise Tax on Distrib.	Income Taxes on Dist./(cont.)	Excise Limit at Death	Additional Estate Tax at Death	Income Taxes at Death	Accumulated P.V. of Net Withdraws	Year
148,500	0	(13,239)	1,393,401	224,490	1,176,290	1,472,460	1994
154,440	0	(13,239)	1,428,250	267,113	1,298,255	1,524,027	1995
160,618	0	(13,239)	1,462,913	314,548	1,432,174	1,578,702	1996
167,042	0	(13,239)	1,497,331	367,284	1,579,239	1,636,575	1997
173,724	0	(13,239)	1,531,483	425,849	1,740,765	1,697,747	1998
180,673	0	(13,239)	1,565,333	490,829	1,918,198	1,762,321	1999
187,900	0	(13,239)	1,598,799	562,872	2,113,124	1,830,405	2000
195,416	0	(13,239)	1,631,842	642,685	2,327,294	1,902,113	2001
203,233	0	(13,239)	1,664,251	731,070	2,562,620	1,977,560	2002
211,362	0	(13,239)	1,695,818	828,905	2,821,208	2,056,864	2003
219,816	0	0	1,726,255	932,668	3,094,118	2,141,612	2004
228,6p9	0	0	1,755,354	1,047,463	3,394,029	2,230,058	2005
237,753	0	0	1,782,918	1,174,405	3,723,637	2,322,357	2006
247,263	0	0	1,809,003	1,314,677	4,085,925	2,418,680	2007
257,154	0	0	1,833,539	1,469,599	4,484,167	2,519,199	2008
267,440	0	254,094	1,856,556	1,554,242	4,705,991	2,645,445	2009
278,138	13,237	285,285	1,877,837	1,637,353	4,923,217	2,766,997	2010
289,263	62,634	311,922	1,897,214	1,720,325	5,139,258	2,869,204	2011
300,834	73,509	349,020	1,914,220	1,799,631	5,345,084	2,968,965	2012
312,867	82,683	381,321	1,928,368	1,876,573	5,543,735	3,066,322	2013
325,382	95,581	424,791	1,939,315	1,947,125	5,724,996	3,160,573	2014
338,397	105,746	460,438	1,946,897	2,013,285	5,893,788	3,251,867	2015
351,933	121,855	513,807	1,951,039	2,068,550	6,033,817	3,339,269	2016
366,010	137,066	564,770	1,952,040	2,112,553	6,144,296	3,422,617	2017
380,651	153,899	620,751	1,950,278	2,142,357	6,218,049	3,501,482	2018
395,877	174,743	688,759	1,946,313	2,152,316	6,241,205	3,575,154	2019
411,712	192,854	749,065	1,940,518	2,143,001	6,215,354	3,643,591	2020
428,180	215,552	823,110	1,933,182	2,107,730	6,123,914	3,706,066	2021
445,307	232,917	881,757	1,924,217	2,049,132	5,973,422	3,762,744	2022
463,120	246,446	929,419	1,913,193	1,968,648	5,767,291	3,813,740	2023
481,645	249,986	948,008	1,900,969	1,873,812	5,524,740	3,859,780	2024
500,910	251,978	962,372	1,888,737	1,764,428	5,245,804	3,901,027	2025
520,947	246,896	956,261	1,876,171	1,646,049	4,944,228	3,938,057	2026
541,785	239,978	945,105	1,861,823	1,519,703	4,621,943	3,971,116	2027
563,456	231,091	928,524	1,844,769	1,386,549	4,281,438	4,000,477	2028
	3,138,653	12,846,225					

T A B L E   3–4

Ranking of Table Based on Income Taxes Paid

Table	Estimated Tax Payments
3–1	$12,119,365
3–2	$8,908,964
3–3	$12,846,225

that the client sell his stock, eliminate the unsystematic risk exposure, and pay the capital gains tax? Or, do you recommend that he defer the tax and hold the stock? Considering the importance of the issue, there has been surprisingly little practical research.

The answer to the question depends on a number of factors:

- The relative volatility of an individual position versus that of a diversified portfolio (e.g., the volatility of IBM versus Vanguard S&P 500).

- The relative returns of a single position versus that of a diversified portfolio (e.g., the relative returns of IBM versus Vanguard S&P 500).

- The subsequent holding period if the stock is not sold.

RELATIVE VOLATILITY

One of the better papers on the subject is included in *Taxes and the Private Investor.*[2] Following are some concepts from this paper that are useful in assisting your client in making a decision.

- Single positions are inherently more volatile than diversified portfolios. As discussed later in Chapter 6, Mathematics of Investing, and as illustrated in Table 3–5, the variance due to increased volatility may decrease long-term growth. That explains why the average stock in the market underperforms the stock market. This factor alone is a strong argument for liquidating a single position and diversifying the proceeds.

- The decision to hold a position and defer the gain in a stock in order to achieve a step up in basis may not be within the client's control. Based on a 20-year study, Bernstein found that 35 percent of the companies had failed, liquidated, or merged. In most cases, the activity caused a

T A B L E   3–5

$100 Original Investment with 10 Percent Average Return

Portfolio	Year 1	Year 2	Ending Value
Volatile Stock A	40%	−20%	$112
Diversified Portfolio	10	10	121

T A B L E   3–6

Relative Risk of an Equity Portfolio
("Worst Case"–One Standard Deviation)

One-Year Holding Period			Five-Year Holding Period		
Diversified Portfolio	Typical Stock	Risky Stock	Diversified Portfolio	Typical Stock	Risky Stock
−9%	−18%	−30%	10%	−16%	−40%

taxable event for the stock owner. The subsequent price appreciation of these stocks so underperformed that of a diversified portfolio that their poor returns would have eroded any tax savings.

  ▪ Sanford Bernstein quantifies the relative risk of holding a nondiversified position in Table 3–6.

CLIENT ISSUES

Considering the results of Bernstein and those of another researcher, Richard Applebach, Jr.,[3] the following guidelines are useful in assisting clients to make the hold/sell decision:

  ▪ For long-term investors,* selling 20 percent of the position per year over a five-year period will significantly reduce annualized standard deviations and, in most cases, not reduce returns. The longer the expected time period until step-up, the more favorable the strategy of diversification will be.

---

*Defined as a life expectancy of 15 years.

T A B L E   3-7

Prudent Level of Low-Basis Stock

Life Expectancy	Invested in a Single Stock*
10 years	10%
15	6
20	4
25	4
30	3

*Assumptions: Cost basis = 10% of market value
50% of the portfolio is in equities
Step-up in basis at death

- Based on Bernstein's studies, I recommend the guidelines set in Table 3–7 for determining the maximum percent of net worth to be held in a single low-basis stock
- An additional technique that the wealth manager may find useful to demonstrate to his client the increased volatility of a single stock as compared to a diversified portfolio is to refer to the pricing of put options. For example, in November 1995, the annualized cost of a put option at the market price for blue chip stocks (Kodak, Phillip Morris, and Ford) ranged from 12 to 18 percent. The same cost for a similar option on the S&P 500 was about 6 percent. Intelligent and sophisticated professional investors, voting with their pocketbooks, were willing to pay a 6 to 12 percent premium to protect against the risk of not diversifying. Professionals recognize that there is a real risk to owning a single company, no matter how "blue chip."

STOCKS, BONDS, IRAS, AND OTHER SHELTERED ACCOUNTS

Assume you are advising your client regarding stocks and bonds, and the client has an IRA and/or self-directed pension. In what do you recommend investing? Conventional wisdom suggests stocks in the personal accounts and bonds in the sheltered accounts. This recommendation is based on a number of points:

- The investor should place "safe" investments (i.e., bonds) in the sheltered account.
- The investor should place the highest income-generating investment (i.e., bonds) in the sheltered account.
- Stocks generate capital gains, which are taxed at a lower rate than ordinary income.
- Capital gains can be deferred.

Once again, conventional wisdom is wrong. The argument for safe investments in the sheltered account has real appeal for the naive investor. It seems reasonable not to take risk with retirement money. Unfortunately, this simplistic focus on unsystematic risk misses the power of diversification and the reality of systematic risk (e.g., inflation). It also fails to recognize that the sheltered account is simply a part of the investor's total portfolio and a loss is a loss is a loss. Presumably, an investor in a diversified equity portfolio, over the long holding periods typical of sheltered accounts, is not expecting, and is not likely to sustain a permanent capital loss. Hence, the inability to use capital losses in a sheltered account is of little concern.

The balance of the arguments focuses on the issue of taxable income. They miss two important points—total return and tax-free alternatives. The goal should be to maximize the efficient use of the shelter. This can be accomplished by putting the investments that will generate the highest taxable total return in the sheltered account. Although it is true that capital gains are generally taxed at a lower rate than ordinary income, in the investment world, there is a choice between bonds that pay taxable income and bonds that pay *tax-free* income. There is no similar choice for equities. The real choice is therefore between sheltering equities taxed at the low capital gains rate or bonds taxed at the "municipal bond" rate (i.e., 0 percent).

The following tables have been prepared using what I believe to be reasonable assumptions for asset class returns and the components of total return for stock (i.e., dividends and capital gains). I then calculated the after-tax values for a $100,000 investment for a large number of scenarios. Table 3–8 is a work template for one series of calculations. The columns labeled "Total A/T" reflect the terminal value of the client's portfolio after withdrawing all funds from the sheltered account and paying the taxes due. Table 3–9 is a summary of a number of scenario calculations.

T A B L E   3–8

Stock or Bonds in a Sheltered Account? A Work Template

1973–1992	Taxes		Components of Total Return	
Muni 7.7% (Chase) Stoc 11.3% (Ibbotson) Corp 9.5% (Ibbotson)	Ordinary Capital Gain	31% 28%	Ordinary Capital Gain	30% 70%

	Stock in Plan Muni Personal				*Corp in Plan Stock Personal*			
Year	Pers	Plan	Plan Tax	Total A/T	Pers	Plan	Plan Tax	Total A/T
0	$50,000	$50,000	$15,500	**$84,500**	$50,000	$50,000	$15,500	**$84,500**
1	53,850	55,650	17,252	**92,249**	54,017	54,750	16,973	**91,795**
2	57,996	61,938	19,201	**100,734**	58,357	59,951	18,585	**99,723**
3	62,462	68,937	21,371	**110,029**	63,046	65,647	20,350	**108,342**
4	67,272	76,727	23,786	**120,214**	68,111	71,883	22,284	**117,710**
5	72,452	85,398	26,473	**131,376**	73,583	78,712	24,401	**127,894**
6	78,030	95,048	29,465	**143,613**	79,495	86,l90	26,719	**138,966**
7	84,039	105,788	32,794	**157,032**	85,882	94,378	29,257	**151,002**
8	90,510	117,742	36,500	**171,752**	92,782	103,343	32,036	**164,089**
9	97,479	131,047	40,625	**187,901**	100,236	113,161	35,080	**178,317**
10	104,985	145,855	45,215	**205,625**	108,290	123,911	38,413	**193,788**
11	113,069	162,337	50,324	**225,081**	116,990	135,683	42,062	**210,611**
12	121,775	180,681	56,011	**246,445**	126,389	148,573	46,058	**228,904**
13	131,152	201,098	62,340	**269,909**	136,544	162,687	50,433	**248,798**
14	141,250	223,822	69,385	**295,687**	147,514	178,143	55,224	**270,432**
15	152,127	249,114	77,225	**324,015**	159,366	195,066	60,470	**293,961**
16	163,840	277,263	85,952	**355,152**	172,170	213,597	66,215	**319,552**
17	176,456	308,594	95,664	**389,386**	186,002	233,889	72,506	**347,386**
18	190,043	343,465	106,474	**427,034**	200,946	256,109	79,394	**377,661**
19	204,677	382,277	118,506	**468,448**	217,091	280,439	86,936	**410,594**
20	220,437	425,474	131,897	**514,014**	234,533	307,081	95, 195	**446,418**
21	237,410	473,553	146,801	**564,162**	253,376	336,253	104,239	**485,390**
22	255,691	527,064	163,390	**619,365**	273,733	368,197	114,141	**527,789**
23	275,379	586,623	181,853	**680,149**	295,725	403,176	124,985	**573,917**
24	296,583	652,911	202,402	**747,092**	319,485	441,478	136,858	**624,104**
25	319,420	726,690	225,274	**820,836**	345,153	483,418	149,860	**678,711**
26	344,016	808,806	250,730	**902,092**	372,884	529,343	164,096	**738,130**
27	370,505	900,201	279,062	**991,644**	402,842	579,630	179,685	**802,787**
28	399,034	1,001,924	310,596	**1,090,361**	435,208	634,695	196,756	**873,147**
29	429,759	1,115,141	345,694	**1,199,207**	470,174	694,991	215,447	**949,718**
30	462,851	1,241,152	384,757	**1,319,246**	507,949	761,016	235,915	**1,033,050**

T A B L E   3–9

Stock or Bonds in a Sheltered Account?
Terminal After-Tax Values: A Summary

Taxes	Ord = 30%/C.G. = 15%		Ord = 30%/C.G. = 20%	
Holding Period	Stock in Plan Muni Personal	Corp in Plan Stock Personal	Stock in Plan Muni Personal	Corp in Plan Stock Personal
10 years	$ 207,084	$ 206,158	$ 207,084	$ 201,899
20 years	518,269	500,181	518,269	480,198
30 years	1,331,657	1,213,942	1,331,657	1,143,619
Taxes	Ord = 30%/C.G. = 25%		Ord = 31%/C.G. = 28%	
Holding Period	Stock in Plan Muni Personal	Corp in Plan Stock Personal	Stock in Plan Muni Personal	Corp in Plan Stock Personal
10 years	$ 207,084	$ 197,777	$ 207,084	$ 201,899
20 years	518,269	461,549	480,198	518,269
30 years	1,331,657	10,803,339	1,331,657	1,143,619
	Ord = 36%/C.G. = 18%		Ord = 36%/C.G. = 30%	
Holding Period	Stock in Plan Muni Personal	Corp in Plan Stock Personal	Stock in Plan Muni Personal	Corp in Plan Stock Personal
10 years	$ 198,332	$ 193,986	$ 198,332	$184,353
20 years	492,740	459,576	492,740	417,239
30 years	1,257,188	1,090,383	1,257,188	950,753

Assumptions:
Components of stock's total return: 30% from dividends and 70% from capital gains
Asset Class Returns:
    Municipals   7.7% (Chase data 1973–1992)
    Corporate   9.5% (Ibbotson data 1973–1992)
    Stock   11.3% (Ibbotson data 1973–1992)

Note that under all combinations reflecting today's tax code, the investor has a better after-tax return by investing the stock in the sheltered account. Of course, this assumes all things being equal. As clients have unique needs and tax laws change, in some cases it may be appropriate to place fixed income in the sheltered account and stock in the personal account. Examples would include:

- A reduction in the client's capital gains tax.

- A change in the relative returns of different asset classes.
- Significant nonrepositional equities held in the client's personal account. In this case, the asset allocation decision would be of overriding importance.
- Restricted choices in the client's 401K plan. There may not be any equity managers meeting your standards in the asset class and style needed by the client and/or the GIC option may be offered at a premium to current market rates.
- The only sheltered equity options may only be offered as variable annuities (VAs) with unacceptable expenses.

TAX EFFICIENCY AND ASSET ALLOCATION

The tendency of Congress to change tax rates is familiar to all wealth managers. If a wealth manager accepts the importance of asset allocation and is interested in his client's real, after-tax return, it is obvious that the impact of tax changes is important. The question is, what changes should the wealth manager make in the portfolio allocations? The solution is counter-intuitive.

The most obvious impact of an increase in tax rates is a diminution of after-tax total returns. If a client requires a specific return in order to accomplish his goals, the allocation would have to be adjusted in favor of equities to compensate for the increased tax loss. The less obvious impact is the change in the relative desirability of bonds vis-à-vis stock. The counter-intuitive result is the influence a change in tax rates can have on the return/risk relationship of different asset classes. It would seem obvious that if a wealth manager, in response to an increase in taxes, recommends an increase in equities, he will also be recommending a higher risk portfolio. However, once again common sense fails us.

In order to demonstrate this, SEI, in their July 1993 *Capital Market Research Report,* developed a "Real Rate of Return to Risk" ratio for stocks and bonds. This ratio, which I call the *SEI Ratio,* is calculated as:

SEI RATIO = (Portfolio Return − Inflation)/σ

The ratio can be calculated using both before- and after-tax returns. SEI then calculates an "Equity Advantage Factor," a measure of real return per unit of risk, as:

SEI FACTOR = SEI Ratio (Equity) − SEI Ratio (Bonds)

T A B L E   3-10

	Before Tax		After Tax		After Tax—New	
	Equity	Bonds	Equity	Bonds	Equity	Bonds
Real ROR	6.50%	2.50%	3.35%	0.55%	3.35%	–0.10%
Risk	21.00	7.00	14.70	4.90	14.70	4.20
SEI Ratio	0.31	0.36	0.23	0.11	0.23	–0.02
SEI Factor	–0.05		0.12		0.25	

F I G U R E   3-1

The Impact of Inflation After-Tax Returns

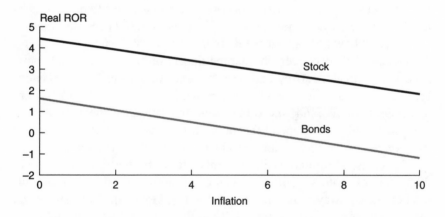

Table 3–10 shows the advantage of equities over bonds. For current taxes, it assumes a 30 percent ordinary and capital gains tax and for new taxes it projects an increase in the ordinary tax rate to 40 percent. Inflation is assumed to be 4 percent. As the table demonstrates, taxes not only reduce returns; they also reduce the relative risk of equities!

One final consideration is the influence of inflation on the relative after-tax returns of stocks and bonds. Analogous to the impact of taxes, inflation reduces the real rate of return of both asset classes but has a disproportionate influence on bonds. Figure 3–1 displays this relationship. The higher the inflation rate, the riskier bonds become relative to stock.

Table 3–10 and Figure 3–1 can be effective tools in communicating to the client another perspective on the "safety" of stocks versus bonds.

THE BIGGEST MYTH—ACTIVE
PORTFOLIO TAX MANAGEMENT

According to *The Wall Street Journal*, in 1913 the entire federal tax code (including commentary) fit neatly into a single 400-page book. In 1995, Commerce Clearinghouse's tax publications comprised 22 volumes with more than 40,500 pages. Taxpayers spend in excess of $350 billion dollars annually just to comply with the requirements of those 22 volumes. It is, therefore, not surprising that since the publication of Robert Jeffrey and Robert Arnott's 1993 article, "Is Your Alpha Big Enough to Cover Its Taxes?"[4] one of the most popular investment issues has been portfolio tax management. What is surprising is how little had been written on the subject before their article, how little practical research has been done subsequently, and how little substance there is to the whole issue.

There is no disagreement that the impact of taxes on a taxable portfolio is significant. Jeffrey and Arnott quote early commentators as observing, "taxes are the biggest expenses that [many] investors face—more than commissions [and] more than investment management fees," and "returns are likely to depend far more on the risk the fund assumes *and more on its tax liability* [emphasis added] than on the accuracy of the analysts' forecasts." Another writer laments, "It has been estimated that over 40 percent of professionally managed balanced portfolios' returns are ultimately taxed away."[5] In a major 1995 study, Goldman Sachs suggested that the investors' growing sensitivity to tax issues might result in major changes for the mutual fund industry, including:

> A flight of assets from funds that mix both retirement and taxable assets and a cultural upheaval when traditional portfolio managers have to deal with the new management guru—the tax strategist.

The conclusion we are to draw from these observations is that portfolio tax management inefficiency is the most significant source of inferior manager performance. By extension, we are led to believe that more effort should be devoted to active portfolio tax management than any other factor under the manager's control. The following discussion will consider, in detail, this conclusion. However, often in debating issues of investment management, much of the disagreement between opposing sides is the result of differing definitions of the subject under consideration. That is certainly the case in the debate over the pros and cons of portfolio tax management. Frequently the benefits attributed to active portfolio tax management are really benefits of other strategies. So, I will narrow the focus of the discussion and begin with my definition of portfolio tax management.

> Portfolio Tax Management (PTM) is the implementation of *active* tax management strategies directly under the control of the money manager. Only those tax savings generated by and under the control of the money manager should be credited as a benefit of the strategy.

Following are a number of other important strategies for tax management available to the wealth manager. However, they may all be implemented independent of the actions of the money manager or the nature of the account (e.g., separate account or mutual fund); therefore, they are not PTM strategies and are not considered as part of this discussion.

- Charitable gifting
- Estate tax planning
- Sheltered vehicles (e.g., annuities)
- Sheltered accounts (e.g., pensions and IRAs)
- Passive management*

It is a pleasant thought that a money manager can significantly minimize taxes without hurting performance. By simply breaking out of the old paradigm of focusing on pretax portfolio returns (a hangover from the emphasis on tax-exempt portfolio management), a money manager can significantly increase the portfolio's bottom line return. Unfortunately, good stories, without good fundamentals, do not necessarily make good sense. As an example, the quote above regarding the poor after-tax performance of professionally managed balanced funds is based on the rather extraordinary assumption that all capital gains are taxed at 39 percent and all ordinary income is taxed at 50.6 percent. Obviously, this inaccurate basis negates the conclusion.

---

*Proponents of passive management should not fret that I am sloughing off the tax efficiency of passive management. It is just that the debate between active and passive management is an entirely different issue. Much of the research regarding portfolio tax management tends to confuse the benefits of active tax management strategies with passive management. I have separated the issues in order to focus on the tax benefits of active portfolio tax management. A discussion of active versus passive styles (including taxes) will be addressed in Chapter 11, Manager Selection and Evaluation—Basics.

For those readers who know the fairy tale of *The Emperor's New Clothes,* the moral is applicable for many old investment truths including portfolio tax management. The fable's moral is, even if everyone says it is true, including the experts, it may not be. Rather than base your truth solely on the experts' opinion, apply reality and common sense.

Summaries of the most influential research on portfolio tax management are included in Appendix B. The following discussion will describe how, for our practice, I evaluated the assumptions and credibility of the major studies and tested them using reality and common sense. My conclusion is that the potential savings from portfolio tax management is largely a myth. This emperor has no new clothes; in fact, he's naked. This controversial conclusion is not based on the quality of the research or the thoughtful effort of the researchers. The real issue is the choice of assumptions (e.g., tax brackets and holding period) and the interpretation of the significance of the results.

EB&K HOMEMADE RESEARCH

When I first read "Is Your Alpha Big Enough to Cover Its Taxes?" I was stunned by Jeffrey and Arnott's conclusions. As a former engineer, my reaction was to whip out my trusty Excel and test their conclusions for myself. When I finished my analysis, I was confused. I simply could not see this emperor's new clothes; he looked naked to me. No matter how I fiddled the data, my simple analysis led me to the conclusion that there was negligible value in any practical form of active portfolio tax management.* The spreadsheet in Table 3–11 is a copy of one of my calculations. The format may be useful should you wish to run your own analysis using your own assumptions. I define *tax efficiency* as the percent of the portfolio's capital gains that the manager defers (in my analysis I assumed a 10-year deferral).** The greater the

---

*Note that I neither disagree with their conclusion that passive indexing is a very tax efficient way of investing nor with their conclusion that holding period, not turnover, is a more sensitive measure of tax efficiency. I do, however, disagree with their conclusion that "there are trading strategies that can minimize these typically overlooked tax consequences."

**It is commonly assumed that the deferral of gains is directly related to portfolio turnover. Research has demonstrated that this simplifying assumption is not correct. A manager who generates a 100% portfolio turnover may in fact have turned over his losses 10 times. As Dickson and Shoven conclude in their study, "there seems to be no significant correlation between the amount a fund turns over its portfolio and the percentage of its pretax value that must be paid in taxes." A better measure of tax efficiency is *effective turnover* as described by William Lewis Randolph. My tax efficiency measurement is the equivalent of Randolph's effective turnover. Refer to Appendix B for a more detailed discussion.

T A B L E   3–11

EB&K Homemade Portfolio Tax Management Efficiency Analysis
50% Tax-Efficient Portfolio

Year	1 Value Begin Yr	2 Div B/T	3 Div A/T	4 CG B/T	5 CG A/T	6 Def Gain	7 Value End Yr	8 Total Taxes	9 Tax Basis Yr End	10 Value A/T Yr End	IRR
1	100,000	3,000	1,920	7,000	6,020	3,500	107,940	2,060	102,900	106,960	
2	107,940	3,238	2,072	7,556	6,498	7,278	116,510	2,224	111,070	114,473	
3	116,510	3,495	2,237	8,156	7,014	11,356	125,761	2,400	119,889	122,582	
4	125,761	3,773	2,415	8,803	7,571	15,757	135,747	2,591	129,408	131,335	
5	135,747	4,072	2,606	9,502	8,172	20,509	146,525	2,796	139,683	140,783	
6	146,525	4,396	2,813	10,257	8,821	25,637	158,159	3,018	150,774	150,981	
7	158,159	4,745	3,037	11,071	9,521	31,173	170,717	3,258	162,746	161,989	
8	170,717	5,122	3,278	11,950	10,277	37,148	184,272	3,517	175,668	173,871	
9	184,272	5,528	3,538	12,899	11,093	43,597	198,903	3,796	189,616	186,696	
10	198,903	5,967	3,819	13,923	11,974	50,559	214,696	4,097	204,671	200,540	7.2%

Assumptions:

Div	3%	1 Portfolio value at the beginning of the year	7 Portfolio Value Year End
CG	7%	2 The Dividend—before taxes	8 Total Taxes Paid by Year End
Div Tax	36%	3 The Dividend—after taxes for the year	9 Tax Basis at Year End
CG Tax	28%	4 The Capital Gain Distribution—before taxes	10 After-Tax Value at Year End Assuming All Gains Realized
		5 The Capital Gain Distribution—after taxes for the year	
		6 Deferred Gains	

deferral, the more tax efficient the portfolio. For example, the 50 percent Tax-Efficient Portfolio is one for which the manager only defers 50 percent of the portfolio's gains.

Table 3–12 shows that a money manager achieving an 80 percent efficiency will outperform his inefficient competitor (i.e., one deferring 50 percent) by only 15 basis points.* Because my conclusions so drastically contradicted the conclusions of Jeffrey and Arnott, I reviewed the available literature on the subject of portfolio tax management. The following is my evaluation of that literature and my conclusions.

---

*As the following analysis of the research demonstrates, in reality, an 80 percent efficiency is not realistic and the maximum benefit of active tax management (net of costs) is about 10 basis points.

T A B L E   3-12

Summary of Tax Efficiency

% Tax Managed	IRR 10-Year Holding Period
100%	7.46%
80	7.36
50	7.21
20	7.06
None	6.96

EVALUATION OF PORTFOLIO TAX MANAGEMENT RESEARCH

In order for the wealth manager to evaluate and to come to his own conclusions regarding the acceptance or rejection of the recommendations emanating from this research, he must have a clear understanding of the numerous issues that influence the research. The following is a summary of those issues followed by a description of their treatment in my evaluation:

- Types of Investments.
- Types of Taxes Considered.
- Restrictions.
- Variables/Assumptions.

Types of Investments

The stock portion of a portfolio is the basis for most of the research and commentary on portfolio tax management. Most taxable equity portfolios are primarily composed of individual stocks and open-end mutual funds; therefore, these are the investment vehicles we are concerned with.

Types of Taxes

Taxes that impact an investment portfolio may be universal (i.e., federal taxes) or unique to the residents of specific states (i.e., state taxes).

Wealth managers in high-tax states must incorporate state taxes into their planning. Taxes may also be imposed on income generated from the investment portfolio (interest and dividends) and subject to ordinary rates; other income is generated by capital gains and taxed as such.

Also, the corpus of the investment portfolio will constitute part of an investor's taxable estate and may be subject to federal and state estate taxes. As wealth managers, we are concerned with the estate tax exposure. We council our clients on the use of estate tax management strategies such as insurance and charitable giving. However, these strategies are neither initiated nor implemented by the portfolio manager and we do not consider these portfolio tax management strategies. Thus, they are not included as part of this discussion.

Restrictions

A major consideration in the use of portfolio tax management strategies is constraints set by the tax code. The most significant is Internal Revenue Code (IRC) Section 1091 (a); Regulation §1.1091-1(a) generally known as *the wash sale rule*. This rule prohibits an investor from realizing a loss on a security sale unless he refrains from repurchasing the same security (or one substantially identical) for a period of 31 days.

A restriction, under Section 852(b)(3), intended for mutual fund managers but impacting individual investors, is the requirement that all realized capital gains be paid annually to the shareholders. If the fund defers the payment of realized gains, it is the fund that will be taxed on the gains.

Finally, an option in favor of a mutual fund shareholder is the determination of the basis of shares sold. IRC Section 1.1012 provides for the following acceptable methods of determining the basis of shares sold.

- **FIFO**—This stands for *first in, first out*. Under this method, when a sale is made, the shares sold are considered to be those first acquired. This is the IRS's assumed default if the investor has not elected one of the other available choices.

- **Identified Shares**—This option allows the investor to specify which shares are to be sold. The advantage of this choice is that it allows an investor to have some control over the tax consequences of a partial sale, by picking and choosing from among his purchases, selecting the highest basis first, thus minimizing his gain and maximizing his tax deferral. This is often referred to as "High In First Out," or HIFO. If the investor has capital losses from another sale, he can sell particular shares according to basis and offset his losses.

In order to meet IRS standards, an investor selecting this method must either deliver to the fund the actual certificates for the shares or provide in writing to the fund a dated letter specifying the shares to be sold, the number of shares to be sold, the original purchase date, and the purchase price. Confirmation of the specifics of the trade should be kept by the investor.

• **Average Cost Method**—Due to its simplicity, the "single category method" is the most popular choice. Under this method, the investor merely averages the cost of all the fund's shares. A somewhat more complex alternative is the "double category" method, which averages separately the investor's short-term and long-term positions. The latter method may be useful in cases where separating short and long term works to the benefit of the taxpayer. Once selected, this method can only be changed with permission of the IRS.

Variables/Assumptions

A number of variables have significant impact on the after-tax returns of an investment portfolio. Not surprisingly, then, the assumptions regarding these variables significantly influence the conclusions.

As noted earlier, I disagree with many of the assumptions made by various researchers. You, the reader, should carefully consider the profile of your client when reading the following and develop criteria that you believe credible for your practice. Having done so, you will find it much easier to translate the research and the conclusions of this chapter into a useful model.

Tax Brackets

Congress seems to enjoy frequently changing tax rates so brackets tend to be moving targets. Appendix A provides a history of marginal tax rates for low, middle, and high tax bracket investors over the last 33 years.

Two main factors affect taxes:

Bracket Into which marginal brackets are your clients likely to fall? Most studies divide taxpayers into low, medium, and high brackets. *Low* refers to a taxpayer at the lowest marginal bracket. *Medium,* under today's code, describes a 28 percent marginal client. High would be today's 39.6 percent marginal client. Also, as noted earlier, depending on your client's state of residence, there might be an additional 3 to 6 percent added for

T A B L E   3–13

Components of Total Return

Fund Objective	Total Return	Yield Component Interest/Dividend S/T Cap Gains	Long-Term Capital Gains
Aggressive Growth	12%	1%	11%
Growth	11	2	9
Growth and Income	10	4	6
Balanced	9	5	4
Taxable Bond	7	7	0
Municipal Bond	5	5	0

state taxes. I believe that the medium bracket is the most appropriate one to use when evaluating the general efficacy of tax management strategies.

Holding Period   This is simply a measure of the length of time a particular portfolio (e.g., a set of individual stocks or a mutual fund) is likely to be held without repositioning. It is used as a measure of the timing of the tax impact. Later I will discuss why I chose a maximum of 10 years as the standard for holding period.

Relative Interest, Dividends, and Capital Gains

The term *relative* in the heading above refers to the assumption made regarding the components of tax returns. For example, if an equity fund has a total return of 12 percent, is it all long-term capital gains, or 2 percent dividends, 3 percent short-term gains, and 7 percent long-term capital gains? Obviously, due to the different tax consequences of each, the relative returns will significantly influence the total after-tax returns.

The matrix in Table 3–13 is a reasonable model to use as a baseline guide.[6]

Trading Costs

Trading costs are difficult to quantify because they are affected by volume and share price, as well as the elusive cost attributable to trading spread.

CONCLUSIONS AND OPINION REGARDING
PORTFOLIO TAX MANAGEMENT (PTM)

With all of the prior material and Appendix B as a reference, what conclusions may the wealth manager draw? You may wish to analyze this information yourself. My thoughts regarding portfolio tax management, which follow, may serve as a useful start. I will first discuss the assumptions I consider appropriate for such an analysis and will end with my recommendations.

Restrictions

Most of the academic studies make light of the wash sale rules. I am less sanguine.

To be sitting on the sidelines for 30 days is a big decision. Further, I do not find it credible to suggest that there are usually fungible individual equities or funds to swap.

The following table demonstrates that returns can vary significantly in 30 days.

Any study that ignores the potential impact of return-drag due to the opportunity cost associated with the wash sale rule may be flawed.

Determination of Basis

The primary conclusion of Dickson and Shoven is that significant tax efficiency can be achieved through the use of Identified Share (HIFO) accounting.

This is the one strategy that is unequivocally persuasive. The question is, Who can use this strategy? Dickson and Shoven only consider its application to an S&P 500 index fund. Vanguard touts it as an "innovative

T A B L E   3–14

Monthly Standard Deviation

S&P 500	1%
Lipper Capital Appreciation Average	2%
Lipper Small Company Average	3%
Phillip Morris	4%

solution" in its promotion material for tax-managed funds. The reality is, HIFO is not innovative. It is not a portfolio tax management strategy; it is a common sense strategy appropriate for *all* portfolios—actively and passively managed as well as managed accounts and mutual funds. HIFO is not related to the nature of the portfolio's assets or the investment-related decisions of the manager. It is a bookkeeping decision. No management style has an advantage. HIFO is available to all. The real question is, Why don't all managers use it for all of their funds? Wealth managers need to encourage their portfolio managers to use HIFO. When comparing HIFO and non-HIFO managers, we apply a 50–75 basis point tax drag penalty to the non-HIFO manager.

Variables

As noted earlier, different choices in variables/assumptions have an enormous impact on the conclusions of the tax management studies.

Tax Brackets

The first screen that a wealth manager should use is the question, Into which tax bracket are my clients likely to fall? Our firm's experience is that few clients fall into either a very low (i.e., 15 percent) or very high (i.e., 39.6 percent) bracket. Most are in the medium brackets, especially those clients for whom we can control the nature of fixed income investments (i.e., municipal bonds). Having determined appropriate brackets, the next decision is which marginal rate to use. Although it may seem sophisticated to use historical rates (Appendix A), there is little reason to believe that they have any predictive value. The most rational and general standard seems to be a marginal rate of 28 percent for capital gains and 28 to 36 percent for ordinary income.

Holding Period

The optimum would be a buy and hold portfolio that is unchanged until the owner's death. In such a case the holding period could well be 30 years, turnover 0 percent, and, due to a full step up in basis, a capital gains tax of $0. This is an unlikely scenario for the clients of most money managers and wealth managers. As a more realistic measure, I consider a passive, low turnover index fund as a standard for the lowest turnover. The obvious example is the Vanguard S&P 500 with a 5 percent turnover (i.e., an average holding period of 10 years). Any actively managed alternative is likely to range from a very low turnover of 25 percent (an average 2-year holding period) to very active at 100+ percent (<1 year holding period). In addition to the turnover attributed to the portfolio manager, there are extraneous considerations such as turnover resulting from management changes, asset class rebalancing, and modifications attributable to the client's needs. According to industry statistics, the average holding period for mutual fund investors, without advisors, is less than three years, for those with advisors, less than four years. In our practice, we have a strong bias against manager turnover. We select managers with the assumption that we are hiring them forever. Unfortunately, reality intrudes. As a result of fund management personnel changes, style drift, or significant and consistent underperformance, we have an annual manager turnover of at least 10 percent. The conclusion I draw is that, at an absolute maximum, the most optimistic holding period to be considered for tax planning is 10 years.

Interest, Dividends, and Capital Gains
As taxable dividends have a significant impact on tax efficiency, they should not be ignored by the wealth manager when evaluating the usefulness of tax management. The best model for the components of total return is that proposed by Randolph and shown earlier as Table 3–13.

Trading Cost
Assuming reasonably large and efficient trading volume for individual equities, a 1 percent one-way transaction cost can serve as a reasonable guide.

SUMMARY: PORTFOLIO
TAX MANAGEMENT RESEARCH

   ▪ Jeffrey and Arnott, even using what I believe to be unrealistic assumptions, have failed to make a case for active tax management. Substantively, the before- and after-tax rankings of actual funds remained almost unchanged. In a study of 72 funds, the ranking for the Vanguard S&P 500 before taxes was 16, the ranking after taxes was 14—less than a 3 percent change!*

   ▪ Dickson and Shoven's data do not show any significant value added by actively managing gains and losses. Contrary to their observations

---

*Before-tax ranking = 16/72 = 22.2 percent; after-tax = 14/72 = 19.4 percent.

regarding the significance of ranking changes, I find the changes for most investors to be inconsequential. For mid-tax-bracket investors the added return was effectively 0 basis points, and for high-tax-bracket investors, less than 10 basis points.*

Although they did demonstrate that HIFO accounting can add value, it does not qualify as a *portfolio tax management strategy*. HIFO is not an active strategy; it is generic. HIFO is implemented by an accounting process, not a trading strategy. It is equally available to all managers, independent of their management philosophy (i.e., active and passive, separate account or mutual fund).

- Sanford Bernstein's data confirms the contribution made by the early recognition of capital losses to be 10 basis points (i.e., 6.56% versus 6.66%). This is the same 10 basis points measured by Dickson and Shoven.**

- Gregory and Litman empirically confirm that the change in rankings of funds based on before- and after-tax returns is insignificant.***

- Jeffrey and Arnott demonstrated the fallacy of focusing on turnover as a measure of tax efficiency and redirected attention to holding period. However, Gregory and Litman, Dickson and Shoven, Randolph, and SEI all suggest that turnover may be a poor way to calculate tax-related holding period. Therefore, I place very little emphasis on portfolio turnover or turnover calculated from turnover.

Recommendations Regarding Portfolio Tax Management

Based on these conclusions, I believe that the wealth manager should not chase the phantom promise of active tax management (remember the emperor's new

---

*See Appendix B, Table B–3.

**These are also the same statistically insignificant 10 to 15 basis points that I had calculated with the spreadsheet analysis in Table 3–12.

***Don Phillips makes the point that Gregory and Litman may have unknowingly biased their conclusions by the selection of a limited historical time period with extraordinary returns. This would bias the results in favor of their conclusions. Although Phillips's observation may be correct, my review of other research suggests that, using appropriate assumptions, Gregory and Litman's conclusions are true for all periods.

clothes). He should instead devote his portfolio management time to asset allocation, manager selection, and monitoring. However, the wealth managers should actively lobby his selected managers to implement HIFO accounting.

Also, although the research has not demonstrated the efficacy of active portfolio tax management, it does provide a very powerful argument for the tax efficiency of a passive portfolio. That is a story in itself and it will be addressed in Chapter 13, Manager Selection and Evaluation—Selection Process.

VARIABLE ANNUITIES

It has been estimated that by 1994, variable annuities (VAs) accounted for over $160 billion in assets. More of a product than a strategy, they are still too important to simply ignore.

It is the responsibility of each wealth manager to determine for himself when, if ever, it is appropriate to utilize VAs. Whatever that decision, he should be able to defend it. All too often the debate has been couched in marketing terms. This section will provide a framework for making these decisions and recommendations for their application.

POSITIVE ATTRIBUTES*

Positive attributes, unique to the VA, follow. Attributes of the underlying investments (e.g., inflation protection by investing in an equity mutual fund) are available to investors independent of an annuity.

- Tax-deferred growth—This is the single most important feature of a VA. The IRS code specifically excludes from current taxation all forms of gain in a VA. Not only can an investor defer taxes, the timing of the deferral is at the option of the investor.
- Tax-free switching—For market timers and tactical allocations, the tax shelter advantages of a VA provide a significant benefit.
- Costs—Many VA proponents suggest that VA funds are more cost efficient than independent funds. Typically the comparison is between the average VA at about 80 basis points and the average fund at 140bp.

---

*These are positive attributes suggested by proponents of variable annuities, not necessarily ones that I agree with. My conclusions will follow.

- Unlimited contributions—Unlike IRAs and qualified plans, there are no limits on the amount that may be invested in VAs.
- Asset protection—In a number of states, investments in VAs are protected from seizure by creditors.
- Guaranteed death benefit—In most policies, the beneficiary of a VA is guaranteed to never receive less than the gross amount originally invested.
- Expense guarantee—In most policies, the contract guarantees that the insurer cannot increase the charges for operating expenses and mortality costs.
- Probate avoidance—As VAs have designated beneficiaries, the proceeds bypass probate upon the annuitant's death.
- Portfolio insulation—As a result of various negative tax consequences and possible insurance company penalties for early withdrawal, the portfolios in a VA are less likely to be subject to extraordinary liquidations.
- Tax-favored distributions—By utilizing an annuity payment option the owner can take advantage of the income exclusion ratio.

NEGATIVE ATTRIBUTES

- Mortality and operating expense—In order to provide their benefits, VAs incorporate mortality and expense fees.
- Marketing costs—Annuities sold on a commission basis include in their expenses a marketing charge. The funding of these charges is through the imposition of additional mortality and expense fees and/or early withdrawal fees.
- Tax penalty—For investors less than 59½ years old, withdrawal of gains from a VA may be subject to a 10 percent tax penalty.
- Loss of capital gains—Although the gains in a VA may be deferred at the owner's option, once withdrawn, they are taxed as ordinary income, not capital gains.
- Loss of step-up—Upon the annuitant's death, all gains remaining in the annuity are subject to income tax at the ordinary income rate. There is no step-up basis.
- Limited choices of investment vehicles—Although some VAs have as many as 20, 30, or 40+ underlying subaccounts (i.e., manager choices), the variety is insignificant compared to the thousands in the open-end fund universe. Further, most annuities have only one or two choices in any particular asset class/style.

▪ Tax risk—The more popular VAs become and the more they are marketed as tax shelters, the more likely Congress will eliminate their tax benefits. Given the history of tax legislation, this could include negative retroactive tax law. Michael Lane, of Providian, reminds me that similar legislation has been proposed four times and never passed; however, this is an issue the wealth manager must evaluate for himself. Even without such doomsday changes, a reduction of the capital gains rate would have a negative impact on the relative efficacy of VAs.

▪ Misleading appearance as a clone fund of a successful public mutual fund—Similar names and objectives between funds and VAs may have little significance. The portfolio managers, as well as fundamental policies, may differ significantly.[7]

EB&K EVALUATION

With the pros and cons as a background, the wealth manager needs to evaluate the viability of VAs based on the nature of his practice. For this purpose, I will use our firm's analysis as an example.

▪ Tax-Deferred Growth—Once again, the conclusions of any comparison depend on the assumptions. Analyses supporting the tax benefits of VAs often use many of the following assumptions:

1. The highest state and federal ordinary income and capital gains rates.
2. Long accumulation periods.
3. Long postretirement withdrawals.
4. Full withdrawals (i.e., no assets left at the owner's death; therefore, no penalty for a loss in step-up).
5. Alternatively, the analysis compares the after-tax growth of a fund investment to the accumulation value of the VA (i.e., no taxes have been paid on the accumulated gains in the VA).
6. A lower postretirement income tax bracket.
7. Relatively high dividend component of total return.

Our clients rarely have long accumulation periods, rarely have long liquidation periods, and generally do not expect to use the bulk of their assets before their death. They also rarely fall into a lower tax bracket after retirement. In those cases when the client may meet one of the criteria (e.g., long accumulation) they do not meet the other criteria (e.g., long postretirement withdrawals and full withdrawals).

In order to evaluate the sensitivity of VAs to these various factors, we ran a series of scenarios, varying the assumptions regarding accumulation and liquidation periods and tax combinations. The results are summarized in Tables 3–15A and 3–15B. Table 3–15A is based on an ordinary income tax rate of 31 percent, a capital gains rate of 28 percent, and an annuity cost of 85bp. Table 3–15B uses the same federal tax rates but assumes a 6 percent state tax rate and an annuity cost of 65bp. The reader may find these results useful in evaluating the use of VAs in their practice.

- Tax-Free Switching—As we do not utilize either market timing or tactical allocation, this is not a benefit for our clients.

- Costs—The standard comparison is a generic comparison of apples and oranges. The question is how VA expenses compare to the wealth manager's alternative. As we use only no-load funds and are extremely sensitive to the expense ratio of our managers, we find the expense ratios of the subaccounts of the better VAs and the individual funds we use are in the same range. Thus, based on fund expenses, neither VAs nor funds have an advantage.

- Asset Protection—Florida is one of the states that provides almost unlimited asset protection for VA investments. As a result, we consider the extra costs and limitations of VAs to be the charges related to insuring our clients' assets against creditor seizure. For clients in high-risk professions or with unique creditor exposure, we find these costs modest compared to their benefit. In such cases we do consider the use of VAs.

- Guaranteed Death Benefit (GDB) and Expense Guarantee (EG)— These seem to have little substantive value. The GDB is the difference between the original investment value and the portfolio value at the time of the annuitant's death, if it is lower than the original investment. Consider the profile of the VA purchaser—a client in his mid 50s with a life expectancy of 30+ years. If the client lives to anywhere near his life expectancy, the probability of the account value at death being less than his investment is statistically zero; exactly equal to the value of the GDB. If the client lives only 10 years after the purchase and had been so unfortunate as to have purchased at a historic high, his heirs' exposure is likely to be less than 10 percent. Under any rational scenario, the real value of the GDB is negligible.

- The value of the expense guarantee is equally negligible. If our client's alternative is to make a purchase that does not require an expense

T A B L E 3–15A

Variable Annuity Performance versus Mutual Funds

Lump Sum Investment* Death—20 Years after Retirement		$100,000	

Systematic Withdrawal—5%

Accumulation Period	Annuity after Taxes**	Mutual Fund Stepped-Up Basis	Mutual Fund Advantage
10 years	$ 602,893	$ 804,299	33%
15	996,892	1,225,878	23
20	1,662,241	1,869,654	12
25	2,854,818	2,846,860	0

Systematic Withdrawal—10%

Accumulation Period	Annuity after Taxes**	Mutual Fund Stepped-Up Basis	Mutual Fund Advantage
10 years	$224,765	$423,682	88%
15	358,386	568,100	59
20	584,032	742,732	27
25	965,081	926,755	−4

Systematic Withdrawal—15%

Accumulation Period	Annuity after Taxes**	Mutual Fund Stepped-Up Basis	Mutual Fund Advantage
10 years	$ 89,332	$298,463	234%
15	135,238	363,397	169
20	207,176	387,516	87
25	328,657	316,764	−4

*Assumes federal ordinary income tax rate = 31%; capital gains rate = 28%.
Mutual fund return = 12%; dividend return from mutual fund = 25%; realized CG = 30%.
Total annuity return = 12%; administration costs = $30; cost of annuity = 85bp.
**Assumes original contribution as basis.

T A B L E 3–15B

Variable Annuity Performance versus Mutual Funds

Lump Sum Investment* Death—20 Years after Retirement		$100,000	

Systematic Withdrawal—5%

Accumulation Period	Annuity after Taxes**	Mutual Fund Stepped-Up Basis	Mutual Fund Advantage
10 years	$ 591,739	$ 604,987	2%
15	983,406	859,360	−13
20	1,651,514	1,208,788	−27
25	2,791,175	1,670,154	−40

Systematic Withdrawal—10%

Accumulation Period	Annuity after Taxes**	Mutual Fund Stepped-Up Basis	Mutual Fund Advantage
10 years	$224,962	$348,164	55%
15	357,791	382,689	7
20	584,373	337,931	−42
25	970,876	97,607	−90

Systematic Withdrawal—15%

Accumulation Period	Annuity after Taxes**	Mutual Fund Stepped-Up Basis	Mutual Fund Advantage
10 years	$ 94,919	$215,190	127%
15	139,146	199,840	44
20	211,382	14,759	−93
25	334,602	—	−100

*Assumes federal ordinary income tax rate = 31%; capital gains rate = 28%; state tax = 6%.
Mutual fund return = 12%; dividend return from mutual fund = 25%; realized CG = 30%.
Total annuity return = 12%; administration costs = $30; cost of annuity = 65bp.
**Assumes original contribution as basis.

factor, he is certainly not going to consider the "guarantee" of no *additional* expense to be of much value.

- Unlimited Contributions—By utilizing the term *contribution,* this advantage implies a unique feature of VAs. The option is actually to "buy more." This advantage is of little consequence unless the tax savings feature provides significant benefit. After all, an investor can make unlimited contributions to most investments.

- Probate Avoidance—To the extent the client finds this a useful feature, investing in a VA restricts the advantage to that single investment. The alternative we suggest is to establish a revocable trust, thus providing probate avoidance for all of his assets as well as significant additional advantages.

- Portfolio Insulation—This is a difficult value to measure and no substantive research has been published on this issue. In any event, we have significant control over our client's exposure by selecting funds (e.g., institutional) that are unlikely to face extraordinary liquidations. During a significant market correction, it is quite likely that nervous naive investors in VA equity subaccounts will liquidate and move to cash, whereas more knowledgeable investors will stay put in the funds we select.

- Tax-Favored Distribution—The value of this opportunity is directly related to the same influences as the VA's tax-deferred growth— long periods of withdrawal and significant withdrawals.

The following observations on VAs—pro and con—are from two commentators whom I highly respect.

> **Con**—An independent analysis of variable annuities was prepared by Bob Veres in the February 1996 issue of *Inside Information.** The study was an update of an analysis that ran in the October 1994 issue. The original study compared the traditional load variable annuities available at the time to investments in index funds. It concluded that the index investment outperformed the variable annuity every year for a 20-year period. The 1996 article revisited the comparison but compared the index fund investment to the new no-load variable annuities. The index funds beat the variable annuity by a slimmer margin but it still won. Veres concluded, "So, let's give praise where it is due. Thank you, Vanguard/Skandia/Fortis/Jack White

---

*A subscription to *Inside Information* is a must for any financial planner. Although I frequently disagree with Veres, he always makes me think. There are a few journalistic stars who write about our profession and I include Veres in this exclusive list. Bob Veres, Mary Rowland, Bob Clark, and Nick Murray—if they write it, I'll read it.

[vendors of no-load annuities] for driving down the costs of a very popular investment . . . We applaud your character, but we also hope that the planning community will decide, collectively, to pass on your VA offerings . . .

Pro—In a letter to Bob Veres, Michael Lane argues that the analysis neglects two critical variables—state taxes and the type of income distribution. He also points out that less than 1 percent of the variable annuities charge front-end loads and suggests that the assumption of a 4 percent charge "really stacks the analysis" against variable annuities. Not too surprisingly, Lane concludes that such analysis may "lead to misconceptions about an important financial tool and can discourage fee planners from recommending what may be the best long-term investment solution for their clients."

CONCLUSIONS REGARDING VARIABLE ANNUITIES

Having considered all the advantages of VAs, we have determined that, all things being equal, VAs are only useful in those cases when our client is likely to spend down the investment during retirement and has long accumulation and withdrawal expectations or where asset protection is a significant issue.

We do not believe that all things are equal. The costs associated with VAs may be significant and the possible tax liquidation penalties restrict their liquidity in emergencies. If our client does not use the funds, the loss of step-up in basis may be significant. Although the risk of retroactive tax legislation is small, the risk of a reduction in the VA's relative return due to a lowering of the capital gains is quite real.

Finally, in spite of the importance of all those negatives, we believe they are insignificant compared to the inflexibility of manager selection. Many VAs have poorly defined asset class managers, making it difficult, if not impossible, for us to control the critical asset allocation balance of our client's portfolio. For those products that offer subaccounts with managers who adhere to a well-defined philosophy and process, there is rarely an alternate within the VA to move to, if either the management changes or the existing manager drifts from his original philosophy.

Although for most of our clients we do not use VAs, we believe that they are viable strategies for certain clients. The development of no-load and low-cost VAs by firms such as Providian, Schwab, Vanguard, and T. Rowe Price have addressed some of our objections. Providian's Advisor Edge is particularly interesting, as its policy includes a selection of both active- and passive-style specific managers. We will continue to evaluate the products available.

OTHER STRATEGIES*

There are occasions when a client would like to defer (or avoid) paying capital gains taxes, yet he wishes to eliminate the risk of a concentrated holding. The discussion so far has implicitly assumed that the only techniques available for managing taxes are directly related to the securities held in the portfolio. There are, in fact, numerous strategies that may be implemented for special cases. The following is intended as an introduction. For the most part, these strategies require expertise beyond the realm of the wealth manager.**

SHORT AGAINST THE BOX

Consider the problem facing Mr. Brown.

> Mr. Brown holds a position in Stock A and wishes to reduce his market exposure. The obvious solution is to simply sell shares. Unfortunately, it is a stock that has appreciated significantly. As Mr. Brown has a low basis, an outright sale will result in the realization of significant capital gains and the related obligation to pay capital gains tax.
> The problem becomes one of reducing market exposure without triggering a required tax payment.

The solution may be a short sale.*** A straight short sale can be very rewarding or very risky. There is, however, a strategy known as *shorting against the box* that transforms the short into a tax strategy.

---

*Congress is currently considering legislation that may eliminate many of those strategies. Known as the *smile test,* the law would consider an investment to have been constructively sold if the investor didn't smile when the value of his security went up or frown when its value dropped.

**My thanks to Twenty-First Securities Corporation, 780 Third Ave., New York, NY 10017 for their assistance in providing background information for this section.

***A short sale is the act of selling shares not owned by the client initiating the sale. Many brokerage firms lend their clients shares for this purpose. This is a trading strategy frequently used by active traders anticipating a future drop in the price of the stock. If correct in their projections, the trader will subsequently repurchase shares (at the then lower price) and return them to the lender (i.e., the brokerage firm that loaned him the shares to sell). The trader's profit is the difference between the original sales proceeds and the cost of replacing the loaned shares.

In our example, even though Mr. Brown owns shares in A, he will not sell his shares. Instead, he will borrow and sell an equal number of shares (*against the box*). Unlike the trader, Mr. Brown cannot profit from a drop in the price of A. After all, if he profits on his short sale, he will have an equivalent offsetting loss in his original position. He also does not face a loss if the shares of A rise precipitously in price. His loss on the short sale would be covered by his gains on the shares he owns. If the net change is zero no matter which way the price of A moves, why bother?

By "bothering," Mr. Brown has accomplished his goals. He has eliminated his market exposure to Stock A. He has avoided the immediate tax impact he would have faced with an outright sale. The short sale did not result in a taxable event as the tax code treats the closing of the short sale as the taxable transaction.

Although generally used as a strategy for deferring gains from one year to the next, there is a growing use of the technique to defer until the owner's death. This totally eliminates the tax gain via a step-up in basis. It has also focused the attention of Congress on the strategy and there is considerable pressure to close this "loophole."

Specific potential problems related to short sales include the ability to borrow responsibility for dividend payments and the risk of forced liquidations (e.g., call, company failure).

COLLARS

Somewhat more complex than a short against the box, *collars* entail a simultaneous purchase of puts and the sale of calls in an amount equal to the number of shares of the stock the client wishes to protect.

As the design of collars is unique for each trade, the options (i.e., puts and calls) used are not those listed on major exchanges. Instead, they are structured with over-the-counter options, custom derivatives sold by the structuring broker-dealer to investors.

The cost of a collar, not including the structuring firm fee, is the difference between the cost of the puts and the proceeds of the calls. The most common structure, called a *zero cost collar,* is designed to have these two amounts exactly offset each other.

Specific risks include counter-party default (e.g., failure to meet the put), lack of emergency liquidity, and forced liquidation (e.g., call).

EQUITY SWAP

There may be occasions when Mr. Brown would like to reduce his unsystematic risk in a single security while avoiding realizing his gains. He would, however, also like to maintain his voting rights. In this case he can implement an equity swap.

This is structured as an agreement with a broker. Mr. Brown would pay the broker the dividends and net appreciation on Stock A while the broker would pay Mr. Brown the dividends and net appreciation on an agreed upon diversified portfolio (e.g., S&P 500). As Mr. Brown continues to be the owner of A, he will maintain his voting rights.

Specific risks include counter-party default and the treatment of dividend and net appreciation payments as ordinary income.

EXCHANGE FUNDS

Typically formed as a limited partnership, the exchange fund serves as a legal bucket for holders of low-basis stock to pool their positions in a tax-free exchange. The result is the transfer of risk from a single position to a multiple security portfolio. In order to meet the IRS requirements, there are numerous restrictions, including a mandatory five-year investment period.

Specific risks, in addition to the holding period include the risk of early fund liquidation and what has been called the *graveyard* effect. As the investor has no control over the other securities added to the portfolio, he may end up a partial owner of a portfolio of dogs.

CONCLUSIONS REGARDING OTHER STRATEGIES

Of the numerous issues to be considered regarding the use of these strategies, a few of the more important are:

- All have a carrying cost, usually in terms of fees paid to the firm assisting in the structuring of the transaction. These costs typically range from 1 to 3 percent per year.
- While the client has immunized his market exposure to the specific equity, he may have eliminated any opportunity of gain (e.g., short against the box) or transferred the risk to a different market exposure (e.g., exchange funds).

- If the position to be deferred is subject to short-term gains (e.g., stock options), there are significant issues regarding the tolling of the holding period for long-term gains. Special supplementary strategies may be necessary (e.g., married put).
- They may disappear with changes in the tax code.

ENDNOTES

1. Sanford Bernstein Research, *Taxes and the Private Investor,* "Gains versus Income" 1995, 2–3.
2. Sanford Bernstein Research, *Taxes and the Private Investor,* "Do I Dare Sell This Stock?" 1995, 8–16.
3. Richard O. Applebach, Jr., "The Capital Gains Tax Penalty" *Journal of Portfolio Management* (Summer 1995), 99–103.
4. Robert H. Jeffrey and Robert D. Arnott, "Is Your Alpha Big Enough to Cover Its Taxes?" *The Journal of Portfolio Management* (Spring 1993), 15–25.
5. Nancy L. Jacob, "Taxes, Investments Strategy and Diversifying Low-Basis Stock," *Trusts & Estates,* May 1995.
6. William Lewis Randolph, "The Impact of Mutual Fund Distributions on After-Tax Returns," *Financial Services Review,* 3(2), 1994, 127–141.
7. Kylelane Purcell, "VA Investors Gain by Knowing How Clone Funds Differ," *5 Star Investor,* April 1995, 12–13.

CHAPTER 4

Data Gathering

Garbage In, Garbage Out

—Anonymous

RISK TOLERANCE

If risk is a four-letter word describing a concept that looks like a reflection in a mirror maze, how can a wealth manager possibly evaluate a client's risk tolerance? The answer is by becoming a great artist with the palette of client psychology, using a variety of techniques and a continuing application of education.

The two basic principles of risk assessment are:

▪ Be aware of the potential conflicts between your objective view of risk and the client's emotional view. This is a major danger when the wealth manager is communicating on an intellectual frequency and the client is receiving on an emotional frequency. Nick Murray notes that a wealth manager "cannot plan around or through someone's definition of risk . . . it must be shared." He goes on to state that if the client has "a diseased concept of risk [he] will have a diseased concept of safety."

▪ Do not assume client knowledge. Even the most successful and sophisticated business or professional client is unlikely to have a rudimentary knowledge of modern investment theory. As discussed earlier, most will certainly be subject to the misuse of heuristics.

The primary purpose of a formal risk tolerance questionnaire is to facilitate a dialogue in order to help the client develop a healthy concept of risk and reach informed decisions. The wealth manager needs to be vigilant in avoiding the imposition of his own psychological biases.

F I G U R E   4–1

Spectrum of Risk Analysis

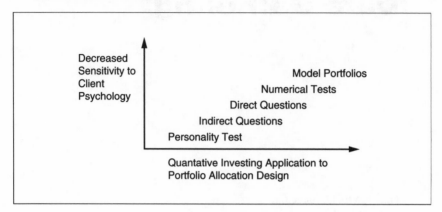

Figure 4–1 above is a graph reflecting the interplay between a client's emotional orientation and a wealth manager's desire to quantify risk tolerance:[1]

Depending on the location in this spectrum, questions may be based on behavioral psychology, finance, investment theory, or decision science (e.g., probability).

RISK EVALUATION QUESTIONNAIRES

PERSONALITY TESTS

A number of proprietary tests are available on the market. Among the most respected is that of Dr. Kathleen Gurney. We do not currently use these forms of tests in our practice.

INDIRECT QUESTIONS

These quasi-psychological questions, although not directly related to a client's core personality (hence, quasi), assist in validating the consistency of the client's answers to more direct and numerical questions. Examples would include:

Which of the following comes closest to your ideal employment compensation structure, involving some mix of salary and commissions?

1. Entirely salary
2. Partially salary
3. Equal mix
4. Primarily commissions
5. Entirely commissions

DIRECT AND NUMERICAL QUESTIONS

Both are similar in that they address issues directly related to portfolio design. Direct questions require nonquantitative responses and numerical questions require quantitative responses. Examples include:

- Is there an immediate or near-term (i.e., within five years) need for income from this portfolio(s)?
- Up to what percentage of this portfolio can be invested in long-term investments (i.e., over five years)?

MODEL PORTFOLIOS

Model portfolios allow the client an opportunity to select his own allocation from a variety of choices. Effective as part of a comprehensive evaluation process, model portfolio selection should never be relied upon as a single criterion. The client's stand-alone answer to a question of this nature is very likely to violate the two principles of risk assessment:

- There is a potential conflict between your objective view of risk and the client's emotional view.
- Do not assume client knowledge.

RISK ASSESSMENT FRAMEWORK

An effective framework for developing a risk assessment program was created by Eleanor Blayney, an expert in the areas of investment theory and client risk assessment. She has participated with the National Endowment for Financial Education in the preparation of a number of useful practitioner guides on these subjects. Table 4–1 was presented to a meeting of the Alpha Group (referenced in Chapter 3, p. 40) in January 1995.

Risk Measurement

Definition	Discipline	Indicator/Measure
Taking chances (e.g., entrepreneurship)	Behavioral psychology	Ability to change
Aversion to loss	Behavioral psychology	Framing exercises
Aversion to uncertainty	Finance	Volatility
Likelihood of outcome	Decision science	Probability

QUALITATIVE SCALE INTERPRETATION

When developing questions to measure issues emanating from finance and decision science, a wealth manager may often wish to use qualitative responses in lieu of numbers. The following are examples of how this might be accomplished.

Parallel Qualitative and Quantitative Responses

This allows the client to select a verbal description but provides a parallel numerical interpretation.

If my risk tolerance is		I would have to accept an occasional loss of	
Short-Term	Long-Term	Short-Term	Long-Term
Low	Low	− 2%	0%
Medium	Low	− 5	0
Medium	Medium	−10	−2
High	Medium	−15	−5

Numerical Conversion Scale

Use a verbal response that can be converted to a numerical scale. At the Alpha meeting, Ms. Blayney also provided the following scale, based on extensive psychological testing, as a useful numerical interpretation for responses to multiple-choice questions:

Client Choice	Numerical Interpretation Based on a Scale of 0 to 100
Very improbable	5
Low chance	20
Possible	70
Very high, almost certain	90

EVENSKY, BROWN & KATZ QUESTIONNAIRE

The questionnaire that we currently use in our firm has evolved over many years beginning at the yellow pad stage to its current five-page, 15-question format. The Risk Tolerance Questionnaire (RTQ) supplements a more traditional financial planning data-gathering guide. Our RTQ is used both to capture specific information regarding risk tolerance and, equally important, to provide a springboard for conversation and client education.

Although the risk tolerance questionnaire assists us in developing an investment policy for the client, that is not its sole use. We believe that the questionnaire should also be used to facilitate a discussion about risk and to help manage the client's expectations. Consequently, the risk tolerance questionnaire is not given to the client to take home and complete. Once we have completed an education program (Chapter 5, Client Education) and feel reasonably confident that we have answered all our client's questions as well as provided him with a solid foundation regarding important investment issues, we sit with the client and complete our RTQ. The following is a detailed discussion of our questionnaire and the issues we raise with our clients.

Usually, we are concerned with all of a client's investment assets. Occasionally, however, our advice may be requested regarding a specific investment portfolio that represents only a portion of his investments (e.g., a pension plan or trust fund). For that reason, the first questions we ask are directed at placing into perspective those investments about which we are being asked to advise.

QUESTION #1

What is the approximate value of this investment portfolio(s)?	$
What percentage of your total investments is represented by this portfolio?	%

We begin with a rather obvious question, that is, the approximate value of the investment portfolio. In order to place this number in the perspective of the client's total financial plan, we follow up with a request for the percentage that the investment portfolio represents of the client's total investments. This question supplements the more detailed, traditional, data-gathering guide in order to determine whether this particular investment portfolio is or is not part of a much larger portfolio. If it is part of a larger portfolio, it is necessary to determine how it should be integrated with the client's other assets. If it is not, it is important to determine the plans that have been made to provide for emergency reserves and short-term cash needs.

QUESTION #2

Is there an immediate or near-term (i.e., within five years) need for income from this portfolio(s)?	Y N
If yes, when will the income be needed?	YRS

Question #2 addresses the need for cash flow. As discussed earlier, our focus on portfolio design is on total return and we address the need for cash flow after having determined the portfolio allocation. We do, however, need to determine the effective cash flow demands (i.e., after taxes) at the beginning of the process for four reasons:

- If the requirement is in excess of what we believe is a realistic total return target, it is an immediate flag to stop the data-gathering process and turn the discussion to the reality of the client's short-term goals.

- If the cash flow need is significant relative to the corpus (e.g., more than 4 or 5 percent), it is a flag to develop a detailed five-year cash flow projection.

- It is a reminder to query for any significant and unique short-term cash flow demands (e.g., wedding, major trip).
- In any case, it provides a measure for us to determine the nature of the "cash flow liquidity reserve" that we need to establish.

QUESTION #3

Will significant cash withdrawals of principal and/or contributions be made over the next five years?	Y	N
If yes, please attach a schedule.		

This is the first of a series of purposely redundant questions. We've already asked about the need for income, but Question #3 addresses the need for any significant principal withdrawals within our five-year period. This is a second opportunity to query for unique short-term cash flow needs. The question also asks about future contributions. This may be an important consideration in developing the asset allocation model. The size of the portfolio may influence the number of asset classes to be considered (e.g., are there adequate assets to add secondary asset class allocations such as small cap international?)

The Evensky, Brown & Katz Client Mantra

Although we have discussed the concept with our client during the educational session, at this point we once again emphasize our firm mantra: "Five years! Five years! Five years!"

We believe in the concept of time diversification.* Further, as a general rule, we believe that five years is a good minimum standard to use as a criterion for investment time diversification. It is important to note that this is a rolling, not a fixed, standard. If a client informs us that he will need the investment funds in exactly 5 years, the portfolio would not meet our standard, for one day later the holding period will have dropped to 4 years and 364 days.

Although we realize that a rolling 5-year standard is much longer than a fixed 5 years, we also know that our client's real-time horizon is typically 20+ years and his psychological time horizon is 10 seconds. If we started off discussing a 20-year period, our clients would balk. Their initial orientation is short term (remember the story about the green banana).

---

*This is a controversial issue, discussed in Chapter 7, Investment Theory.

The art of data gathering (which is one element of managing client expectations) includes obtaining commitment as well as information from clients with 10-second psychological time horizons and 20-year real horizons. We find that the five-year mantra is an effective tool.

The mantra is not a bluff. Unless the client can swear (or affirm) upon penalty of dire consequences that there is no expectation (even remote) of needing the corpus of the portfolio for a period of five years, we do not consider the funds "investment" funds. We will neither develop an investment plan nor assume the responsibility of investing the assets. We do not make the client sign in blood, but we do have him acknowledge, in writing, at the end of the questionnaire his affirmation of the answers he has provided.

QUESTION #4

Is this a taxable or partially taxable portfolio(s)?	Y	N
If yes, what tax rate should be used for planning purposes?		%

Obviously, the design of the portfolio will ultimately be impacted by its tax status. This question provides an opportunity to clarify the tax status of the portfolio. It also provides for a check on the client's marginal tax rate and as a double check on the detailed fact finder.

QUESTION #5

What is the portfolio's Investment Time Horizon?
Investment Time Horizon refers to the number of years you expect the portfolio to be invested before you must dip into principal. Alternatively, how long will the objectives stated for this portfolio continue without substantial modification?
Please mark your choice:

3 years   O
5 years   O
10 years   O
More than 10 years   O

Note: If you have indicated less than 10 years, please state when the funds will be needed:

Questions #1 through #4 set the framework for the dollar amounts to be invested or withdrawn from the portfolio and initiate our emphasis on the importance of the holding period. Question #5 continues the process of educating the client relative to the realities of risk and volatility.

Presumably the client has already answered Question #5 by responding to Questions #2 and #3. We find, however, that when translated into actual holding periods measured in years, the client's 10-second horizon may move front and center. It is not unusual to find someone answering Questions #2 and #3 with a No, only to answer Question #5 with the choice of three years. Such contradictory responses bring the client's concerns out into the open. In order to force the discussion, we recently added an additional statement requesting the client to state when the funds will be needed if anything less than 10 years is selected. As planners, we know that most clients have a very long investment horizon. Even those clients consulting us for retirement planning and postretirement planning, in reality, have their life expectancy as an investment horizon. Question #5 allows us the opportunity to discuss this reality in depth. For example, it forces our 70-year-old retired widow (with an 18-year life expectancy) to acknowledge that she really does not plan on spending much of her principal before her death. Once we have had an opportunity to discuss the concept of a planning horizon based on life expectancy, most clients understand that the bulk of their corpus must remain intact, in order for them to continue to maintain their lifestyles for the balance of their lives.

QUESTION #6

OPTIONAL	
My (our) goal for this portfolio(s) is an annual return of:	%
This is based on an expected inflation rate of:	%
See the appendix for a long-term historical reference.	

In earlier forms of our questionnaire, this particular question did not exist. On occasion, we found that after going through a great deal of analysis and work, the response to our final recommendations might go as follows: "Ms. Mort, we recommend that you reposition your portfolio from 60 percent bonds to 40 percent bonds and increase your stock allocation from 40 percent to 60 percent. We believe that this will provide you with a long-term return of approximately 5 percent over the inflation rate." Ms. Mort responds, "What return would that mean today?" We answer, "In the current 3½ percent inflation environment, that would translate to a total return of 8½ percent," only to be told by Ms. Mort, "Why, that's ridiculous, it's totally unacceptable. I certainly expected that I would be able to get about a 12 percent or 13 percent return . . . my friend said last year that she earned 17 percent."

Obviously, we lost sight of the basic rule to *really* know our client. We performed a great deal of work for naught. We failed to uncover our client's unrealistic but, for us, hidden agenda. Question #6 is intended to uncover any expectations regarding returns that the client may have.

Our first version of Question #6 simply addressed the possibility of a hidden agenda by asking for the client's expected return. If he completed the question (which is optional, and which most of our clients skip) with an unrealistic goal, we found ourselves on the defensive. After all, he asked, "Why couldn't we deliver his request?" By adding a space for the client to provide the inflation assumption that underlies his return goal, we found the burden was shifted. The second part of Question #6 tends to serve as a stumbling block. By providing a table of historical real returns, the burden is now on the client to defend an expectation significantly in excess of what has been achieved in the past.

QUESTION #7

For each of the following attributes, circle the number that most correctly reflects your level of concern. The more important, the higher the number. You may use each number more than once.					
	Most Important			Least Important	
Capital preservation	6	5	4	3	2	1
Growth	6	5	4	3	2	1
Low volatility	6	5	4	3	2	1
Inflation protection	6	5	4	3	2	1
Current cash flow	6	5	4	3	2	1
Aggressive growth	6	5	4	3	2	1

This is our ultimate integration of the art and science of wealth management. The question resembles a myriad of similar matrix questions that have been used by other planners over the years. It has, however, been designed to be a much more structured and comprehensive datagathering question than is reflected on its surface.

First, the client is not constrained in prioritizing the six different attributes. He may rate each one as strongly or as weakly as he desires. For example, he may rank all "most important" or all may be ranked "least important." By not forcing the client to prioritize, we find that it lets him focus on each attribute individually. He is not restricted by the impact a choice for one attribute may have on his ability to weight the remaining attributes.

The next component of the structure is the order in which the attributes are listed.

Capital preservation is very purposefully placed first. It is very rare for a client not to read "Capital preservation" and instantly circle "6" (Most Important). Figuratively, and frequently in reality, the client circles "6," looks at the planner, slams his fist on the table, and says, "There! I'm conservative! I told you so!" Basically, it is an opportunity for the conservative client to clearly and emphatically demonstrate that he is *really* conservative and that capital preservation is of paramount importance. He has placed his conservatism on the table. He now feels much better about the process.

Growth follows Capital preservation. Conservative investors like to have some growth in their portfolio. This is the first "I gotcha" built into the matrix. Even our most conservative investors are aware that safe investments such as CDs and U.S. Treasury securities do not have the attribute of growth. At this point, they begin to realize that they may, in fact, have some contradictory goals. We use the conflicting goals of Capital preservation and Growth as an opportunity to continue our discussion about multiple forms of risk.

Volatility is frequently a confusing concept to the client. Listing "low volatility" provides us an opportunity to discuss risk measurement and to distinguish between volatility and capital loss. At this point we may turn back to the education illustrations* and discuss the volatility of various markets over different time periods. Finally, we relate the concept of volatility to their investment time horizon. We bring the client's attention back

---

*Discussed in Chapter 5, Client Education.

to questions #2, 3, and 5, where he has clearly indicated that his investments have at least a five-year-term horizon. In general, after this discussion, we find that most clients, even the most conservative, select a "low volatility" ranking of between 2 and 4.

"Inflation protection" is the ultimate "gotcha." Almost all clients rank this a 5 or a 6. This is particularly true of retirement and postretirement clients. If we have not previously done so, this is the occasion we use, without fail, to address the conflict between inflation protection and capital preservation. Even the most naive of investors knows that no single investment will psychologically satisfy both these goals. We once again refer back to our education charts. Very few clients rate inflation protection much below a 5 as their level of concern. In most cases, the ranking of inflation protection is the same as that for capital preservation. Occasionally it is even higher.

Current cash flow is our opportunity to call the "bluff" of many of our clients. From the earlier questions, particularly #2 and #3, as well as our general data gathering and other questions, we frequently learn that the client has adequate cash flow from other sources (e.g., a pension). On the other hand, we find that most clients, when asked, automatically default to the assumption that they require cash flow from the investment portfolio. It is not at all uncommon for a client to say, "Well, I need at least 4 percent or 5 percent." We discuss with the client the need for cash flow versus the desire for cash flow. In reality, there is frequently little or no need for cash flow.

The last choice, "Aggressive growth," is purposefully included as the last attribute. We started out Question #7 by making our clients feel good by offering them the opportunity to look us in the face and boldly say that they want to preserve their principal. We end the discussion of Question #7 by discussing aggressive growth. We define the term as it is used in the mutual fund industry. We explain that we are not talking about high growth but rather aggressive strategies, such as short sales and margin, or highly volatile investments, such as commodities. This gives our client the opportunity to once again slam his fist on the table, look us straight in the eye, and say, absolutely not, as he circles #1. He now feels terrific! In our practice, we have a policy of avoiding managers who implement aggressive strategies, so the rejection of aggressive growth has little or no effect on our recommendations other than to provide a level of comfort to our clients.

QUESTION #8

Asset Class Constraints		
ASSET CLASSES	Provided Any Asset Class Limitations (OPTIONAL)	
	Minimum	Maximum
T-bills, CDs, money market	_____	_____
Intermediate government bonds	_____	_____
Intermediate corporate bonds	_____	_____
Intermediate municipal bonds	_____	_____
Long-term government bonds	_____	_____
Long-term corporate bonds	_____	_____
Long-term municipal bonds	_____	_____
Foreign bonds	_____	_____
Domestic equities S&P 500	_____	_____
Domestic equities OTC	_____	_____
Foreign equities	_____	_____
Real estate	_____	_____

Asset Class Constraints is the second of two optional questions in the questionnaire. Very much like Question #6, this question is designed to address any potential hidden agenda that we may otherwise miss in discussions with our clients. It also allows us to take the opportunity to discuss investment classes that may be unfamiliar to our clients, such as Foreign Equities, Foreign Bonds, and Real Estate. On occasion, it provides the opportunity to increase the client's willingness to consider an investment class that might otherwise be rejected, by offering to put a maximum cap on an asset class. For example, a client unfamiliar and/or uncomfortable with the possibility of foreign investing may be willing to consider such an investment if he knows that our recommendations will be limited to a maximum allocation, such as 15 percent. In our practice we find that setting specific caps is rarely problematic in our ability to design what we believe to be a functionally efficient portfolio.

QUESTION #9

What percent of your investments are you likely to need within five years?	%

You will note great similarities between Questions #2, #3, #5, and #9. There is no mistake in this. We are adamant in our insistence that the investment portfolio must have a minimum of a five-year horizon. Once again, we discuss our firm mantra "5 years, 5 years, 5 years." The only acceptable answer to Question #9 is "0 percent."

QUESTION #10

Up to what percentage of this portfolio can be invested in long-term investments (i.e., over five years)?	%

This is simply another way of asking the same question we posed in numbers 2, 3, 5, and 9. The only acceptable answer is 100 percent. Now that the client has entered a 0 percent in Question #9 and 100 percent in Question #10, he is under no illusions regarding the fact that these funds have a long-term investment horizon.

In Question #10 we explain to our clients that the redundancy is not only included to educate, alert, warn, and train them. It is also designed to serve as a comforting reminder in the future. When the markets have turned nasty, we will remind them that the world did not actually come to an end. We knew it would happen, just not when it would happen.

We tell them that when the market does take a big plunge, we will pull out this "old" questionnaire and flip it open to the questions they have just answered. We then remind them that they need not panic. We have anticipated this type of market turmoil. Their portfolios were designed with the knowledge that they would not be forced to liquidate at the bottom. It works. Our experience after Black Monday 1987 was a surprise even to us. We called all our clients, anticipating that many would be very concerned. *All* our clients dutifully repeated back to us, "we know, 5 years, 5 years, 5 years." They knew that the world had not come to an end. They also knew that they had no immediate need for their investment funds. Black Monday served as interesting cocktail party patter, but was a nonevent in our clients' lives.

To drive the point home, I would say, "By the way, we are on the phone." After a few seconds of confused silence, my client would say, "Of course we are, you called me, so what?" to which I would respond, "I guess that means AT&T is in business today and I bet families are taking Kodak pictures at Disney World as we speak. I have no idea what happened to the market but you own AT&T, Kodak, Disney, and thousands of other fine companies around the world. I think they are just as good as yesterday, so relax and enjoy your life." My clients got the point. They slept well while others fretted.

QUESTION #11

Investment "risk" means different things to different people. Please rank the following statements from 1 (the statement that would worry you the most) to 4 (the statement that would worry you the least).				
I would be very concerned if I did not achieve the return on my portfolio that I expected (i.e., my target rate of return).	1	2	3	4
I would be very concerned if my portfolio was worth less in "real" dollars because of inflation erosion.	1	2	3	4
I would be very concerned with short-term volatility (i.e., if my portfolio dropped substantially in value over one year).	1	2	3	4
I would be very concerned with long-term volatility, i.e., if my portfolio dropped in value over a long period of time (i.e., five years and longer).	1	2	3	4

This is an attempt to educate our clients regarding the many manifestations of risk, including the risk of losing their standard of living or not meeting their goals, and the risk of not sleeping well (i.e., market volatility.) The first two items above address the issue of returns. We emphasize that their goals are accomplished by earning an appropriate real rate of return, not by earning an arbitrary fixed target return. Item #3 helps clarify for the client that short-term volatility is a reality that he has to live with.

QUESTION #12

Except for the Great Depression, the longest time
investors have had to wait after a market crash or
significant decline, for their portfolio to return to its
earlier value, has been 4 years for stock and 2 years for
bond investments. Knowing this, and that it is impossible
to protect yourself from an occasional loss, answer the
following question:

If my portfolio produces a long-term return that allows
me to accomplish my goals, I am prepared to live with a
time of recovery of:

Less than 1 year...................................   O

Between 1 and 2 years............................   O

Between 2 and 3 years............................   O

More than 3 years. ....   O

If you select the first or second option above, are you   Y   N
prepared to substantially reduce your goals?

This question goes straight to the heart of market volatility and its emotional power. The description emphasizes that even investors in the bond
market have gone through periods in which their portfolio would have
had to wait a few years for positive returns. Stock markets have had bear
markets lasting for as long as four years. With the historical warning that
there is no way of protecting against bear markets, we then ask how long
they will be able to maintain their wits if their portfolio has an extended
loss. We explain that we are talking in terms of 12-month periods and not
the day after Black Monday. For example, if they invested their money on
January 1, 1997, a two-year down market would mean that the portfolio
value would be less on January 1, 1999.

We then allow the client to choose "less than 1 year," "between 1 and
2 years," "between 2 and 3 years" or "more than 3 years." Note that if anything less than "between 2 and 3 years" is checked, we ask the question,
"Are you prepared to substantially reduce your goals?" We explain that if
he checks anything less than 2 years, our recommendation would have to be
that his funds be placed in fixed-income investments with maturities of less

than 2 years. Clearly, if historically the markets have required as long as 2 years for bonds and 3 years for stocks to recover, any investment in either of those asset classes, or a combination thereof is likely to exceed the client's risk tolerance.

QUESTION #13

Please check the statement that reflects your preference.

I would rather be out of the stock market when it goes down than in the market when it goes up (i.e., I cannot live with the volatility of the stock market).	○
I would rather be in the stock market when it goes down than out of the market when it goes up (i.e., I may not like the idea, but I can live with the volatility of the stock market in order to earn market returns).	○

Question #13 is perhaps my personal favorite and my clients' least favorite of all our questions. We do not believe in market timing and we require our clients to acknowledge that they are prepared to accept the reality that they cannot market-time. This question simply points out that if the client wishes to participate in the positive periods of the market he must be prepared to also accept the down periods. Should a client ever indicate that he cannot live with the volatility of the stock market, we explain that the only alternative is an all-bond portfolio which, in all likelihood, will not provide a return adequate to meet his long-term goals.

QUESTION #14

This question was added a number of years ago to provide some way for our clients to select, on the investment spectrum, a risk/return intersection that best represents the balance between their goal for returns and their tolerance for risk. We have divided the risk level into two time frames, short-term (1–3 years), and intermediate-term (more than 3 years). We then give them the choice to select, in qualitative terms, their risk tolerance. For example, if a client indicated he was very conservative and very-low-risk tolerant, he would check "low/low." We believe that, most of the time, during a 12-month period, his return is likely to be near break-even or better. During a severe bear market, we believe his portfolio would drop in value less than 5 percent. We also explain that assuming a long-run inflation rate of 3½ percent, we believe that a realistic total return expectation is 6½ percent. The point of providing a "low/low" alternative is to demonstrate to the client that we can design a conservative portfolio, but we believe it will provide a very low total return.

Several portfolio performance projections are listed below. Assuming that inflation averages 3½ percent, check the portfolio that most nearly reflects your goal for your portfolio.

Overall Risk Level	Expected Compounded Return (Inflation = 3½%)	Expected Annual Range of Returns*			Worst Case**	
Low/Low	6.5%	−2.0%	To	13.0%	−4.0%	O
Mod/Low	7.5%	−3.0%	To	16.0%	−9.0%	O
Mod/Low	7.7%	−4.0%	To	19.0%	−10.0%	O
Mod/Low	8.0%	−4.5%	To	20.0%	−11.0%	O
Mod/Mod	8.3%	−5.0%	To	21.0%	−13.0%	O
High/Mod	8.5%	−6.0%	To	22.0%	−14.0%	O
High/Mod	9.0%	−7.0%	To	24.0%	−20.0%	O
High/Mod	9.5%	−8.0%	To	25.0%	−24.0%	O

*These estimates are based on a statistical measure of one standard deviation. This means that based on the assumptions used in developing these projections, the portfolio returns will fall within these ranges 2 out of every 3 years.
**We use the term *worst case* to describe the worst annual return that a portfolio is likely to experience 90 percent of the time.

The second column is based on our current projections determined from our optimization work. The numbers are adjusted to take the fund expenses and our management fee into account. Note that we anchor the projections with a specific estimate for inflation. When we develop a policy, our target is a real ROR, not a fixed return. For example, if we designed a policy to meet the return expectation noted as 8½ percent, the target return would be 5 percent real ROR, not 8½ percent.

Columns 3 and 4, "Expected Annual Range of Returns," is based on one standard deviation. Rather than use the technical term *standard deviation,* we describe normal volatility as most of the time. We explain that this means 2/3 of the time.

Column number 5, "Worst Case," is based on two standard deviations. As noted in the footnote, we tell our clients that this is the worst return that we believe they are likely to see 1 out of 10 years, or 10 out of 100 years, based on 12-month intervals.

In preparing this table, we make adjustments and tend to overemphasize what we believe are the real downside risks. For example, we incorporate a "volatility fudge factor" and increase the calculated standard deviations by 10 percent to 20 percent. Also, the probability of experiencing a 2-standard-deviation-negative return is significantly less than 90 percent; however, we still use 90 percent as our descriptive criterion.

QUESTION #15

Now you have a test to take. There are two parts to the test. For each question, please check (a) or (b).

Question #1. Choose (a) or (b).

(a) You win $80,000.   ○

(b) You have an 80% chance of winning $100,000   ○
    (or a 20% chance of winning nothing).

Question #2. Choose (a) or (b).

(a) You lose $80,000.   ○

(b) You have an 80% chance of losing $100,000   ○
    (or a 20% chance of losing nothing).

Modified from the work of Tversky, this is another "Aha" question and perhaps the most effective question in the Risk Tolerance Questionnaire. We generally give this to the client by first hiding Question #2 and then allowing him to choose (a) or (b) from Question #1. We have recently changed the question from $8,000 to $80,000 to make sure that our more wealthy clients still consider this a significant decision. It is very rare, indeed, that the client does not choose (a).

We then uncover Question #2 and ask him to make a choice between (a) and (b). For Question #2, it is very rare that the client does not choose (b). We use this as an opportunity to explain the difference between *risk averse* and *loss averse*. We tell our clients that we understand their concern with risk. But, we believe by answering (a) in Question #1 and (b) in Question #2, that they have, in fact, demonstrated that they are not risk averse but are loss averse. We show them that choosing to win $80,000 is a very clear demonstration that they do not wish to take a risk in order to earn more money. However, in choosing (b) in Question #2, they have obviously elected to take a risk. They have elected to take this risk in order to avoid losing money. We explain that this is in keeping with our philosophy. When we recommend investments that our clients might be uncomfortable with (for example, a higher proportion of investments in equities, or a portion of their investments in international and small company stock), we do so not to make them richer, but rather to assist them in maintaining their standard of living.

After going through this discussion, we find that clients who for perhaps 60 or 70 years of their lives have considered themselves very conservative CD investors, all of a sudden light up and say, "Aha, I understand. I may not be comfortable making the investments that you suggest, but I am prepared to make those investments now that I understand the reason why. It makes sense to me."

We point out the difference between our recommendation and that of a traditional stock broker. Brokers recommend the purchase of equities because they will make money; we recommend the purchase of equities so that our clients can maintain their standard of living.

HISTORICAL RETURNS

ANNUAL RETURNS 1926–1994*		
Asset Class	Compounded Return (%)	Standard Deviation (%)
U.S. Treasury bills	3.7%	3.3%
Intermediate Govt. bonds	5.1	5.7
Common stock	10.2	20.3
Small company stock	12.2	34.6
Inflation	3.1	4.6

ACKNOWLEDGEMENTS

By completing and signing this questionnaire you agree that its contents were discussed and explained and you agree that your answers are correct to the best of your knowledge. You also understand that this questionnaire does not make or imply any guarantee regarding the attainment of your investment objective. Please make us aware of any changes in your personal or financial circumstances.

Clients_____

Date_____

Planner _____

*Ibbotson data

The last page of our questionnaire is a table of summary statistics for long-term returns. It serves as a reality anchor for our clients. Throughout the process we explain to them that our investment philosophy is based on the belief that over the long term, they can expect historical real rates of return. This table shows what historical real rates of return are. Finally, we ask our clients to sign an acknowledgment that they have participated in the process and that they are committed to the answers that they have given.

Although their acknowledgment may serve as a defense for us in the event of a disagreement, that is not its purpose. We tell our clients that the completed questionnaire will be their psychological life saver when the market drops.

When they start to panic, we can prove to them that they "saw it coming." We anticipated volatility. They are simply suffering through the unpleasant portion of normal market cycles. We know they do not like to worry and we will assure them that we know they are worried. Still, they made a commitment a long time ago to persevere; not to get rich, but to maintain their quality of life. We have been doing this long enough, and have enough experience to know that it is very comforting for our clients to see proof that they had anticipated a bear cycle. They will not be happy but they will go about their business confident that the world has not come to an end and that tomorrow will be a brighter day.

OTHER RISK-TOLERANCE MODELS

There is no shortage of risk-tolerance models available for use by the wealth manager, but one deserves special mention.

THE AMERICAN COLLEGE—PERSONAL FINANCIAL RISK TOLERANCE[2]

Designed by Michael Roszkowski, a licensed psychologist and faculty member of the American College, the system (composed of a hard-copy guide and a number of computer disks) has a number of unique and valuable features.

The questionnaire itself includes many psychological questions, tested by the American College, for reliability and validity. In addition, the client's response to the questions can be evaluated against an extensive database of responses from clients of graduates of the College's Master program. Obviously, these questions are far superior to those designed by an advisor with no training in psychology and no database to validate the significance of the responses.

The formal report is provided in the form of a client letter. In addition to a familiar raw-score ranking based on a scale of 0 to 100, it provides a number of interpretive graphs.

The first graph (Figure 4–2) relates the client's risk tolerance to the college's extensive database (the details of this reference graph are included in the client letter).

Psychologists tell us that a person's risk-taking behavior may vary across situations. The survey captures information necessary to evaluate and measure the client's consistency. The second graph is the most unique

F I G U R E   4–2

Your Risk Tolerance Score as Compared to Other People's

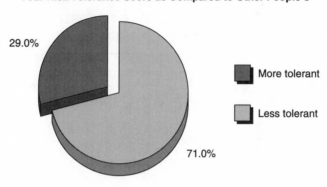

F I G U R E   4–3

Your Consistency as Compared to Other People's

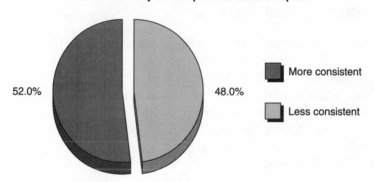

feature of the system. It is a pie chart, measuring a client's consistency in answering the survey as compared to others who have completed the survey. It is reported in Figure 4–3.

The final analytical tool (Figure 4–4) displays the combination of the client's risk tolerance and consistency.

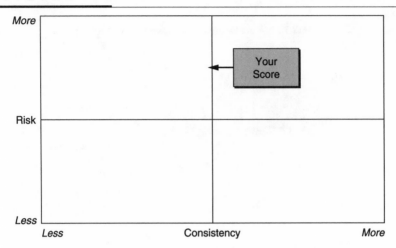

CAPITAL NEEDS ANALYSIS

Capital needs analysis or capital accumulation planning (CAP) is a time value calculation, based on explicit assumptions. When used for retirement planning, the analysis is a present value calculation that factors in the client's unique investments, risk tolerance, tax status, income, and expense factors. By determining the return requirement necessary to balance the client's current portfolio with his future needs (subject to his unique constraints), CAP analysis is the analytical tool used to quantify the return requirement for retirement planning.

COMPREHENSIVE

An effective CAP analysis is a comprehensive approach to evaluating the client's retirement goals. Specifically, it should incorporate an evaluation of the unique composition of the client's portfolio. As an example:

▪ Unique Asset Classes. The client's investments need to be subdivided into economically unique asset classes. A quasi-class, such as limited partnerships, is useless as it describes an investment's legal structure, not its economic exposure. Asset classes are discussed later in this chapter.

▪ Tax Environment. Investments must also be classified according to their tax consequences. For example, an investment in the tax-sheltered environment of a pension will have a significantly different long-term after-tax return from a similar investment held in a personal account. A CAP should account for the tax benefit of shelters.

▪ Liquidation. At some point it may be necessary to sell an asset in order to provide cash flow for a client's living expenses. Some assets can be partially liquidated such that the portion not needed can remain invested (e.g., mutual funds); others may have to be completely liquidated even if only a small percent of the asset value is required (e.g., real estate). As the re-investment rate of a fully liquidated asset may be less than that projected for the original investment, a CAP needs to account for this contingency.

▪ Distribution. Some investments may have required distributions independent of a client's cash flow needs (e.g., pensions and IRAs for clients reaching age $70\frac{1}{2}$). The required distribution may have tax consequences and re-investment constraints resulting in lower future return expectations. A CAP should account for these events.

▪ Interim Expenses. Many clients will have to make demands on their investment portfolio prior to retirement (e.g., subsidize current standard of living, college expenses, weddings). A CAP must account for the timing of these expenses and the impact of inflation. It must also allow for the flexibility of determining from which asset classes these funds will be drawn. They are rarely drawn equally from across the client's portfolio. The result is a change in the portfolio allocation that must be accounted for as the change in allocation may significantly change future return expectations.

▪ Savings. This is the flip side of distributions. The CAP must account for the timing, magnitude, and changes in savings as well as their asset classes and tax environment (e.g., pension contributions).

▪ Postretirement Income and Expenses. As discussed earlier, these cash flow streams must be delineated in detail with respect to timing, magnitude, changes, and tax consequences.

CAP, like our clients' lives, is not a simple process and, if successfully applied, is a mathematically holistic view of our clients' resources and needs.

REAL RATE OF RETURN

When utilizing CAP, there are a number of fundamental issues that must be addressed as part of the design process. Perhaps the most critical is an incorporation of the concept of real rate of return. The mathematics of a CAP analysis requires an input of specific rates of return for each asset class and specific inflation factors for inflatable expenses. Unfortunately, over a typical projection period of 20+ years, returns are likely to vary significantly. All current research concludes that historical total returns provide no predictive value for future returns. However, we can assume, with at least some confidence, that over these extended time horizons, real rates of return will remain relatively consistent.* As a result, instead of using historical total returns, the wealth manager should develop his return input by constructing his projections from real ROR. The constructed projections should equal the projected real ROR for the asset class added to the wealth manager's projected inflation rate.

For example, a CAP analysis in 1989, relying on historic 10-year returns as data input, would use inflation at 4.6 percent, long bonds at 16.2 percent, and equities at an incredible 31.5 percent. Conclusions of a CAP analysis based on this input are likely to be dangerously optimistic. The 10-year period ending in 1989 provided historically extraordinarily high real rates of return. The following are the return inputs currently used by EB&K:

> Bonds—Factoring in our estimate of premium returns added by active management and our use of a laddered maturity distribution, we use a projected 2.8 percent real ROR for the bond allocation.
>
> Stock—For this estimate, in addition to active management and taxes, we take into consideration the fact that we will be allocating not only to large cap domestic equities, but also to small cap domestic, international, and emerging market equities. Our estimate for a blended stock return is a 7.5 percent real ROR.
>
> Inflation—We currently use a long-term inflation assumption of 4 percent.

Take a look at the following table to see what the differences are. Unless the advisor is prepared to defend the assumption that, in the future, real rates of return are likely to significantly exceed historical returns, a CAP analysis should incorporate these lessons of history.

---

*This will be discussed in more detail in Chapter 9, Optimization.

Real Rates of Return

	1985–1994	EB&K Estimates	1926–1994
Bonds	5.8%	2.8%	1.7%
Stock	10.8%	7.5%	7.1%

CONSERVATIVE ASSUMPTIONS

The next issue to consider is the client's inclination to request that the wealth manager use *conservative* assumptions. Unfortunately, the concept of conservative assumptions in a CAP analysis is illusionary. The consequences of using *conservative* assumptions are aggressive investment recommendations.

No Invasion of Capital

Consider the client who requests that the analysis not allow for invasion of principal. You are certainly familiar with the lament, I don't ever want to dip into capital! As conservative as the requests may seem to the client, the result will be a naively conservative portfolio or a much larger allocation to growth investments (which clients think of as risky). The following examples may be useful in explaining the problem of erroneously equating "conservative" with "preserving capital":

> Ms. Moore has a portfolio of $200,000 currently invested in money market funds. After accounting for other sources of income during retirement (e.g., Social Security), she has determined that she will require a living expense supplement for 20 years of $11,000 per year. In addition, she agrees that an inflation factor of 4 percent per year seems reasonable. Her choices are limited to fixed-income investments that are expected to return an after-tax, real rate of return of 1 percent and equities that are expected to provide an after-tax real rate of return of 6 percent. By investing in a balanced portfolio (i.e., 50 percent fixed income and 50 percent equity), Ms. Moore can expect to meet her goals and preserve her portfolio principal. On the other hand, if she chooses to be *conservative* and attempts to preserve her corpus, and invest 100 percent in fixed income, she would eventually be forced to use over 80 percent of the original investment to continue to fund her income needs.

Other Conservative Illusions

Other assumptions that may be illusory-conservative and result in inappropriate, aggressive portfolios include, "I don't trust Social Security, so let's be conservative and leave it out," or, "Well, let's be conservative and ignore that inheritance," and the perennial favorite, "Well, taxes always go up, so let's increase your tax bracket."

Conservative Assumptions—My Opinion

Conservative CAP analysis is based on utilizing the best available information. It is the responsibility of the wealth manager to use his utmost professional judgment in determining when to include or exclude certain assumptions. Such decisions should not be made based on a simplistic belief that an assumption of lower income is inherently conservative. It is not. The estimation of the probability of the future income stream should be based on the wealth manager's informed judgment.

MORTALITY

As discussed earlier, even if the wealth manager avoids all of the problems above, the conclusions of a CAP analysis will be nonsense unless reasonable mortality assumptions are made in the process. Our questionnaire includes a section requesting the age of death of our client's siblings, parents, and grandparents, or, if still living, an evaluation of their general health. The goal is to accumulate enough data to make an educated judgment regarding how long-lived our clients are likely to be. At a minimum, we use a 70 percent mortality standard. For clients from very-long-lived families, we may use a 90 percent standard.*

PROCESS

Data-Gathering/Input Guide

Figure 4–5 is a simplified version of a data-gathering and input form used to capture the information needed to complete a CAP analysis. It will serve as a guide for the following discussion:

---

*For example, a 70 percent standard means that we would use as our estimate for the client's mortality, an age by which 70 percent of the population, the same age as our client, will have died. Our current mortality table matrix is included in Chapter 1, Client Goals and Constraints.

Capital Needs Analysis Data Gathering & Input Guide

Each Spouse:	Current Age
	Retirement Age
	Mortality Age
Pre- & Post-Retirement:	Inflation
	Marginal Tax Bracket
Assets:	Asset Class
	Tax Status, Returns
	Liquidation Constraints
	Payout Sequence
Pre-Retirement Cash Flow:	Contributions & Distributions
	Annual Amount
	Growth
	Beginning & Ending
Post-Retirement Cash Flow:	Income & Expenses
	Source
	Tax Status
	Annual Amount
	Growth
	Beginning & Ending

CAP Software

The first use of this data-gathering guide is as a tool to judge the analytical software the wealth manager plans to use to perform the calculations. Don't spend days, or even hours, constructing massive spreadsheets to evaluate various software vendors' products. Instead, use Evensky's Screening Process. Although originally conceived of to evaluate comprehensive financial planning software, it is a simple and invaluable technique for selecting mutual fund software, asset allocation software, and CAP analysis software. The idea is simple. Do not bother looking in detail at software that will not meet your minimum requirements. Suppose that you were looking for a new car and saw a beauty that you thought you might like to own. What would be your reaction if you discovered that, inexplicably, the manufacturer omitted a speedometer and there was no way to add one. Would you really spend time inquiring about city and highway mpg and choice of colors? Of course not. So, if a CAP analysis program will not let you enter data in the detail you consider necessary, do you really care how beautifully it can produce colored charts and graphs? Again, of course not! Reject software that will not accept data in the detail you deem necessary. Then, eliminate any software that will not meet your practice-specific criteria (e.g., color graphics- or Windows-based). Finally, select the best from the survivors of the prior screens. When you consider that the results of a CAP analysis drive the investment portfolio allocation, and determine the future quality of life for the client, it should be obvious that short-cut or simplistic analysis is not only inadequate, it's unprofessional.

Unrealistic Expectations

Before even beginning the CAP analysis, there is one client issue that must be addressed as it can potentially torpedo all of the wealth manager's future work. Determine whether your client has unrealistic expectations regarding assets in his current investment portfolio. We have all had clients who believe that their heavy concentration in their very favorite stock will grow at an unrealistic rate ("I work for the company, I know a good thing when I see it"), or own an apartment that they believe will have returns exceeding all other real estate ("Well, this apartment is in the best neighborhood in the city—it can't go wrong!") In these cases, you have two alternatives. One is to run a CAP analysis using the client's estimates and then re-run it with your more realistic estimates. Show the client his risk of a reduced standard of living if unsystematic risk catches up with him or if his optimism turns out to be unfounded. The second alternative is to do a simple economic analysis and demonstrate to your client how much more return he is projecting than the experts have historically been able to achieve.

Data Gathering—Step by Step

Personal Data
First, start with the determination of the client's current personal status. In addition to the obvious questions such as current age, spouse's age, and expected retirement dates, the wealth manager needs to capture information helpful in determining a mortality age.

Existing Portfolio

Asset Classes   Next, we need to consider the client's existing portfolio. As discussed earlier, the investments need to be separated by function. Most software provides for a single investment class. This simplified approach is woefully inadequate. Among other things, a single portfolio with a blended return cannot account for additional investments in or withdrawals from an asset class. It cannot account for different tax consequences or varying liquidation priorities. Some software solutions purport to separate investments but use pseudo classes: pensions, mutual funds, and partnerships. As investments in each of these pseudo classes could be in almost any true economic class (such as short bonds, long bonds, domestic stock, international stock, and gold), pseudo classes are useless.

Return Assumptions   Having separated the investments by true economic classes, the wealth manager needs to make assumptions regarding the returns for each class. Next he must determine the tax status of those returns. Investments in a client's personal account will be currently taxed at some mix of the ordinary rate and the capital gains rate, whereas investments in IRAs, pensions, or annuities will grow tax deferred and be subject to ordinary taxes on future distributions. This requires a careful review of each investment. The wealth manager cannot simply assume that taxable gains are correlated with turnover. This was discussed at length in Chapter 3. For example, investments in actively traded equity accounts may generate less taxable income than a low-turnover mutual fund.

Reinvestment Risk   In order to account for reinvestment risk, each investment must be considered in terms of its marketability. For example, suppose your client has a half million dollars invested in a floating rate real estate mortgage. The mortgage was placed at a rate quite favorable for the client. It is paying a real ROR of 8 percent. Ten years from now, the mortgage matures. The proceeds may be invested at a much lower rate.

Savings and Liquidations   Clients do not take savings and invest them in "their portfolio." That is, the savings are not reinvested pro rata over the existing portfolio but are, in fact, being invested in specific asset classes. If funds are withdrawn before retirement for interim goals (such as college funding or paying for a child's wedding), the funds are also drawn from specific asset classes, not pro rata across the portfolio. As noted earlier, this ever-changing asset mix does not allow for simply assuming a fixed-proportion blended portfolio.

Preretirement additions to the portfolio may come from numerous sources such as savings, lump sums (e.g., gifts and inheritances), and sales of businesses. Hence, the wealth manager needs to factor in any expected changes (such as a gradual increase in savings) and determine what asset class is likely to be used for investment.

Withdrawals are the mirror image of investments. We need to account for preretirement withdrawals for such interim goals as supplementing preretirement living conditions or college funding. As with investments, we need to determine when and from which asset classes the withdrawals are likely to be made.

Postretirement Assumptions   These can be divided into two categories:

- Income sources independent of the investment portfolio

  The primary factors are the source and amount (e.g., pensions), changes in that amount (e.g., pension payment with a COLA), the timing, and the tax consequences (e.g., Social Security taxation).

- Postretirement expenses

  The necessity to classify postretirement expenses into at least four classes was discussed at length in the earlier section on client goals.

  Given this multiplicity of postretirement income classes, perhaps one day the media will take NEFE's course and stop recommending such worthless rules of thumb such as "You need 70 percent of preretirement income."

The following examples may be helpful in evaluating a software package's ability to handle these issues. The question in all cases is, Can the software handle the client's unique circumstances?

- Clients frequently invest their retirement savings in an allocation different from their personal assets. They may, for example, invest their retirement plan assets 30 percent in bonds and 70 percent in stock while maintaining a personal allocation of 60 percent bonds and 40 percent stock.

- Clients may have significant personal investments in fixed and variable annuities.

- A significant portion of the client's portfolio is in a single piece of real estate. He believes that when the real estate is sold he will not be able to replace it with an investment providing the same return.
- In four years, the client will be drawing down a significant portion of his personal savings before retirement to fund his child's college education. These funds will largely be drawn from his short-term bond investments (that's why he's been accumulating these funds). These withdrawals will significantly change his overall portfolio allocation over the next few years.
- A client estimates that he will receive an inheritance in 10 years. As it is a portion of a family business, it will pay an increasing amount yearly. He plans to sell his interest three years after the inheritance.

Analysis

Once the number crunching has been completed, the wealth manager will have determined the ability of his client's current portfolio to meet his retirement goal. Basically, the CAP analysis will lead to 1 of 4 conclusions; the client can, with his existing portfolio allocation, just achieve his goals; he will fall short of his goals; he needs to change the allocation to reflect a higher percentage of growth assets in order to meet his goals; or his goals are so modest compared to his resources that he may increase his fixed-income allocation and still achieve his goals.

In our practice, the results of the CAP analysis are a major component in the next stage of the wealth management process—the portfolio allocation. We will revisit this idea a little later.

CAP CAVEAT

We are firm believers in the use of a detailed and comprehensive capital needs analysis to assist our clients to quantify their retirement planning goals. In October 1994, however, I read an article that led me to revisit our approach. The article was "Determining Withdrawal Rates Using Historical Data," by William P. Bengen, published in the October 1994 issue of the *Journal of Financial Planning*.

The article was a wake-up call and a reminder for our practice that our use of long-term "conservative" real rates of return in our CAP analysis will not protect our client from becoming a *black hole* investor. The *black hole* investors are the ones who had the misfortune to begin the drawdown of their retirement funds just at the beginning of a major market correction (e.g., 1937, 1946, 1969, 1973, and 1974). For those unfortunate souls, an early erosion of corpus may make it impossible for the portfolio to recover sufficiently to maintain their standard of living. After reading the article, we realized that we had fallen into the trap of believing that using long-term average returns implied we were being conservative. We forgot that averages can be dangerous. A man with his head in the oven and his body in a freezer may have an average body temperature of 98.6 degrees, but he is not comfortable.

In addition to refocusing our attention on reality and not just averages, Mr. Bengen's article included a number of exceptionally useful graphs. The series that our clients find particularly meaningful are those showing, for a specific withdrawal rate and portfolio allocation, the number of years the portfolio would last before becoming totally depleted. Three of his graphs that we find most useful are presented here as Figures 4–6 through 4–8.

Our Number	Bengen's Number	Graph
Figure 4–6	Figure 1(c)	5% withdrawal/50% stock
Figure 4–7	Figure 1(d)	6% withdrawal/50% stock
Figure 4–8	Figure 2	Minimum years

F I G U R E   4-6

**Number of Years Portfolio Assets Will Last
(Withdrawals Vary Each Year with Inflation)**

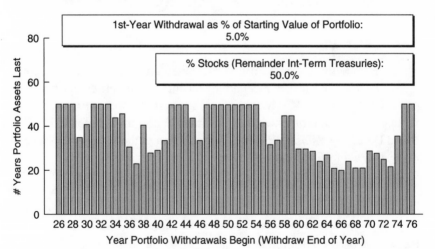

FIGURE   4-7

Number of Years Portfolio Assets Will Last
(Withdrawals Vary Each Year with Inflation)

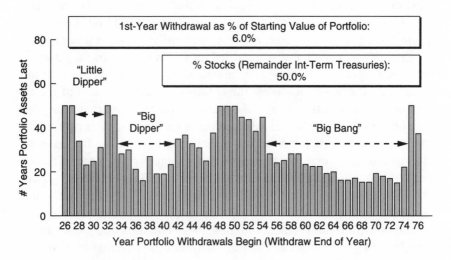

FIGURE   4-8

Minimum Number of Years Withdrawals Will Last
(Assuming Worst Case from 1926–1976 Ibbotson Data)

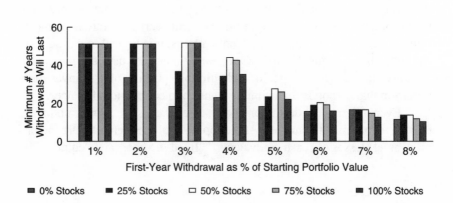

Bengen's article was, in effect, a generalization of a strategy that Larry Bierwirth wrote about in the January 1994 issue of the *Journal of Financial Planning*. Titled "Investing for Retirement: Using the Past to Model the Future," it introduces the concept of a dynamic ledger. Using the recommended allocation for the client and the client's projected cash flow requirements (in real dollars), beginning in 1926, a year-by-year personal historical ledger is developed. In fact, a series of these ledgers is developed. Each new series assumes retirement in a later year. Bierwirth describes the results as a family album of the actual experience of the client's 42 relatives whose resources and goals mirror the client's. The only difference is the year of their retirement. We found Bengen's paper an important influence on our implementation of our CAP analysis and Bierwirth's dynamic ledger an effective way of communicating the issues to our clients. Based on these papers, the conclusion our investment committee reached was that we would continue to use CAP as our primary analytical tool; however, we would constrain our recommendations based on the conclusions of the article. Also, we would add to our client education program a special discussion to address the differences between historical averages and historical reality.

ASSET CLASSES

In order to intelligently gather data regarding a client's investments, it is necessary to agree on a definition of an asset class. As the conceptual basis for optimization is diversifying investments across different segments of the economy that move in different patterns, it is logical to define asset classes in those terms. *Wealth Management* therefore uses the phrase *asset class* to describe a specific, identifiable portion of the investment spectrum that responds, in a similar manner, to economic influences.

Even utilizing the definition above, asset classes are a fuzzy notion, as they have multiple hierarchies. At the top level of the hierarchy are the primary asset classes of "cash equivalents," "fixed income," and "equities."

CASH EQUIVALENTS

This primary class has no subclasses. For investment purposes, the choices are T-bills, money market, cash reserves, and similar highly liquid investments. As a general default, we use a one-year maturity as a cut-off, although, for most purposes, we consider T-bills and money market mutual funds the cash equivalents of choice.

FIXED INCOME

- **Issuer** The issuer of the fixed-income instrument will determine in which of a number of possible subclasses the instrument might be classified in issuer-related considerations.
- **Tax Status** The obvious differentiation regarding taxes is between:

Corporate and Foreign Governments—fully taxable.

U.S. Government—exempt from state taxes.

Municipal—exempt from federal taxes and possibly state taxes.

States levying taxes differ in their treatment of municipal bonds and each must be reviewed individually. In addition, some bonds may provide shelter from ordinary income taxes but subject the holder to AMT taxes. Even rarer, but possible, are municipal bonds fully subject to ordinary federal income taxes.

As a general rule, the wealth manager might find it useful to separate a client's fixed-income assets according to the client's tax status. The wealth manager should, however, remember that the real issue is not how much the client pays in taxes but, rather, what the client's after-tax return is.

- **Quality** The issuer, or, as bond traders say, the "name," generally determines the investment quality of the bonds. However, there are numerous forms of security enhancements that might increase the perceived quality.
- **Country** Although it is true that the bonds of foreign issuers differ significantly in their performance depending on the country of issue, I recommend that the wealth manager simply divide the universe of global bonds into domestic and foreign. A wealth manager who considers foreign bonds for a client's portfolio will find his time most efficiently spent selecting a foreign bond manager who can be delegated the responsibility of determining the country allocations. The general convention in classifying mutual funds is to consider the term *global* as all-inclusive, i.e., all countries including the United States, and *international* as exclusive, i.e., all countries except the United States. I will use that convention in this text. Note that domestic is synonymous with U.S.; foreign is synonymous with international.

■ **Maturity/Duration** As we'll discuss in more detail in Chapter 6, Mathematics of Investing, an even more important distinction for purposes of asset class assignment is fixed income's sensitivity to interest rate changes. As an example, the Solomon 1- to 3-year Corporate Bond correlation with the Solomon Treasury 1- to 3-year Bond is 0.98, but with the Lehman Municipal Bond index the correlation is only 0.83.

For purposes of evaluating the interest rate exposure of individual managers or specific bonds, the most appropriate measure is duration. For general classification purposes, I find it useful to think in terms of four broad ranges:

	Maturity in Years	Maximum Duration in Years
Short Term	1–3	2.5
Short/Intermediate	3–5	3.5
Intermediate	5–10	6.0
Long Term	>10	>6.0

■ **Structure** Fixed-income securities are among the most complex of all security investments. The complexity may derive from the basic payout structure inherent in the security (e.g., mortgage-backed securities) or as a result of financial engineering (e.g., CMOs). Although it is not necessary for the wealth manager to become an expert in these areas, it is important that he understand enough of the dynamics of fixed-income structure to properly allocate those investments according to their natural asset classes. One of the less scientific aspects of structure is what I call *surprises.* An awareness of these possible problems is also important in order to avoid misclassification of a client's fixed-income investment.

One type of surprise is an event that might result in the security being redeemed earlier than anticipated. This is a serious risk if the potentially hidden surprise is built into an existing bond portfolio (e.g., a mutual fund or closed-end fund) or a previously issued bond. In these cases, it may be difficult, if not impossible, to locate the surprise by a simple review of the investment's description and ratings.

Another example of a potential surprise is the risk of a bond facing a possible rating downgrade. With tens of thousands of issuers, it is unlikely that any wealth manager will know that a particular issuer is at risk of having its current rating downgraded. Bond traders, however, are likely to be aware of this exposure and will demand a premium for bonds with a "bad" name. If the bond is part of a mutual fund portfolio, it certainly will not be highlighted in the fund's promotional material.

The solution to protection against surprises is to follow the sage advice, "If it's too good to be true, it usually is." In other words, trust the efficiency of the markets. Applying this to the problem of locating potential surprises in fixed-income investments means that the wealth manager should compare the current market yield of the bond or portfolio to current market yields of ostensibly comparable quality/duration issues. If the item under consideration is being offered at a significant premium to the current market, there is very likely an embedded surprise.

It is clear from the discussion above that there are numerous possible sub-asset class divisions for fixed-income investments. To simplify the taxonomy, it may be unnecessary to divide each and every one into all its possible components. I recommend that the minimum classifications include:

> Cash equivalents
> Corporate/Government and municipal
>> Short-term fixed income
>> Short-intermediate-term fixed income
>> Long-term fixed income
> International fixed income

For larger portfolios it might be appropriate to consider further subdivision by tax status and investment quality (e.g., investment grade and below investment grade) and strategy (e.g., hedged and unhedged). However, as indicated by the list above, even the smallest portfolio should be divided into the classifications listed above.

EQUITIES

The primary equity class division is into stocks, real estate, natural resources, and tangibles. Stocks represent an investment in an asset class that one would expect to perform well in positive economic environments with low to moderate inflation. Real estate would typically perform well in moderate to high inflation. Natural resources generally respond well during high inflation and tangibles and collectibles during very high and hyperinflation.

As most investors concentrate the bulk of their equity funds in stocks, it is necessary to further divide that asset class.

▪ **Domestic** Individual domestic companies may have significant international operations. For simplicity, these should still be considered domestic equities.

However, this simplifying assumption is not applicable with regard to pooled assets. Increasingly, domestic equity managers, particularly domestic mutual fund managers, are branching out to include significant positions in foreign companies.* To the extent the allocation becomes significant (we use 20 percent as a guide), it may be necessary to split the portfolio allocation for these managers between domestic and international.

▪ **Capitalization** As there is no legal or regulatory definition of capitalization, there are numerous definitions. The following represent the most common:

1. >$5 billion—This is the usual large cap break point for classifications that consider three size categories (large, medium, and small).

2. > $1 billion—The traditional split for those using only two size categories (large and small).

3. >½ billion—This is a logical standard for small cap for those using three tiers.

4. Recently, there has been research suggesting that very small firms, referred to as micro-cap, should be considered as a separate class. The measure usually set to define micro-cap is <$100 million.

I recommend a two-tier classification:
Large Cap > $1 billion and Small Cap < $1 billion.

▪ **Style** There has been a great deal written regarding style and we will discuss this later in greater detail. At this stage, for purposes of establishing a general and useful taxonomy, I recommend the following classifications:

Core–A market holding (e.g., the Vanguard S&P 500 or the Schwab 1000.) Although any position, including a market portfolio, can be separated into styles, clients have an emotional tie to the "market."

---

*As an example, according to Morningstar reports for December 1995, Fidelity Capital Appreciation held more than 40 percent in foreign stock; Scudder Value and T. Rowe Growth Stock both held more than 20 percent.

This is exacerbated by daily (if not hourly) exposure to the financial media. As a result, it is useful to provide some allocation to a core position.

Growth–Using book to market as the measure of style, we define growth stocks as those with a book-to-market ratio lower than the mid-decile of the stock on the NYSE.

Value–Rather obviously, those stocks or portfolios with book-to-market ratios greater than the mid-decile of the stock on the NYSE.

Top Down/Bottom Up–Although I consider this a secondary aspect of style and one that overlaps with growth and value, it is important to know a manager's basic philosophical bias. From an institutional perspective, *top down* describes an organizational structure that develops an approved allocation model and related asset class/country constraints and expects the individual managers to invest within these parameters. A *bottom up* structure allows far more flexibility for the individual managers to concentrate on the attributes of individual companies. As an example, the Montgomery Emerging Markets fund develops a country allocation model based on a proprietary optimizer. Although managers have the authority to override the model to some extent, there are basic policy constraints that mandate a portfolio weighting of at least one-fifth of the IFC Global index and not more than five times the IFC Global index weighting (and not to exceed 25 percent). Harbor International Growth is bottom up. Country and industry allocations are entirely determined by stock selection.

▪ **Other** Numerous additional possible classifications exist. Major examples include yield, sector, metals, and REITs.

Yield stock generally correlate closely with value. Although there is some preliminary research suggesting that utilities might be usefully considered as a separate asset class, the results are not definitive enough at this time to justify a separate classification.

I believe sector allocations are more of a marketing concept than investment class. Wealth managers who believe that sectors are true asset classes must develop their own criteria for incorporating sector funds into their classification system.

Precious metals are a primary equity class. The question is, how to invest in these metals. Many stocks represent ownership in metals-related ventures and many managers suggest that they manage metals funds. It would seem reasonable to include metals as a separate class and invest via these metals-related stocks or funds. In our practice, unfortunately, our own studies indicate that, at least among the available mutual funds, none provide an economic exposure that correlates with the price of precious metals.

As a minimum, I would recommend an equity classification taxonomy that includes the following:

Large capitalization domestic.

Small capitalization domestic.

Large capitalization international developed.

Emerging markets.

REITs.

For larger portfolios it might be appropriate to consider further subdivisions including small cap international and micro-cap.

Table 4–2 is a detailed summary of the possible asset classes and subasset classes a wealth manager might consider. As the table clearly demonstrates, even for a minimally diversified portfolio, there is a requirement of selecting a large number of asset classes.

So far, we have considered those aspects of our clients that are quantifiable. We have considered time and dollar quantification and goal prioritization. We looked in detail at the multiple classes of postretirement expenses, investment tax consequences, and allocations of additional savings to asset classes. Even if we must make tenuous estimates, all of these issues eventually are converted to numbers that we can process with some form of mathematical engine. Next we will discuss the most important aspect of client communication and expectation management—education. So, put down your calculators, turn off your computers, and turn to the next chapter.

T A B L E   4-2

Taxonomy of Asset Classes/Styles*

I. **Cash Equivalents**
II. Fixed Income
    A. Short term
        1. **Corporate**
        2. **Government**
        3. **Municipal**
        4. International
    B. Short/Intermediate
        1. Corporate
            a. **Investment grade**
            b. Below investment
                grade
        2. Municipal
            a. **Investment grade**
            b. Below investment
                grade
    C. Intermediate
        1. Corporate
            a. **Investment grade**
            b. Below investment
                grade
        2. Municipal
            a. **Investment grade**
            b. Below investment
                grade
        3. International
            a. **Developed nations**
            b. Emerging markets
    D. Long-Term
        1. Corporate
            a. Investment grade

            b. Below investment
                grade
        2. Municipal
            a. Investment grade
            b. Below investment
                grade
        3. International
            a. Developed nations
            b. Emerging markets
III. Equities
    A. Stock
        1. Large capitalization
           domestic
            a. **Growth**
            b. **Value**
            c. **Core**
        2. Small capitalization
           domestic
            a. **Growth**
            b. **Value**
            c. Microcap**
        3. International
            a. Developed countries
                (1) **Top down**
                (2) **Bottom up**
                (3) Small company
            b. **Emerging markets**
    B. Real Estate
    C. Tangibles
        1. Precious metals
        2. Collectibles

---

*Those items in bold are the ones we currently use for our clients.
**We include this in "value."

E N D N O T E S

1. Eleanor Blayney, "Assessing Your Client's Tolerance for Risk," IAFP Advanced Planners Conference, 1995.
2. The American College, 270 Bryn Mawr Avenue, Bryn Mawr, PA. 19010.

CHAPTER 5

Client Education

You have to pick what you're going to be worried about.
Markets are volatile, but retirement is certain.

—Nick Murray

Uncared wealth is one risk you can't afford. Money has
plenty of natural enemies—inflation, politics, ignorance.

The ultimate success of any client relationship begins with the appropriate education of the client. No matter how astute or sophisticated the client may be in his own profession, without prior education by his advisor, he will rarely, if ever, have an understanding of the issues necessary to become a successful participant in the wealth management process. Clients, without this preparation, will not understand the terminology of the wealth manager. If the advisor begins the goal-setting and data-gathering process before the education process, he may think he is speaking English, but to the client it may sound like Sanskrit. There is a significant probability that either the necessary information will not be captured and/or the client will not accept the wealth manager's final recommendations.

MINI-EDUCATION PROGRAM

Before having the client complete a risk tolerance questionnaire, we provide the client with a mini-educational program. Depending on the client's questions and the digressions that the conversation may take, this program typically takes between one-half and one and a half hours. We have it prepared to be presented either by flip chart or computer display.

The purpose of the program is threefold:

- To introduce the client to the basic concepts of modern investment theory (e.g., asset allocation, manager style).

- To provide a basic vocabulary framework (e.g., volatility, style, risk).

- To make our client aware of our philosophy and biases (e.g., our belief in the work of Brinson, Hood, and Beebower, and a total rejection of traditional market timing).

The following pages include examples and explanations of many of the tables and illustrations we use, examples of the issues covered, and the presentation style.

Figure 5–1 The Investment Process

After a few slides that introduce our firm, we begin the education process with this flow chart of the investment process. Modeled after one developed by Don Trone,* we find it an effective introduction to our philosophy.

We begin with a description of the top left-hand box, "Investor Objectives and Constraints." This is an opportunity to discuss the need to define each of the client's objectives with time and dollar specificity and to rank them in order of priority. We explain to our student-client that constraints can include any restrictions on the investment process that the client may desire. Examples might include keeping the stock they inherited from Grandma, setting aside $20,000 for mad money, or restricting any allocation to international stock to no more than 15 percent of the portfolio. The point we wish to make is that our client drives the investment process. Our job is to educate and assist him to achieve his goals, not to tell him what his goals should be.

Included in the discussion at this stage is an introduction to our data-gathering process. We want the client to understand that we follow a very structured process. This enables us to obtain the information necessary to adequately and accurately reflect his objectives and constraints. We want

---

*Trone, Allbright and Taylor, *The Management of Investment Decisions,* Irwin, 1996. Also Trone, Allbright, and Madden, *Procedural Prudence,* SEI, 1991.

F I G U R E   5-1

The Investment Process

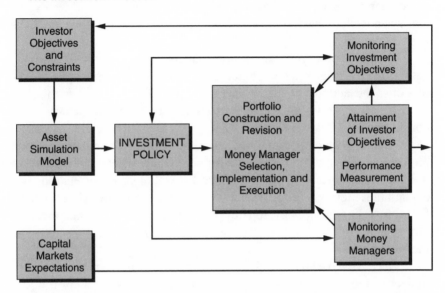

him to know how important it is to thoughtfully and completely assist us in completing the data-gathering forms. Equally important, we want him to be proactive and bring to our attention anything he believes we may have neglected to ask.

Over and over (probably ad nauseum) we emphasize that he is the sole reason for this whole process and this first step is the most important.

"Asset Simulation Model" and "Capital Market Expectations" are usually discussed together. After a brief description of the concept of portfolio diversification, we explain that we use a sophisticated mathematical model that provides guidance for the most efficient combinations of investments. Because the model requires a number of assumptions, we explain that it is our job to develop these assumptions. We begin by listing those asset classes that our client has agreed to consider. Once we have that list, for each of the asset classes we make three estimates. The first estimate concerns the returns we believe our client is likely to earn over the next 3 to 5 years. Our second estimate is a measure of how confident we are of our first. For example, although we may expect large cap growth stock to *average* 13 percent per year, we do not expect *exactly* 13 percent per year. There will be good and bad years. So, we might estimate a risk factor of 20 percent. That means, most of the time, we would expect the stock returns to range from –7 percent to +33 percent, and we expect that when we look back five years from now, the average return will have been 13 percent.

Third, we point out that all investments do not go up and down together (this is usually accompanied by moving my hands in opposite directions; the action helps to wake them up). To account for this, we estimate each asset class movement relative to all of the others we've considered.

Although we do not go into great detail regarding our capital market projections, we do discuss the basis for our estimates. We explain that we use historical projections for the standard deviations and correlations (we explain these terms) but we do not believe in using historical projections for returns. Instead, we develop our own estimates based on historical return relationships and our expectations regarding the economy over the next 3 to 5 years.

Once we have all our estimates, we feed them into our computer optimizer and after lots of thinking and fiddling, we arrive at a portfolio allocation that we believe will best suit our client's needs. In discussing the "Asset Simulation Model," I liken it to playing the piano. I tell the client that while we are exceptionally good technicians and scientists and use the most sophisticated computer hardware and software, 90 percent of the process is art. I add that we are also exceptionally fine artists. The end result is not an answer from a black box. It is a recommendation from our brains and heart, based on information developed by a mathematical model that we have selected and understand.

With the results of this analysis in hand, we then prepare a comprehensive and detailed road map, the "investment policy." This is a custom document unique for our client. It will not only tell him where to invest, it will explain why (i.e., detail his goals and constraints). It will also describe the assumptions. In the future, this will provide standards to measure the performance of the policy.

We explain that with the road map in hand, we can then select the best managers for each piece of the portfolio. After all, we know what asset classes we wish to invest in and the policy tells us how much to place in each. We also know what kinds of returns we expect of the manager of each class and how much risk we expect him to take. That information is also in the policy.

Once we have implemented the policy, we monitor the process. We monitor the managers against the standards established in the policy. We monitor the overall goal of the policy and we monitor the policy against the client's current objectives and constraints.

If a manager fails to meet the standards set for his or her performance, he or she is fired and a new manager is hired. If the portfolio fails to meet the goals of the policy, it is modified. If the client's goals and/or constraints change, the policy is reviewed and possibly revised. The process is ongoing and it begins and ends with our client.

F I G U R E   5-2

The Most Important Determinant of Portfolio Performance Turns Out to Be Asset Class Selection

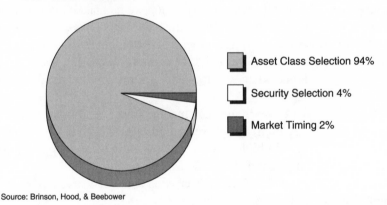

Source: Brinson, Hood, & Beebower

Figure 5-2 Asset Allocation Pie Chart

As the Brinson, Hood, and Beebower study is so important to the core of our philosophy, we spend time describing the nature of the work. Depending on the client, we may even review with him the tables from the study.

We emphasize that we are experts in portfolio allocation. We explain that we understand the real excitement is in selecting managers but we want our clients to always keep in mind the importance of the allocation decision.

Frequently we will use this chart as an opportunity to discuss the trauma of buying low and selling high. Everyone agrees that there is no better way to success in the market. We point out that, unfortunately, it may not feel like the best system. We use the following example to help our clients understand.

In August 1987, when the stock market was reaching a peak, we were selling stock and buying bonds. We were not doing this because we were market timers. We did not anticipate a crash. We had no idea the market was going to take a dive. We were only rebalancing. If a client had started with a portfolio split, 50 percent bonds and 50 percent stocks, by August 1987, his or her portfolio might have become 40 percent bonds and 60 percent stocks, simply as a result of the run-up in stock prices. As our policy said 50/50, we sold stock and bought bonds to bring the portfolio back into balance. Occasionally, the question arose, Are you nuts? Selling stock and buying bonds in one of the best bull markets? The answer was, No, we're not crazy, we're just doing what we do—very unemotionally rebalancing back to the policy.

In October 1987, when the market hit bottom, some 50/50 portfolios were closer to 60/40. Not because of any action we had taken but because stocks were worth less. Naturally, we started buying stocks to rebalance back to 50/50. This time the question was, Are you nuts? Buying stocks when the world's coming to an end? The answer was, No, we're not crazy, we're just doing what we do—very unemotionally rebalancing back to the policy.

After this vignette, we invite the student-client to tell us if we sold high or low (obviously high) and if we had purchased high or low (obviously low). Aha! We sold high and bought low. Just what we wanted to do. It just did not feel so good at the time.

Generally, this is an interesting discussion and a new perspective for the client. He begins to understand the power of an investment policy and the benefits of being an intelligent contrarian. He also understands that there is no free lunch. Good long-term performance is paid for with the coin of fear and worry. Not only does diversification almost always guarantee that he will have some investment that is doing poorly, but that's the one we'll be buying more of.

The next three illustrations all relate to market timing. We usually place these just after the asset allocation pie chart. Frequently, the discussion about selling high and buying low leads to the question of why not just avoid the market lows by getting out of the market. These illustrations are part of our answer. Before going further, however, a note to any timer fan. You may want to skip to the next discussion as we are timing skeptics.

We usually begin the discussion of market timing by relating it to a Ouija Board (we have one in the office). Our conclusion is that we place far more faith in the Ouija Board.

We tell our clients that we have three major objections to market timing:

- Almost all studies, academic and practitioner, conclude that, over time and after transaction costs, market timing does not add value. The few studies in support of timing are almost all based on hypothetical backing testing, prepared by marketers of timing services.

- Market returns, both positive and negative, frequently occur in short spurts. Successful market timing requires not one but two correct "calls"—getting out of the market before it goes down *and* getting in before it goes back up.

- If anyone ever did develop a system for successful market timing, it stretches credulity to believe that they would share it.

T A B L E   5–1

Why Market Timing Doesn't Work
1991 Market Performance

	S&P 500 Appreciation	# of Trading Days
Entire year	26.3%	253 days
Jan 16–Feb 13	17.6	21
Last 7 days	9.0	7
Rest of 1991	−1.5	225

Table 5–1 Why Market Timing Doesn't Work

This table demonstrates the difficulty of catching market spurts. In 1991, almost all the year's positive return occurred during 28 of the 253 trading days. Almost 70 percent was attributable to a 21-day market run-up from January 16 to February 13.

T A B L E   5-2

Market Timing Is Risky
Missing a Few Good Days Substantially Reduces Return

1989–1994	S&P 500 Annualized Returns (%)
All 1,275 trading days	10.30%
Minus 10 best days	4.28
Minus 20 best days	0.14
Minus 30 best days	−3.29
Minus 40 best days	−6.56

Figures assume that when not invested in stocks, assets were earning interest at the average of a 30-day Treasury Bill over the 1989–1994 period.
Source: Ibboston Associates and Sanford Bernstein & Co.

T A B L E   5-3

Market Timing Should Be Avoided as an Investment Strategy for an Entire Portfolio
For the 88-Year Period between 1901 and 1988

Buy and Hold Stock Return	9.4%
Perfect Forecasting of All Bear/Bull Markets	15.8%
Correct Forecasting 50% of the Time	6.6%
Correct Forecasting of Bear Markets, 50% Bull Markets	8.7%
Correct Forecasting of 71% of Bear/Bull Markets	9.4%

Table 5-2 Market Timing Is Risky

This table demonstrates the same problem over a 10-year period. As we point out during the discussion, there is a real likelihood that a timer will miss the upsurgings. They frequently occur when the market is bouncing back from a low. This is when timers often stay on the sidelines waiting for a "trend" to be established. For anyone old enough to remember Joe Granville, his poor performance after successfully calling the 1987 crash is a powerful example.

Table 5-3 Market Timing Should Be Avoided

This table is a long-term study that debunks the statement, I only have to be right 51 percent of the time. In fact, to match the performance of a buy-and-hold portfolio, you would have to be correct 70 percent of the time.

F I G U R E   5-3

Modern Portfolio Theory

How Do We Decide Which Asset Classes to Utilize and In What Combination?	
Since 1952, major institutions have been using a money management concept known as Modern Portfolio Theory. It was developed at the University of Chicago by Harry Markowitz and later expanded by Stanford University Professor William Sharpe. Markowitz and Sharpe won the Nobel Prize in Economics for their investment methodology. Although the process is mathematical in nature, it is important to note that math is nothing more than the expression of logic. As you examine their process, you can readily see the common-sense approach that they have taken.	The Five Steps of Developing a Strategic Plan Using Modern Portfolio Theory • Risk Tolerance • Expected Return • Standard Deviation • Correlation Coefficients • Efficient Frontier

Source: John Bowen

Figure 5-3 Modern Portfolio Theory

Having made clear our position regarding market timing, we once again return to a discussion of asset allocation. This illustration more formally lists the steps we go through to arrive at the client's policy. The commentary about Sharpe and Markowitz provides an opportunity for us to discuss some of the history behind the theory and to introduce our client to the personalities involved and their impressive credentials. We find that this background adds an element of comfort for our clients.

We follow up this discussion with the next two figures.

Figure 5-4 Standard Deviation

We find that a picture of a standard bell curve helps us explain the concept of long-term expected returns and the risk of intermediate volatility. We refer to one standard deviation as "most of the time" and two standard deviations as "worst case."

From this discussion, we want our clients to understand that volatility does not necessarily equal permanent loss. We want them to begin to distinguish between volatility and disaster.

F I G U R E   5-4

Standard Deviation as a Measure of Risk
Average Annual Expected Return

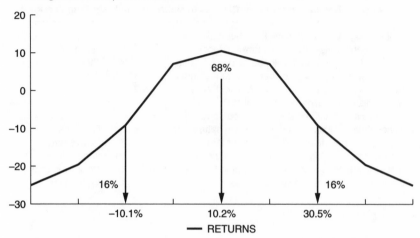

— RETURNS

Figure 5–5 Correlation Coefficient at Work

The second illustration is used to describe correlation. We show that if they bought either investment A or B, over time the investment would grow in value but the ride would be unpleasant. If instead they bought some of both, then the out-of-sync ups and downs would cancel out. The client's blended portfolio return would almost match the return of A or B but with much less volatility. We remind them, however, that reduced volatility has a price. If they own both A and B, they give up the opportunity to make a killing. If A is up, B is down. They can never be at the top. Of course, they also give up the opportunity to get killed.

Frequently we use the following story to expand on the concept:

Suppose you need a 10 percent return to maintain your lifestyle and you had only three investment choices: A CD paying 8 percent and two stocks. One stock is Snap's Swimwear and the other is Boone's Bumbershoots. If the sun comes up all year, you earn 20 percent in Snaps. Of course, you better hope it doesn't rain. When it rains, Snap's earns zero.

If you think it will rain, you should buy Boone's! The bumbershoot company will earn 20 percent when it rains (and "zero" when the sun shines).

Now, as you have consulted a professional money manager, he's hired the world's best meteorologists and statisticians to help design a portfolio. His recommendation is a portfolio of 65 percent Snap's and 35 percent

F I G U R E   5-5

Correlation Coefficient Cycles

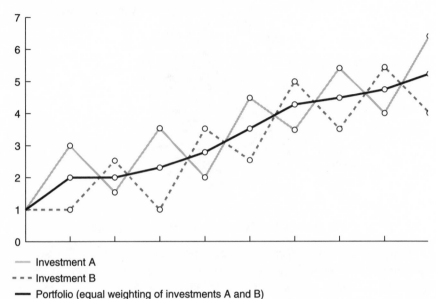

— Investment A

- - - Investment B

— Portfolio (equal weighting of investments A and B)

Boone's. With that combination he believes that you will have a 70 percent chance of earning 14 percent. The small print at the end of his recommendation points out that there is a 30 percent probability of a 5 percent return.

At this point, most clients react with the question, Where do I find the CD? A wealth manager would recommend a 50/50 split for a no-risk 10% return.

We find this story to be a very effective way to explain correlation and Markowitz's discovery of the safety provided by diversifying assets. It is also useful in demonstrating the difference between a money manager's goal of maximizing return and a wealth manager's goal of assisting his client to achieve his own personal goal.

Like most advisors, we use the Ibbotson mountain charts to demonstrate the significantly higher returns of stocks over bonds. However, we find that they do not seem too persuasive. The client would like the stock returns but his perceptions of the risk of stocks dampens his enthusiasm.

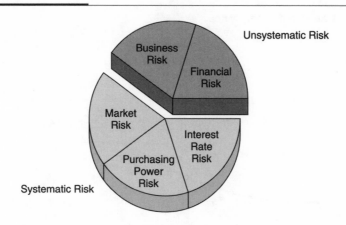

Figure 5–6 Investment Risk

Risk is a concept we never stop discussing with our clients. We discuss it during our data gathering, when we meet for quarterly reviews, and in our newsletter. This slide is simply an introduction to risks.

We point out that the investment risk pie is sliced into many wedges to show that risk has many faces. The pie is separated into two pieces to show that there are two major classes of risk. We explain that most investors worry about only one type of risk, the one we have labeled *unsystematic risk*. This is the familiar fear, I'm not worried about the return on my investment, I'm worried about the return of my investment.

We point out that there are two general reasons a business might default on its obligations to an investor. The business might go broke due to bad management. The company was in the typewriter business and failed to move into word processors. Alternatively, the company might be well managed and reasonably leveraged. Unfortunately, the sales price of their product might fall at the same time their cost of borrowing skyrockets (e.g., oil and gas firms during the early 1980s). The resulting financial squeeze puts them out of business. The first scenario is business risk and the second is financial risk. We know that our client wouldn't care why the investment failed, only that it did. We explain that both of these risks are unique to the specific investment and they are a form of unsystematic risk. We continue our explanation to include a discussion of the elimination of unsystematic risk through diversification.

To convey the concept of the safety obtained by diversification, we use a myriad of examples. One effective example is comparing the risk of a single vacancy if they owned a single family home versus a 10-unit apartment. My most effective example was a stroke of luck. I read an article in *The Wall Street Journal* about toxic waste dumps just before my clients arrived. The clients, a husband and wife, held a large position of inherited stock in a single company. I recommended they sell in order to diversify and eliminate the unsystematic risk. They believed that their stock was in "a really good" company and were reluctant to sell. Remembering the article, I used, as an example, an investment in a company that had built a major manufacturing plant on an undiscovered toxic waste dump. The error was discovered long after completion of the plant and, due to the excessive costs of any remedial solution, the plant had to be abandoned and the company went bankrupt. My clients blushed, turned to each other, nodded, turned back to me and said, "OK, we'll sell." It seems that a number of years before, the husband had been a senior executive for a major manufacturer and he was scheduled to run their latest and largest facility. That is, until it was discovered that the facility had been constructed on a toxic waste dump. The plant was abandoned, the company didn't fold, but cut back substantially and he was out of a job.

Because we believe so strongly in the dangers of unsystematic risk, we typically spend a good deal of time discussing the concept of diversification. Just like the five-year mantra, we believe that quantifying the risk helps our clients relate to and remember the lesson of diversification, so we tell them that 10 is a good standard to remember. We tell them that if they get a good stock tip, don't buy until they get nine more tips. The point we emphasize is that a portfolio of less than 10 diversified securities is likely to expose them to unnecessary loss because of lack of exposure to enough positions.

Having made such a big deal about the safety provided by diversification, we tell our clients they may wonder why they should worry if they follow our advice and diversify.

We ask them to picture a diversified portfolio of not 10 stocks but of 30 of America's largest industrial companies. In October 1987, that portfolio lost 30 percent in less than one week. The portfolio was comprised of the 30 stocks in the Dow Jones Industrial Average. Obviously, there was a risk other than lack of diversification. This risk is represented by the "Market Risk" wedge, namely, the risk that all investments in the market will drop.

We point out that it is just this type of risk that scares many investors away from the stock market. Instead, they invest in safe investments (i.e., bonds). Unfortunately, this move simply throws them into the slice labeled "Interest Rate Risk." Depending on the client, we may use historical charts but usually we remind him that investors who purchased triple-A, long-term bonds when rates were low, did not feel so safe a few years later when rates were much higher. And their even more conservative friends who continually rolled over one-year CDs, did not feel so safe when rates dropped and their income stream was significantly impaired.

Finally, we turn to purchasing power risk. We tell our clients that this is likely to be their biggest risk and it is certainly the most insidious. Purchasing power erosion is like soil erosion. It works quietly and almost invisibly. Twenty-four hours a day, slow but steady, it can convert mountains of value into mole hills.

When we have finished discussing this illustration and related vignettes, we want our clients to understand the many aspects of risk. We want them to know that there is no such thing as a safe investment; there are only investments with different types of risk. Not wanting to depress them, we tell them the good news is that there are safe portfolios. And, as wealth managers, our expertise is in combining risky investments to design custom-tailored safe portfolios for our clients.

Figures 5–7A and 5–7B Inflation

These are graphic supplements to the purchasing power risk wedge of the previous illustration. Using Figure 5–7A, we point out that over a one-year period an investor is just as likely to beat inflation no matter which investment he chooses. However, over a lifetime, the risk of losing real dollars disappears for stock investors and approaches 50 percent for bond investors. These are bad odds for planning the quality of the rest of their life.

Figure 5–7B shows how a "safe" bond investor would have fared since 1980. The scenario assumes an investment of $500,000 each, into Vanguard Fixed Income—GNMA fund and Vanguard Fixed Income—Long-Term Bond fund. The illustration assumes a 28 percent capital gains tax, a 31 percent ordinary income tax, and actual inflation rates. As the illustration shows, the frightening reality is that the $1,000,000 portfolio value would have increased only marginally to $1,108,000, while the purchasing power of the income stream would have dropped from $74,133 in 1981 to $24,556 in 1994!

F I G U R E   5–7A

Probability of an Asset Class Exceeding Inflation

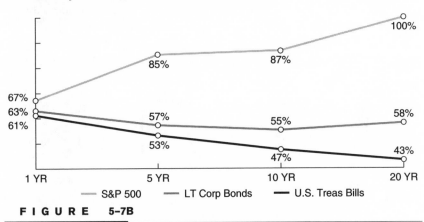

F I G U R E   5–7B

Fixed Income Portfolio and Decreasing Purchasing Power

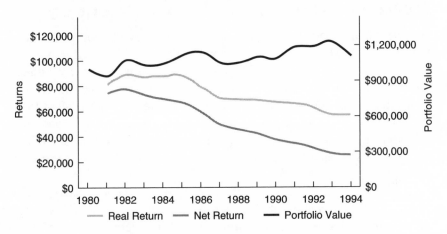

Figure 5–8 Equity Styles

Our firm's investment philosophy places a heavy emphasis on diversification, including diversification of manager style and strategies. As most prospective clients are not familiar with manager styles and strategies, we introduce them to the concepts at this stage. The first illustration we use is the equity style illustration. As our asset class taxonomy includes "growth" and "value" as major classifications, we primarily focus on these two styles.

F I G U R E   5-8

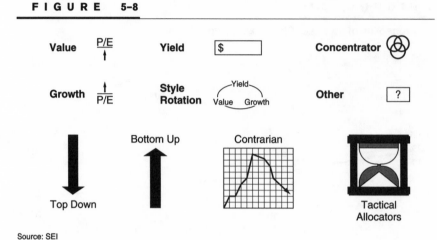

Source: SEI

Table 5-4 Comparison of Investment Styles

We use this illustration to emphasize the importance of style diversification. Based on SEI data, the data show an annual differential return, attributable to style, in excess of 8 percent! Beginning in 1987, we direct the client's attention to the frequent flip-flopping of value and growth style returns. We ask the client how he would have felt from 1988 to 1991 if, as his criterion, he had selected the 1987 performance winner—the value manager. Then we ask, how would he have felt in 1992 and 1993 if, in 1991 he switched to the four-year performance winner—the growth manager?

Clearly, picking the best would have been tough (we believe impossible). A simple strategy of investing equally in each would have provided a much less volatile return series and an average return of 11.7 percent, only 30 basis points below the eight-year winner—value.

This is just one more opportunity to emphasize the risk of following hot trends and the safety derived from diversification.

Figure 5-9 Efficient Frontier

The simplified illustration of efficient frontier is one of the last concepts to be discussed. We ask the client to consider an investment world in which there are only three choices—Treasury bills, an investment grade

T A B L E   5-4

Comparison of Investment Styles

1987 Rankings	Return	1988 Rankings	Return	1989 Rankings	Return	1990 Rankings	Return
1 Value	21.67%	1 Growth	6.50%	1 Growth	36.40%	1 Growth	0.20%
2 S&P 500	16.23%	2 S&P 500	5.10%	2 S&P 500	31.40%	2 S&P 500	–3.27%
3 Growth	11.95%	3 Value	3.68%	3 Value	26.13%	3 Value	–6.85%
Differential	9.72%	Differential	2.82%	Differential	10.27%	Differential	6.45%
1991 Rankings	Return	1992 Rankings	Return	1993 Rankings	Return	1994 Rankings	Return
1 Growth	38.37%	1 Value	10.53%	1 Value	18.60%	1 Growth	3.13%
2 S&P 500	30.47%	2 S&P 500	7.61%	2 S&P 500	10.02%	2 S&P 500	1.32%
3 Value	22.56%	3 Growth	5.07%	3 Growth	1.68%	3 Value	–0.63%
Differential	15.81 %	Differential	5.46%	Differential	16.92%	Differential	2.50%

Average Annual Differential = 837 bp
Differential represents the difference between the top ranked and the bottom ranked investment styles.

bond index, and the S&P 500. We then explain that there is an almost infinite number of portfolios we might construct. For example, a portfolio might be 99 percent T-bills/1 percent bonds/0 percent S&P (or 99/1/0), or 99/0/1, or 0/99/1, or 1/99/0, or 2/98/0, etc, etc. The client quickly gets the point. We then introduce Harry Markowitz and the concept of determining a portfolio's location as a graph plotting risk and return. As an example, the left end of the curved line might represent all T-bills (100 percent /0/0), little return, and no risk. The far right end of the curve might be all stock (0/0/100), maximum return and maximum risk. We tell our client that we know everyone would like the stock return and no risk. Unfortunately, in the real world, any combination of T-bills, stocks, and bonds would represent a risk/return intersection on or below a line connecting the most efficient portfolios, i.e., the efficient frontier.

We point to the portfolio designated A, and explain that it represents an inefficient portfolio. It is inefficient because if the client is comfortable with the portfolio's risk, we can design portfolio B with the same risk and *increase* the return from 10 percent to 12 percent. Or, if the client is happy with the current portfolio's return, we can maintain the return but

F I G U R E   5-9

Efficient Frontier

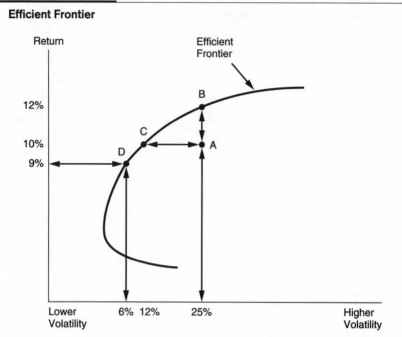

significantly reduce the risk. Neither portfolio B nor portfolio C is better than the other. They are both efficient and better than the original.

Our job, we explain to the client, is not to maximize his portfolio return but rather to design the most efficient portfolio for his unique needs. As an example, if he came to us with portfolio B, an efficient portfolio, but we determined that he needed only a 9 percent return, we would recommend changing his investments to portfolio D. This would result in a significant reduction in his returns. However, it meets his return needs *and* it has much lower risks, and that's our job.

CHAPTER 6

Mathematics
of Investing

Two things cause a stock to move—the expected and the unexpected.

—Gary Helms*

The incredible pace of both academic and practitioner research in investment theory during the last 30+ years can be attributed to four forces: theoretical breakthroughs, the development of comprehensive and accurate market databases, the refinement of analytical tools, and the availability of high-power personal computers.

Although the wealth manager need not become an expert in all of these areas, there are many analytical concepts that he should understand and numerous academic theories he should be familiar with. A sound knowledge of these issues is one of the attributes that distinguishes a wealth manager from the nonprofessional.

The ultimate responsibility of the wealth manager is to integrate these issues, concepts, theories, and models into an investment philosophy that he will use as a guide in designing plans and providing recommendations for his clients.

For example, does the wealth manager accept Fama's weak, or perhaps the semi-strong efficient market hypothesis? Does he agree with Sharpe's CAPM and other asset-pricing theories that unsystematic risk should be avoided? Should the conclusions of Markowitz's MPT be followed? Is the

---

*I discovered a treasure trove of pithy quotes by Gary Helms in the 1978 January/February *Financial Analyst Journal,* reprinted in *Classics* by Charles Ellis, Dow Jones-Irwin, 1989.

market leptokurtic?* Will the wealth manager determine his allocation rec-ommendations by using a parametric quadratic optimizer, optimizing for semivariance? Is multiple repression factor analysis a useful tool in manager evaluation? Should he supplement the capital needs analysis with Monte Carlo simulation?

The following section will neither resolve all these questions nor even address all the issues. It will, however, provide a comprehensive founda-tion. After completing this section, you will have a familiarity with many of the mathematical and analytical issues of importance for the wealth man-ager. You also will know the historical underpinnings of our profession and will meet many of the pioneers who brought us to where we are today. You will have been introduced to the major research and become familiar with the significant terminology. Enough said. Let's start.

There is some rhyme and a little reason behind the order of the fol-lowing mathematical tid-bits, but if you fail to see it do not despair. My goal is to provide the wealth manager with at least a basic understanding of some of the primary measures, tools, and techniques he is likely to en-counter in his readings on investments. Skip those you are familiar with and turn to the references listed earlier for areas that you feel a need to un-derstand in greater depth.

NORMAL DISTRIBUTIONS
AND RELATED MEASURES

Market returns do not occur in a simple, orderly, and consistent manner. Although we might expect the annual return on a particular asset to be ap-proximately 12% over the next five years, we would not expect it to grow by 1% per month. The general default assumption in investment theory is that returns will be normally distributed. This assumption provides for simplification in the analytical process.

VARIANCE AND STANDARD DEVIATION

As actual returns are likely to be higher or lower than the expected return, a variation will exist around the expected return. If we simply measured the deviation between the expected return and the measured real returns

---

*Defined along with other related terms on page 159.

and added up the results, the solution would equal zero. In a normal distribution there are an equally distributed number of positive returns and negative returns; hence, they will cancel out.

The solution is to square the deviations. When squaring, all quantities become positive and this eliminates the self-canceling effect. The result of the average of the squares of the deviation is known as the *variance*. Mathematically, the variance is expressed as:

$$\text{Var}_A = \text{Average value of } (R_A - \overline{R}_A)^2$$

For example, consider a portfolio with the following returns:

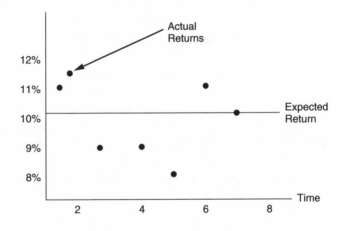

Time	Actual Return(%)	Expected Return(%)	Deviation	Deviation Squared
1	11%	10%	1	1
2	12	10	2	4
3	9	10	−1	1
4	9	10	−1	1
5	8	10	−2	4
6	11	10	1	1
7	10	10	0	0
Total			0	12

Unfortunately, by solving one problem we've created a second. Squaring the deviation eliminated the negative values, but our new measure, variance, is in units of $\%^2$. No useful information is conveyed by knowing that a portfolio has an expected return of 10% and a variance of $1.71\%^2$ (i.e., $12/7 = 1.71$).

We can fix this new problem by simply reversing the process. If squaring the deviation caused the problems, what will happen if we now take the square root of the variance?

$$\sqrt{\text{Var}} = \sqrt{1.71\%}^2 = 1.31\%$$

The square root of $1.71\%^2$ is 1.31%. At least we've eliminated the bothersome $\%^2$ and now have a number in % units. Does the 1.31% convey any information?

Actually, quite a bit. The square root of variance is the familiar measure, *standard deviation* (σ), and is calculated as:

$$\sigma = \sqrt{(R_A - \bar{R}_A)^2} = \sqrt{1.71\%}^2 = 1.31\%$$

We can now interpret the results as an expected return of 10% with a standard deviation of 1.31%.

Now that the measure of volatility has been converted to standard deviation, the real power of the assumption of a normal distribution comes into play. We know from statistics that 67% of the time returns will fall within a range of ± 1 standard deviation of the expected return and ± 2 standard deviations about 98% of the time. Therefore, in the example above, we would expect that 67% of the time the portfolio return would fall between 8.3% and 11.7%, and 98% of the time, we would expect returns between 6.6% and 13.4%.

COVARIANCE AND CORRELATION COEFFICIENT

As will be discussed in Chapter 7, Investment Theory, Harry Markowitz demonstrated that although the return on a combination of assets is equal to their weighted returns, the risk of a portfolio is usually less than the weighted average of each asset's risk. This reduction in risk is due to diversification. The magnitude of the risk reduction is dependent on the degree of similarity in movement between the returns of the portfolio's assets. The measure of this co-movement is the *covariance*.

Covariance is calculated by the formula:

Cov_{ij} = Expected Value of $(R_i - \bar{R}_i)$ × Expected Value of $(R_j - \bar{R}_j)$
$\text{Cov}_{ij} = E[R_i - \bar{R}_i] \times E[R_j - \bar{R}_j]$

Suppose we were interested in two stocks, Snap's Swimwear and Boone's Bumbershoots. We are interested in determining how the prices of these two stocks are likely to perform relative to each other. Therefore, we used the preceding formula and calculated the covariance to be –15.1. Unfortunately, we're facing a familiar problem. A mighty fine number that conveys very little information. We cannot tell from the value –15.1 if this is high or low. Is the common movement between Snap's and Boone's significant or insignificant? All we know is that because the number is negative, the two stocks are negatively related (i.e., their prices are likely to move in opposite directions.) That's interesting but not very surprising given the nature of their products. What we would like to know is the strength of that relationship.

In order to garner more useful information about the relationship between the price movements of A and B, we need to use a technique mathematicians refer to as normalizing. This process will result in a measure that can range only between a value of +1 and –1.

To develop this solution consider the case of two assets, A and B, with prices that move in exactly the same pattern. In effect, what is the covariance of an asset with itself. The calculation would be:

$$\text{Cov}_{AA} = (R_A - \overline{R}_A) \times (R_A - \overline{R}_A) = (R_A - \overline{R}_A)^2$$

If that looks familiar, it should. It is simply the formula for calculating the variance of A! In other words, the covariance of a variable with itself is its variance.

We also know that variance = standard deviation squared, so for two identical assets:

$$\text{Cov}_{AA} = \text{Var}_{AA} = \sigma_A \times \sigma_A$$

Now, suppose we created a new measure calculated by dividing the covariance of two assets by the product of their standard deviations. The measure would be calculated as follows:

$$\text{Cov}_{AB} / \sigma_A \sigma_B$$

If we applied this formula to the example above for two identical assets, the result would be the following:

$$\text{Cov}_{AA}/\sigma_A\sigma_A = \text{Var}_{AA}/\sigma_A\sigma_A = \sigma_A\sigma_A/\sigma_A\sigma_A = 1$$

We've demonstrated that if we use this new measure, the result is exactly what we desire. A maximum value of 1 for two assets that move exactly together. Following the same process, we would find that if the assets moved exactly opposite each other, the division would result in –1. All other patterns of movement will result in a value between +1 and –1.

The name given to this standardized measure is the *correlation coefficient*. As shown on the preceding page, it is calculated as:

$$Cor_{AB} = Cov_{AB}/\sigma_A\sigma_B$$

For many analytical purposes, the correlation coefficient provides a more meaningful measure. Covariance, however, remains important. Correlation measures only direction and degree of association. Unlike covariance, it provides no information regarding magnitude. For portfolio optimization analysis, information regarding magnitude is critical and covariance is an important tool.

R²: THE COEFFICIENT OF DETERMINATION

Harry Markowitz, William Sharpe, and others focused attention on the concepts of systematic and unsystematic risk. As discussed later, the laws on fiduciary investing are beginning to direct the court's attention to the importance of minimizing nonmarket (i.e., unsystematic) risk. Obviously, it would be convenient to have a method of separating and measuring these two components of risk.

One approach to determining these two components of risk is based on Sharpe's Capital Asset Pricing Model (CAPM). According to CAPM, the systematic component of total risk can be determined by multiplying the market variance by the square of a factor known as *Beta* (Beta and CAPM are discussed in Chapter 7, Investment Theory). The unsystematic component of total risk is simply the difference between the market risk and the systematic risk. These relationships are shown below:

Systematic Risk   = Security Market Variance
Unsystematic Risk = Security Nonmarket Variance
                          = Var_{market} − Security Market Variance
                          (i.e., what's left over)

Unfortunately, the answer is in terms of variance. As we've seen earlier, variance conveys limited information. The solution is quite simple. Divide the Security Market Variance by the Total Market Variance. The result is a number ranging from 0 to 1. Expressed as a percentage, it provides a clear measure of the variability (or risk) of an asset explained by the market.

This measure is known as the *coefficient of determination* or, more commonly, the R^2. It can also be calculated by simply squaring an asset's correlation coefficient with the market. About now, a few examples would probably be handy.

Asset	Market	Correlation	R^2
Vanguard S&P	S&P 500	100	100
American Mutual	S&P 500	92	85
Fidelity Magellan	S&P 500	78	61
Merrill Lynch Corp. Investment Grade	Shearson/Lehman Bond	97	95

It's comforting to see that all the risk associated with the Vanguard S&P 500 can be explained by the risk of the S&P index. Presumably, that's why someone would invest in a market index. It's not surprising to find that a blue chip, top down fund like American Mutual also has a risk exposure largely explained by the S&P 500. However, for some investors, it would probably come as a surprise that their investment in the behemoth of Fidelity Magellan has a significant risk exposure not explained by the S&P 500. Finally, it's probably not surprising to find that the Merrill Lynch Corporate Investment Grade Fund's variability can be explained by the Shearson Lehman Bond Index. The reason for including this last example is to remind the reader not to fall into the trap of always equating *the market* with *the S&P*. See the following example, in the section "Use of R^2."

The analytical tools available to wealth managers are not restricted to one market. They allow us to focus on the market or markets of interest.

USE OF R^2

In discussions of performance measurement, it is common for advisors to toss around terms such as *Beta* and compare a manager's performance relative to various indexes such as the S&P 500. The terms and indexes are valid but frequently misused. It's of no value to measure the risk of a portfolio by its Beta, if the Beta is based on an inappropriate market. The problem arises when an attempt is made to measure the systematic attributes of a poorly diversified portfolio. Too much of the risk is attributable to the unsystematic exposure of the portfolio.

For example, in the 11/95 publications of Morningstar and Value Line, the following statistics were provided:

Foreign Stock Funds Relative to the S&P 500

	β	R^2
Morningstar	.77	24
Value Line	.70	24

Based on the low Beta, many investors may be misled into believing that foreign funds are much less risky (i.e., volatile) than domestic funds. The wealth manager should be able to explain to his client why such a conclusion is wrong.

The wealth manager might first show his client the following table:

	Standard Deviation
Vanguard S&P 500	8.1
Foreign Stock Funds	13.0

Based on standard deviation, the foreign stock funds are actually much more volatile than the S&P 500. The reported Beta, using the S&P as the market comparison, is a misleading statistic. It compares apples to oranges. This can be seen by looking at the R^2. In this example, only 24% of "what's going on" is explained by the S&P.

In order to properly evaluate the international funds, we need to compare them to an appropriate benchmark. Morningstar has addressed this issue. Their reports now include modern portfolio statistics based on more closely related markets (they refer to this as the "best fit" index.) For some foreign stock funds, Morningstar uses the Morgan Stanley All Country Index.

	MS All Country	
	β	R^2
Foreign Stock Funds	1.12	.80

Finally, the wealth manager might use the following data to show his client how he uses this information to choose between two excellent international managers for a client's portfolio.

| | S&P 500 | | 3-Yr | MS All Country | |
	β	R^2	Returns	β	R^2
T. Rowe Price Int'l Stock	.80	26	14.6%	1.16	86
Warburg Pincus Int'l Eq	.86	20	18.5	1.31	75

Referring to the Beta based on the S&P, these two funds seem to be taking similar risks, but Warburg has a far better three-year return. If the wealth manager ended his analysis there, he would select Warburg for the client's portfolio. However, the wealth manager recognizes that with a low R^2, the S&P 500-related Beta does not provide a fair measure of relative risk. Instead, he will look at the MS All-Country-related Beta. He discovers that both funds are volatile relative to their market, but Warburg has a significantly greater volatility than T. Rowe Price. Checking further, he finds that Warburg's extra returns (and volatility) can largely be attributed to the manager's willingness to allocate more to emerging markets than T. Rowe Price. Based on this information and a knowledge of his client's tolerance for risk, the wealth manager selects T. Rowe Price as the most appropriate international manager for this particular portfolio.Unlike the Sharpe and Treynor measures described next, the coefficient of determination is not good or bad, it simply conveys useful information. Although there is no magic number, as the R^2 falls below 100 (i.e., totally diversified against the benchmark), measures based on a diversified portfolio become less and less significant. In our firm we use a minimum of 75. Whatever minimum you elect to set for your analysis, consider also using additional measures based on total risk (e.g., standard deviation and the Sharpe ratio).

RISK MEASURES[1]

Returns, returns, and returns . . . It often seems that this is the only measure that counts when evaluating the performance of a manager or a portfolio. Advisors may argue over the return measure to use, e.g., AIMR standards, time weighted, dollar weighted, average, compounded, etc., but always "returns." Unfortunately, focusing solely on returns is akin to ordering gumbo and forgetting the Tabasco—nice but not enough. The necessary missing ingredient is a measure of risk.

Suppose we offered our clients a choice between two mutual funds (or individual managers). Manager A has a five-year compounded annual return of 12% and manager B's return has been 14%. Is there any doubt which manager would garner the bulk of the investment dollars?

Now suppose we added the information that manager A has been investing in a portfolio of diversified, large cap domestic equities and manager B has invested in a highly leveraged portfolio of small cap emerging market securities. For many, if not most investors, manager A now looks to be the more attractive. As simple as this example may seem, in "the real world" investment decisions are far too frequently made in favor of the manager Bs of the world. The element of risk is not factored into the decision process.

It is necessary to recognize that risk is not one-dimensional. Risk is multidimensional. Academics continue to argue over those dimensions (e.g., Fama and French's explanation of the risk associated with high book-to-market investing. We'll discuss that later). For now this section will focus on total investment risk and its components, systematic and unsystematic risks.

STANDARD DEVIATION

Described earlier, standard deviation is a measure of the variability of returns of an asset compared to its average or expected return. Thus, it serves as a measure of total risk. Standard deviation may be a misleading measure if the evaluation period is not long enough to cover a manager's risk exposure (e.g., the standard deviation of bond funds that were aggressively using derivatives before January 1992). Its use has also been criticized for rewarding poor and mediocre performance and penalizing upside volatility. The counter-argument to this latter objection is that significant upside standard deviation may be a warning of subsequent downside risk (e.g., junk bonds, Japanese stocks, and high-tech stock funds).

SHARPE RATIO

The Sharpe ratio belongs to a class of measurements known as "efficiency ratios." These are measures that indicate the amount of return earned per unit of risk (i.e., how efficiently the returns were earned). Focusing on the total portfolio risk (as does the standard deviation), Sharpe designed a ratio he termed the reward-to-volatility ratio,[2] now more commonly known as the *Sharpe Ratio*. Based on his earlier work on the CAPM, Professor Sharpe suggested that an appropriate way to

rank the risk-adjusted performance of various portfolios was by calculating their excess return per unit of risk. His ratio is simply:

Sharpe Ratio$_i$ = (R$_i$ – R$_f$) / σ_i

where

R$_i$ = the portfolio return for period i

R$_f$ = the risk-free rate of return for period i

σ_i = the standard deviation of the portfolio during period i

Thus, portfolios with higher Sharpe ratios provided superior excess
returns per unit of risk over the period measured compared with portfolios
with lower Sharpe ratios.

A later version of this ratio, the *New Sharpe Ratio,* is designed to adjust the return to reflect the risk of an appropriate portfolio benchmark.
Numerically, it is the ratio of the portfolio's average differential return
between a fund and its benchmark divided by the historical standard deviation of differential return, or:

$$\text{New Sharpe Ratio} = (\Sigma(R_i - R_b)/N)/ \sqrt{\Sigma(D_i - D_b)^2}$$

Although the mathematics of calculating the Sharpe ratio is not particularly daunting, it is still comforting to know that it is available for
most mutual funds from a number of sources. Among others, both Morningstar and Value Line now include Sharpe ratios for the last 36-month
period in their printed reports. Morningstar includes the ratio in its CD
ROM. Wilson's CAMS program goes one step further and allows the
planner to calculate and rank most mutual funds by their Sharpe ratio for
any time period selected.

Before we move on to the next measure, it's worth remembering
that there are risks of misinterpreting the significance of all investment return and performance measures. The Sharpe ratio is no exception.

- Efficiency ratios do not incorporate information related to
  correlation; therefore, Sharpe ratios should only be used to
  compare similar asset classes and styles.

- Assume that you currently use a passive manager in this asset
  class and you are considering replacing the passive manager with
  an active manager named Levitt. The passive portfolio has a
  Sharpe ratio of 0.4. Levitt's most recent performance follows:

Quarter	Excess Return over Benchmark
1	−1%
2	3
3	−1
4	3
5	−9
6	27
7	−9
8	27

For the first four quarters, Levitt implemented a low volatility policy and, based on a conscious policy shift, a more aggressive strategy for the second year. In the first year Levitt's average excess return was 1%, the standard deviation was 2%, and the Sharpe ratio was 0.5. Thus, Levitt's Sharpe ratio was 20% better than the passive manager's 0.4 Sharpe. In the second 52-week period, the portfolio's higher returns made up for its greater volatility and Levitt once again achieved a Sharpe measure of 0.5. This suggests that the active manager continued to outperform, on a risk-adjusted basis, the passive manager.

However, if we decided that a longer period would provide a better measure, Levitt's Sharpe calculated for the two-year period was only 0.37, slightly worse than the passive manager. How could she have superior performance each year but subperformance for the two-year period? Clearly, she cannot. What happened was that the shift in strategy was not reflected in the two one-year calculations. Combining the two years together results in a mathematically misleading conclusion that the portfolio had a greater volatility resulting in a downward bias for the Sharpe ratio. What's the moral? Don't accept simple rules of thumb or measurements at face value, even if they are named after a Nobel laureate.

TREYNOR INDEX

About the same time that Sharpe developed his ratio, Jack Treynor developed another measure of portfolio performance that combined both risk and returns[3] (actually, Treynor developed the first composite reward/volatility measure, but someone who has been awarded the Nobel Prize gets top billing). Building on capital market theory, Treynor developed a ratio similar to that later designed by Sharpe. The *Treynor index,* however, measures excess returns per unit of systematic risk (remember, the Sharpe ratio measures per unit of total risk).

Treynor Index $= (R_i - R_f) / \beta_i$

where

R_i = the portfolio return for period i

R_f = the risk-free rate of return for period i

β_i = the Beta of the portfolio during period i

Like the Sharpe ratio, the Treynor is easily calculated although less directly available from services such as Morningstar and Wilson. This lack of availability is less troublesome than it might seem, for as you'll note in the next section, it's also less frequently applicable.

ALPHA—JENSEN'S DIFFERENTIAL RETURN MEASURE

The last of the triumvirate of major risk-adjusted performance measures is Jensen's differential return measure or, more popularly, the portfolio *Alpha (α)*.* Like Treynor's index, the Alpha is based on CAPM, and its significance is related to the diversification of the portfolio. All assume that the relationship between risk and return remains linear throughout the entire range. Unlike Sharpe and Treynor, the return for each period, not averages, must be used.

Alpha$= (R_i - R_{fi}) - \beta_i(R_{mkti} - R_{fi}) - U_i$

where
R_i = the portfolio return for period i

R_{fi} = the risk-free rate of return for period i

R_{mkti} = the market return for period i

β_i = the systematic risk of the portfolio for period i

U_i = a random error term

The Alpha is easily understood as it measures, in terms of %, the contribution of the portfolio manager. Stated more formally, it is a measure of the incremental rate of return per period in excess of the return attributable to the risk the portfolio has assumed.

---

*Michael Jensen, "The Performance of Mutual Funds in the Period 1945–1964," *Journal of Finance* 23, no. 2 (May 1968), 389–416.

Alphas are handy and available. They're included in most fund reports, including Morningstar, Value Line, and Wilson, and they're easy to explain to clients. Unfortunately, they belong to the real world and naturally there's a catch or two.

- The use of Treynor and Alpha assumes that systematic risk is the proper measure of risk of the portfolio. Catch #1 is a warning that unless the portfolio is reasonably diversified, these measures are meaningless at best and potentially dangerously misleading.

- Catch #2 is more insidious. Even for a well-diversified portfolio (remember, a high R^2), the Alpha value may be correct but statistically meaningless. Frequently the random error factor, noted in the Alpha formula above, is of such a magnitude that it renders the calculated Alpha meaningless. As Magnin and Tuttle warn in *Managing Investment Portfolios,** "Statistical error is so large, because of large fluctuations observed in a limited sample of data, that statistically significant alphas seldom occur."

SEMIVARIANCE

When Markowitz wrote his paper on Modern Portfolio Theory (MPT), he noted that a measure of distribution known as *semivariance* would, theoretically, be the best measure of risk. At the time, most computers did not have the computational power to handle semivariance. Consequently, Markowitz opted for the more practical measure of mean-variance. Today, with greater computational power available at very low cost, there is an increasing interest in considering more complex solutions to investment issues, including the use of semivariance.

Earlier, variance was defined as the square of the deviation of distributions from the mean. The reason given for squaring the deviations was that otherwise, those below the mean would cancel those above the mean. A sum of the deviations would be zero. In other words, we were concerned with *all* the deviations from the mean.

As many academics and practitioners point out, variance resulting from upside deviations (i.e., making a lot more than anyone expects) should not result in branding a manager as a high-risk taker. They argue

---

*John Magnin and Donald Tuttle, *Managing Investment Portfolios,* Warren, Gorham & Lamont, 1990, 14–21.

that portfolio design should only be concerned with unwanted deviations, not all deviations.

One of the definitions of the word semi is partial. So the easy way to think of semivariance is as partial variance, i.e., the "bad" part. Consider the example in Figure 6–1.

F I G U R E   6-1

Semivariance

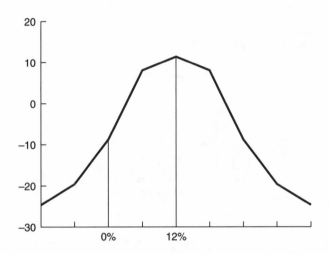

Figure 6–1 represents a hypothetical normal distribution for a market's expected return. Traditional risk analysis would concern itself with deviations, both above and below the 12% mean return. In reality, your client might be much more concerned with losses. His focus of attention would be those returns below 0%. A risk analysis based on this standard is an example of target semivariance with a target of "0." The issue of semivariance will be discussed in more detail in the section on optimization.

MOMENTS

The following discussion will introduce you to a new mathematical vocabulary. Although it is unlikely that the wealth manager will ever have to calculate these measures, it is important that he understand their meaning. Investment research continues to expand the knowledge base regarding market forces. Only wealth managers who read and understand this research will be able to apply it for their clients' benefit.

If market returns resemble the familiar bell shape of a normal distribution, the median value and the mean value will be identical, and the balance of the data points will fall symmetrically about the mean.

Unfortunately, the handy assumption that distributions are normally distributed is frequently inaccurate. Just the process of compounding returns results in a non-normal distribution. The shape resulting from the effect of compounding is called a *log normal* distribution. The result of the uneven distribution is shown by Figure 6–2.

F I G U R E   6-2

Positive Distribution Skew

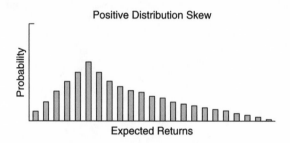

Source: D. Katz

Divergence from the symmetrical bell shape of the normal distribution is called *asymmetry*. *Skewness* is the term used to describe a shift in the relationship between the median and mean and disproportionate distribution tails. If, as shown in Figure 6–2, there is a long tail to the right, the distribution has a positive skew. If, as Figure 6–3 shows, the long tail is to the left, it is negatively skewed.

F I G U R E   6-3

Negative Distribution Skew

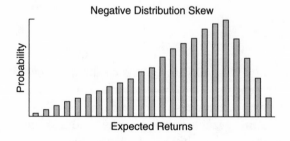

For a normal distribution, the only information necessary to completely describe the shape of the distribution curve is the mean and the standard deviation. As financial textbooks and journal articles frequently use statistical terms to refer to these measures, it's handy to know that the mean is referred to as the *first moment* of the distribution. Generally, as measurements are against the mean, the standard is to set the mean equal to "0." This is referred to as the *first central moment.* Standard deviation (i.e., the square of the deviations) is called the *second central moment.*

If the distribution is skewed, more information is required to determine the shape of the distribution curve. The measure containing this additional information (i.e., the skewness), is based on the cube of deviations from the mean. Skewness, hence is called *the third central moment.*

There remains one more aspect of the shape of distributions that it may be necessary to consider, i.e., the *peakedness.* All of the earlier figures, even if skewed, looked pretty much like the same mountains, some just pushed to the left, others to the right. As shown by the following distribution illustrations, there are other possibilities.

These distributions reflect different relationships between the peaks and tails. Figure 6–4, with fat tails and an especially peaked peak is called *leptokurtic.* Figure 6–5, without much tail and a relatively flat peak is a *platykurtic* distribution. As the measure of this difference in peakedness involves raising deviations to the fourth power, it is not surprising that this measure, *kurtosis,* is called the *fourth central moment.*

F I G U R E   6–4

Leptokurtic Kurtosis

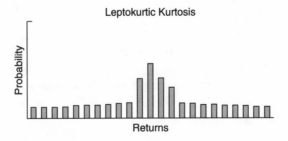

F I G U R E   6-5

Platykurtic Kurtosis

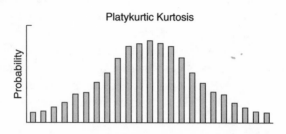

Because current market research suggests that market returns are positively skewed and leptokurtic, it is easy to see why there is so much criticism of the use of the simplified assumption of normal distributions. For example, Markowitz's selection of mean-variance as a measure of risk not only requires restrictive assumptions regarding investor behavior (i.e., a measure of loss based on below-median performance), but also the restricted assumption of normal distributions.

REGRESSION

Frequently in the process of investment analysis, the question arises regarding the influence of one variable on another. For example, how much does a change in earnings growth rate influence a stock's price to earnings ratio (P/E)?

We'll start by using a simplified assumption that the relationship can be mathematically described as:[4]

P/E = Function of earnings growth (G)
   = a + b (G)
a = P/E if growth rate = 0
b = a factor reflecting the change in P/E as a direct change in growth

With enough data, an analysis using a technique known as linear regression can determine the likely value of a and b. Suppose the work has been completed and the solution arrived at is:

P/E = 7 + 0.85 (G)

The formula above is an example of a regression equation. It was based on the original assumption that the relationship between P/E and G could be plotted as a straight line. As it is based on the assumption of a linear relationship, it is a linear regression equation.

The preceding solution was developed from historical data; hence, it is only an estimate of the future relationship between two variables based on past performance. Using statistical measures, it is possible to determine if the regression relationship is statistically significant. If these tests determine that the regression is significant, to determine how useful this formula may be in predicting future values, we may use calculations discussed earlier, namely R^2 and standard deviation.

We find that in this case:

$R^2 = 83$

Standard Deviation = 0.8

We now know that much of the P/E can indeed be explained by the earnings growth rate. Because of the low standard deviation, we can also be confident that the actual P/E is likely to fall within a relatively narrow range around the formula's projected value.

Suppose we concluded, after reviewing the literature, that the P/E ratio was not only dependent on earnings growth rate (G) but was also likely to be influenced by the company's use of financial leverage as measured by its debt-to-equity ratio (D/Eq). The problem now becomes one of determining the influence of a number of independent variables (i.e., G and D/Eq) on a dependent variable (P/E). The mathematical technique used in this case is a multiple regression.

Using a multiple regression analysis, we might find that:

$P/E = 10 + 0.6 (G) + 0.4 (D/Eq)$

$R^2 = .99$

Standard Deviation = 0.09

By adding new information, we have developed a model that shows almost all the P/E can be explained by G and D/Eq. We can now project the expected P/E with significant confidence.

COMPOUNDING

At face value, this seems like a trivial concept to include amidst a discussion of kurtosis and multiple linear regression. Still, the seemingly simple decision of when to use arithmetic compounding and geometric compounding is not so simple. Most wealth managers are trained ad nauseum in the use of the HP-12C and other time-value calculators. We tend to scoff at the concept of arithmetic returns as being at the prekindergarten level math. Real wealth managers talk in terms of internal rates of return and dollar-weighted returns. Unfortunately, finance experts tell us that in many instances, for predicting future values, correct estimating is arithmetic, not geometric.

Mark Kritzman,* author of the *Financial Analyst Journal*'s regular column "What Practitioners Need to Know . . ." best described the confusion in his May–June 1994 column, ". . . About Future Value." He writes:

> Some analysts argue that the best guide for estimating future value is the arithmetic average of past returns. Others claim that the geometric average provides a better estimate of future value. The correct answer depends on what it is about future value that we want to estimate.

GEOMETRIC VERSUS ARITHMETIC

Consider a very simple two-period example for a $1,000 investment:

Period	Return	Portfolio Balance
1	100%	$2000
2	−50	1000

Average Return   = 25%

Geometric Return = 0%

If we use the geometric future return as our guide, it suggests that the future expected return is 0. That does not seem logical given this manager's record. In fact, it's not 0, it is 25%. It is the arithmetic return that is the best estimate of the expected future value for the following year.

Consider a somewhat more detailed 10-period example. In this example the manager has a record that demonstrates he has just as much chance of gaining as losing. Starting with an investment of $1,000:

---

*If you read nothing else in the *Financial Analyst Journal* make sure you at least read his columns. They are **always** worth reading. I copy them and keep them as an ever-growing reference book. As noted in Chapter 7, Investment Theory, the earlier columns have been collected in Mark Kritzman, *The Portable Financial Analyst* (Burr Ridge, IL: Irwin, 1995).

Period	Return (%)	Portfolio Balance ($)
1	− 50%	$500
2	50	750
3	−10	680
4	10	740
5	−30	520
6	30	680
7	−20	540
8	20	650
9	−40	390
10	40	540

Average Return   =   0%

Geometric Return = −6%

If in the future, as in the past, it is just as likely that the portfolio will go up in value as it will drop in value, one would think that the expected return would equal the arithmetic return of 0%. On the other hand, with a history of a 6% compounded loss, it just does not seem reasonable to expect that the investor has a 50/50 chance of a positive return. As in the foregoing example, this discrepancy is real.

The reason for the discrepancy relates to the asymmetric distribution of compounded returns noted earlier. The result of this skew is that geometric compounding will yield a future value that is less than the expected future value.

The arithmetic return is an unbiased estimate of a portfolio's expected future return. Therefore, if the goal is to estimate future value, arithmetic return is correct. The geometric return represents the fixed return required to achieve a specific return over a given period of time. It is, therefore, the best measure of past performance. We will revisit this discussion late in the section on optimizer inputs.

VARIANCE DRAIN[5]

Recognizing that if there is any variance in the return series, the geometric return will always be less than the arithmetic return. Tom Messmore wrote a useful paper in the Summer 1995 *Journal of Portfolio Management,* titled "Variance Drain." The descriptive term *drain* was selected to draw attention to the fact that an active manager will usually generate a variance in excess of a passive alternative. In order to add value, the active manager must not only cover fees and transaction costs but also must cover the cost of the drain attributable to variance. Although the paper is directed at money managers and suggests numerous strategies for managing the drain, the following approximation formula for calculating the variance drain is a useful addition to the mathematical tool kit of the wealth manager:

$C \cong R + \sigma^2/2$ or Variance Drain $= \sigma^2/2 = C - R$

where C = Arithmetic Return and R = Geometric Return

For example, for the five years between 1990 and 1995:

Fund	Geometric Return	Arithmetic Return
20th Century Ultra	21.6%	28.7%
Acorn	21.0	23.4

The approximate "variance drain" for 20th Century Ultra was 7.1% compared to Acorn's 2.4%. In order to achieve approximately the same compounded return as Acorn, 20th Century had to achieve a 23% better average return.

FIXED-INCOME RISK MEASURES

DURATION*

Assuming that for most readers duration is a familiar topic, this brief review is included for the sake of completeness. Maturity, the standard measure of interest rate exposure, is often a poor guide. Maturity measures only the time until the principal is due. Duration incorporates both the magnitude of the interest and principal payments and the timing of those payments.

The original measure, the *Macaulay Duration* (named after its creator), is a direct measure of the relationship between the magnitude and

---

*Although limited, there has been work in developing the concept of duration for use in evaluating the interest rate sensitivity of nonbonds such as stock and REITs. Known as the *implied duration*, it is empirically derived as: Implied Duration = (–% Price Change) / (Yield Change)

timing of the payments for interest and principal. Unfortunately, the Macaulay duration tends to over- or understate a bond's interest rate sensitivity. In order to reduce this error today, analysts use a modification of Macaulay's duration calculation. Known as the *Modified Duration*, it is frequently simply called *duration*.

This is the slope of the price/yield curve at a given yield and, within a narrow range of interest rate change, modified duration serves as a reasonably accurate measure of interest rate sensitivity. Expected price changes can be calculated by the following formula:

Price Change = (Modified Duration) × (−Yield Change)

Duration has the following attributes:

- It is positively related to maturity.
- It is inversely related to coupon.
- It is inversely related to yield.
- It is significantly influenced by calls and sinking funds.

Duration has the following limitations:

- As noted in the discussion of convexity below, duration is only useful over a limited range of yield change.
- Price changes due to changing quality spreads and changing sector spreads are not considered.
- Duration assumes that yield curves will remain unchanged when, in fact, they do change.
- Durations may change as a result of changing the basis for calculation from call to maturity. This insidious but real risk was brought to my attention by an article prepared by Brian McMahon, lead manager for a number of the excellent Thornburg Funds. With Thornburg's kind permission, the following is adapted from McMahon's article:

Duration—A Warning

Most mortgage, corporate, municipal, and government agency bonds with final maturities longer than 10 years can be redeemed before maturity. Market conventions regarding how duration is reported on callable bonds may mislead investors by understating the downside risk of a callable bond, or of a portfolio of callable bonds such as a mutual fund.

The Portfolio Today

Consider two bonds: the *long bond* has a 6% coupon, matures on May 1, 2024, and is callable May 1, 2004, at 102% of par. The *intermediate bond* matures in eight years on May 1, 2004, has a 5.5% coupon, and is noncallable. If each bond has a market price of 100 for a May 1, 1996 settlement date, the respective durations of these bonds are shown below:

Long Bond—28 Years to Maturity
6% Bond 5/1/2024 Maturity Date
Callable 5/1/2004 at 102 percent of par

Mkt Yield	Mkt Price	Adjusted Duration	Duration
6.00% YTM	100	13.48 Years	Runs to Maturity

Intermediate Bond—8 Years to Maturity
5.5% Bond 5/1/2004 Maturity Date
Noncallable

Mkt Yield	Mkt Price	Adjusted Duration	Duration
5.50% YTM	100	6.40 Years	Runs to Maturity

Note that the duration of the long bond is more than twice that of the intermediate bond.

The Market Changes—Returns Drop

If interest rates decrease by a modest amount, however, the picture changes considerably. A 30 basis-point decrease in the market rate to 5.70% causes the long bond to price to the 2/1/2004 call date. The standard practice in calculating bond duration is to base the computation on the date to which the bond is priced. If the "yield to call" is lower than the "yield to maturity" (as is the case here) the duration calculation will assume that the bond is called in 2004 at 102% of par. The new duration, 6.32 years, is that which corresponds to the call date, not the maturity date. From this point forward, if interest rates decline the upside price appreciation potential of the long bond is actually less than that of the intermediate bond!

Long Bond—28 Years to Maturity
6% Bond 5/1/2024 Maturity Date
Callable 5/1/2004 at 102 percent of par

Mkt Yield	Mkt Price	Adj Duration	Duration
5.70% YTC	103.181	6.3 2 Years	Runs to Maturity*
(5.77% YTM)			

*The duration to maturity is 13.70 years at this price.

Intermediate Bond—8 Years to Maturity
5.5% Bond 5/1/2004 Maturity Date
Noncallable

Mkt Yield	Mkt Price	Adj Duration	Duration
5.20% YTM	101.943	6.43 Years	Runs to Maturity

The Market Changes—Returns Spike Up

Suppose now that you are considering two bond mutual funds. One holds a portfolio of callable long bonds with a profile similar to the long bond example above. The other fund has a portfolio of intermediate noncallable bonds with a profile similar to the intermediate bond above. If interest rates were to increase by only 1%, the investor in the longer maturity bond fund would get a nasty surprise. The long bond portfolio value would plummet to 91.202, a change of about 12%. The duration of the long bond at a 6.70% YTM would be 12.83 years! The intermediate bond would lose only about 6.3% of its market value.

Long Bond—28 Years to Maturity
6% Bond 5/1/2024 Maturity Date
Callable 5/1/2004 at 102 percent of par

Mkt Yield	Mkt Price	Adj Duration	Duration
6.70% YTM	91.202*	12.83 Yrs	Runs to Maturity

*Change in Price from Increase: 103.181 − 91.202 = 11.98 pts

Intermediate Bond—8 Years to Maturity
5.5% Bond 5/1/2004 Maturity Date
Noncallable

Mkt Yield	Mkt Price	Adj Duration	Duration
6.20% YTM	95.637*	6.34 Years	Runs to Maturity

*Change in Price from Increase: 101.943 − 95.637 = 6.31 pts

F I G U R E   6-6

Convexity

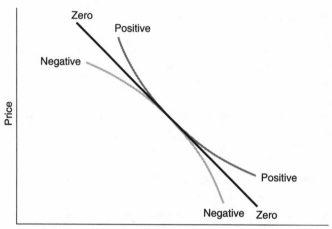

Interest Rate

What conclusions can a wealth manager draw? First, the shrinking duration of a callable bond in a declining interest rate environment causes these bonds to underperform noncallable bonds of similar or even shorter maturities when rates are dropping. Second, a duration measure that runs to an expected call date will understate the downside price risk of a callable bond if interest rates rise. Thus, it frequently makes more sense to buy noncallable bonds. The stable durations of noncallable bonds evidence a better balance between price appreciation potential and price depreciation risk in changing markets.

CONVEXITY

Although a handy measure, duration assumes a linear relationship between the change in yields and bond prices. This assumption is only accurate over small changes in interest rates (less than 1%). If the change is greater, it is necessary to know something about the shape of the relationship. The measure of a bond's price sensitivity to change in yield is called *convexity*. As shown in Figure 6–6, convexity describes the curvature of the price-yield curve for a given bond.

The concave price-interest rate curve is referred to as positive convexity. This attribute describes the relationship for most traditional bonds. Positive convexity is a desirable characteristic. As rates fall, the effective duration of a bond with positive convexity increases, thus increasing the rate of the bond's price appreciation. If, however, rates rise, the effective duration of a bond with positive convexity will fall, reducing the rate of the bond's price erosion. The convex curve is described as negative convexity and is typical of mortgage-backed securities.

Market traders are aware of the benefits of positive convexity. The prices of bonds with this attribute include a premium. Purchasers of negatively convex bonds are generally compensated with higher yields. Although the basic risk-reward balance is accounted for by these market price adjustments, for active bond managers there is the potential opportunity to add value through yield curve strategies. By designing a portfolio with the convexity most likely to benefit from changes in the shape of the yield curves, managers can increase total return. Thus, convexity, as well as duration, is an issue of concern.

REALIZED COMPOUNDED YIELD

PIMCO, one of the nation's preeminent bond managers, provides a wealth of educational material for wealth managers. One of the issues they frequently emphasize in their publications is the importance of focusing on the total return of a fixed-income portfolio. Related to the comment above regarding changing yield curves, a major aspect of total return is the impact of the reinvestment rate. The relationships between yield-to-maturity, reinvestment rate, and realized compounded yield are noted below:

- If reinvestment rate < yield-to-maturity,
  then realized compounded yield < yield-to-maturity
- If reinvestment rate = yield-to-maturity,
  then realized compounded yield = yield-to-maturity
- If reinvestment rate > yield-to-maturity,
  then realized compounded yield > yield-to-maturity

OTHER MATHEMATICAL TOOLS AND TECHNIQUES

In the tool boxes of financial analysts and a new breed known as financial engineers, there is an ever-increasing array of mathematical tools and techniques.

MONTE CARLO SIMULATION

In discussing numbers with clients, wealth managers tend to speak in terms of absolutes (e.g., a life expectancy of 85 or an expected investment return of 8.5%). This can give the client an unrealistic impression of precision. To address the shortcomings of this single-point decision process, a wealth manager may employ the technique of Monte Carlo simulation. This process involves the assignment of probabilities to the various inputs of a model and explores potential scenarios by running multiple cases (hundreds to thousands) to develop a probabilistic profile of the various outcomes.

There are many situations for which Monte Carlo simulation might be usefully employed by wealth managers. Lynn Hopewell, in his presentation to the 1995 IAFP National Conference titled "Decision Making under Conditions of Uncertainty," provided the following example:

Mr. Adrian requests that his wealth manager advise him regarding the funding for his daughter's college education. She will enter college in eight years.

If the wealth manager is an experienced practitioner, the solution is easy. Using his standard educational funding assumptions:

Today's cost = $15,000/year

College inflation = 8%

Discount rate = 6%

He quickly calculates a present value funding requirement of $71,671 and presents that answer to his client. Unfortunately, the client is the same engineer who met with Lynn back in Chapter 6 and he asks, "Does that mean if I put aside that amount today, I can be pretty confident of having enough for my daughter's college costs?"

The answer is, Not exactly. Traditional educational funding analysis is a classic example of a single-point decision process. The single answer provided the client is what's possible, not how probable. In effect, it is the midpoint of the planner's intuitive estimate of best and worst outcomes. As a result, $71,671 represents an amount that has a 50% chance of meeting the client's goal. Rephrased, it represents a 50% chance of failure!

Using the technique of Monte Carlo Simulation, the wealth manager can build in information reflecting his uncertainty regarding his estimates. For example:

He believes education inflation is likely to be 8% but is extremely confident it will fall between 6% and 10% (1% standard deviation).

He believes the investment earnings discount rate is likely to be 6% but is extremely confident it will fall between 4% and 8% (1% standard deviation).

With those expectations and a Monte Carlo Simulation, the wealth manager can develop the following probability distribution table:

Education Cumulative Distribution Table
Forecast: PV of Future Education Costs

Percentile	Approximate PV Costs
5%	$ 47,804
20	65,826
40	69,860
50	71,671
60	73,481
80	77,983
100	105,923

Now, the wealth manager can discuss an appropriate funding level in terms of likelihood.

Lynn suggests the following sources for Monte Carlo Simulation spreadsheet—"add-in" software.

Crystal Ball, Decisioneering, Inc.
Boulder, Colorado
800–289–2550
@ Risk, Palisade Corporation
800–432–7475

In our practice, we are just beginning to experiment with the use of Monte Carlo simulation. Our initial application will be for capital needs analysis. We then expect to apply the technique to our process for developing optimizer input.

ARTIFICIAL INTELLIGENCE

One of the earlier applications of cutting edge technology was *Artificial Intelligence (AI)*. The concept of AI is to develop a comprehensive flow chart of rules based on the input of content experts. For example, a simplified

version of an AI rule for determining a client's recommended emergency
reserve allocation might go as follows:*

Are you married?—No.

- Have you been employed at the same job over five years?
- No—Then set aside four months worth of living expenses.
  Yes—Then set aside three months worth of living expenses.

Are you married?—Yes.

- Is your spouse employed?
- No.
- Have you been employed at the same job over five years?
- No—Then set aside five months worth of living expenses.
  Yes—Then set aside four months worth of living expenses.

Are you married?—Yes

- Is your spouse employed?
- Yes.
- Has your spouse been employed at the same job over five years?
- No—Then set aside three months worth of living expenses.
  Yes—Then set aside two months worth of living expenses.

Our firm had the privilege of participating in the first major effort to
apply AI to financial planning. The program was developed by a Boston
firm named APEX, a pioneer in the field. Through the efforts of a few of
the country's top planners and industry experts** and a cadre of AI programming whiz kids, APEX developed an incredible AI program to assist
planners in developing comprehensive plans. Unfortunately, due to a number of factors, including high costs and, at the time, limited computational
power at an affordable price, the effort was abandoned. The experience,
however, left us with a respect for the power that AI and related technology might bring to the aid of a wealth manager. So, although there may not
be a package currently available off the shelf, it is important to be aware of
the capabilities of AI and other technologies.

---

*Remember, this is an example. It is neither a recommendation for setting reserve requirements nor a
    suggested form for an actual AI program.
**The effort was headed by Richard Austin, now at T. Rowe Price, and the "brains in the box"
    included Jim Joslin and Virginia Applegarth.

FUZZY LOGIC

One of the limitations of AI, more fundamental than cost or the need for computer power, is that the rules of AI are based on binary logic, i.e., a choice between 0s and 1s. Basically, this translates to having a choice between yes or no. There is no place for possibly, maybe, or probably so. The solution to handling gray in addition to black and white, is a technique known as *fuzzy logic*. In a fuzzy logic system, the rules do not have to be hard and fast, they can be fuzzy, just like the natural world.

NEURAL NETWORKS AND GENETIC ALGORITHMS

For the analysis of the kinds of markets described by the chaologists,* new nonlinear techniques are necessary. The most popular is the use of an AI-related technology known as *neural networks.* Designed to mimic the neural network process of a human brain, and trained to recognize patterns, a neural network is the ultimate "black box." The neural network ingests a huge volume of data and generalizes from it. The conclusions of an analysis (e.g., the market is going to go up) may be accurate; however, there is no easy audit trail for the analyst to retrace in order to determine what factors specifically influenced that conclusion.

As neural networks learn from historical data, they are dependent on the quality and appropriateness of the data input. Fuzzy logic is one technique used to add an element of sensitivity to neural net programs. Another technique is *genetic algorithms.* The term genetic is used, for it is an apt description of the underlying concept. Basically, once data are entered and a result is obtained, the algorithm randomly changes an element of the solution and feeds the new data back into the system. If the new solution is better (i.e., predicts more accurately), it becomes the surviving network. This process continues until no new solution replaces the reigning survivor. Darwin would certainly be proud of this system.

The theory and technology of nonlinear quantitative analysis is not limited to academia. Practitioner journals are devoted to the subject, and billions of dollars are being spent for research and development by firms such as Fidelity and Morgan Stanley. *The Economist* wrote in

---

*In the 1970s a number of respected scientists began to suggest that the classical foundation of science was built on an exception to the rules of nature. This new breed of scientist, the chaologist, believes that order, as we know it, is the exception, and that chaos, a new dynamic concept of order, is the rule.

1993 that Fidelity was utilizing neural networks to help select stock for seven of their funds totaling over $2.6 billion in assets.[6] At the time of this writing, research alliances were being announced between leading investment banks and investment management firms and research organizations staffed with physicists, mathematicians, economists, and financial engineers.*

Although much of this technology is available to wealth managers at modest cost for use on their own PCs, few wealth managers are likely to find an immediate need to purchase software. However, that delay may be short-lived. In our practice, we made a preliminary attempt to utilize a neural network but concluded that, due to its experimental nature, it was too early for us to implement effectively at this time. We do, however, continue to follow the work in this area and would expect to begin some use within the next 12 to 24 months. Possible applications that might be improved include developing input for an optimizer, determining rebalancing parameters, determining fixed-income duration ranges, and making tactical allocation decisions.

ENDNOTES

1. Harold Evensky, "A Total Look at Returns," *Financial Planning,* December 1994, 87–88.
2. William Sharpe, "Mutual Fund Performance," *The Journal of Business* 39, no. 1, Part 2 (January 1966), 119–138.
3. Jack Treynor, "How to Rate Management of Investment Funds," *Harvard Business Review* 43, no. 1 (January–February 1965), 63–75.
4. Jerome L. Valentine and Edmund A. Mennis, "Regression, or How to Express the Relationships among Variables," *Quantitative Techniques for Financial Analysis, Revised Edition* (1980), 121–158.
5. Tom Messmore, "Variance Drain," *Journal of Portfolio Management,* Summer 1995, 104–110.
6. "The Mathematics of Markets," *The Economist,* October 9, 1993.

---

*Recent examples include Swiss Bank, Prediction Co. (Santa Fe), Batterymarch (Boston), Olsen & Associates (Zurich), G. K. Capital (Houston), and Eventus R&D (Tel Aviv).

CHAPTER 7

Investment Theory

"More people have read Sylvia Porter than Paul Samuelson."

—*Gary Helms*

In the professional media and at educational meetings of wealth managers, the different approaches to investment management are frequently debated. These debates may range from the pros and cons of using a mathematical optimizer to the value (or lack thereof) of active versus passive managers. Generally, open discussion of these issues is healthy for a profession. Unfortunately for wealth managers, there is frequently a problem. Perhaps because the profession is new, all too often participants in these debates have little or no knowledge of the issues. Even worse, the audience frequently does not have the knowledge necessary to separate the wheat of the argument from the chaff of ignorant criticism.

After speaking at a Schwab National Conference, I was teased (and occasionally cursed) for saying:

> Bernstein [Peter Bernstein] concluded by saying: 'Today, the classical capital ideas are suspected of suffering from kurtosis, skewness, and other less familiar malignancies. They are under attack from nonlinear hypotheses, overwhelmed by fears of discontinuities rather than pricing volatility.' I submit to you that if you don't understand that paragraph in total and if you could not explain to your clients what that means, you should probably not be charging your clients money for managing their assets.*

---

*This was quoted in the guest speaker column of the 50-year anniversary publication of the *Financial Analyst Journal*, January/February 1995. Be sure to add a copy of that issue to your library.

The intention of my comment was not to belittle anyone unfamiliar with those esoteric terms. It was (and is) intended to be a wake-up call for those aspiring to be professional wealth managers. It is easy to reject an emphasis on academic theory as intellectual snobbishness and to suggest that use of sophisticated analytical tools is no more than an effort to market the cache of a famous academic name. Unfortunately, these criticisms are often valid. The solution, however, is not to reject the lessons of academia and avoid the teachings of Nobel laureates. Rather, the wealth manager should develop a familiarity with the very latest information and knowledge available from all appropriate professions, including finance, economics, investments, and psychology, and make decisions based on this knowledge and his own personal experience. The wealth manager assumes the responsibility of helping real people to achieve their life goals through the intelligent management of their financial resources. That is an awesome responsibility. It cannot be met by advice based on "common knowledge" and rules of thumb.

The wealth manager does not have to agree with the conclusions of academic research (e.g., the predominance of the value factor or the inefficiency of active management), and he may reject the conclusions of Nobel laureates;* however, he should have a sound basis for acceptance** or a sound basis for rejection.

Lynn Hopewell was perhaps the first to alert financial planners, practicing wealth management, to this problem. As editor of the *Journal of Financial Planning,* he wrote in his July 1995 editorial:

> If, as I argued in the last issue's editorial, financial planning is becoming dominated by asset management services [wealth management], a question must be raised as to whence cometh asset-management education for planners.
>
>   . . . just as financial planning is an amalgam of the technical matter from other disciplines such as insurance, tax, and estate planning, our asset-management knowledge base lies largely outside the financial planning profession.
>
>   As asset management becomes more dominant in our business, asset-management education must likewise follow. If planners are to stay out of trouble

---

*See, for example, the section on "time diversification" later in this chapter. In that discussion I reject the advice of not one, but two Nobel laureates.

**My thanks to an unnamed reviewer who pointed out that my original criterion of only requiring a "sound basis for rejection" could well lead to the naive adoption of inadequately tested techniques and strategies.

by not being in 'over their heads' in the asset-management game (a definite danger now), we need some concentrated offerings that focus on just this subject.

Echoing my Schwab comments, in the October issue of the *Journal,* Lynn wrote:

> I will go even further—if you don't thoroughly understand the material in Padgette's article [a technical article on performance reporting], you may call yourself a financial planner, but you cannot call yourself an asset manager or investment professional. The essence of asset management is investment policy, portfolio design, and performance measurement. The technical tools are modern portfolio theory and statistics. If you don't master this material, you are like someone who claims to be a physician but who doesn't know about the body's circulatory or immune systems. We would not call that person a physician, we would call him a 'quack.'

As Lynn pointed out, currently there is no single source for the technical and academic background necessary for wealth managers. The following section is intended solely as an overview. It will place in historical perspective today's predominant and evolving theory. It, along with the material in Chapter 6, will provide a working knowledge of the key mathematical and analytical tools that should be a part of the wealth manager's repertoire.

REFERENCE SOURCES

For more detailed guidance, the following are valuable sources:

JOURNALS

Five journals that should be on the subscription list of a wealth manager are:

Financial Analyst Journal. P.O. Box 3668, Charlottesville, VA 22903. The official publication of the Association for Investment Management and Research.

   The Journal of Investing. Institutional Investor, Inc., 488 Madison Avenue, NY, NY 10022. One of a series of journals published by Institutional Investor. Its mission is to "provide in-depth technical exploration of the most provocative theories in portfolio management."

   The Journal of Portfolio Management. Institutional Investor, Inc., 488 Madison Avenue, NY, NY 10022. Another publication of Institutional Investor, edited by Professor Frank Fabozzi, with Peter Bernstein as consulting editor. In spite of its imposing name, this journal is frequently the one most fun to read. Given the editors' attitudes, that's not too surprising. To quote from the guide for submission of manuscripts:

We publish this journal so that its subscribers will read the articles we select . . . we aim for simple sentences and a minimum number of syllables per word . . . The editors have a passionate and well-known abhorrence of passive sentences as well as long-standing dislike of extensive introductions, and carefully crafted summaries are essential. Follow equations with English translations.

The Journal of Financial Planning. 3801 East Florida Avenue, Suite 708, Denver, CO 80210. The official publication of the Institute of Certified Planners is designed to be a "forum for the free exchange of ideas, facts, and information relevant to the financial planning profession."

Financial Services Review—The Journal of Individual Financial Management. 55 Old Post Road, Greenwich, CT 06836. The journal of the Academy of Financial Services. The mission of the journal is to "provide a forum for high quality research in the field of individual financial management."

BOOKS AND REFERENCE MATERIAL

Investment Theory

A wealth manager's library should include books on investment theory. Three core books are:

Frank Reilly, *Investment Analysis and Portfolio Management,* Harcourt, Brace, Jovanovich College Publishers, 1989.
   Professor Reilly brings to his work more than the credentials of traditional academics. His perspective is well beyond the ivory tower. He has served as president of the Academy of Financial Services and as a long-term board member of both AIMR and the CFP Board of Governors.
   William F. Sharpe, *Investments,* Prentice-Hall, Inc., 1985.
   Classics, An Investor's Anthology, edited by Charles Ellis, Dow Jones-Irwin, 1989.
A collection of 86 fascinating classic articles on investment theory. Includes "The Concept of Intrinsic Value," by Graham and Dodd; "Portfolio Selection," by Harry Markowitz; "Capital Asset Prices: A Theory of Market Equilibrium under Conditions of Uncertainty," by William Sharpe; and "The Loser's Game," by Charles Ellis.

Practitioner Basics

For the practitioner, no bookshelf will be complete without:

Roger Gibson, *Asset Allocation,* Irwin, 1990.
   Gibson's text is the definitive work on asset allocation for the wealth manager.
   Don Trone, William Allbright, and Philip Taylor, *The Management of Investment Decisions,* Irwin, 1995. This is the definitive text on the development of an investment policy.
   Carl Reinhardt, Alan Werba, and John Bowen, *The Prudent Investor's Guide to Beating the Market,* Irwin, 1994. This book, although designed for the retail market, provides a useful introduction to asset-class investing.

Mark Kritzman, *The Portable Financial Analyst,* Irwin, 1995. In addition to managing an active investment practice and serving on the editorial board of the *Financial Analyst Journal,* the author writes a regular "must read" column for *The Financial Analyst Journal,* titled "What Practitioners Need to Know . . ." Those columns serve as the basis for this book.

Data

Stocks, Bonds, Bills, and Inflation Yearbook, Ibbotson Associates.

This annual book of market data belongs on the shelf of every wealth manager. However, he should certainly look beyond this publication and consider subscribing to Ibbotson's extensive software database. Their various programs, along with Wilson's CAMS optimizer, serve as the foundation for my firm's analytical software.

Chase Investment Performance Digest.

This annual publication provides performance results, rankings, and risk analyses for more than 75 major investment classes. When available, the data provide detailed information from as far back as 1960. An even more powerful source is the *Chase Investment View software.* A Windows-based program, it enables the wealth manager to compare and analyze over 200 major investment indexes as well as Lipper Analytical Services mutual fund indexes.

History and Philosophy

There are two books that should not only be on the shelf, but should, if not yet read, be the next books on a wealth manager's reading list.

Peter L. Bernstein, *Capital Ideas,* The Free Press, 1992.

This is the eminently readable tale of the modern financial revolution. Much of the following discussion on investment theory history is gleaned from *Capital Ideas.*

Charles Ellis, *Investment Policy? How to Win the Loser's Game,* Dow Jones-Irwin 1985.

This is a small book and that is good, as it should be frequently re-read. It is fair to say that had my partners and I not read *Investment Policy,* our practice would not be what it is today.

Commercial Organizations

Research material from major commercial organizations is often available for the asking, a few of the better organizations include:

SEI
680 East Swedsford Road
Wayne, PA 19087
(610) 254–2328

Frank Russell Company
909 A Street
PO Box 1616
Tacoma, WA 98401
(206) 572–9500

Sanford C. Bernstein & Co., Inc.
767 Fifth Avenue
New York, NY 10153
(212) 756–5806

CONFERENCES

Attending gatherings of experts is an obvious and traditional way of extending knowledge. Unfortunately, for the wealth manager, it is still chancy. Many conferences that address issues of importance do so at far too basic a level. Some conferences that are designed to meet the needs of experienced practitioners address issues from the perspective of institutional money managers, not wealth managers. With prior due diligence, the following organizations offer programs that may be of value to the wealth manager.

Professional Organizations

International Association for Financial Planning (IAFP)
National Convention and Conference for Advanced Planners
5775 Glenridge Drive, NE, Suite B–300
Atlanta, GA 30328
(404) 845–0011
(800) 945–4237

Institute of Certified Financial Planners (ICFP)
Annual Retreat
3801 East Florida Avenue, Suite 708
Denver, CO 80210
(303) 759–4900

Association for Investment Management & Research (AIMR)
Conferences
5 Boar's Head Lane
Charlottesville, VA 22903
(800) 247–8132
(804) 977–6600

Academy of Financial Services
Annual Conference
C/O Robert McLeod
College of Business
P.O. Box 870224
University of Alabama
Tuscaloosa, AL 35487–0224
(205) 348–8993

American Institute of Certified Public Accountants (AICPA)
Investment Conference
Harborside Financial Center
201 Plaza Three
Jersey City, NJ 07311
(201) 938–3000

Commercial Organizations

An increasing number of private organizations are providing high-quality, nonmarketing programs to qualified wealth managers. The best include programs offered by:

National Endowment for Financial Education (NEFE)
National Conference
4695 S. Monaco Street
Denver, CO 80237
(303) 220–1200

Schwab Institutional
Charles Schwab & Co., Inc.
101 Montgomery
San Francisco, CA 94104
(415) 627–7000

Wilson Associates International
21300 Victory Blvd.
Suite 920
Woodland Hills, CA 91367
(818) 999–0015

Federated Investors
Federated Investors Towers
Pittsburgh, PA 15222
(800) 245–5000

Ibbotson Associates
225 North Michigan Avenue
Suite 700
Chicago, IL 60601
(312) 616–1620

Obviously, there are innumerable other sources, but those listed should provide a solid beginning. Let us now turn to an overview of investment theory.

EARLY HISTORY

Perhaps the earliest recorded work that can be said to relate the concepts of theory and investment markets was a doctoral dissertation completed in 1900 titled *The Theory of Speculation,* by the French mathematician Louis Bachelier. His conclusions seem incredibly contemporary.[1]

> Past, present and even discounted future events are reflected in market price . . . the determination of these fluctuations depends on an infinite number of factors; it is therefore impossible to aspire to mathematical predictions of it.
> The mathematical expectation of the speculation is zero.

Unfortunately, at the time his work went unnoticed, and was not rediscovered until the mid-1950s. Whether knowledge of Bachelier's work would have made any difference will remain unknown. By the 1920s, however, there were dozens of soothsayers marketing systems for predicting the stock market.

In 1932, Alfred Cowles III, an early pioneer in the accumulation and measurement of market data, established the Cowles Commission for Research in Economics. Since that date, the Cowles Commission has been the home of many distinguished academics including Nobel laureates James Tobin and Harry Markowitz.

One of the commission's first publications was Cowles's own research on the efficacy of market forecasting. Based on a study of the predictive ability of leading subscription service market forecasters (including the still touted Dow Theory), Cowles, unknowingly echoing Bachelier, concluded, "It is doubtful." Cowles's research confirmed the conclusion that the market outperformed advisors. Many years later, Cowles made the following sobering observations.[2]

> I had belittled the profession of investment advisors. I used to tell them that it isn't a profession and of course that got them even madder.
>
> Market advice for a fee is a paradox. Anybody who really knew just wouldn't share his knowledge. Why should he? In five years, he could be the richest man in the world. Why pass the word on?

For the most part, however, the work of Cowles was as influential as that of Bachelier, i.e., ignored. The period of the 30s and 40s belonged to the fundamentalists, led by Graham and Dodd.

FUNDAMENTALISTS—GRAHAM AND DODD

The publication of *Security Analysis* in 1934, by Benjamin Graham, a partner in a Wall Street brokerage firm, and David Dodd, a Columbia University professor, heralded in the age of fundamental analysis. Graham and Dodd focused attention on the evaluation of the intrinsic value of a stock. With a strong emphasis on balance sheet analysis (hence, fundamentalists), they argued that a stock should only be purchased when its fundamentals met or exceeded a series of specified criteria. The focus was the individual equity, not the portfolio. Risk was subsumed in the concept of intrinsic value.

Many successful investment managers today remain strong adherents of the fundamental concepts presented in *Security Analysis* over 60 years ago. The most famous and the most successful is Warren Buffett. He very articulately presented this philosophy in 1984, in a speech he gave at the Columbia Business School, in honor of the 50th anniversary of the book's publication. Responding to the statistical argument that in a normal distribution there will always be a few lucky managers with extraordinarily good records, he commented:

> I think you will find a disproportionate number of successful coin-flippers in the investment world come from a very small intellectual village that could be called Graham-and-Doddsville. A concentration of winners that simply cannot be explained by chance can be traced to this particular intellectual village.

He describes the common intellectual theme of investors from this village as:

A search for discrepancies between the *value* of a business and the *price* of that business in the market. Essentially, they exploit those discrepancies without the efficient market theorist's concern as to whether the stocks are bought on Monday or Thursday, or whether it is January or July . . . Our Graham & Dodd investors, needless to say, do not discuss beta, the capital asset pricing model or covariance in returns among securities. These are not subjects of any interest to them. In fact, most of them would have difficulty defining those terms. The investors simply focus on two variables: price and value.

While they differ greatly in style, these investors are mentally always *buying the business, not buying the stock.*

His personal observations on the work of academics may serve as a thoughtful introduction to the next section's discussion on modern investment theory:

Of course, the reason a lot of studies are made . . . is that now, in the age of computers, there are almost endless data available . . . It isn't necessarily because such studies have any utility; it's simply that the data are there and academicians have worked hard to learn the mathematical skills necessary to manipulate them. Once these skills are acquired, it seems sinful not to use them, even if the usage has no utility or negative utility. As a friend said, to a man with a hammer, everything looks like a nail.

Buffett's record and the common sense philosophy of "buy value; buy the company not the stock" is compelling. In developing a personal investment philosophy, the wealth manager must carefully consider the premise of the fundamentalists. Now the rebuttal.

MODERN PORTFOLIO THEORY

The spark that started the modern revolution in investment theory (what Peter Bernstein more colorfully calls the "Fourteen Pages to Fame") was the *Journal of Finance's* March 1952 publication of "Portfolio Selection" by 25-year-old Harry Markowitz, a graduate student at the University of Chicago.

Markowitz's ultimate fame, including the 1990 Nobel Prize in Economics, stemmed from his notion that "you should be interested in risk as well as return." That notion led to the insight that risk is central to investing and that the portfolio, not the position, is the fundamental entity for investment management.

Although today these insights seem less than revolutionary, consider the investment world in the 1950s. Bachelier had been forgotten and Cowles all but ignored. Graham and Dodd were revered. They considered the individual position paramount, and risk, a secondary concept. Even John Maynard Keynes, the father of modern economics, and for many years manager of Kings College, Cambridge's endowment fund, had left a legacy consistent with Graham and Dodd's focus on the individual asset.

> I am in favor of having as large a unit as market conditions allow . . . to suppose that safety first consists in having a small gamble in a large number of different [companies] where I have no information to reach a good judgment, as compared with a substantial stake in a company where one's information is adequate, strikes one as a travesty of investment policy.[3]

Even when Markowitz defended his dissertation, Federal Reserve Board Chairman Milton Friedman, then a professor at Chicago and a member of Markowitz's examining committee, challenged:

> Harry, I don't see anything wrong with the math here, but I have a problem. This isn't a dissertation in economics, and we can't give you a Ph.D. in economics for a dissertation that's not economics. It's not math, it's not economics, it's not even business administration.[4] [P.S. They did award Markowitz the Ph.D.].

With this academic and practitioner environment, it is not surprising that Markowitz's work was not an instant success. In 1966, a 20-year index of *Financial Analyst Journal* articles listed 41 articles on growth stock, 24 on gold, and only 4 on security analysis.[5] There was no separate listing for portfolio management.

Harry Markowitz's original article evolved into his thesis in 1955. The full evolution of his work was published in 1959 as *Portfolio Selection: Efficient Diversification*. It is now referred to as *Modern Portfolio Theory (MPT)*.

COVARIANCE

As Harry Markowitz began to think through his notion that risk was important, he first considered the portfolio construction process of the fundamental investor.

An investor concentrating on fundamentals is primarily concerned with constructing a portfolio of stocks that maximize their expected discounted earnings. Markowitz concluded that this approach would result in a concentration of stocks in a few economic sectors. The resulting portfolio would be nondiversified.

In the 1950s, it was well-known that the expected return of a portfolio of assets was the simple weighted average of the expected returns of the individual assets in the portfolio. Harry Markowitz recognized that a similar calculation, simple weighted average of risk, would not result in a correct measure of the total portfolio risk. He determined that, in fact, total portfolio risk, as measured by standard deviation, is a function of covariance.

The mathematical statement of this relationship may be somewhat intimidating:

$$\sigma Port = \sqrt{\sum_{i=1}^{N} W_i^2 \sigma_i^2 + \sum_{i=1}^{N} \sum_{\substack{j=1 \\ i \neq j}}^{N} W_i W_j Cov_{i_j}}$$

$\sigma_{Portfolio}$ = the standard deviation of the portfolio

W_i = the weight of the individual assets in the portfolio

σ_i = the standard deviation of asset i

COV_{ij} = the covariance between returns for assets i and j

where $COV_{ij} = \sigma_i \times \sigma_j \times r_{ij}$

r_{ij} = correlation coefficient for assets i and j

Although the wealth manager need not be able to derive Markowitz's formula, he should understand its import. Professor Frank Reilly, in his text, provides a useful example:

Consider a portfolio equally divided between stocks ABC and EFG. We know the following about these stocks:

Stock	Expected Return	Standard Deviation
ABC	20%	10
EFG	20	10

With this information we can easily calculate the portfolio's expected return to be 20 percent, but what about the standard deviation? For that, we need to know the correlation of ABC and EFG.

Suppose the two stocks are perfectly correlated; i.e., the correlation coefficient = 1. Then, using the earlier formulas:

$$\text{Covariance} = 1 \times 0.1 \times 0.1 = 0.01$$

Standard Deviation of the Portfolio
$$= \sqrt{(.5)^2 \times (.1)^2 + (.5)^2 (.1)^2 + 2 \times (.5) \times (.0.01)}$$
$$= 0.10$$

The solution is not too surprising. As both ABC and EFG are totally correlated, mixing the two stocks in the portfolio has no impact on the portfolio's standard deviation.

Now consider the case where the correlation between ABC and EFG = 0.5.

$$\text{Covariance} = 0.5 \times 0.1 \times 0.1 = 0.005$$

Standard Deviation of the Portfolio
$$= \sqrt{(.5)^2 \times (.1)^2 + (.5)^2 (.1)^2 + 2 \times (.5) \times (.0.005)}$$
$$= 0.087$$

Now we can see the power of diversification! The volatility of the two stocks did not change one iota. The only change in the calculation was the last number, i.e., the covariance. The expected return of the portfolio is still 20 percent but the portfolio is 13 percent less volatile than either ABC or EFG!

One of the key insights of Markowitz's work is that the risk of a portfolio is usually less than the weighted average risk of the individual assets. A little diversification provides a lot of risk reduction. As demonstrated by Figure 7–1 (useful for client education), 10 to 12 poorly correlated stock positions can significantly reduce portfolio risk.

METHODOLOGY

Markowitz believed that there is a trade-off that investors make between risk and reward. Investors either accept higher risk for greater returns or sacrifice returns in order to reduce risk. In addition, he believed that once an investor determined either his return goal or his risk tolerance, there was a single superior portfolio that would meet the investor's goal.

His interest in developing a rational solution to the problem of selecting this portfolio led to the development of a theoretical framework for portfolio design and diversification, i.e., MPT. Included in his work

F I G U R E   7-1

Diversification

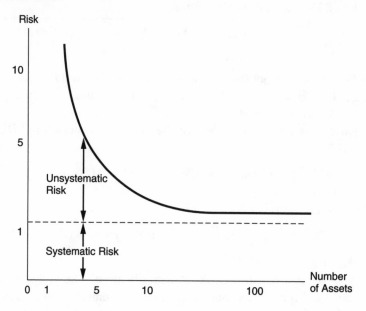

was a formal methodology for determining the specific asset combination that was superior to all other alternatives.

ASSUMPTIONS

Underlying MPT are a number of important assumptions:

- Investors are rational; hence, they want to maximize the expected utility of their investments.
- In order to accomplish this goal, they select investments solely according to their evaluation of their risks and returns.
- For a given return, rational investors derive the lowest risk, and for a given risk, rational investors prefer the highest return.
- Return is measured as total return.
- Risk is defined as the uncertainty of the return and is measured by variance.
- Expected returns are normally distributed.

- Investors select their assets from a universe of risky assets.

The major criticisms of these assumptions are:

- Investors may not be rational, as defined by economic theory. They may either be irrational or rational as defined by psychological theory.
- Market returns are not normally distributed.
- Investors have choices other than risky investments, e.g., Treasury bills.
- There is no accepted "universe of risky assets."

E-V MAXIM

Based on these assumptions, Markowitz developed a rule for selecting investments that he called the *Expected Return-Variance Maxim,* or *E-V Maxim.* The rule is a mathematical formulation of the design of portfolios with the highest return for a given level of risk.

In the development of this rule, Markowitz considered a number of risk measures, including semivariance. He concluded, however, that the other alternatives were computationally unrealistic and selected variance as a measure that was fundamentally sound and practical for calculations.

As variance is the measure of risk Markowitz selected, the solution is not linear, but rather quadratic. The utility function also requires a quadratic solution. Further, the goal is to determine not one solution, but solutions for a series of risk levels. To accomplish this, a parametric quadratic program is used. This is the mathematical engine that drives the better of the oft maligned 'black box' optimizers.

The output of a Markowitz optimizer is usually presented in graphic form. The curve (Figure 7–2) is called the Efficient Frontier and it is plotted by connecting a series of positions representing the most efficient portfolio for each level of risk.

Using the following generalized efficient frontier as representative of that generated for a combination of real investment choices, the curve can be interpreted as follows:

Point A represents a client's current portfolio. His expected return is 10 percent with a risk of 25. As it lies below the efficient frontier, it is an inefficient portfolio for a rational investor. Remember the definition of a

F I G U R E   7–2

Generalized Efficient Frontier

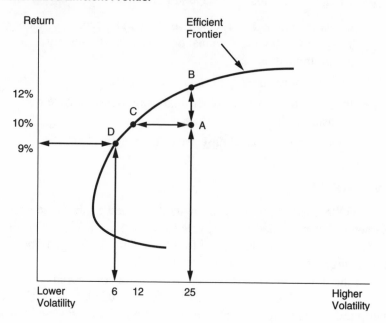

rational investor. For a given return, he will seek the lowest risk, and for a given risk, he will seek the highest return.

In this example, if the client is prepared to maintain his current risk level, he can reposition his assets to match Portfolio B, increasing his return by 2 percent without increasing his risk. If the client is happy with the return of his current portfolio, he can reallocate to match Portfolio C and decrease risk while maintaining his return. Finally, if the client only needs a return of 9 percent, he would reallocate to Portfolio D, the most efficient allocation for that specific return.

Markowitz's efficient frontier can be a very effective tool for educating clients. As discussed above, it demonstrates a number of important concepts:

- There is no perfect portfolio. There is an infinite series of perfect (efficient) portfolios.
- These efficient portfolios fall along the efficient frontier.

- A client's current portfolio (A) may be improved by rebalancing it to fall on the efficient frontier such that the client can maintain his expected return while reducing risk (C) or increase his expected return without increasing his risk (B).

- Neither Portfolio B nor C might be appropriate. If the client does not require the return expected by B or C, it may be appropriate to design a portfolio with *less* return than the current one (e.g., Portfolio D). Even though Portfolio D is expected to underperform the current portfolio, it is more efficient and it meets the client's return goal.

As a final note, it is important to remember that MPT is based on a number of debatable assumptions. However, the efficient frontier is a tool, not a guarantee. Empirical evidence, as well as academic research, suggests that it provides better guidance than alternative methods.

CAPITAL MARKET THEORY

The next major contribution to investment theory is generally credited to William Sharpe, a student of Markowitz's, and a corecipient with Markowitz of the 1990 Nobel Prize.*

Sharpe's work was an extension of Markowitz's portfolio theory to general market theory. The culmination was the publication in the September 1964 *Journal of Finance* of "Capital Asset Prices: A Theory of Market Equilibrium under Conditions of Risk."

Sharpe's theory provided a model for determining how financial assets are valued (i.e., priced) by the market. This model has become known as the Capital Asset Pricing Model (CAPM). Based on MPT, Sharpe utilized Markowitz's assumptions, and added a number of significant new ones:

CAPM ASSUMPTIONS

There is a risk-free asset (i.e., one with no uncertainty regarding the expected rate of return).

- Investors can borrow and lend at the risk-free rate of return.

---

*Independent work of a similar nature was concurrently developed by John Litner and Jan Mossin. Their names are frequently linked in discussions on this subject.

F I G U R E   7–3

The Efficient Frontier and the Capital Market Line

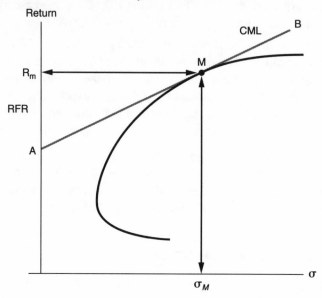

- There are no taxes and no transaction costs.
- All investors have the same investment time horizon.
- All investors have identical expectations for asset returns.

In addition to the objections to the Markowitz assumptions, criticism of Sharpe's new assumptions include:

- Inability of investors to borrow at the risk-free rate.
- The reality of taxes and transaction costs.
- Investors do not have uniform time horizons.
- Investors do not have identical expectations of returns.

CAPITAL ASSET PRICING MODEL

Sharpe concluded that, based on the assumptions above, the efficient frontier for all investors would look like a graph of the Capital Market Line (Figure 7–3).

The point of tangency (M) of a line drawn from the return of the risk-free asset (A) represents the single best portfolio for the world of homogeneous, Markowitz-efficient investors. Logically, if this portfolio represents what every investor *would* own, it must represent what they *do* own; hence, *M* is the *world portfolio.*

Taking the logic of the CAPM illustration one step further, all investors would obviously choose to own a portfolio of only two investments—the risk-free asset and the market portfolio. Under the assumptions of CAPM (i.e., the ability to lend or borrow at the risk-free rate at no cost), an investor could construct a portfolio anywhere along the line AM by lending a portion of his funds at the risk-free rate and investing the balance in the market portfolio. For an investor who wishes to ratchet up his returns above the "average" of the market portfolio, it is easily accomplished. He would simply leverage his investment by borrowing at the risk-free rate and investing the borrowed funds, along with all of his own assets, in the market portfolio. How much he borrows will determine where along the line MB his leveraged portfolio will fall.

The line AB is known as the *Capital Market Line.* The next important concept of CAPM is the Security Market Line.

SECURITY MARKET LINE

In MPT, risk is a function of the covariance of one asset with the other portfolio assets. In Sharpe's world, there is only one market asset, the market portfolio. Thus, the only covariance of importance is the asset's covariance with the market portfolio. This covariance is effectively the systematic risk in Figure 7–3. Thus, according to CAPM, for diversified portfolios, total risk is irrelevant. Unsystematic risk is diversified away and all that remains is systematic risk, i.e., the risk of the market.

To make the following easier to follow, we'll first mathematically define a number of terms:

Cov_{ij} = Covariance of two assets, i and j
Cov_{im} = Covariance of an asset with the market
r_{ij} = Correlation coefficient of i and j
R_i = Return of asset i
R_{RF} = Risk-Free Return
σ_i = Standard Deviation of asset i
σ_i^2 = Variance of asset i

We know that:

From the Markowitz formula discussed earlier, $\text{Cov}_{ij} = \sigma_i\sigma_j r_{ij}$

The market covariance with itself is equal to 1.

In CAPM, covariance with the market is the single measure of risk. Add to this two basic math concepts:

A straight line can be defined by two points.

The algebraic formula for a straight line is: $Y = a + bX$

This equation provides for determining the value of Y for any value of X.

$$a = \text{the value of Y if } x = 0$$
$$b = \text{the slope of the line}$$

Returning to CAPM, we can now develop a line graph describing the relationship between return and risk. Start with a generalized formula:

$$R = a + b \text{ (risk)}$$

We also know that $\text{Risk} = \text{Cov}_m$

$$R_i = a + b \text{ (Cov}_{im})$$

Now let's locate two points in order to draw a line. We know that for a risk-free asset, covariance with the market equals zero; therefore:

$$R_{RF} = a + b \text{ (0)} = a$$

That provides our first point. For our second, we know the correlation of the market with itself is equal to 1; therefore:

$$\text{Cov}_m = \sigma_m \times \sigma_m \times 1 = \sigma_m^2$$

Therefore, with:

$$a = R_{RF}$$
$$\text{Cov}_m = \sigma_m^2$$

Then the SML can be described as:

$$R_m = R_{RF} + b \times \sigma_m^2$$

Using basic algebra, we can see that the slope of the SML is:

$$b = (R_m - R_{RF})/\sigma_m^2$$

Rearranging the formula to make it a little easier to read, the result is:

$$R = R_{RF} + (Cov_m/\sigma^2) \times (R_m - R_{RF})$$

Although this is a pretty simple description of the SML, CAPM takes it one step forward. As market risk is the primary exposure for a diversified portfolio, it would obviously be convenient to somehow have it serve as a standard against which the risk of other assets can be measured. The simple and elegant solution was the creation of a new term called *beta* (β), where

$$\beta = (Cov_m/\sigma_m^2)$$

Now our formula can be rewritten as:

$$R = R_{RF} + \beta \times (R_m - R_{RF})$$

Even better, if we calculate the β of the market (β_m):

$$\beta_m = (Cov_m/\sigma_m^2) = (\sigma_m^2/\sigma_m^2) = 1$$

With this SML, we can predict the exact relationship between β and expected return and draw this relationship as Figure 7–4.

F I G U R E   7-4

Security Market Line

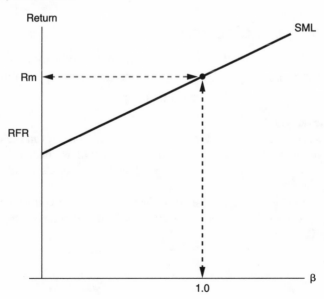

A CAUTION ON THE USE OF β

Using the formula for the SML, we can now determine the expected return for an asset if we know the risk-free return, the expected market return, and the beta of the asset. For example, assume that we expect:

$$R_{RF} = 3\% \text{ and } R_m = 12\%$$

For Stock A with $\beta_A = 1.2$ and Stock B with $\beta_B = 0.7$, we can calculate the expected return:

$$R_A = 0.03 + 1.2\ (0.12 - 0.03) = 13.8\%$$
$$R_B = 0.03 + 0.7\ (0.12 - 0.03) = 9.3\%$$

For some wealth managers these results may come as a surprise. It is common to use beta as a single factor relating risk and return. Most investors would have calculated a different expected return:

	Common Use of Beta	CAPM Expectation
Stock A	12% × 1.2 = 14.4%	13.8%
Stock B	12% × 0.7 = 8.4%	9.3%

Obviously, the error is in not adjusting for the risk-free rate. As the differences may be significant, a wealth manager using beta as a guide to risk must be sensitive to the possible misuse by others.

IMPLICATIONS OF CAPM

- An investor should invest in a combination of only two investments—the risk-free asset and the market portfolio.
- Risk is composed of two components:

Market Risk
This is the risk associated with the market (i.e., economy) and cannot be diversified away. Hence, market risk is also known as nondiversifiable risk and is a form of systematic risk. β is the measure of a securities-market-related risk.

As market risk cannot be diversified away, some investors are prepared to pay a premium in order to avoid the risk. Those investors willing to accept the risk are thus compensated.

Nonmarket Risk

This is the risk unique to the security or portfolio. It can be eliminated through diversification; hence, it is also referred to as *diversifiable risk.* As it can be eliminated by diversification, investors are not prepared to pay for assuming this risk.

FINAL THOUGHT

By now the reader might enjoy a brief respite. So I'll take this opportunity to place this theory in some perspective.

As Markowitz, Sharpe, and many other academics whose names are synonymous with modern investment theory were educated and/or teach at the University of Chicago's School of Economics, the following illuminates one of the school's fundamental beliefs.

How many Chicago School economists does it take to change a light bulb? None. If the bulb needed changing, the market would have done it already.

OTHER ASSET-PRICING MODELS

The goals of asset-pricing models are to:

- Assist managers to understand the dynamics of asset pricing.
- Direct managers' efforts to those issues that can affect future returns.
- Help managers to assess risk.
- Assist in the evaluation of portfolio performance.

To the extent that CAPM is seen to fail in meeting these goals, there have been alternate pricing models proposed. The most important is:

ARBITRAGE PRICING THEORY (APT)

In 1976, Stephen Ross published his APT, a new asset-pricing model, that became a significant catalyst for new research.

Whereas CAPM is a single-factor model (the market portfolio), APT is a multifactor model. In addition to being more robust than CAPM by allowing for the influence of multiple factors, it does not require a number of the assumptions of CAPM.

FINAL THOUGHTS ON ASSET-PRICING MODELS

No model on theory has become the Rosetta stone of asset pricing. As with the Efficient Market Hypothesis (EMH), research papers criticizing various asset-pricing models have become a cottage industry. Objections include criticism of underlying assumptions and claims that empirical tests demonstrate their lack of predictive value.

Still, these models serve as a major catalyst for market research and an influence on market practice. They remain powerful theoretical concepts that continue to influence market theory and practice.

The wealth manager should neither accept pricing models as gospel nor reject them out of hand. With respect to individual asset selection, it is the role of the portfolio manager to determine the influence of pricing models in his philosophy. The wealth manager's job is to intelligently evaluate the manager's philosophy.

One of the key lessons of both CAPM and APT is that unsystematic risk is not rewarded by the market. Unsystematic risk should be avoided. Chapter 15, Fiduciary Investing, a discussion of fiduciary investing, will show how ignoring this advice may expose the wealth manager to significant personal liability.

RANDOM WALK

Random walk, along with its close relation the *efficient market,* are phrases that tend to start active managers frothing at the mouth. Most investors believe that these terms describe a market in which stock prices move in a totally random manner. Although some observers have suggested just such a conclusion, the concept does not depend on stock prices being statistically random; only that they are random in the sense that information about the history of prices cannot be used to predict future prices.

The early work in this area by Bachelier (1900), Working (1934), and Cowles (1933) was largely ignored. The concept of market randomness was not revisited until the 1950s. Renewed interest in the 1950s started not in finance or economics but with statistician M. Kendall's "The Analysis of Economic Time Series," Harry Roberts's "Stock Market Patterns," and astrophysicist M. F. M. Osborne's "Brownian Motion in the Stock Market."[6] These studies suggested that market prices had "no memory." Any information in the past sequence was reflected in the current price.

In the 1960s the economist picked up the gauntlet. In 1964 Paul Cootner published *The Random Character of Stock Prices,* and in 1965 Nobel laureate Paul Samuelson published "Proof that Properly Antici-pated Prices Fluctuate Randomly." In this paper, Samuelson hypothesized an efficient market with normally distributed prices. He concluded that in such an environment, market prices would be random. The major synthe-sis of this evolving work is credited to Eugene Fama.

Fama, a newly minted Ph.D., began teaching at the University of Chicago in 1964. His doctoral thesis was concerned with the question of market efficiency. It was published in the January 1965 *Journal of Busi-ness* as "The Behavior of Stock Market Prices." The work was so persua-sive that an abridged version was published in the *Financial Analyst Journal* as "Random Walks in Stock Market Prices," as well as in a 1968 issue of the trade journal *Institutional Investor.* At the end of 1969, Fama presented a paper to the American Finance Association and published "Efficient Capital Markets: A Review of Theory and Empirical Work" as the definitive synthesis on the subject in the May 1970 issue of *Journal of Finance.*

EFFICIENT MARKET HYPOTHESIS (EMH)

The *EMH* is concerned with the relationship of stock prices and the ac-tions of buyers and sellers. The premise of the EMH is that "security prices fully reflect all available information."

Fama suggested that this hypothesis could be more easily addressed if the test of its validity were divided into three subthemes (referred to as *forms*). Each form reflects a different definition of "information" against which the hypothesis might be tested.

The most stringent test is the *strong form.* This tests whether all rel-evant information, public and nonpublic (including insider information), is reflected in security prices.

The *semistrong form* asserts that all useful publicly available infor-mation is immediately used by investors. Stock prices discount the infor-mation and the market will instantaneously reach equilibrium.

The *weak form* assumes that current stock prices reflect all stock market information. It tests the hypothesis against information provided by historical market data (e.g., prices and trading volume). The weak form can be explained by the random walk theory. If price movements are in fact random, historical market information would obviously not provide any useful information. However, the weak form may still be valid even if markets are not random. The question is whether historical data can provide useful information, not *why* they can or cannot.

If the weak form is correct, then adherents of traditional technical analysis cannot add value. The information utilized by technical analysis will have no predictive value. The weak form neither supports nor rejects the notion that other forms of information (e.g., good research) may be helpful in predicting future prices. If a wealth manager accepts the weak form, he will ignore managers who employ technical analysis and he will ignore the siren song of market timing. Regarding a wealth manager's use of active managers who use fundamental analysis, the weak form says, You're on your own; this hypothesis has no opinion.

A wealth manager accepting the strong or semistrong hypothesis will not only avoid market timing and technically oriented managers; he will avoid all active managers. As good as they may be, they simply cannot add value.

THOUGHTS ON EMH

During the last 30+ years, academics have empirically tested these hypotheses continually. Almost uniformly, the results support the weak market hypothesis and generally reject the strong hypothesis. There is no agreement on the results of the test of the semistrong.

A wealth manager who employs managers using technical analysis, concentrates positions, or uses market timing may want to reconsider his philosophy. If challenged by an unhappy client, the wealth manager will find himself having to defend his actions against an impressive and overwhelming history of research that clearly says he is wrong! It may be legally safe to manage your own funds based on an unpopular theory. It is riskier to challenge generally accepted theory when advising others.

For wealth managers who employ active managers who base their investment policy on fundamental research, there is better news. One of the major problems with the EMH is the interpretation of the word *information*. The earlier discussion addressed only one aspect of information, namely the source. Left unresolved is the nature of *information*. If information is simply data, it is available to all interested parties almost instantaneously. If information depends on interpretation, the role of an intermediary, such as a fundamental analyst, may be significant.

A wealth manager selecting active fundamental managers currently has significant academic support for his decision; however, research on the subject continues. A wealth manager should stay apprised of the results of new studies because one day the support for active management may disappear.

TIME DIVERSIFICATION

One of the truisms branded into the soul of most wealth managers is that time diversifies risk. The original formulation of this belief is attributed to Peter Bernstein. His two basic premises were:

- The longer the investment horizon, the larger the percentage of the portfolio that should be invested in stock and other high-return assets.
- In the long run, an investor can be reasonably sure that a higher-volatility portfolio will earn more than a lower-volatility portfolio.

This belief has led wealth managers to preach to their clients that it is nonsense to say that the market is risky. It is risky in the short term and safe in the longer term. Time diversification is the basis for the EB&K mantra, "five years, five years, five years."

This faith in the salutary effect of time on risk was not created from naive optimism. Over time, it seems that above-average returns should offset below-average returns. Logically, the longer the time horizon, the more effective this dampening effect. Mathematically, for normally distributed returns, standard deviation declines with the square root of time. For example, if an equity fund has a 25 percent annual standard deviation, the expected standard deviation for a three-year cycle is 14.4 (i.e., $25/\sqrt{3}$).

As comforting as it is to believe that time diversification is working in the client's favor, the wealth manager needs to be aware that some observers argue that this is another investment myth. It might be tempting to ignore these objections, but as the list of critics includes Robert Merton and Paul Samuelson (both Nobel laureates), it is wise to at least understand why they argue that time diversification is specious.

In 1969, publishing independently but reaching the same conclusions, Merton and Samuelson demonstrated that although the standard deviation of average annual returns may decrease over time, the standard deviation of cumulative returns *increases.* More recently, Zvi Bodie[7] forcefully argued the same general conclusion. In other words, although the probability of loss decreases over time, the magnitude of losses increases. As a result, an investor's asset allocation decision should be independent of the time horizon. Mathematically, Merton's and Samuelson's conclusions are indisputable. How, then, does a wealth manager incorporate time diversification into his own personal philosophy?

Recognize that the rejection of time diversification rests on various assumptions including the academic economists' favorite person, the "rational" investor. One of the attributes of a rational investor is a utility function that translates into a desire to maximize terminal wealth (actually the log of terminal wealth). Real clients of a wealth manager seldom have such simple goals. The academics' definition of a rational investor may be academic.

For most clients, the long-term goal is to earn a return adequate to maintain their standard of living. They have neither a reason nor a desire to take excess risks to earn returns in excess of their target. Also, the investor is likely to be relatively indifferent as to whether he is earning one-fourth or one-half of his required return. Any return significantly below the required is likely to decimate the client's standard of living.

The significance of this in terms of time diversification is that the wealth manager's client is far more sensitive to the probability of meeting his goal than the relative magnitude of a shortfall. For him, time diversification may work.

The following example[8] and tables[9] may be useful in demonstrating this concept to clients.

Ms. Rhinehart Time Diversifies

Ms. Rhinehart has $1,000 to save for retirement. She has a choice between two investments:

- A risk-free investment with an expected return of 4 percent and a standard deviation of 0 percent.

- A risky investment with an expected return of 12 percent and a standard deviation of 16 percent.

Table 7–1 compares the probability of terminal values for the risky and risk-free investments.

T A B L E   7-1

Time Diversification—Risk-Free versus Risky Investments

		Risky Investment Value			
Time Horizon in Years	Risk-Free Investment Value*	Mean	10th Percentile	90th Percentile	Probability of Underperformance
1	$1,000	$ 1,000	$ 900	$ 1,400	30.9%
5	1,200	2,000	1,200	2,900	13.2
10	1,500	3,800	1,700	6,400	5.7
20	2,200	14,200	4,400	27,600	1.3
40	5,000	202,800	33,200	444,500	0.1

*Rounded to the nearest $100

After 10 years, there is a 90 percent probability that the risky investment return will exceed the risk-free return by at least 13 percent. There is only a 5.7 percent probability that it will underperform the risk-free asset. After 20 years the probability of underperformance drops to 1.3 percent. For a 40-year time horizon (common in retirement planning), the probability of underperformance drops to 0.1 percent!

Asset Allocation and Time Diversification

Combining the benefits of asset allocation and time diversification makes for an even stronger "story."

Suppose that the client has the choice of investing in three portfolios—all bonds, all stock, or a diversified portfolio.

If we wish to evaluate the risk the investor faces with these different investment choices, we can compare the expected portfolio returns to Treasury bill returns. Tables 7–2 and 7–3 explore the probability that the portfolio returns will exceed Treasury bill returns.*

---

*The table is based on an assumption of a mean-reversion model but the results are essentially the same for the random walk model.

T A B L E   7-2

Investor Portfolio Choices

	T-Bills	T-Notes	Bonds	S&P 500	Small Cap
Portfolio A	0.0%	0.0%	0.0%	100.0%	0.0%
Portfolio B	0.0	0.0	100.0	0.0	0.0
Portfolio C	5.0	12.5	22.5	50.0	10.0

T A B L E   7-3

Time Diversification and Asset Allocation—It Works
Probability of Exceeding T-Bill Returns

Holding Period in Years	Portfolio A Stock	Portfolio B Bonds	Portfolio C Diversified
1	61%	59%	66%
10	85	72	91
20	93	79	97
30	96	84	99

Time Diversification—A Caveat

Where the client's goal has an intermediate time horizon (i.e., one requiring a specific terminal wealth value), Merton and Samuelson may be right. The following example illustrates such a case:

> Mr. Godchaux has money set aside to fund his child's education in five years. He is considering investing in an equity fund with an expected return of 15 percent and a standard deviation of 30 percent. He is concerned with the high volatility of the fund. When Mr. Godchaux expressed his concerns to his advisor, the advisor explained that as the portfolio is designed to be held for five years, the expected ROR per year for five years is still 15 percent but the standard deviation is only 13.4 percent (i.e., $30\%/\sqrt{5}$). The client is relieved. This is time diversification in action. Is his sense of security warranted?
>
> Unfortunately, the answer is no! The problem is that although the standard deviation of the *annualized rate of return* is reduced to 13.4 percent, the volatility of the terminal value of the portfolio is not. If the client's average return is off by just one standard deviation (a very real possibility), *his terminal wealth will be less than half the expected value.* Figure 7–5 demonstrates how significantly the terminal wealth can diverge over time.

F I G U R E   7–5

Deviation of Terminal Wealth

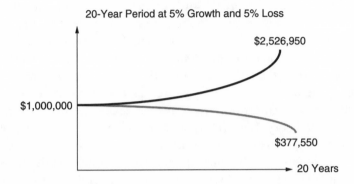

Investment Growth

20-Year Period at 5% Growth and 5% Loss

$2,526,950

$1,000,000

$377,550

20 Years

ASSET ALLOCATION

Harry Markowitz, with the development of MPT, refocused investment managers' attention away from specific securities and on the portfolio. Markowitz demonstrated that asset allocation was important, but not how important. Many managers and investors continued to believe the advice given in the mid-1930s by Henry Loeb. "The greater safety lies in putting all your eggs in one basket and watching that basket."[10]

The publication of "Determinants of Portfolio Performance" in the July–August 1986 issue of *Financial Analyst Journal*[11] was a seminal event in portfolio management. The concepts of investment policy and asset allocation have, largely as a result of that article, become part of the common investment lexicon for retail as well as institutional investors. I believe that the contribution of Gary Brinson, Randolph Hood, and Gilbert Beebower (BHB) is of such importance that every wealth manager should be familiar with their process and conclusions.* The next chapter will discuss their work in detail.

---

*I think it's so important, I've named one of our cats Brinson. Of course, the other two are Sharpe and Markowitz.

CHAOS THEORY

Webster's dictionary defines chaos as "a state of things in which chance is supreme; a state of utter confusion." It would seem, then, that Chaos Theory is the ultimate oxymoron. How can there be a theory about chance and confusion? The answer is to redefine chaos. In mathematical terminology, chaos is a form of a deterministic nonlinear dynamic process.

Most of the science of the 20th century is based on the work of ancient and classical scientists (e.g., Euclid, Galileo, and Newton). For the most part, the universe has been viewed as a smooth and continuously evolving process. This world view also serves as the basis for modern capital market theory. Linearity is built into the concepts of efficient markets and rational investors. Information is readily reflected in security prices and return distributions approximate normal distributions. Although there is increasing discussion of non-normal distributions reflecting different levels of skewness and kurtosis, the analysis of these asymmetric models is still based on statistical concepts rooted in a linear universe.

In the 1970s a number of respected scientists began to suggest that the classical foundation was built on an exception to the rules of nature. This new breed of scientist, the chaologist, believes that order, as we know it, is the exception, and that chaos, a new dynamic concept of order, is the rule. They believe that this new order, called chaos, has three major attributes:

- First, nature is deterministic, i.e., the past mechanically governs the future. There is an exact mathematical relationship between the future and the past. There is *no* randomness.
- Second, the mathematical relationships relating the future to the past are *non-linear,* i.e., they are not related in a directly proportional way.
- Third, the process is dynamic and changes over time.

Chaotic systems can be recognized by a number of attributes: Although not random, they may appear random according to standard statistical tests. Chaotic systems have an extreme sensitivity to their initial conditions. As a result, specific future states are unpredictable.

The most familiar example of a chaotic system is the weather. Although on a day-to-day basis the weather may seem random, it obviously has a certain predictability. No one is likely to get sunstroke in Syracuse in January. It is equally unlikely that it will snow in Miami in September. Thus, it is perhaps no surprise that the real impetus for current research in Chaos Theory began with the work of an MIT meteorologist, Edward Lorenz.

In the early 1960s, weather forecasting was considered guesswork. Computers were still big, slow, ungainly conglomerations of vacuum tubes. As told in the book *Chaos,*[12] by James Gleick, Lorenz was experimenting with a make-believe world and its weather system by programming his computer with 12 God-like rules regarding temperature, pressure, and wind speed. His program produced a graph of continually undulating lines representing the rise and fall of the temperature in his make-believe world. In the winter of 1961, Lorenz decided he would like to continue a study of a series he had begun earlier. Rather than starting over, he simply entered the data obtained from his last computer run and started once again crunching numbers. Having used exactly the same data as the earlier run, the graph should have generated a pattern similar to the original graph. It didn't! The new graph rapidly diverged in shape from the original. After a few "months," his new world's weather pattern bore no resemblance to the weather pattern in his earlier analysis.

According to Gleick, Lorenz at first assumed that a vacuum tube had gone bad,* but soon realized that the cause of the dramatic changes was a tiny change in the data starting point. His computer calculated to an accuracy of 6 decimal places, but only printed 3. So, if the ending point of the original run was 0.602193, it printed 0.602. When Lorenz entered the data for the second run, he typed 0.602 and the computer read it as 0.602000. Although the difference, one part in a thousand, seemed inconsequential, it had a profound effect. In other words, there was an extreme sensitivity to initial conditions.

A more colorful and useful (if explaining the concept to clients) description of extreme sensitivity is the Butterfly Effect; the notion that a butterfly flapping its wings today in Hong Kong can decide the difference between a beautiful weekend or a hurricane for Miami a month later.

Thirty years after Lorenz's original work, meteorologist research facilities with vast resources, including the latest supercomputers, continuously crunching close to a million concurrent equations, can only predict with useful accuracy, up to a week ahead. Even if the world's weather prognosticators could blanket the world at one-foot intervals with 100 percent accurate sensors, measuring temperature, humidity, and any other

---

*If you do not know what a vacuum tube is, you're disgustingly young, and I'm not going to tell you

desired quantity every 60 seconds, they couldn't accurately predict rain or sun in New Orleans one month later. The Butterfly Effect is too powerful. This is an important lesson to keep in mind as you read about chaos and the capital markets.

CHAOS AND THE CAPITAL MARKETS[13]

Historically, investment theory has been based on the assumption that, for the most part, financial market relationships were linear. As an example, in the 1980 edition of *Quantitative Techniques for Financial Analysts,* it was stated: "A truly nonlinear regression is seldom encountered in actual practice." However, even then there were doubters.

Benout Mandelbrot, one of the original chaologists, suggested in the early 60s that stock movements were chaotic. More recently, the publication of *Chaos and the Capital Markets,* by Edgar Peters (along with *Chaos,* by Gleick, a "must read" for the wealth manager), focused increasing interest and research on the implications of chaos theory for investment professionals.

Chaos World

Peters provides a simple and credible example to demonstrate how capital markets may very well function as a chaotic system.

Consider, he suggests, a penny stock (i.e., one selling for under \$1). If the market was only composed of buyers, the price of the stock would rise only as a function of buyers entering the market. The price of the stock in the future could be calculated by the simple formula:

$$P_{(t+1)} = a \times P_t$$
P_t = Price at time t
$P_{(t+1)}$ = Price at time t + 1
a = the rate the price would rise as a function of demand

To make the case more realistic, Peters adds "sellers" to the market. The actions of these sellers will tend to reduce the price down as a function of P_t^2.

We can now develop a formula that mechanistically determines future stock prices.

$$P_{(t+1)} = a \times P_t - a \times P_t^2$$
$$= a \times P_t \times (1 - P_t)$$

This seems to be a pretty simple world. Let's call it "Penny World" and investigate how the price of a stock, issued at 30¢, might vary over time, depending on the single variable a.

When a = 2

Time	Price
0	30¢
1	=2×0.3×(1–0.3)= 42¢
2	49
3	50
4	50
5	50
100	50

Obviously, in this nice, clean world, our stock reaches a fair price of 50¢ and stabilizes there.

World in which a = 3

Time	Price
0	30¢
1	63
2	70
3	63
4	70

At this higher growth rate, there is an oscillation between two "fair values." Where the price reaches 70¢, the sellers begin to dump. The price drops until at 63¢ the buyers jump back in and push it back up to 70¢.

With very minor changes in the rate function a, the simple world can turn very strange. The equation we developed for Penny World is a form of what is known as the Logistic Equation. The following diagram, plotting all the possible values for our stock for varying values of a is called a bifurcation diagram.

Bifurcation Diagram for Penny World

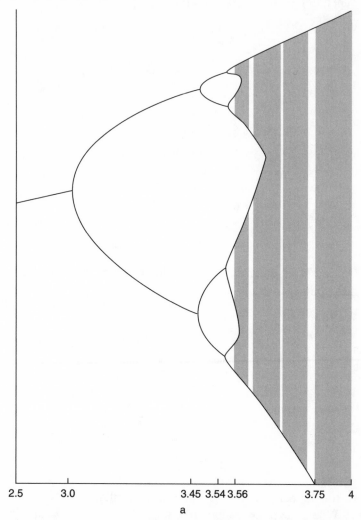

Peter's example demonstrates that it is easy to conceive of feedback mechanisms that would result in chaotic financial markets. The bifurcation diagram is a classic picture of a chaotic system. It is also a powerful demonstration of the impact minute changes in initial conditions may have on future events, even in a "simple" financial world. His work, along with other practitioners and academics, provides strong evidence of chaotic dynamics in the capital markets. Still, it is far from an acknowledged fact that capital markets are chaotic systems.

Implications of Chaos in the Capital Markets

Although still subject to debate, the implications of chaotic markets are so significant that the possibility should not be ignored. The implications include:[14]

- Chaotic markets appear to be the rule, not the exception. As demonstrated by Peter's preceding example, complex markets may appear to be random when, in fact, they are following a few simple mathematical rules that incorporate an element of information feedback.

- It is not possible to accurately forecast, for anything but a very short horizon, expected returns and values. Even the most complex and sophisticated of econometric or timing models will fall prey to the same butterfly effect that cripples meteorologists' forecasts.

- Chaotic systems frequently seem to be highly structured and to have regular cycles only to explode into unpredictable behavior (e.g., a snow-covered mountain just before an avalanche, or the stock market in October 1987). This is the trap of quasi-periodicity that may lead to false faith in successfully backtested trading systems.

- Traditional portfolio theory assumes no trends or cycles. However, as chaotic systems are not random, there are also positive implications for our ability to quantify reality:

1. Market return series may be bounded. For example, even if the specific temperature in New Orleans in the summer cannot be predicted, it can be predicted that it will be hot.

2. Previously inexplicable market behavior (i.e., leptokurtic distributions) may become explainable.

3. The array of linear-based analytical tools currently used by investment analysts may be successfully supplemented by nonlinear analytical systems resulting in improved portfolio performance and/or a better ability to manage client expectations.

- The concepts of efficient markets, value investing, and tactical asset allocation may be consistent with chaos theory.

SUMMARY

Change is everywhere. What changed? What didn't?

—Alan Pariese

What is a wealth manager to do with all of this theory? The following is from Michael Corning's review in the July 1994 issue of the *Journal of Financial Planning* of Edgar Peters's book, *Fractcal Market Analysis: Applying Chaos Theory to Investments and Economics.* I thought that Corning did such a fine job of answering this question that I will close this section with his "Final Thoughts":

> We risk making two types of errors when faced with a new and provocative world view. Type I: We too quickly *appropriate* a new idea or theory. Type II: We too quickly *dismiss* a new idea or theory. With Type I errors we agree without understanding; with Type II we disagree without appreciating. The former is naive, the latter is insolent. With Type I errors we are not fully utilizing our critical faculties; with Type II errors we are forgetting our intuitive capacity. Ignorance is non-market risk. We have an obligation to our clients to diversify it away, and the best way to do that is with an open and critical mind.

E N D N O T E S

1. Peter Bernstein, *Capital Ideas, The Improbable Origins of Modern Wall Street,* The Free Press, 1992.
2. Ibid.
3. Ibid.
4. Ibid.
5. Ibid.
6. Bernstein.
7. Zvi Bodie, "On the Risk of Stocks in the Long Run," *Financial Analysts Journal,* May–June 1995.
8. Steven R. Thorley, "The Time Diversification Controversy," *Financial Analysts Journal,* May–June 1995.
9. William Reichenstein, CFA, "Introduction," *Time Diversification Revisted,* Dovalee Dorsett, February 1995, 1–8.
10. Gerald Loeb, "Is There an Ideal Investment?" Charles Ellis, Editor, *Classics: An Investor's Anthology,* Dow-Jones Irwin, 1989, 266–276.

11. Gary P. Brinson, L. Randolph Hood, and Gilbert L. Beebower, "Determinants of Portfolio Performance, *Financial Analysts Journal,* July–August 1986.

12. J. Gleick, *Chaos: Making a New Science* (New York: Viking Press, 1987).

13. Edgar E. Peters, *Chaos and Order in the Capital Markets: A New View of Cycles, Prices, and Market Volatility,* John Wiley & Sons, Inc., 1991.

14. James J. Angel, "Implications of Chaos for Portfolio Management," *The Journal of Investing,* Summer 1994, 30–35.

CHAPTER 8

Asset Allocation

Not to decide is to decide.

—Gary Helms

To set this chapter in perspective, I'll begin with a quote from the introduction to *Global Asset Allocation,* one of the most technically rigorous and comprehensive texts on the subject of asset allocation.

"Asset allocation remains more art than science and will probably remain so as long as the models used are only approximations of a reality that is in a constant flux."[1]

Obviously the authors believe in the importance of technical competence; else why write the book? However, once again the wealth manager is cautioned to become a competent artist.

WHY BOTHER?—DETERMINANTS
OF PORTFOLIO PERFORMANCE (BHB)

In "Determinants of Portfolio Performance,"[2] the question that the authors set out to answer was, as the article title stated, What determines portfolio performance? For their study, the authors used the SEI large plan universe database. The basic screen for a plan's inclusion in the study included:

- A corporate plan with the investment decisions resting solely with the corporation.
- A large asset base.

- The study excluded public and multiemployer plans. This was to eliminate plans that might be subject to legislative or legal constraints on the investment managers' activities.
- 40 quarters of data (1974–1983).

The final database used for their study included 91 plans ranging in size from $700 million to $3 billion in assets. The plan assets were separated into three asset classes: cash, bonds, and common stock. It was decided that the approximately 8½ percent of plan assets not falling into these classes (e.g., real estate, venture capital, and private placements) were too small an allocation to be treated separately. They were prorated over the three major asset classes.

As a beginning premise, the authors determined that there were only three decisions that a portfolio manager could make that would have an impact on a portfolio's performance.

- Security Selection. The active selection of a specific security within an asset class (i.e., active management).
- Timing. The active decision to over- or underweight a specific asset class relative to the manager's long-term (i.e., "normal") allocation. The decision to change weightings could be based on a desire either to increase returns or decrease risk.
- Investment Policy. This third decision is not optional. An investor cannot avoid implementing an investment policy. Either implicitly or explicitly there is a policy. Generally referred to as "asset allocation," this includes the decision of what classes to include and the decision regarding the weights of each selected class.

Starting with the investment policy and the option of implementing timing and security selection strategies, the authors developed a graphic matrix of the decision process.

Figure 8–1, from the article, is a simple representation of these relationships.

- Quadrant I represents the impact of the portfolio based on the impact of policy alone.
- Quadrant II represents the performance of the portfolio based on the impact of the policy and timing decisions.

F I G U R E   8-1

A Simplified Framework for Return Accountability

Selection

		Actual	Passive
Timing	**Actual**	(IV) Actual Portfolio Return	(II) Policy and Timing Return
	Passive	(III) Policy and Security Selection Return	(I) Policy Return (Passive Portfolio Benchmark)

Active Returns Due to:

Timing	II – I
Selection	III – I
Other	IV – III – II + I
Total	IV – I

- Quadrant III represents the performance of the portfolio based on the impact of the policy and security selection decisions.

- Quadrant IV represents the performance of the actual portfolio.

The analytical process employed was to run a regression analysis of each of the portfolios against the returns of quadrants I, II, and III. The final reported results were for the 91 regression series. In order to determine the effective return of the 91 portfolios attributable to the strategies implemented in quadrants I, II, and III, the calculations reflected in Figure 8–2 were made.

The returns for the policy portfolio (I) were calculated assuming that the portfolio funds were invested at the original asset class percentage and passively invested in indexes. The Shearson Lehman Government Corporate Index was used as the asset class return for bonds, the S&P 500 for stock, and 30-day T-bills for cash. The result of these calculations was the return of the portfolio solely attributable to the policy decision.

The influence on return of the security selection strategy was determined by running an analysis similar to the one for policy returns, but substituting the portfolio's actual asset class returns for the passive returns. By

F I G U R E   8–2

Computational Requirements for Return Accountability

Selection

		Actual	Passive
Timing	Actual	(IV) $\Sigma_i(Wai - Rai)$	(II) $\Sigma_i(Wai - Rpi)$
	Passive	(III) $\Sigma_i(Wpi - Rai)$	(I) $\Sigma_i(Wpi - Rpi)$

Wpi = policy (passive) weight for asset class i
Wai = actual weight for asset class i
Rpi = passive return for asset class i
Rai = active return for asset class i

holding the policy allocations steady (i.e., ignoring the manager's actual timing decisions), the results provided a return measure attributable to the policy and security selection decisions (III). By subtracting from this result the returns solely attributable to policy, the remainder was the return solely attributable to security selection.

The last calculation used the index returns for the asset classes but adjusted the allocation percentages to reflect the timing decisions made by the portfolio manager. The result of this analysis was the return attributable to timing and policy (II). The timing contribution was isolated by, once again, subtracting the policy contribution.

The results of this process, as shown in Figure 8–3, were disturbing. By applying the brains and talent of many of the best and brightest of the nation's portfolio managers to actively manage an investment portfolio, the returns were reduced! Active security selection reduced the returns below a passive portfolio by 0.36 percent, active timing "lost" 0.66 percent, and together the underperformance was 1.10 percent. Although not the purpose of the study, these results should certainly be considered by the wealth manager when developing his own philosophy regarding the use of active and passive strategies.

In order to determine the importance of the policy decision, the final analysis was a regression of each portfolio's actual returns against the returns

F I G U R E   8–3

Mean Annualized Returns by Activity 91 Large Plans, 1974–1983

Selection

		Actual	Passive
Timing	Actual	(IV) 9.01%	(II) 9.44%
	Passive	(III) 9.75%	(I) 10.11%

Active Returns Due to:

Timing	–0.66%
Security selection	–0.36
Other	–0.07
Total active return	–1.10%

in quadrants I, II, and III. The R^2 of the 91 regressions were averaged and the final results were reported as shown in Figure 8–4.

As the authors observed, "The results are striking." "Startling" might have been an even more descriptive adjective. Over 93 percent of the variation in portfolio returns is attributable to policy. According to BHB, active security selection and timing play minor roles in determining portfolio performance.

The conclusion of the study was;

> Although [active] investment strategy can result in significant returns, these are dwarfed by the return contributions from investment policy—the selection of asset classes and their normal weights.

In August 1991, Brinson, Brain, Singer, and Beebower published "Determination of Portfolio Performance II: An Update" in the *Financial Analyst Journal*.[3] Based on a study of data from 82 large pension plans for the period between 1977 and 1987, they reconfirmed the earlier research. In the second study they concluded:

> For our sample of pension plans, active investment decisions by plan sponsors and managers, both in terms of selection and timing, did little to improve performance over the 10-year period from December 1977 to December 1987.

F I G U R E   8–4

Percentage of Total Return Variation Explained by Investment Activity
Average of 91 Plans, 1973–1985

	Selection	
	Actual	Passive
Timing — Actual	(IV) 100.0%	(II) 95.3%
Timing — Passive	(III) 97.8%	(I) 93.6%

	Variance Explained			
	Average	Minimum	Maximum	Standard Deviation
Policy	93.6%	75.5%	98.6%	4.4%
Policy and timing	95.3	78.7	98.7	2.9
Policy and selection	97.8	80.6	99.8	3.1

THE VALUE OF ASSET ALLOCATION DECISIONS (HEI)

Although William Sharpe and Fidelity accept these conclusions,* BHB is not without its critics. The most cogent was a Frank Russell Research commentary, *The Value of Asset Allocation Decisions,* by Chris Hensel, Don Ezra, and John Iekiw (HEI), published in March 1990 and republished in the July–August 1991 *Financial Analyst Journal* as "The Importance of the Asset Allocation Decision."[4]

The Russell authors contend that the BHB study started with an inappropriate default portfolio (i.e., one not invested in any capital assets). If, however, a more realistic beginning (or "naive") portfolio were selected for

---

*William Sharpe states: "It is widely agreed that asset allocation accounts for a large part of the variability in return on a typical investor portfolio." Art Lutschauing, VP Fidelity, likewise states: "We, like the rest of the industry, believe that 90 percent of return comes from the asset allocation decision."

analysis, HEI concluded that the determinants of portfolio performance are quite different from BHB.

HEI argues that a reasonable choice for the naive portfolio is not an all-cash portfolio, but one resembling the average asset allocation held by large pension plans. This information is readily available and it entails little cost or effort to design a policy based on what everyone else is doing. For purposes of HEI, this becomes the Russell naive portfolio.*

The HEI concluded that:

- If T-bills rather than the Russell naive portfolio was selected as a beginning point, the BHB position was correct.
- If the starting point is the Russell naive portfolio, the potential impact of security selection is almost equal to the influence of the specific policy allocation. Both have more influence than the potential attributable to timing.
- As a result, "Decisions regarding active management (market timing and security selection) can be just as worthy of a sponsor's attention [as the asset allocation decision]."

THE IMPORTANCE OF MANAGING ASSET ALLOCATION–MY OPINION

The influence and acceptance of the work of BHB is so pervasive that a wealth manager should not ignore their conclusions. Even the Russell study does not contradict BHB's conclusion that the policy decision is of paramount importance. It simply suggests that policy may explain "only" 40 to 50 percent of the variation in returns instead of 90+ percent. Also, the Russell study is based on institutional portfolios where a 60 percent/ 40 percent allocation is a reasonable assumption for a naive allocation. Wealth managers know that, in their retail world, an all-cash portfolio (e.g., T-bills or CDs) is often the real naive portfolio. Thus, for clients of wealth managers, the BHB assumptions may be closer to the truth.

Many of the illustrations in the previous section can be useful in client education. Continually reinforcing the concept of diversification in the client's mind is part of the ongoing process of managing a client's risk tolerance and expectations.

---

*In fact, the study noted that a simple policy of 60 percent stock and 40 percent bonds would achieve the same results.

Assuming a wealth manager incorporates at least an element of managing the asset allocation, he must adopt a process to develop allocations appropriate to the client's needs. For those not yet convinced of the necessity of establishing an asset allocation policy, I will briefly consider the alternative.

THE ALTERNATIVE TO A MANAGED ASSET ALLOCATION POLICY

In the management of an investment portfolio, there are only three categories of decisions that influence the portfolio performance:

- The asset allocation.
- The security (manager) selection.
- The market timing.

All other decisions are subsumed by these. All portfolios have "policies" regarding each of these decisions. Financial planners frequently tell their clients that everyone has an estate plan. A client's failure to execute a will does not eliminate estate planning; it simply substitutes the state's plan for the client's. An asset allocation policy is analogous to an estate plan; by design or by default all portfolios have a policy. A portfolio without a managed asset allocation policy still has a policy—a randomly determined policy. The question for the wealth manager, then, is whether to design and manage a policy or to let chance design a policy.

A lack of understanding regarding the unavoidability of an allocation policy has led to unfounded concern over the concept of asset allocation. As an example, Robert Clark, one of our profession's most astute media commentators, discussing asset allocation, asked:

> But what if we're wrong? . . . What if we're positioning our clients in exactly the wrong assets, setting the state for another debacle that would make limited partnerships seem like pocket change?[5]

WHAT IF EVERYTHING GOES WRONG?

The answer to the question is that it would be terrible! But it would be wrong to conclude that wealth managers should not make the effort to design reasonable allocations. Random allocations are more likely to lead to the disaster envisioned by Clark. The responsibility of the wealth manager

F I G U R E   8–5

Worst Rolling Period Return

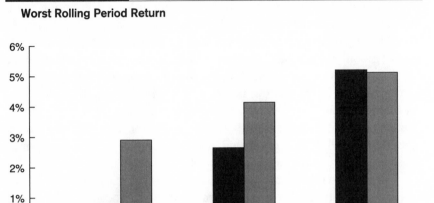

Source: P. Brown

is not to guarantee future returns but rather to use his experience and knowledge to maximize the probability of achieving the client's goal.

I was curious as to how an investor might have fared in the past during "bad" times had he followed this advice. Figure 8–5 compares the performance of an all T-bill portfolio and an all-stock portfolio to that of a diversified portfolio, invested as follows:

T-bills	10%
Intermediate Bonds	30
Large U.S. Stock	40
Small U.S. Stock	20

During the worst period for each portfolio the results show that asset allocation has indeed been a very effective strategy.

CONFUSION OF THE CONCEPT WITH THE IMPLEMENTATION

Some critics of asset allocation confuse the concept with the application. For example, an oft-repeated criticism is that many planners develop asset allocation models based on unsubstantiated input resulting in unrealistic expectations.[6] Although this is undoubtedly true, the error is in the selection of the input, not the attempt to manage allocations.

Occasionally, the concept of asset allocation is criticized for ignoring global catastrophe. Examples include worldwide nuclear war, a catastrophic virus killing much of the world population, or global economic collapse. I must admit that our firm's implementation of our asset allocation policy does not incorporate these issues, but the 'fault' is in our implementation, not the concept of allocation. A wealth manager, haunted by fear of global disaster, can certainly incorporate those nightmares into an allocation policy.

Rather obviously, my conclusion is that the only alternative to a managed asset allocation policy is a random-asset allocation policy. And, as allowing the gods of chance to direct our clients' fiscal lives is not in keeping with professional wealth management, all wealth managers should develop an asset allocation strategy.

ASSET ALLOCATION IMPLEMENTATION STRATEGIES

The balance of this chapter will discuss a number of strategies for asset allocation that a wealth manager might consider.

MODEL PORTFOLIOS

Perhaps the simplest solution for the wealth manager is to adopt the use of one of the myriad of asset allocation models provided by the purveyors of investment product. One example of this approach is the series of SEI Financial Services' "Strategies." These are thoughtful and sophisticated asset allocation models designed by two of the nation's leading financial services firms: SEI, a sponsor of over $30 billion in investment portfolios, and Wellington, managers of over $35 billion in assets. The strategic series includes 18 different models ranging from all fixed income to all equity. Reviewed and revised quarterly, the models are clearly delineated by style and asset class allocation. Although these models are among the best available, they still are of no use for the wealth manager.*

---

*My criticism is directed at all packaged models, not SEI. We respect and actively work with SEI and SEI funds.

Limitations of Models

▪ *Lack of Customization.* Wealth managers are professionals, not vendors. They use their expertise and knowledge and make professional judgments. Packaged products will not suffice. Although some models, such as the SEI Strategy's 18 choices, attempt to provide an element of customization by offering many choices, they are still not flexible enough to meet the needs of wealth managers. For example, our firm's investment philosophy currently excludes the use of high-yield bonds, while the SEI Institutional Moderate Growth and Income Portfolio includes an 11 percent allocation to high-yield bonds. For our purposes, the model is worthless.

▪ *Black Box.* As Chapter 9, Optimization, states, one of the most frequent criticisms of wealth manager optimization is the use of a complex computer program, frequently referred to as a *black box.* This pejorative description suggests that the wealth manager is implementing an asset allocation policy without understanding how the allocations were determined. The presumption is that the black box, not the wealth manager, is making the decision. Unfortunately, this is often a valid criticism.

When a wealth manager uses someone else's model, this is *always* a valid criticism. Instead of using his skills to balance the myriad of factors necessary to design unique models for his clients, the advisor has simply elected to choose from among a limited number of boilerplate products. No matter how sophisticated the thought process that led to the model, from the advisor's perspective, each model is, in effect, the product of a black box. The model developers might briefly describe the global issues influencing their design (i.e., "Bond yields are close to fair value"); however, the advisor has no real feel for the specifics of the models underlying assumptions (i.e., expected returns, standard deviations, and correlation).

▪ *Asset Class Benchmark.* Model portfolios are divided into asset classes and, occasionally, styles. If a wealth manager elects to use a model portfolio, and implements with managers of his own choosing, he must determine how closely his managers match the assumptions of the model. As these assumptions are usually not disclosed, overlaying someone else's model allocation on the wealth management universe of approved managers is as scientific as using the results of the Superbowl as a market timing trigger.

▪ *Tax Efficiency.* In spite of the earlier criticism of many portfolio tax management strategies, there is at least one that always needs to be considered; the use of municipal bonds in a taxable account. Unfortunately, most models do not incorporate even this basic consideration.

Third-Party Models—My Opinion

For wealth managers, an asset allocation strategy should be an integral part of their personal wealth management philosophy. Packaged models, no matter how credentialed the creators, are a product. For all the reasons noted above, they are not an appropriate solution for the wealth manager. Wealth managers provide professional service; they do not market product.

This does not, however, mean that the wealth manager should not create his own models. In doing so, he can still address the unique needs of his client base. He will have determined all the assumptions used in the models design. He will know what benchmarks were used and he will know when his own models do not meet the needs of a particular client.

JUDGMENTAL INTUITION

This is an approach that, while acknowledging the necessity of an asset allocation policy, approaches the solution as 100 percent art.

A clear example was provided by a trust officer at an AIMR conference on Asset Allocation for Individual Investors. Explaining that his trust company had toyed with a black box quantitative approach, they ultimately concluded that the intuition of their experienced staff was a more comfortable and credible strategy.

Their process is to categorize the U.S. economy into four generic inflation environments—deflation, price stability, disinflation, and rapid inflation. Looking back over the last 100 years, they consider the interaction of inflation and various asset classes during each form of inflation environment.

The investment committee, composed of the most experienced members of the investment staff, meet for several hours twice a year. Based on the belief that the most important decision is to call the "turning points in various asset categories and being in the right place at the right time," the investment committee "simply sift[s] through where we feel the environment will take those assets and arrive at our judgment."

As an example, during 1985 the focus was on eight major classes. The target allocations are noted in Table 8–1.

Judgmental Intuition—My Opinion

Although I believe that wealth management (and the process known as asset allocation) is 90 percent art (i.e., judgment and intuition), I also believe that it is 10 percent science and that science is the foundation for the judgment.

T A B L E   8-1

Recommended Asset Allocation

Asset	Possible Range	Current 3- to 5- Year Targets	Prior Targets	
			Jul–85	Jan–85
Reserves	2–30%	6%	4%	3%
Bonds	10–40	24	26	33
Stocks	20–60	45	36	42
Real Estate	5–30	10	14	14
Oil & Gas Ptnr	0–15	1	4	4
Venture Capital	0–10	2	2	2
Precious Metals	0–15	5	4	2
Foreign Securities	0–15	7	10	—

It is difficult to rationally comment on an approach that rejects academic research and quantitative analysis. I would only suggest that there are a number of problems a wealth manager might face by adopting such an approach:

■ Reallocating. Based on the example of Table 8–1, the frequency and magnitude of reallocation can result in significant transaction costs and tax consequences.

■ Heuristics. Without a well-defined underlying policy, an asset allocation model based on judgment and intuition is likely to be significantly influenced in a negative way by all the heuristics discussed earlier. For example, "representativeness" may result in an inappropriate influence of short-term trends (reflected by significant short-term changes in allocations), "availability" may result in an inappropriate weighting in hot asset classes. And, "regret, pride, and shame" may result in an unfounded defense of "intuitive judgment" decisions.

■ Liability. Intuition may be a weak defense for a failed allocation policy. As Trone, Allbright, and Madden emphasized in their book *Procedural Prudence,* the primary defense of an investment fiduciary is procedural prudence, not performance. In my opinion, 100 percent reliance on judgment and intuition fails the test of procedural prudence.

MULTIPLE SCENARIO ANALYSIS

Multiple scenario analysis (MSA) is an approach familiar to most financial planners. In its simplest form, it is based on projecting a best case and worse case and, from within that range, selecting a "most probable." As applied to asset allocation, the most visible firm applying this technique is Bailard, Biehl, and Kaiser (BBK). For the wealth manager interested in implementing MSA, there is no better model than BBK.[7]

BBK describes their approach as a disciplined method of applying quantitative analysis to problems of uncertainty. The process is divided into a number of steps:

- Define investments.
- Determine starting points.
- Create future alternatives (scenarios).
- Forecast returns for each scenario.
- Assign scenario probabilities.
- Choose optional portfolios.

Each scenario is an economic projection defined by expectations for major economic factors:

- Real GNP
- CPI
- Short-term interest rates
- Long-term interest rates

Once a scenario has been defined, estimates are made for returns for each asset class. BBK typically uses six scenarios. They believe the simple default of two scenarios, pessimistic and optimistic, is too constraining, and more than six, too excessive. The time horizon for the scenarios is four years. This approximates an economic cycle.

Only after completing this detailed quantitative procedure does BBK begin a judgmental/intuitive overlay. The first step is for each investment committee member to assign a probability to the various scenarios. The first scenario is the average of these weightings. The next step is for each member, using the consensus scenario as a base, to modify the weightings based on current relative asset-class returns, the current yield curve, and investor sentiment. The head of the asset allocation committee uses these optional portfolios to arrive at the firm's recommended policy.

This comprehensive process is completed annually. The work, beginning in January, requires about six weeks and results in a policy looking forward four years. Although reviewed quarterly, there is a strong institutional bias against short-term changes. In addition, individual portfolio managers are generally held to the firm's 3 percent rule, i.e., discretion to vary from the policy by only 3 percent.

BBK believes that their careful blending of the science and art of investment management avoids the pitfalls noted earlier for a pure judgmental/intuitive approach and the rigidity associated with mathematical optimizers. They refer to this process as a "confirmed" decision based on a rational process that heightens risk awareness and expands investment possibilities.

Multiple Scenario—My Opinion

Intermittently, over the past few years, our investment committee has considered implementing an MSA strategy modeled after BBK. We have not done so for a number of reasons:

- As Chapter 9, Optimization, will address, the process of estimating expected returns for one scenario is difficult; estimating six scenarios seems overwhelming.
- In addition to the compounding effect of multiple scenarios on uncertainty, MSA requires an additional series of estimates regarding the probability of each scenario.
- Although the final overlay of relative market yields, yield curves, and investor sentiment is intended simply as the fine-tuning of a quantitative process, we fear that it is too susceptible to the heuristic problems associated with the judgmental strategy.
- We believe that the detail of the multiple assumptions and the application of economic probabilities results in an unfounded level of confidence in the results.
- Finally, BBK's Diversion Fund, managed in accordance with their MSA strategy, has an inconsistent performance record, often attributable to the allocation policy.

Still, BBK has been most gracious in sharing the details of their process with their investment peers and there are many thoughtful and potentially useful ideas in the BBK strategy. Wealth managers would be well rewarded in reading about the BBK process.

MATHEMATICAL OPTIMIZERS

Depending on your orientation, mathematical optimizers are the solution or the problem. The debate, pro and con, occasionally becomes vituperative and is often silly. In almost all cases, the critics of the black box fall into the trap of wanting to kill the messenger. Optimizers are only tools; they are neither good nor bad. The responsibility of the wealth manager is to have an adequate knowledge base to evaluate their efficacy in his practice. If the use of optimizers is rejected by the wealth manager, the decision should be based on a rational and prudent analytical process. The decision should not only consider the absolute benefits and disadvantages of an optimizer but also the benefits and disadvantages of mathematical optimization relative to other alternatives.

Benefits

The benefits of using optimizers are many.[8]

- They are exact.
- They provide solutions for an infinite number of efficient portfolios.
- They offer a convenient structure for integrating a client's goals and constraints.
- They provide a mechanism for controlling portfolio exposure to various components of risk.
- They allow the wealth manager to determine the portfolio's sensitivity to changes in expectations of returns, risks, and correlations.
- They assist in the design of a procedurally prudent policy.

Objections

Eleanor Blayney colorfully described optimizers as diversification gone high tech. As she so cogently pointed out, optimization implies a scientific right and wrong. This arrogance of absolutes is at the core of most objections to optimization:

- Optimizers present a misleading exactness. The inputs are subject to significant statistical errors and the mathematical process of optimization maximizes the errors.
- The conclusions of optimizers are frequently counter-intuitive and occasionally down-right stupid.

Other less fundamental and more operational objections include the following:

- Optimizers are difficult to use and they require substantial amounts of quantitative input.
- They require a significant knowledge of quantitative concepts.

Mathematical Optimizers—My Opinion

The argument against formal asset allocation and mathematical optimization boils down to two major issues:
- Asset allocation places too much emphasis on academics and science. It ignores the real world.
- Asset allocation may be important but mathematical optimization is at best overkill, and at worst a danger.

Perhaps the most prominent and respected proponent of the first objection is Don Phillips of Morningstar.* The September/October 1995 *Fee Advisor* included a special article, featuring Don Phillips, on just this issue.

Phillips also had strong words regarding asset allocation. 'I really question how much value all of this asset allocation analysis brings to the table. I think that there are a handful of important lessons to learn from asset allocation, and you could probably fit them all onto one sheet of paper. A lot of it is, take your age and subtract that from 100, and that gives you your stock versus bond allocation, and I think that gets you pretty far. That may be 95 percent of the utility of asset allocation, coming from that one decision.'

In fact, Phillips suggested the whole notion that 95 percent of the portfolio decision-making process rests on asset allocation was 'one of the grave disservices that academia inflicted upon financial advisors. You can look to

---

*As I am about to totally disagree with Don on these issues, let me note that, in addition to considering Don a good friend, largely through his efforts Morningstar has become the preeminent information source for the wealth manager. I have harangued friends and acquaintances, almost from the inception of Morningstar, that no one can call himself a wealth manager and/or financial planner without having Morningstar publications on his shelf and in his computer.

the academics and get that, or you can look to the real world and say, where have people made money?'

I believe that Don's conclusions are wrong for many reasons.

▪ As I discussed in the introduction, an allocation formula such as 100 – age results in inappropriate recommendations. To suggest such a simplistic solution for planning an individual's financial future reflects a lack of understanding of investors' unique goals and constraints.

The assertion that the "notion that 95 percent of the portfolio decision process rests on asset allocation" was the work of academia is nonsense. It was the conclusion reached by investment practitioners* based on "real world" data. The confirmation and acceptance of the original research has also come from investment practitioners (e.g., SEI, Fidelity, Federated, Callan, Vanguard).

▪ The focus on "where people made money" also reflects a misunderstanding of the goals of most individual investors and the role of the wealth manager. People "make money" by building bridges or widgets, performing operations, starting or managing businesses, managing mutual funds, or creating and selling mutual fund database information. Investors don't "make money;" they invest and earn reasonable returns for the risk they are prepared to take in order to become financially independent.

Part of the education we provide our prospective clients is to explain that we can't "make them rich" (if we knew the secret, as much as we love our profession, we would not be working—we'd be sipping mint juleps in the South Seas) but we will not make them poor. We will assist them in achieving financial independence. Maximizing returns may be the goal of institutions; it is not the goal of our clients. They want to enjoy the quality of the balance of their lives. They could care less if someone else "makes more money."

If a client's goal was solely to "make more money" from investments, I would agree with Don that asset allocation was probably irrelevant. However, I would not waste my time looking for the best large cap domestic manager; I would concentrate the portfolio in small cap value and emerging market funds. However, I don't. My clients care about "sleeping well" as much as they care about "eating well."

---

*At the time the BHB study was prepared, Gary Brinson was president and chief investment officer of First Chicago Investment Advisors; L. Randolph Hood was assistant vice president of First Chicago Investment Advisors; and Gilbert Beebower was senior vice president of SEI Corporation.

A portfolio built out of the sticks and straw of simplistic allocations and "make them rich" may survive good times but it will not survive a bear market. For that, the investor needs a portfolio built of the bricks and mortar of artful and scientific wealth management.

▪ Those objecting to the use of optimizers, are, for the most part, objecting to a technology that they cannot, do not, or have not bothered to understand. Similar objections were made to the use of the first computers (and probably to the abacus and slide rule). The term GIGO (garbage in garbage out) predated optimizers but the concept is the same. Even the best of technology cannot turn garbage input into good output. But, the villain is the input (and "inputer"); not the technology. Equally troubling, those objecting to the use of optomizers fail to suggest a better alternative.

I believe that most of the objections to mathematical optimization reflect inappropriate implementation by the user; not fatal flaws with the concept. Comparing the benefits and disadvantages of optimizers to other asset allocation strategies, I've concluded that the knowledgeable use of optimizers is the superior alternative. The following chapter will discuss my perceptions and suggestions regarding a "knowledgeable" use.

E N D N O T E S

1. Scott L. Lummer, PhD, CFA and Mark W. Riepe, "Introduction: The Role of Asset Allocation in Portfolio Management," *Global Asset Allocation,* John Wiley & Sons, Inc., 1994, 1–6.

2. Gary P. Brinson, L. Rudolph Hood, and Gilbert L. Beebower, "Determinants of Portfolio Performance," *Financial Analysts Journal,* July–August 1986, 39–44.

3. Gary P. Brinson, Brian D. Singer, and Gilbert L. Beebower, "Determinants of Portfolio Performance II: An Update," *Financial Analysts Journal,* May–June 1991, 40–48.

4. Chris R. Hensel, D. Don Ezra, and John H. Ilkiw, "The Importance of the Asset Allocation Decision," *Financial Analysts Journal,* July–August 1991.

5. Bob Clark, Editor's Note, *Investment Advisor,* September 1995, 8.

6. Robert Veres, "Apocalypse When?" *Investment Advisor,* September 1995, 113–120.

7. David R. Rahn, "Implementing and Managing the Investment Asset
    Allocation Process for the Individual, Part 1," *Asset Allocation for the
    Individual Investor,* The Institute of Chartered Financial Analysts, 1987, 99–
    105; Peter M. Hill, "Global Asset Allocation," *Global Asset Allocation,* John
    Wiley & Sons, 1994, 264–281.

8. Richard O. Michaud, "The Markowitz Optimization Enigma: Is 'Optimized'
    Optimal?" *Financial Analysts Journal,* January–February 1989, 31–40.

CHAPTER 9

Optimization

Any security specific selection decision is preceded either
implicitly or explicitly by an asset allocation decision.

—Scott Lummer and Mark Riepe

Chapter 8, Asset Allocation, considered a number of strategies that a
wealth manager might use in order to develop an asset allocation model.
At EB&K, we believe that the most appropriate strategy is the thoughtful
and knowledgeable use of mathematical optimizers.

I recognize and agree with much of the criticism directed at "black
boxes." The software available for wealth managers generates projections
5, 10, or even 20 years into the future, carried to the 5th decimal place,
with probability measures to the 10th decimal place. These results are
clearly ludicrous. Any wealth manager who unquestioningly accepts the
allocations recommended by an optimizer is likely to be a threat to his clients' financial well-being.

The solution, however, is not to default to an inferior strategy, but
rather to recognize that good optimization is a blend of art and science. Integrating complexities such as parametric quadratic programming with the
uncertainties of future events is not an exercise in pure science. In fact, I believe that art, not science, is the predominant factor.* However, an acknowledgment of this reality does not excuse a slipshod understanding of

---

*I use the term *art* as a catch-all description to include a wealth manager's professional intuition,
experience, and common sense.

the academic and technical aspects of optimization. Instead, it demands a solid grasp of the elements that drive the analysis. It is only by understanding these issues that the wealth manager can know when and how to apply his art.

As with many topics covered by this book, there are a number of excellent books dedicated solely to asset allocation and optimization. A few of the most important include:

Roger Gibson, *Asset Allocation,* Irwin, 1990, 1996.
Mentioned earlier, this is a "must read." It is *the* text on asset allocation and optimization for the wealth manager.
Lederman & Klein, *Global Asset Allocation,* John Wiley Publishers, 1994.
One of the newest (and most readable) of the texts on the subject. It is comprised of many essays by knowledgeable commentators and is full of practical information.
Robert Arnott and Frank Fabozzi, editors, *Active Asset Allocation,* Probus, 1992.
A wealth of thoughtful and informative contributions on asset allocation and optimization from luminaries such as Peter Bernstein, William Sharpe, Robert Arnott, and Frank Fabozzi.
Financial Planning Perspectives: Asset Allocation Viewpoint Series, College for Financial Planning Tape Series, 1992.
A series of 12 tapes and scripts discussing asset allocation and optimization from the perspective of the wealth manager. Contributors include William Droms, Gerald Perritt, Jeremy Black, and Harold Evensky.

To avoid redundancy with these excellent references, this chapter will address only a few special topics, namely, those that I believe of particular importance to the wealth manager.

- Optimizer input
- OP_{SOP}
- Rebalancing
- Downside risk

OPTIMIZER INPUT

The wealth manager should remember that we "cannot depend on strict mathematical expectations since the basis for making such calculations does not exist; and that it is our innate urge to activity which makes the wheels go round our rational selves choosing between the alternatives as best we can, but falling back for our motive on whim or sentiment or chance."[1]

I've prefaced this section with this sobering quote, as it reflects the feelings of many advisors. I simply remind the reader that it is our professional responsibility to concentrate on the "as best we can," while minimizing "whim or sentiment or chance."

To ignore all efforts to rationally determine allocations is defaulting 100 percent to chance. To rely solely on judgment and intuition is to rely on whim and sentiment. So, "doing the best we can," how do we develop input for our optimizer?

REQUIREMENTS

At this stage of the discussion we will consider the classic Markowitz mean-variance model and the use of an MVO (mean-variance optimizer). An MVO requires the wealth manager to make a decision regarding the investment time horizon and, for each asset class included in the portfolio, an estimate of the:

- Expected return.
- Expected standard deviation.
- Expected correlation with every other asset class.

TIME HORIZON

This is a critical assumption, as it will affect the wealth manager's estimation of expected returns and risk. For most wealth manager clients, the investment portfolio is expected to remain largely intact for many, many years (i.e., for the balance of their life). Therefore, from a purely academic perspective, a period of 10 or even 20 or 30 years might be appropriate. However, for our clients, volatility is a schizophrenic concept. When markets are going up, the client has an infinite time horizon. When markets drop, they have a one-day horizon. Black Monday, October 19, 1987, was a classic example. It was the rare investor who looked at his portfolio and said, "looks pretty good compared to 10 years ago!" Most investors lamented: "Oh! What a disaster I lost 10 percent since Friday!"

Realistically, I believe that five years is at the outer limit of a client's psychological commitment to the investment market. It is also long enough to encompass most economical cycles. Hence, our five-year mantra. As a result, with one notable exception, our optimizer inputs are based on five-year estimates. The notable exception is the time horizon for standard deviation. For standard deviation we use a one-year horizon. This decision is clearly the triumph of art over science. I would be the last person to defend, scientifically, the mixing of 5-year-return estimates with 1-year estimates for standard deviation. In a world of logic it is equivalent to eating ice cream with pickles. In a world of emotions, it is a cup of hot chocolate on a cold day. I know it works because it's been tested.

Soon after the market debacle in October 1987, I met with each of my clients for a session of comfort. I had (and still have) no idea why the market collapsed so precipitously, but I believed that, for my clients, it was a nonevent. We remained confident that our clients were well invested and, except for rebalancing, made no changes in our clients' portfolios. The purpose of the meetings was to let our clients know that we were aware of their concern but that their investments remained on course. We told them they could ignore the frenetic headlines and that they could continue with their lives and sleep soundly.

For the first few clients I met with, I reminded them of their long-time horizon and our five-year mantra and said, "Look how much more you have than five years ago." They looked at me and said, "Five years! Look where I was last Friday!" After that, I changed my presentation. I did discuss their long-time horizon and our five-year mantra, but I added: "Let's put this in a little more perspective than just a few days or months. Look where you were only one year ago." Not one client objected. Although not happy with having seen their portfolio drop, all of them recognized that it was not quite as terrible as the headlines trumpeted. One year is an emotionally credible time frame for risk; five years is not. Obviously, using a 1-year standard deviation and a 5-year time horizon exaggerates the expected risk exposure. I believe, however, that clients do not think in terms of 5-year standard deviations; the "error" we incur by using 1 year instead of 5 years is a valuable component in the management of our clients' expectations.

RETURNS

From dart boards to ouiji boards, there are innumerable ways of estimating expected returns. However, the most common are:

- Historical projections.
- Relative real rates of return.
- Prospective estimates.
- Risk premiums.

Historical Projections

This is probably the most frequently employed strategy. In its simplest form, the assumption made is that future returns will equal past returns. There are a number of problems with such an approach.

- It requires a decision regarding "what past returns," i.e., what period to include in the historical series. Some practitioners suggest that the longest available series should be used as it will span the maximum number of different kinds of cycles. Others argue that long series include periods that do not reflect major structural changes in the economy and hence, include misleading information.

- If the wealth manager selects a relatively short time horizon for his optimization (e.g., five years), projections far into the future may be totally inappropriate. Projections based on short-time horizons (e.g., five years) are also extremely sensitive to the choice of the starting date.

To demonstrate the problem, consider a wealth manager on January 1, 1995, using the following historical information from Ibbotson's database for Large Company Stocks (Table 9–1):

Based on this information, what return should he use as in input for large company stocks in an optimizer? Who knows? I certainly don't. Extrapolation of historical returns assumes that return series are stable. Unfortunately, they are not. Research to date suggests that simple historical projections do not offer

T A B L E   9–1

Large Company Stock Historical Returns

Period	Return
1926–1994	10.2%
1974–1994	12.2
1979–1994	14.8
1984–1994	13.6
1989–1994	12.2
5-Year Rolling Returns for 1926–1994	
High	23.9
Low	–12.5

T A B L E   9-2

Large Company Stock Historical Real Rates of Return

Period	Return
1926–1994	7.1%
1974–1994	6.4
1979–1994	9.7
1984–1994	10.0
1989–1994	8.4
Best and Worst **5-Year Rolling Returns for 1926–1994**	
High	21.4
Low	−7.1

an acceptable solution for return projections. I do not believe that a wealth manager should use them as a basis for optimization input.

Relative Real Rates of Return

For long periods, real rates of return have been more consistent than total returns; however, for short-term projections (i.e., five years), the problems associated with historical returns still apply. Table 9–2 is similar to Table 9–1, but reflects real rates of return:

For longer-term projections (e.g., capital needs analysis) where the time horizon may be 20 or 30 years, the use of historical real rates of return might be a viable option. It is, in fact, the basis for developing our capital needs analysis assumptions.

Prospective Estimates

This approach uses a CAPM to estimate future returns based on earnings projections. Using consensus forecasts and making assumptions regarding price to earnings multiples, a wealth manager might develop estimates of future returns.

However, in addition to the estimation errors associated with any attempt to predict unknowns, the wealth manager might want to review a study of 66,000 consensus earnings forecasts reported in the *Financial Analyst Journal.*[2] The authors concluded that forecasts differed significantly from actual earnings and that the average error seemed to be increasing.

Risk Premiums

Investment theory says that investors demand returns for taking risk. If an investor can earn 5 percent from a T-bill, he is unlikely to invest in a stock with an expected return of only 5 percent. As different assets expose investors to varying levels of risk, the extra returns associated with these investments vary with their risk. These "extra" returns are referred to as *risk premiums.*

As the original research in this area was by Roger Ibbotson and Rex Sinquefield,* and the primary proponent is Ibbotson Associates, I will discuss Ibbotson's "Building Block"[3] approach as the primary model. Figure 9–1 is a graphic description of the building blocks.

F I G U R E   9–1

Building Blocks

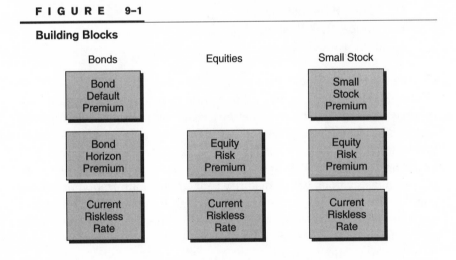

*Roger Ibbotson and Rex Sinquefield, "Stocks, Bonds, Bills, and Inflation: Simulations of the Future (1976–2000)," *The Journal of Business,* The University of Chicago, Volume #49, Number 3, July 1976, 313–338.

Historical Risk Premium—Theory

The building block begins with historical risk premiums. The assumption underlying this strategy is that not only do investors demand incremental return for additional risk; their expectations of what the incremental return should be are determined by past incremental returns. Therefore, past incremental returns (i.e., the derived risk premia from the Ibbotson/Sinquefield research) can serve as the basis for estimating future return expectations.

This historical benefit for taking extra risk (i.e., the historical risk premiums) is calculated by subtracting the risk-free return from the asset-class return. In a simplified form, the three major risk premiums are calculated as follows:

- Equity risk premium = Equity return—T-bill returns
- Horizon premium   = T-bond return—T-bill returns
- Default premium   = Corporate bonds returns—T-bond returns

Using the building block strategy, future expected returns are determined by adding the historical risk premium to the current risk-free rate.

Forecasted Expected Return$_{\text{Asset Class A}}$
= Historical Risk Premium$_{\text{Asset Class A}}$
+ Current Risk-Free Rate

Current Risk-Free Rate

The usual default for risk-free returns is the T-bill rate. Although an appropriate standard for determining historical risk premiums, it is not the factor used in building forecasted expected returns. Instead, the treasury yield curve serves as the basis for the riskless rate. The riskless rate used as the first element of the Ibbotson building block is the return on a zero coupon treasury bond with a maturity equal to the optimization time horizon. The basis for this choice is quite logical. If the time horizon is five years, it is reasonable to consider a five-year T-bond as "risk free," since zero coupon treasury bonds eliminate the credit and reinvestment risk over the defined time horizon.

Once the risk-free rate has been determined, it would seem that the forecasted expected return can be calculated by simply adding it to the historical risk premium. Not so fast. The earlier discussion was purposefully titled "Historical Risk Premium—*Theory*." Now we have to address:

Historical Risk Premiums—Art

Ibbotson's development of the historical risk premiums to be used in building block calculations is an excellent example of the intelligent application of investment art.

In theory, the historical return series would be the longest available with good data. For bonds, this period is over 60 years. However, Ibbotson notes that some asset classes (including bonds) have undergone significant structural changes during the last 60 years. For example, the U.S. fixed-income market was subject to an unprecedented structural change in 1979 when the federal reserve formally shifted its policy to managing the money supply instead of rates. Unfortunately, shortening the series reduces the statistical validity of the analysis. The solution (the art) to balancing the need for a statistically significant series, and yet accounting for the structural change in the bond market, was to begin the analysis in 1970 (a little before the structural shift) and use a monthly rather than an annual series.

Another example of an artful overlay on science is the strategy used to develop an appropriately long historical series for calculating a small company premium. As the benchmark used, the Russell 2000, is relatively new, Ibbotson developed a hypothetical historical return series by applying a size premium to existing large company market data going back to the 1920s.

An even more recent example supporting my contention that wealth management is 90 percent art is from Ibbotson's 1991 *Quarterly Market Report: Forecast Edition.* The following is a description of how the analysts handled the fact that, without modification, their theoretical model would have had strange results.

> Historically, the last observation of the annual real riskless rate has been used as the starting value in the above equation to generate this forecast. However, applying this method in the unusual interest rate environment of late 1991 achieved nonsensical results for the forecast period. Nominal rates plunged in 1991, reverting to a level near their historical mean of 3.75 percent. Because inflation rates were relatively stable, it is reasonable to assume that real rates plunged in similar fashion, to a level near their historical mean of 0.5 percent. Applying the year-end estimates instead of the actual real rates observed over the course of the year results in a more meaningful forecast.*

Obviously, the selection of specific time series, the selection of different compounding periods, and the construction of hypothetical series

---

*Ibbotson, *Stocks, Bonds, Bills, and Inflation 1991 Quarterly Market Report: Forecast Edition (1992–2011),* pp. 3–4, Ibbotson Associates, 1992.

requires many assumptions based on judgment and intuition. The goal, however, is to reduce the estimation error in the results of the final estimations. It is the responsibility of the wealth manager to understand what these assumptions are and to decide whether or not to accept the conclusions they lead to.

Arithmetic and Geometric

The last issue to consider in the building block strategy is the use of arithmetic and geometric returns. Ibbotson's building block strategy is based on the simple addition of *arithmetic* returns. This recommendation may be counter-intuitive to many readers (it was for me). The argument in favor of using arithmetic is covered in Chapter 6, Mathematics of Investing. To summarize that discussion, because arithmetic returns reflect the distribution of probable ending wealth values, Ibbotson considers it the more appropriate measure.

Ibbotson Building Block Returns—Summary

The argument in favor of the building block strategy is that by combining a historical risk premium and the current risk-free rate on the results will:

- Account for current market conditions.
- Implicitly include the economic expectations of investors.
- Implicitly include forecasts of economists and financial analysts, as their forecasts are reflected in the building block input.
- Correct for shifts in market fundamentals.
- Correct for market anomalies.

The result will not be a perfect point estimate of future returns but rather a consensus forecast that reflects "what the market expects."

STANDARD DEVIATIONS

Unfortunately, expected returns are not the only estimates necessary for optimization. The wealth manager must also estimate standard deviations and correlations. Frequently, the estimates of these measures are sloughed off based on the belief that, unlike returns, they are generally consistent over time and a wealth manager only needs to use a simple

T A B L E   9-3

Historical Standard Deviations and Correlations
20-Year Periods from 1926–1994
Ibbotson Data

	Correlations						Standard Deviations	
	Stocks		Bonds		Bills			
	Low	High	Low	High	Low	High	Low	High
Stocks	1.00	1.00	−0.18	0.49	−0.43	0.13	13.60	28.70
Bonds			1.00	1.00	−0.28	0.15	3.60	13.60
Bills					1.00	1.00	0.40	3.00

historical projection. This simple assumption is questionable, as Table 9–3 demonstrates.

Solutions to the estimation of standard deviation include:

- Ibbotson[4]—Beginning with historical data, eliminate inappropriate periods (e.g., U.S. fixed income) or develop hypothetical series (e.g., U.S. small-capitalization stock).

- Frost National Bank[5]—Use a combination of historical series in order to avoid an overemphasis on the very long-term series. For example, Frost uses an average of the 60-year, 20-year, and 5-year series.

Standard Deviation Estimates—Special Issues

Inflation

One important issue that seems to be overlooked by most strategies for projecting standard deviations was brought to my attention by Don Chambers of Mercer. Chambers notes that the standard deviation of a historical series has an underlying inflation factor. Thus, when projecting future standard deviations they should be adjusted to reflect the impact of this inflation factor. He provides the following example:

Historical series used last 20 years

Inflation = 6%

Expected inflation next 20 years = 5%

Adjust standard deviation down by 1%

Misleading Series

Another problem with historical series is that they may not accurately measure real volatility. The most obvious example is real estate. Most real estate return indexes are appraisal based. The nature of the appraisal process results in a smoothing of changes in valuations. As a result, the real estate indexes suggest a low volatility that contradicts observable market behavior. In other words, the standard deviation of real estate, based on traditional real estate indexes, seems absurdly low.

The following story tells of my introduction to the art of investment theory. A number of years ago, my partner Deena Katz and I attended, in New York, one of the first Ibbotson Seminars on Asset Allocation. It was a very expensive program, limited to about 30 attendees. We signed up because we wanted to know what the "big boys" were doing. I was very impressed. In addition to Professor Ibbotson and his associates, the other attendees represented major organizations from around the world—Bank of Tokyo, Chase Manhattan, and the World Bank, among others. I felt very much a little fish in a very big pond.

On the second day of the seminar, we had a discussion on input projections for an optimization program. When considering the asset category of real estate, a long discussion ensued regarding the historical standard deviation of real estate. The gist of the discussion was that, as noted earlier, real estate prices used in developing the historical index data were based on institutional sources. Institutional data are based on appraisals, and appraisals tend to have relatively low variance over time. Further, in bear markets, major holders of institutional real estate, such as insurance companies, tend to hold onto real estate; hence, the real variation in market value is unlikely to be reflected in the historical data. At the conclusion of this detailed explanation, Professor Ibbotson recommended that the standard deviation of real estate should "be at least doubled, and possibly tripled!"

I was stunned! Until then, I had been careful to refine my projections, frequently to two decimal places, believing that somehow I could generate extremely sound, if not totally accurate, allocation models. Now, here was one of the world's most respected experts telling not only me, but a room full of world-class investment managers, responsible for billions of dollars, that we should take one of the major input criteria for a very major asset class and arbitrarily double or even triple it! From that time on I became a believer in the importance of professional art over science in the implementation of wealth management.

CORRELATIONS

Correlations require less discussion, but not because they are historically more consistent or easier to project. As my brother is fond of saying, "au contraire." They are not historically more consistent and they are not easy to project. The discussion is short because there is no alternative to historical projections other than good judgment. The good news is that optimizers are less sensitive to estimation errors for correlations than for returns or standard deviations.

OPTIMIZER INPUT—CAVEAT

One temptation that many advisors succumb to is the use of mutual fund performance data as the input for their optimization—don't! Although the Wilson CAM's optimization software has a superior database of historical individual fund and manager performance, the creator of the program, and one of the most knowledgeable asset allocation experts in our industry, Phil Wilson, has this to say:

> Optimizing among managers of one asset class will generally result in the selection of the manager with the highest return since the managers will all have a very high positive correlation to each other. Reporting the expected returns of a portfolio comprising the actual managers rather than the surrogate indexes may result in high expectations and negative surprises. If the benchmark return for a surrogate index is 14 percent and the manager is expected to return 16 percent, the investor may be disappointed if the actual return is 14 percent when in fact that is the more likely return. Remember that the actual performance of the manager is relatively inconsequential when related to the performance of the asset class. **We do not recommend that funds be optimized using the optimization programs. Further, we do not recommend that portfolio returns comprising the managers be used in place of benchmark estimates** [my emphasis].

EB&K OPTIMIZATION INPUT

In our practice we use mathematical optimizers, so we face the problems of developing appropriate input. After considering all the alternatives, we have elected to use the following process:

Time Horizon

As discussed earlier, we use a time horizon of five years for our estimation of returns and correlations but one year for standard deviation.

Returns

We believe that the use of historical projections is fundamentally unsound and that, for the short time horizon of our optimization (i.e., five years), relative real rates of return are inappropriate. We find both prospective and risk premium strategies to be credible alternatives. Recognizing that our resources are limited, we elect to leverage off of the work of Ibbotson Associates and other respected vendors of economic data. We use Ibbotson building block projections, which we purchase from Ibbotson Associates, as our preliminary basis. We then accumulate estimates from other sources in whose work we have confidence,* and apply our own art by occasionally adjusting the experts' estimates. Our investment committee then reviews these estimates along with our general economic expectations and our approved manager list. We then go through the process of "sensitivity analysis" and make our final adjustments.

There are two policies we apply to our use of the Ibbotson base estimates.

▪ We use the geometric, not the arithmetic estimates. Although we recognize the academic argument for the use of the arithmetic mean, we also recognize that it will always reflect a higher return estimation than the geometric. Also, at least one recent study concludes that although arithmetic projections are better, based on the study of the last 66 years, they were only dominant 63 percent of the time.[6] Our conclusion is that tempering our client's expectations far outweighs the marginal additional accuracy of arithmetic returns.

---

*This would include Value Line, Wilson, and Callan.

- When we modify returns, we only adjust downward. Thus, the Ibbotson data not only serve as a base; they serve as a maximum.

Standard Deviation

We begin with historical projections based on the arithmetic average of the previous 10 years. We then look at 3- and 5-year standard deviations for the managers (i.e., mutual funds) we use in each asset class. In determining our final input, we place heavy emphasis on the managers' standard deviations. The policies we apply are:

- Use of one year as the horizon.
- The Ibbotson expectations serve as minimums. If we make changes, it is only to increase standard deviations.

Correlations

As the base we use historical 10-year asset-class correlations. We then look at 3- and 5-year correlations for our selected asset class. Our only policy is to assume, when in doubt, that the asset classes will be more, rather than less, correlated. Also, because we find that active international managers tend to be more correlated with domestic active managers than historical index correlations would suggest, we almost always increase the correlations between domestic and international equities. Typically the adjustment is about a 15 percent increase (e.g., from a correlation of 0.6 to 0.7).

General

"The big money is never in the buying or selling.
The big money is in the waiting"

—Jessie Levemore (1920s trader)

As chair of the firm's investment committee, it is my responsibility to develop the preliminary data input for the optimizer. Once I have completed my preliminary recommendations I provide them, along with the supporting data, to my two partners. Approximately one week later we meet formally as an investment committee and finalize our assumptions. We follow this process semiannually. We have a strong belief in strategic allocation and a great skepticism regarding market timing. The overriding policy of the investment committee is to minimize changes in allocations. During our semiannual review, there are usually modifications to the assumptions. These may result in adjustments to expectations regarding portfolio risk and returns. There is an occasional adjustment between styles (e.g., growth and value) or between maturity distributions (e.g., a shift from short to intermediate). However, significant shifts between broad asset classes (e.g., stocks to bonds) occur much less frequently. Theoretically, our goal would be to make such adjustments only every three to five years; in practice it is closer to two years.

Although we do not believe in market timing, we still have an open mind regarding tactical allocation (I will discuss this more, later); however, to date, we have not adopted tactical allocation as an overlay strategy. Our hesitancy is partly due to concerns regarding transaction costs and taxes (for nonsheltered accounts) but is primarily due to our not having found a model we consider credible.

Although I have described, in some detail, our process for determining input into an optimizer, this only addresses the surface of our optimization process. The real heart (and art) of our process is what I call OP_{SOP}*

OP_{SOP}

As noted in earlier discussions, optimizers are powerful mathematical "machines" that purport to produce optimal portfolios. In fact, they are the application of an optimization algorithm with a sophistication far beyond the quality of the input estimates.[7] To compound the problem, the mathematics of an optimizer algorithm exaggerates the importance of extreme measures. Thus, especially high or low returns or standard deviations and exaggerated differences in correlations have a disproportionate effect on the recommended allocation.

As a result, errors in estimations of input data are magnified. Asset classes with misestimated high returns and/or low standard deviations will be overweighted. Asset classes for which the error understates returns or overstates risk will be underweighted or eliminated. Without adjustment, the output of an optimizer is very often the nightmare that

---

*For those of you who enjoy dropping sophisticated terms of modern investment theory in order to impress your less enlightened peers, OP_{SOP} is pronounced "ahhP saahP."

"black box" critics fear—a nondiversified or inappropriately allocated portfolio with overestimated returns and underestimated risk. This "worst of all worlds" is a result of *error maximization.*[8]

As I have recommended that every wealth manager have Roger Gibson's *Asset Allocation* on his shelf, I'll use an example from that book to illustrate the problem.

▪ Table 9–4, optimization #1 shows the recommended allocation for a portfolio consisting of seven asset classes. The assets considered include T-bills, corporate bonds, common stock, small company stock, international stocks, international bonds, and equity REITs. You will note the allocation results in almost half the portfolio in equity REITs with zero allocation to common stocks, small company stocks, and international stocks. Since the results don't (or at least shouldn't) jive with professional common sense, let's consider how rigid a wealth manager should be in adhering to this model by investigating the impact an error in the input assumptions might have on the recommendations.

▪ Assume that, in spite of all the incredible hurdles that we have to surmount to develop accurate estimates, somewhere we discover the ultimate sage economist, and, with his help, we accurately predicted the standard deviations and correlations and we only overstated the expected return of the equity REIT class by 1 percent. With such incredible foresight, you really wouldn't expect there to be much of a change in the allocation if the portfolio were re-optimized with the modest change to the REIT rate of return. If you look at Optimization #2, you'll see that this almost token adjustment dramatically altered the allocation model. The corporate bond allocation changes from 15.2 to 21 percent (a 38 percent increase); international stocks (absent in the original allocation) kick in with an allocation of 8.2 percent; and most of the reduction came from the REIT asset class, with the REIT asset allocation falling by 36 percent.

▪ Now assume that the estimates for expected return and correlations are right on target, but we underestimated the standard deviation by 1 percent. Look at Optimization #3 and you'll see that the impact is, once again, significant. In this case, the equity REIT allocation drops by 20 percent to 33 percent.

▪ In the original optimization, the cross correlation between small company stocks and equity REITs, was assumed to be .85. If we run the analysis, assuming that our projections for expected return and standard deviations were correct, but that the correlation between the small stock and equity REITs is actually 1, we then get the substantial changes shown

T A B L E   9–4

Optimization Results and Sensitivity Analysis for a Client Who Specifies a
Risk Premium of 10.0%*

Asset Class	1 7 Asset Classes	2 Expected Return of Equity REITs Decreased by 1%	3 Standard Deviation of Equity REITS Increased by 1%	4 Equity REITs Perfectly Correlated with Small Stocks
(1) Treasury bills	23.8%	26.1%	27.4%	0.9%
(2) Corporate bonds	15.2	21.0	18.4	20.2
(3) Common stocks	0.0	1.8	0.0	0.0
(4) Small stocks	0.0	0.5	0.0	0.0
(5) International stocks	0.0	8.2	4.4	0.0
(6) International bonds	18.2	14.8	16.0	31.2
(7) Equity REITs	42.8	27.6	33.8	47.7
	100.0%	100.0%	100.0%	100.0%
Portfolio Characteristics				
Expected Return	11.0%	10.2%	10.6%	12.2%
Standard Deviation	8.7	8.0	8.3%	9.6
Probability of achieving a positive return	90.2	90.4	90.3	90.3

*The optimization results shown have been produced using Vestek Systems, Inc. software.

in Optimization #4. The T-bill allocation drops by 96 percent; the corporate bond increased by 33 percent; and the international bond allocation
increased by almost 72 percent.

By this time you may be wondering, "What's the point?" If there is
so much doubt in the input data and if small changes in the input can result in large differences in optimum portfolio composition, what is the
point of going through the optimization process in the first place? The answer is, the risk of error maximization is a danger only for the nonprofessional. For the wealth manager, it is risk to be managed. To reject

optimization as a strategy because it has risks makes as little sense as rejecting stocks because they have more risks than bonds. To suggest that clients with well-diversified portfolios are unlikely to benefit from optimization is simply not supported by current research. The issue is not avoiding optimization but managing the process.

The two techniques—sensitivity analysis and asset-class constraints—that we use in combination allow us to design portfolios that incorporate the best thinking of the Ibbotsons, Wilsons and Callans of the world and our application of professional art. The final portfolios are both rational and intuitive; however, they are *not* optimal!

Well, now, there's an oxymoron for you. Page after page of defense of optimization, only to conclude that wealth managers should tinker with the system, only to end up with a nonoptimal portfolio? Does that make any sense? The answer is yes and no. No, it does not make sense as stated; however, if I simply change nonoptimal to suboptimal, it makes very good sense. The job of the wealth manager is not to design the optimal portfolio—that's an academic concept. Instead of picturing an optimal portfolio as infinitely better than all others, visualize it more realistically, as only marginally better than many other possible combinations. Consider the analogy of a large college graduating class of 10,000 students. Although the valedictorian is unquestionably number one, the 10th or even 100th ranked student demonstrated superior accomplishment.

The point is, the universe of suboptimal portfolios still includes many superior portfolios. Leave perfection to a higher authority. Our responsibility is to design the most efficient, rational, *optimal-suboptimal* portfolio that meets our clients' goals and constraints. In other words, OP_{SOP}. Now let's consider how to design an OP_{SOP} portfolio.

SENSITIVITY ANALYSIS

Even suboptimal optimization requires rational input assumptions for the optimizer. It also requires that the wealth manager have a feeling for the influence his input has on the optimizer's allocations. The process of developing rational input estimates begins with the issues discussed in "Optimizer Input" but it ends with the modifications made as a result of sensitivity analysis.

Sensitivity analysis is the process of developing a feeling for the influence small changes in input have on the optimization output. The process begins once the wealth manager has selected the asset classes he will consider and has determined the preliminary expected returns, standard deviations, and correlations for each of the asset classes. He now has all the data necessary to run an optimization.

When I first went through this process, I ran innumerable optimizations. For each input item I changed my assumption by 5 percent, holding all other factors constant and reoptimized. For example, if my return assumption for U.S. equity was 10 percent, I would change it to 10.5 percent. I then ran changes at 10 percent, 15 percent, and 20 percent, as well as –5 percent and –10 percent and "worst case" estimates. I did this for returns, standard deviations, and correlations (although I only assumed higher volatility and higher correlations). After each run I reviewed the output to see what and how much the allocations had changed, and how the modified assumptions had affected the risk/return relationships. This is a long and grueling process but one every wealth manager should probably do at least once with a new optimizer. On a regular basis, I recommend a modified version of this process. Namely, rather than begin with an unconstrained model, start with the wealth manager's minimum constraints in place. This process will be equally meaningful but much quicker.

Sensitivity analysis provides guidance for the final adjustments to input data (subject to the policies discussed earlier) and allows the wealth manager to develop a sensitivity for the biases of the optimizer.

ASSET-CLASS CONSTRAINTS

If run unconstrained, an optimizer will generally exclude many asset classes and concentrate the portfolio allocations into a relatively few classes. This concentration is the result of an optimizer's tendency to exaggerate the extremes (i.e., error maximize). The most powerful tool that the wealth manager has to control "error maximization" and asset-class concentration is the ability to set asset-class constraints. The fundamental dynamic that makes this a reasonable solution is that small allocations to a new investment class have a significant impact. In order to provide some feeling for the process, consider the following simple 3- and 4-asset-class example and then the 9-asset-class "real world" vignette describing a hypothetical portfolio design for a new client:

Simple Example
Example #1 in Table 9–5 shows the results of a 3-asset-class optimization that has been run totally unconstrained. Example #2 reflects the addition of a 4th asset class (foreign bonds) and reoptimizing the unconstrained portfolio re-

T A B L E   9-5

Optimization Example

Example #1 Optimization—3 Asset Classes— Unconstrained			
Holdings	**Treasury Bills**	**Intermediate Government**	**S&P 500**
Current	100	0.0	0.0
Optimum	0.5	45.0	54.5

	Expected Return	**Standard Deviation**	**Sharpe**
Current	5.3	1.7	0.35
Optimum	9.4	10.2	0.46

Example #3 Optimization—4 Asset Classes— Constrained (Foreign <—17%)				
Holdings	**Treasury Bills**	**Intermediate Government**	**S&P 500**	**Foreign Bonds**
Current	100	0.0	0.0	0.0
Optimum	6.5	20.5	56.0	17.0

	Expected Return	**Standard Deviation**	**Sharpe**
Current	5.3	1.7	0.35
Optimum	9.7	10.4	0.48

Example #2 Optimization—4 Asset Classes— Unconstrained				
Holdings	**Treasury Bills**	**Intermediate Government**	**S&P 500**	**Foreign Bonds**
Current	100	0.0	0.0	0.0
Optimum	8.5	0.0	57.5	34.0

	Expected Return	**Standard Deviation**	**Sharpe**
Current	5.3	1.7	0.35
Optimum	10.1	11.0	0.49

Example #4 Optimization—4 Asset Classes— Constrained (Foreign <— 5%)				
Holdings	**Treasury Bills**	**Intermediate Government**	**S&P 500**	**Foreign Bonds**
Current	100	0.0	0.0	0.0
Optimum	2.5	37.5	55.0	5.0

	Expected Return	**Standard Deviation**	**Sharpe**
Current	5.3	1.7	0.35
Optimum	9.5	10.2	0.47

sults in increased expected return along with an increased standard deviation. These results were obtained by a total elimination of the allocation to intermediate government bonds and the allocation of over one-third of the portfolio to foreign bonds. Suppose we balk at placing all those foreign bonds in the portfolio and as shown in Example #3, we arbitrarily cut the foreign bond allocation by 50 percent. What does that do to the risk-adjusted return? Incredibly, it only reduces it by 10 basis points. Let's go a step further and, as shown in Example #4, constrain the foreign bond allocation to a maximum of 5 percent. In other words, we'll run an optimization, but we'll run it with the restriction that we'll allow no more than 5 percent allocation to the foreign bond category. Referring to Example #4, this new constraint only reduced the Sharpe ratio by 2 basis points. The point is, the wealth manager needs to investigate the consequences

F I G U R E   9-2

Efficient Frontier

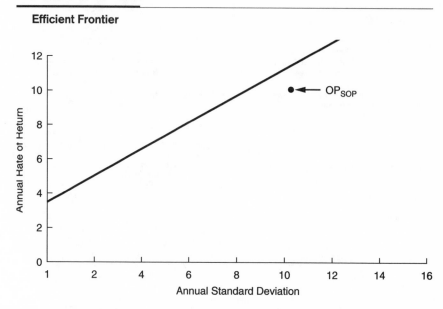

of forcing a more diversified portfolio allocation on a preliminary, unconstrained portfolio.

Figure 9–2 is a graphic representation of the OP_{SOP} portfolio (Example #4), plotted against the unconstrained efficient frontier. The asterisk representing the current portfolio isn't smack dab on the efficient frontier but, as we said when I was in the Army, "It's good enough for government work!" Actually, that's not fair—it's very efficient *and* it's diversified. Not a bad example of an optimal-suboptimal portfolio.

A Vignette

Based on our discussions, my client and I have decided that the universe of investments to be considered will include money market funds, short/ intermediate government bonds, intermediate municipal bonds, intermediate to long-term foreign bonds, value funds, growth funds, S&P 500 index, small company funds, and international equity funds. We have also mutually determined a need for a target total return of approximately 9.5 percent and a moderate risk tolerance (i.e., no more than 60% in stock).

Running the optimizer unconstrained, I find that there is an efficient portfolio "C" that seems to meet my client's needs. According to the optomizer (Table 9–6) this efficient portfolio requires an investment of 18 percent in money market funds, 28 percent in foreign bonds, 29.5 percent

T A B L E   9-6

Optimization—9 Asset Classes

Portfolio	Money Market	Intermediate Government	Municipal Bonds	Foreign Bonds	Mut Fnd Growth	Mut Fnd Value	Mut Fnd S&P 500	Mut Fnd Small Cap	Mut Fnd Int'l
A	79.5	0.0	0.0	9.5	0.0	0.0	4.0	7.0	0.0
B	49.0	0.0	0.0	18.0	0.0	0.0	16.0	13.0	4.0
C	18.0	0.0	0.0	28.0	0.0	0.0	29.5	19.5	5.0
D	0.0	0.0	0.0	27.5	0.0	0.0	38.0	23.0	11.5
E	0.0	0.0	0.0	14.5	0.0	0.0	42.5	21.0	22.0
Scenario									
#1	23.0	11.0	0.0	5.0	0.0	0.0	36.5	19.5	5.0
#2	7.5	28.5	0.0	5.0	0.0	0.0	34.5	19.5	5.0
#3	7.5	17.5	10.0	5.0	0.0	0.0	34.5	19.5	5.0
Recommended	7.5	17.5	10.0	5.0	10.0	20.0	10.0	10.0	10.0

Portfolio	Expected Return	Standard Deviation
A	6.8	2.5
B	8.3	6.0
C	9.8	10.0
D	11.0	13.0
E	11.5	14.6
Recommended	9.7	10.5

in S&P 500 stock, 19.5 percent in small company stock, and 5 percent in international stock funds. There is no allocation to domestic bonds or growth or value funds. The portfolio has an estimated expected return of 9.8 percent with a standard deviation of 10 and a fixed-income/equity ratio of 46 percent/54 percent.

I don't know about you, but in spite of the theoretical perfection of the portfolio, I would neither recommend such a concentrated portfolio nor such a large allocation to foreign bonds. Also, since I believe in staggered maturity, fixed-income portfolios, the barbell maturity distribution (i.e., money market and foreign bonds), is unacceptable. As I cannot accept the optimizer's unconstrained recommendation, I will place my own constraints.

My first step is to redesign the fixed-income allocations. First, I constrain the foreign bond allocation to 5 percent and reoptimize. The result of my new run (Scenario #1) is to shift the foreign bond allocation to money market government bonds and S&P 500 equities. That results in an overall balance of 39 percent Fixed/62 percent Equity. Looking at the new fixed-income allocation, I realize that the heavy allocation to money market (a low-return asset class) is forcing a greater allocation in equities in order to reach my client's target return. So, I set a constraint of 7.5 percent on money market and rerun the optimizer (Scenario #2). Sure enough, the result is to reduce the allocation to S&P 500 equities and increase the intermediate government bond allocation. The overall balance is now 41 percent/59 percent. As I rerun the optimizer, I continually review the change in both expected return and standard deviations in order to assure myself that I am neither significantly reducing expected returns nor significantly increasing volatility. This is the process of sensitivity analysis discussed earlier

Although the input data driving the optomizer is mine, I still do not find it credible that my 28 percent tax bracket client should have all taxable bonds. So, I set a minimum allocation of 10 percent for municipals and rerun the optimizer (Scenario #3). This does not change my fixed-income/equity allocation; it simply moves 10 percent from governments to municipals. At this stage, I decide I am comfortable (for now) with my fixed-income allocations, so I turn to the equities.

I am prepared to accept the 41/59 fixed-income/equity balance but that's my equity limit, so I set a maximum constraint of 59 on equities in order to prevent future optimizations from recommending increase in equity allocations. I would now like to diversify the equity allocation but my client is uncomfortable with small-cap and international stock. So after some discussion, we have agreed to consider them as part of the portfolio but to limit them to 10 percent each. I also decide that I want to limit my S&P 500 core holding to 10 percent. I set these caps and rerun the optimization (recommended).

The result is that all of my constrained asset classes are filled to the limit, forcing the balance of the funds to be allocated equally between growth and value. Based on my belief in the Fama/French research, I decide to force a split of two-thirds value and one-third growth. My tentative proposed portfolio is now complete.

By adding upper and lower constraints, I continually rerun the optimization program until I arrive at a portfolio that meets both my professional common sense and my client's emotional tolerance. The proposed final portfolio shown in Table 9–6 is such a solution. Let's look at it in some detail. I've allocated 7.5 percent to money market (to meet my client's liquidity requirements), 17.5 percent in short/intermediate government bonds (to provide a second tier of liquidity), 10 percent in intermediate municipal bonds (to add longer maturities and provide the tax-free return my client is looking for) and 5 percent in foreign bonds (remember, a small allocation provides significant diversification). I've also diversified between growth and value equity by placing 10 percent in growth and 20 percent in value. I've placed 10 percent in the S&P 500 as a core holding, and, finally, by my agreeing to limit the allocations, my client has agreed to an investment of 10 percent each in small-cap and international mutual funds.

Now is the time to test the validity of OP_{SOP}. After applying all these constraints, how efficient is the proposed portfolio? The answer is, very efficient. After making all of the changes, the proposed portfolio provides a return within 10 basis points of the optimum portfolio C, with a standard deviation that is almost the same. The proposed portfolio is certainly an optimal suboptimal portfolio—and it is one both the client and I can live with.

My Recommendations

The vignette above described the thought process involved in developing an OP_{SOP} portfolio for an individual client. In practice, I have run innumerable sensitivity analysis scenarios and have developed a series of our asset-class constraints. The following is a description of the reasoning my partners and I follow and the specifics of these constraints.

Fixed Income

Cash Equivalent/Money Market   In order to provide for some flexibility in rebalancing, a reserve for a client's unanticipated emergency cash needs and for billing, as well as a short-term anchor for our duration ladder, we typically set a 2 to 3 percent allocation to cash equivalents.

Domestic Fixed Income   Our approach to constraining the domestic fixed-income allocation is much less structured than for cash equivalents and foreign bonds. The first step is to determine the total fixed-income allocation. Once this is set, the total commitment to domestic fixed income is simply the total fixed-income allocation less the allocations to cash/money market and foreign bonds. For nonsheltered accounts, the next step is to determine the split between municipal and taxable bonds.* This is usually set by the results of the optimizer. The final allocation is to maturity ranges.

As indicated in Chapter 4, Data Gathering, our asset-class taxonomy currently provides for three maturity ranges: 1 to 3 years, 3 to 5 years, and 5 to 10 years. The process of setting allocations between these ranges is determined more by projected yield curves than by the optimizer. As we have a strong bias in favor of laddered maturities, we will rarely accept a bullet or barbell allocation.

Our default allocation is one-fourth the domestic fixed-income allocation to the 1-to-3-year and 5-to-10-year ranges, and one-half to 3 to 5 years. Each of these may be over- or underweighted by one-half of the default allocation depending on our evaluation of the yield curves. We leave it to the money managers to make duration bets within these ranges.

International Bonds   During an investment committee meeting a number of years ago, we concluded that the research was persuasive that foreign bonds represented a unique asset class within fixed income. Therefore, we wanted to have an exposure to the international bond market. We also knew that although we would restrict our allocations to managers who purchased high-quality, intermediate-term bonds, the investment class would be foreign to most of our clients. Since even a small allocation provides significant diversification benefits, we settled on a 5 percent allocation. We felt that 5 percent was small enough for even our conservative clients to accept.

We also recognized that if we only set a 5 percent cap as foreign bonds, we could prevent the optimizer from allocating any more than 5 percent but it might result in no allocation to foreign bonds. Having little confidence in our ability to develop input estimates accurate enough to distinguish the contribution of foreign bonds at the 5 percent level, we have elected to set a 5 percent floor. In other words, we do not ask the optimizer to make decisions about foreign bonds. We simply allocate 5 percent.

---

*Remember, good tax management is to maximize after-tax returns, not minimize taxes. Depending on the relationship between taxable and municipal yield curves, a combination of taxable and municipal bonds may result in the optimum after-tax returns.

Equities

REITs   The process we used to arrive at our REIT allocation was quite similar to foreign bonds. For many years we eschewed REITs as an asset class. Although we wanted a commitment to real estate, REITs did not seem to provide a real estate exposure. Our analysis of REITs, regressing their returns over various periods against real estate and equity market benchmark returns, indicated that REITs represented a small-cap equity exposure. They did not correlate well with the real estate index. Subsequent to that early decision, Ibbotson drew our attention to the problems with real estate indexes, and studies out of Wharton, commissioned by DFA, indicated that REITs could in fact serve as an exposure to the real estate market.* Anxious to include real estate in our portfolios and impressed by the research, we elected to include REITs. However, deciding that if change is good, slow change might be better, we elected to cap our initial allocation to 5 percent. As with foreign bonds, we always want this small allocation so we also set the floor at 5 percent, i.e., we allocate 5 percent to REITs in all our portfolios.**

International and Emerging Markets Equities

Philosophically, our investment committee believes in a significant commitment to foreign equities. Intellectually, an allocation of one-half to two-thirds of the equity portfolio to foreign stocks seems reasonable. However, we opt for realistic over reasonable.

For most of our clients, foreign equities, like foreign bonds, are *foreign*. No matter how big the company or how strong its financial statement, if they can't pronounce its name and they don't see its products on TV or in stores, its stock does not feel as safe as a GE or Kodak. Based on interviews and discussions with many clients over the years, we concluded that a 20 percent allocation might be acceptable but 15 percent was a much more comfortable constraint for a foreign developed country equity commitment.

---

*Joseph Gyourko and Donald Keim, "Risk and Return in Real Estate: Evidence from a Real Stock Index," *Financial Analysts Journal,* September–October 1993.

**Actually, that's not quite true. If our client has significant independent real estate investments, we do not include REITs; instead, we reallocate the REIT commitment, 3 percent to small-cap value and 2 percent to small-cap growth.

Based on an extensive series of optimization tests, varying allocations, expected returns, standard deviations, and correlations, we concluded that a 15 percent foreign developed country equity allocation
would, in most cases, result in our achieving 80 percent of the risk-
adjusted benefit of an unconstrained allocation. Increasing the cap from
15 to 20 percent added very little marginal value. Combining the results
of our client interviews and our optimizer tests with a goal of balancing
our clients' perception of risk exposure and the value contributed by additional diversification, we concluded that a cap of 20 percent on total
international equity was appropriate. Although it has never been a controlling factor, we set a minimum of 10 percent allocation to developed
countries and 3 percent to emerging markets to assure some exposure.

The next decision was the division of developed nations and emerging market allocations. Recognizing that emerging market investments
are likely to be quite volatile, we were very sensitive to their allocation.
On the other hand, we believe that it is an important asset class and belongs in every client's portfolio. Our decision was to set a minimum allocation of 3 percent to emerging markets and 10 percent to developed
countries is matched with a maximum of 15 percent to developed and 7
percent to emerging markets. This limits foreign equity allocations to the
narrow range shown in Table 9–7.

Domestic Equities The process of setting asset-class constraints on domestic equities is guided by a number of factors. Reflecting
our belief in passive as well as active forms of equity management, all our
portfolios have a core domestic equity allocation (typically to an index
fund such as the Schwab 1000 or the Value Line S&P 500). In order to
guarantee at least some allocation to this core holding we set a minimum

T A B L E   9–7

Foreign Equity Allocation Ranges

Developed	Emerging Market
10%	3%
15	5
13	7

constraint of 5 percent. We also have a class we call tactical for which we set a minimum 3 percent allocation.*

For small-cap domestic equities, we set two constraints. The first is a minimum allocation of 10 percent. This guarantees at least some allocation to the class. The second is a cap equal to one half of the large capitalization allocation. Although we accept the results of the Fama/French research regarding the return premium attributable to the small company factor, we constrain the allocation to reflect our evaluation of our clients' risk tolerance.

Our final constraints relate to the allocation between growth and value. We have closely followed the work of Fama and French and the related research of Dimensional Fund Advisors, and we are largely persuaded that our clients can benefit from the high book/market factor.** However, we also recognize that the research is not conclusive and, even if it were, styles still move in and out of favor. By not totally committing our domestic style allocation to value, we may (or may not) be sacrificing an incremental premium but we will also reduce the portfolios' interim volatility. Our current solution is to use a constraint allocating 66 percent to value and 34 percent to growth. The following table summarizes our optimization constraints:

EB&K Asset-Class Constraint Summary

	Constraint	
	Minimum	**Maximum**
Fixed Income	None	None
Cash/MMA	3%	3%
Domestic		
Short Term	1/4 domestic	1/4 domestic
Short/Intermediate	1/2 domestic	1/2 domestic
Intermediate	1/4 domestic	1/4 domestic
Foreign	5%	5%

(continued)

---

*Don Phillips often asks how a wealth manager can incorporate an eclectic manager such as Jean Marie Eveillard in an optimized model. Easy, use professional art. Our tactical class was specifically created to provide an excuse to include Sogen (i.e., Jean Marie Eveillard) in our portfolios.

**Chapter 11, Manager Selection, includes a discussion of the Fama/French research.

EB&K Asset-Class Constraint Summary *(concluded)*		
	Constraint	
	Minimum	**Maximum**
Equity	None	None
Large Cap		
Core	5%	15%
Tactical	3%	7%
Style		
Value	2/3 Style	2/3 Style
Growth	1/3 Style	1/3 Style
Small Cap	10% Large Cap	1/2 Large Cap
Value	2/3 Small Cap	2/3 Small Cap
Growth	1/3 Small Cap	1/3 Small Cap
International		
Developed	10%	15%
Emerging Market	3%	7%
REITs	5%	5%

One final note. Our standards serve as a guide, not a bible. These constraints are moving targets. Over the years we have added asset classes (e.g., foreign bonds and REITs) and modified constraints (e.g., growth and value), and expect to continue doing so. For example, currently under consideration by the investment committee is the addition of small-cap international, an increase in the constraint on international and emerging markets equities, and a revision of the relationship between growth and value styles.

REBALANCING

In the discussion of portfolio design, the phrase *asset allocation* has been used in a number of ways:

- Asset allocation—establishing the "normal" asset class weights.
- Strategic asset allocation—the long-term structure of a portfolio.
- Policy asset allocation—the long-term "normal" asset mix.

Obviously, in all of these uses, the emphasis is on the elements of "normality" and long term. As asset classes grow at different rates, portfolios, without adjustments, do not remain "normal." Allocations may change radically over time. The wealth manager must decide on a policy regarding the management of market-driven changes in the asset-class weightings. He has two general choices:

BUY AND HOLD

This is a euphemism for "do nothing, allow the market to determine the policy." Advantages of this passive strategy are low management and low transaction costs and tax efficiency. The disadvantage is the risk of results significantly different from those projected.

For example, consider a portfolio originally allocated 40 percent debt/60 percent equity, that had drifted to 20 percent debt/80 percent equity after a sustained market run up, only to be followed by a sharp 20 percent correction (e.g., 4th quarter 1987). The cost of the allocation drift would be 4 percent.* Even with a relatively modest 10 percent drift followed by a 10 percent market correction, the cost would be 1 percent. The flip side is also a risk. An allocation short of its target would suffer an opportunity cost if that asset class were to make a major positive move.

The final risk associated with 'buy and hold' is psychological. During volatile markets and after runs (either up or down), passive investors are likely to succumb to fear or greed, ignore their buy and hold strategy, and become ill-timed market timers, i.e., buying high and selling low. I believe that a much better alternative is to develop a systematic rebalancing strategy.

SYSTEMATIC REBALANCING

Rebalancing is the action of readjusting a portfolio's asset-class allocations from its current weightings, determined by market forces, back to the policy's "normal" weights. The decision rules for systematic rebalancing fall into one of two categories—calendar or contingent.

Calendar rebalancing calls for rebalancing the portfolio back to its policy asset class weights on a predetermined calendar period. Typically,

---

*A portfolio balanced according to the policy would have a loss of 12 percent (i.e., $0.6 \times 20\%$). A 20/80 portfolio would have a loss of 16 percent (i.e., $0.8 \times 20\%$). A 4 percent greater loss.

the trigger is monthly, quarterly, or annually, although it could be measured in years (e.g., every five years). Contingent rebalancing is dependent upon a predefined trigger that is independent of time. For example, rebalancing may be triggered by a 10 percent change in the weighting of any asset class.

RESEARCH

To date, the research on rebalancing has been limited and inconclusive. One of the earliest articles to address the issue was "Let It Ride," by Kaufman and Goldstone, in the December 1988 issue of *Financial Planning*. The authors found that the overall performance of the buy-and-hold portfolio was superior to contingent rebalancing. They concluded that the "fatal flaw in the rebalancing strategy [was]: A portfolio shouldn't be constantly selling out of appreciating assets and increasing its stake in depreciating assets."

Subsequent research has not supported the superiority of "buy-and-hold." In the April 1992 *Journal of Financial Planning*, Stine and Lewis published "Guidelines for Rebalancing Passive Investment Portfolios.[9] Based on a comprehensive study of rebalancing strategies, for investment horizons of 3, 5, 10, 15, and 20 years, they concluded that a contingent strategy, providing for rebalancing when stock weights varied by 7½ to 10 percent from their policy allocation, was the optimum choice. During that same month, SEI reported in a position paper that their research also concluded that a contingency strategy was optimum. Later SEI research recommended a 6 percent target threshold at the asset class level and a 3 percent target threshold at the style level.[10]

In May 1992, Jeremy Black revisited much of the earlier research in his "Asset Rebalancing" tape for NEFE's Series, "Financial Planning Perspectives: Asset Allocation Viewpoint."[11] Black made two significant observations regarding the earlier studies.

He noted that the conclusions of the studies were so dependent upon the asset classes selected and the weights allocated to each, that these conclusions may not be universally true. For example, the Kaufman and Goldstone portfolios included a significant allocation to gold during a historical period unique for gold prices. Stine and Lewis's study only included three asset classes and was heavily influenced by estimates of transaction costs.

T A B L E   9–8

**Results of Alternative Rebalancing Strategies
for 15-Year Investment Horizon[12]**

Rebalancing Strategy	Holding Period Return	Average Number of Times Portfolio Rebalanced	Stock Weights Average	Minimum	Maximum	Average Commission Costs
Buy & Hold	7.54%	0.00	52.2%	27.6%	85.3%	$ 0
Annual	6.79	15.00	40.9	29.1	49.8	2,201
Semiannual	6.69	30.00	40.5	31.4	47.7	4,088
Quarterly	6.47	60.00	40.4	32.7	44.8	7,560
2.50%	6.61	34.99	40.4	32.7	45.3	4,901
5.00%	6.70	21.13	40.5	31.4	46.0	3,183
7.50%	6.83	14.32	40.8	31.2	46.0	2,264
10.0%	6.86	9.62	41.1	29.6	47.3	1,581
12.5%	6.83	6.34	41.4	28.7	47.9	1,063
15.0%	6.89	5.00	41.5	28.4	48.9	879

Most important, Black refocuses attention on the wealth manager's financial planning orientation. Money managers measure success by relative performance; wealth managers' success is measured by their ability to assist clients in meeting their goals. A significant aspect of this success is related to managing the client's expectations. To illustrate this issue, Black refers to the results of Stine and Lewis's 15-year horizon analysis, reproduced in Table 9–8.

As Table 9–8 shows, the return for the buy-and-hold strategy is clearly superior to all other strategies. However, using data from 1970 through April 1992, Black estimates the standard deviation of a portfolio rebalanced to the policy is 7.7 percent compared to 9.7 percent for a buy-and-hold portfolio with a 52 percent commitment to stock. That is a 25 percent increase in volatility. Even more sobering is the extreme where a buy-and-hold resulted in an 85 percent commitment to stock. The estimated standard deviation of that portfolio is 14.6 (a 90 percent increase in volatility) and the downside risk in any one year is –17 percent. Black's conclusion should serve as a guide to any wealth manager deciding on a rebalancing strategy:

> If you sold your client on an asset balance with specific risk-reward characteristics and gave the impression that this would not change that much over the years, then not rebalancing could cause some serious misunderstanding and a loss of clients.

Subsequent studies generally support some form of contingent rebalancing. Art Lutschaunig of Fidelity reported at an AIMR Conference[13] that after reviewing the empirical studies and based on internal studies, Fidelity uses a contingent trigger of 10 to 12 percent for major asset classes. One interesting addition to the discussion on rebalancing was the observation by Douglas McCalla[14] that percent rebalancing does not consider that different classes have different volatilities. McCalla suggests using a factor of 1.2 standard deviations as a rebalancing criteria.

Still, calendar rebalancing has its proponents. At the same AIMR Conference that Fidelity described their contingent strategy, Frost National indicated that they use a quarterly calendar rebalancing. In her seminar, "Portfolio Optimization and Rebalancing" at the NEFE 1995 National Conference, Eleanor Blayney recommended that although in theory a 7½ to 10 percent contingent rebalance is appropriate, in practice the best strategy is calendar rebalancing on a semiannual or annual cycle.

MY OPINION ON REBALANCING

Once again, this is a decision that emphasizes art over science. Balancing the issues of performance, client risk tolerance,* tax consequences, transaction costs, and management costs, I have concluded that the most appropriate trigger for rebalancing between the broad asset classes of fixed income and equities is a ±7 percent absolute drift. The more difficult decision is the setting of a contingent rebalance strategy for subasset classes and styles.**

Our artful process used to arrive at the solution to this second level of contingent triggers was to heed Jeremy Black's advice and the suggestion of Douglas McCalla and concentrate on the risk factor. Therefore, the rebalance criterion was influenced by the asset-class standard deviation.

---

*The less frequent the rebalancing, the further the portfolio is likely to drift from the policy's expected volatility.

**See the discussion on the taxonomy of asset classes in Chapter 4, Data Gathering.

Also considered was the size of the average commitment to the class and the correlation between the asset classes and styles and SEI's recommendations regarding subasset class rebalancing. Our firm's contingent rebalancing strategy follows:

EB&K Rebalancing Policy
Allocation Drift

	Style	Subclass	Major Class
Fixed Income			±7
Equity			±7
U.S Large Cap		±5	
U.S. Large-Cap Growth	±3		
U.S. Large-Cap Value	±3		
U.S. Small Cap		±5	
U.S. Small-Cap Growth	±3		
U.S. Small-Cap Value	±3		
International		±5	
Emerging Market		±3	
Real Estate		±3	

For practical purposes, we also overlay a quasi calendar rebalance trigger. As all our clients' portfolios are unique, we do not globally rebalance our accounts. Each client's portfolio is scheduled for a formal review on a quarterly basis. The specific quarterly cycle is determined by our attempt to keep an equal balance of reviews every month. The goal is to have one-third of our reviews on a January, April, July, and October cycle; one-third on a February, May, August, and November cycle, and so on. Our rebalance strategy is to review portfolios quarterly and, during that review, apply the contingent rebalancing policy. With only three months between reviews, it is unlikely that a portfolio will ever significantly exceed our rebalance policy. In the event of an exceptional short-term move (e.g., October 1987), we immediately reevaluate all portfolios.

DOWNSIDE RISK

The work of Harry Markowitz and the general principles of MPT are largely accepted by today's investment community. Markowitz's optimization algorithm serves as the basis for most mathematical optimizers;

acceptance, however, is not universal. The seeds of discontent can be found in Markowitz's own work.

As discussed in the chapters on Theory and Math, Markowitz settled on mean-variance as a risk measure over other alternatives (including semivariance) as a compromise. He acknowledged that a model based on semivariance might be theoretically better but concluded that, at the time, it was an unrealistic computable alternative. Since then over 40 years have passed and some commentators argue that making the compromise is no longer valid. They contend that there are two major reasons for revisiting mean-variance.

- A central tenet of MPT is that investors' decisions are guided by a desire to optimize their risk/return trade-off. The Markowitz optimization model equates risk with standard deviation. Modern research in investment theory and cognitive psychology has demonstrated that standard deviation, even for normal distributions, is not necessarily an acceptable measure of risk.

- Mean-variance is an adequate description only for normal distributions. As innumerable studies have demonstrated, return distributions of financial assets are not normally distributed. Thus, the E-V Maxim does not reflect the actions of real markets.

RISK MEASURES

The following illustrations may be useful in demonstrating to your clients the fallacy of simply equating volatility to risk.

Figure 9–3 compares the performance of Manager A and Manager B. Manager A has, during the last 7 years, achieved a mean return of 12.8 percent with a standard deviation of 4.8 percent. Manager B has achieved a 6.1 percent return with a standard deviation of 2.0. Although as measured by standard deviation Manager A takes more risks, she is obviously the best chioce.

Figure 9–4 is a second example that also demonstrates the inadequacy of standard deviation as a measure of risk. In this case, I have assumed that both asset classes have normal distributions.

Asset A, with a standard deviation equal to 2 is, by that standard, a much less risky investment than B, with a standard deviation of 10. If, however, the investor requires a return of 8 percent in order to meet his goals, we had better revisit the definition. Under this scenario, Investment A is always likely to fail to meet the investor's needs. For the investor, it

F I G U R E   9–3

Standard Deviation ≠ Risk Example #1

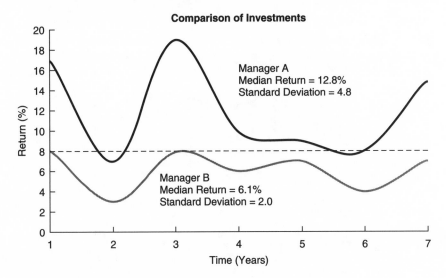

Comparison of Investments

Manager A
Median Return = 12.8%
Standard Deviation = 4.8

Manager B
Median Return = 6.1%
Standard Deviation = 2.0

F I G U R E   9–4

Standard Deviation ≠ Risk Example #2

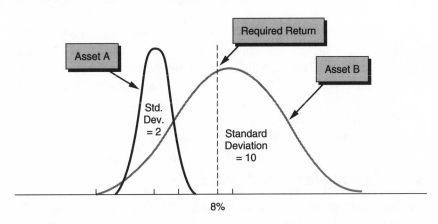

is clearly the riskier of the two choices. Obviously, in terms of defining risk, critics of mean-variance have a valid objection.

F I G U R E   9-5

Returns for Three Managers (%)

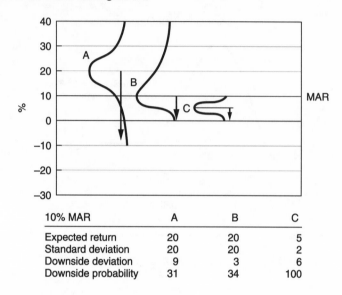

10% MAR	A	B	C
Expected return	20	20	5
Standard deviation	20	20	2
Downside deviation	9	3	6
Downside probability	31	34	100

ASYMMETRIC RETURNS

Consider Figure 9–5, a return distribution graph for managers A, B, and C.[15]

Manager A's distribution is skewed to the left and Manager B's to the right. Only Manager C's returns are normally distributed. If the measure of risk is standard deviation, we would conclude that C is significantly less risky than B. This seems like a strange conclusion given that the returns of C will almost always be less than the average returns for B, and B is never expected to have returns less than C. Once again, the critics of mean-variance seem to have a good point.

A NEW RISK/RETURN PARADIGM

The proposed solution to the weakness of MVP optimization is to expand the concept of risk. Instead of equating risk with uncertainty (i.e., the variability of returns around the mean) and using standard deviation as its measure, it is necessary to recognize that risk is not a universal concept. Although there had been a number of earlier articles addressing this issue, the seminal event in the consideration of downside risk was the publishing of an article titled "Post-Modern Portfolio Theory Comes of Age," by Brian Rom and Kathleen Ferguson in the Winter 1993 issue of *Journal of Investing,* followed by a series of related articles in the Fall 1994 issue,* and a conference sponsored by the Center for Investment Research in February 1995.

Postmodern Portfolio Theory

Rom and Ferguson are principals of Sponsor-Software (SS), the developers of the first software capable of optimizing using a form of downside risk optimization. The phrase *postmodern portfolio theory (PMPT)* was coined by Rom and Ferguson to describe the new "expanded risk/return paradigm"[16] that could be implemented through Sponsor-Software technology. The SS optimizer is based on an algorithm developed by Frank Sortino, the director of the Pension Research Institute and one of the first investment theorists to address practical alternatives to the MV assumption of MPT.

PMPT asserts that investment risk should "be tied to each investor's specific goals and that any outcomes above this goal do not represent economic or financial risk . . . In PMPT only volatility below the investor's target return means risk."[17] The target return is referred to as the minimum acceptable return (MAR).

Unlike MPT, which is based on the assumption of symmetrical distributions, PMPT can be used to optimize asymmetrical distributions. Downside risk in PMPT is measured by target semideviation, the square root of target-semivariance.** It also provides for two measures of downside risk:

- Downside probability (also referred to as shortfall risk) is a measure of the probability of not meeting the MAR.

- Average downside magnitude measures, in those cases when the MAR is not achieved, the magnitude of the failure.

As an example, Rom and Ferguson compared two "equivalent risk"*** portfolios, one using traditional MPT optimization (mean-variance) and one using PMPT optimization (downside risk). The results of the comparison are shown in Table 9–9:

---

*Wealth managers should include a copy of the Fall 1994 issue in their reference library.
**Now you know why Chapter 6, Math, discussed such an esoteric concept.
***The two portfolios are designed to have risks equivalent to a globally diversified independent reference portfolio.

T A B L E   9-9

Asset Class Allocation of Equivalent Risk Portfolios
Five-Year Holding Period, 10 percent MAR[18]

Portfolio Mix	Based on Mean Variance	Based on Downside Risk
Large-Cap Stock	50%	65%
Small-Cap Stock	0	0
Foreign Stock	29	18
Bonds	21	17
Cash	0	0
Portfolio Characteristics		
Expected Returns	14.4%	14.6%
Risks		
Downside	1.8	1.8
Standard Deviation	11.9	13.0
Efficiency Ratios		
Sortino	2.5	2.6
Sharpe	1.2	1.1

Note: The two portfolios are designed to have risks equivalent to a globally diversified, independent reference portfolio.

The authors note that the differences in allocations reflect the ability of PMPT to account for the differences in skewness for the various asset classes. While MPT treats all classes equally, PMPT takes advantage of the positive skewness of large-cap stocks (i.e., more surprises on the upside than the downside) and overweights that class, while penalizing negatively skewed foreign stocks and bonds by underweighting those classes. Measured by the downside risk efficiency ratio,* PMPT designs the best allocation.

---

*The downside risk efficiency ratio used is the Sortino Ratio and is equal to (Expected Return—MAR)/Downside Deviation.

T A B L E   9-10

Risk/Return Statistics 1982-1992

Asset	Return	Standard Deviation	Downside Deviation (DD)	Sharpe Ratio	Sortino Ratio
20th-Century Fund	17.6%	21.60	10.00	0.58	0.95
Money Market	7.1	0.50	1.10	4.12	-0.88
NYSE Index	11.5	15.30	8.40	0.42	0.41
MSCI World Index	15.0	15.40	7.70	0.65	0.91
RCM Growth Eq Fund	16.7	15.60	6.30	0.75	1.39

Ranking		
	Sharpe Ratio	Sortino Ratio
1	Money Market	RCM
2	RCM	20th Century
3	MSCI World	MSCI World
4	20th Century	NYSE Index
5	NYSE Index	Money Market

DOWNSIDE DEVIATION

Included in the Fall 1994 *Journal of Investing* is an article by Sortino and Price specifically addressing the measurement of downside risk. Referring back to Figure 9–5, I have already demonstrated that Manager B is a better choice than Manager C. How does Manager A compare to Manager B?

Referring to the expected returns and standard deviations, they look identical, and if downside probability is used as a criterion, Manager A looks better. The authors point out that the downside probability only considers the chance of failure; it ignores the magnitude of failure. They suggest using a measure referred to as downside deviation (i.e., the deviations below the MAR).[19] Using this as a standard, Manager B looks better. In their article, Sortino and Price analyze a number of familiar investment vehicles and indexes to make their point. Table 9–10 is an abbreviated version of this analysis.

The authors observe that the Sharpe ratio ranking of money market, as the best risk-adjusted investment for the decade ending in 1992 reflects the Sharpe "blindness" to an MAR. They conclude that a focus on downside risk is a step in the right direction but that downside deviation is the only alternative with strong theoretical foundations.

MY CONCLUSIONS REGARDING DOWNSIDE RISK

The work of Rom, Ferguson, Sortino, and others is very persuasive. The question for the wealth manager is how to incorporate it in his practice. In thinking about how to incorporate downside risk into our practice, I considered the following:

- The algorithm for PMPT optimization requires estimates regarding asset class skewness in addition to estimates regarding returns, standard deviation, and correlations. According to an earlier paper by Sortino,[20] skewness for an asset class can change dramatically with the methodology of calculation and the economic environment. Calculations of skewness for the S&P 500 from 1960 to 1988 using different methods of calculation and different economic scenarios resulted in the following range of measures shown in Table 9–11.
- Skewness obviously adds another dimension of estimation error. PMPT recognizes that clients' goals vary, and replaces standard deviation as the risk measure with a more client-dependent measure, the

T A B L E   9–11

Measurement of Skewness

Methodology of Calculation	Skewness
Annual Observations	−1.11
Bootstrap	1.09
Economic Scenario	
Deep Recession	4.37
Mild Recession	3.20
Mild Inflation	1.27
High Inflation	−1.80

MAR. Unfortunately, capturing a client's goals may require more than a single fixed MAR. For example:

Goals are frequently variable, e.g., a minimum return over inflation.

Goals vary depending on the economic environment, e.g., high returns in good markets and capital preservation in bad markets.

Goals are subjective, e.g., maintain a standard of living.

There may be multiple goals, e.g., an MAR as well as a maximum risk of loss.

Goals may vary over different economic horizons, e.g., short-run goals may differ from long-term goals.*

The analytical process seems to still be in the academic and experimental stage.

The clients of wealth managers typically have long investment time horizons. One paper suggests that downside risk is applicable for investors with short- and intermediate-term horizons. It concludes "whether the semivariance approach is superior for longer holding periods is not addressed here."[21]

Finally, the decision to use downside variance requires a balancing of its problems (such as those noted above) with its benefits. For this, refer back to the example in Table 9–9 (Rom and Ferguson's equivalent risk portfolios). The downside risk portfolio resulted in an increase in the equity allocation for less than a 20 basis point increase in expected return, and only a 4 percent increase in the efficiency ratio.

My conclusion, at least for now, is that the wealth manager should become familiar with downside risk and incorporate the concept as part of his art, not his science. In spite of my strong defense of Markowitz's optimization, it should be clear that I consider an MV optimizer *a potentially dangerous instrument,* one that needs to be heavily constrained by a knowledgeable wealth manager. Simply developing the input for an MV optimizer requires a significant leap of faith in one's ability to divine an image of the future. To step beyond

---

*The question of multiple scenario asset allocation optimization is an interesting related technique discussed by Gifford Fong and Frank J. Fabozzi, in Robert Arnott and Frank Fabozzi, editors, *Active Asset Allocation,* Probus, 1992.

this—add the issues of semivariance—seems to me to be a role for Captain Kirk and the crew of the Enterprise, not the wealth manager (at least not yet).

ENDNOTES

1. George M. Frankfurter and Herbert E. Phillips, "A Brief History of MPT: From a Normative Model to Event Studies," *Journal of Investing,* Winter 1994, 18–23.

2. David Dreman and Michael A. Berry, "Analyst Forecasting Errors and Their Implications for Security Analysis," *Financial Analysts Journal,* May–June 1995, 30–41.

3. Roger Ibbotson and Rex Sinquefield, "Stocks, Bonds, Bills and Inflation: Year-by-Year Historical Returns (1926–1974)," *The Journal of Business,* January 1976, 11–47; Roger Ibbotson and Rex Sinquefield, "Stocks, Bonds, Bills and Inflation: Simulations of the Future (1976–2000)," *The Journal of Business,* July 1976, 313–338; SBBI, "Forecasts of the Future," *Ibbotson,* 1995, 1–5; "Expected Returns in the 1990's," *IAFP National Conference,* 1995 Success Forum; Ibbotson Associates, "Differences of Means: Interpretation," *SBBI 1994 Risk Premia Report 1994,* 1–3; Lori Lucas, "Building Bener Inputs: A Guide to the Methodology and Value Added of Ibbotson's Optimizer Inputs," April 11, 1995.

4. Lori Lucas, "Building Better Inputs: A Guide to the Methodology and Value Added of Ibbotson's Optimizer Inputs," Ibbotson, April 11, 1995.

5. Jeanie Rabke Wyatt, CFA, "Quantifying Risk in the Asset Allocation Process," AIMR ICFA Continuing Education, *Managing Assets for Individual Investors,* February 28–March 1, 1995, 50–57.

6. Mahamood M. Hassan, "Arithmetic Mean and Geometric Mean of Past Returns," *Journal of Investing,* Fall, 1995, 83.

7. Richard Michaud, "The Markowitz Optimization Enigma: Is 'Optimized' Optimal?" *Financial Analysts Journal,* January–February 1989, 31–40.

8. Richard Michaud, "The Markowitz Optimization Enigma: Is 'Optimized' Optimal?" *Financial Analysts Journal,* January–February 1989, 31–40; Scott Lummer, Mark Riepe, and Laurence Siegal, "Taming Your Optimizer: A Guide through the Pitfalls of Mean-Variance Optimization," *Global Asset Allocation,* Jess Lederman and Robert Klein, Editors, John Wiley & Sons, 1994, 7–25.

9. Bert Stine and John Lewis, "Guidelines for Rebalancing Passive-Investment Portfolios," *Journal of Financial Planning,* April 1992, 80–84.

10. SEI Corporation, "Asset Allocation for Taxable Investors: Maximizing after Tax Returns," SEI, March 1996, 27–31.

11. Jeremy Black, "Asset Rebalancing," *Financial Planning Perspectives: Asset Allocation Viewpoint,* College for Financial Planning, May 1992.

12. Stine and Lewis, 80–84.

13. Art Lutschaunig, "Optimal Asset Allocation II," *AIMRICFA Continuing Education Managing Assets for Individual Investors,* February 28– March 1 1995, 44–49.

14. McCalla, *Global Asset Allocation,* 55–74.

15. Frank Sortino, and Lee N. Price, "Performance Measurement in a Downside Risk Framework," *The Journal of Investing,* Fall 1994, 61.

16. Brian Rom and Kathleen Ferguson, "Post-Modern Portfolio Theory Comes of Age," *Journal of Investing,* Fall 1994, 11.

17. Brian Rom and Kathleen Ferguson, *Journal of Investing,* Fall 1994, 12.

18. Rom and Ferguson, *Journal of Investing,* Fall 1994, 16.

19. Frank Sortino, and Lee N. Price, *The Journal of Investing,* Fall 1994, 59–64; Frank Sortino, and Hal J. Forsey, "On the Use and Misuse of Downside Risk," *The Journal of Portfolio Management,* Winter 1996, 35–42.

20. Frank A. Sortino, "The Look of Uncertainty," *Journal of Investing,* Winter 1990, 30–33.

21. Harry E. Merriken, "Analytical Approaches to Limit Downside Risk: Semi-variance and the Need for Liquidity," *The Journal of Investing,* Fall 1995, 71.

CHAPTER 10

Policy

Plan the plan, play the plan.

—Harold Evensky

In the framework of wealth management, an investment policy is, in effect, a focused financial plan (i.e., an investment plan). At EB&K, we have elected to use the term *policy* rather than *plan* in order to avoid any possible misunderstanding by the client regarding the scope of our work. Still, as I indicated in the Introduction, I believe that wealth management is a financial planning process and the steps leading to the development of the policy should follow that process.

There are a number of excellent guides regarding the development of an investment policy,* however, their focus is on the institutional client (e.g., pension plans). The purpose of this chapter is to provide an example of an investment policy designed for an individual (i.e., noninstitutional) client and to discuss the rationale behind the wording and structure of the policy.

The earlier chapters of this book discussed many of the activities and decisions that must occur before developing a policy. To recap, the wealth manager must

---

*I would particularly recommend Chapter 10 of John Guy, *How to Invest Someone Else's Money,* Irwin, 1994, and Chapter 5 of Trone, Allbright, and Taylor, *The Management of Investment Decisions,* Irwin, 1996. The earlier work of Trone, Allbright, and Madden, *Procedural Prudence,* SEI, 1991, serves as the basis for EB&K policies.

- Work with and educate clients in order to determine, with time and dollar specificity and in priority order, their personal goals (including the hidden goals).
- Evaluate existing investment assets.
- Determine projected cash flow needs (or surplus).
- Determine the constraints (e.g., asset-class limitations, nonrepositionable assets, taxes, legal).
- Determine the client's risk tolerance.
- Develop an asset allocation.

Once this has been completed, the wealth manager can then draft a customized policy for his client. This chapter provides sample sections of my firm's current investment policy statement, followed by commentary on their roles. Note that these examples include excerpts from the policies of many different clients. They are included solely to provide the reader with ideas for use in developing his or her own policy statement.

PREFACE

This is our first warning that a policy is a guide, not a guarantee. It also draws the client's attention to the assumptions that form the basis for our recommendations.

Mr. and Mrs. Client, many of the illustrations in this plan involve the use of numbers because they are the most effective means of presenting a financial picture. These figures can lend an aura of false precision. Sets of numbers dealing with financial issues five years (and longer) down the road are not intended to be viewed as predictive but rather represent projections, based on a certain set of assumptions. Although real-life events can rarely be predicted with accuracy (e.g., your decision to retire at age 50; if and when you will sell your boat and second condo; your part-time work and the anticipated inheritance; the return on your land development; or the return on your currency hedge program), these projections are useful in comparing the likely results of different approaches and plans of action. If, upon reviewing this plan, you have any questions regarding the data or assumptions, please bring them to our attention.

Investment Policy Summary

SAMPLE CLIENT
JANUARY 1996

Type of Assets	Personal & IRA Assets
Current Assets	Approximately $1,275,000
Investment Time Horizon	Greater than 10 years
Expected Return	4.5% over CPI
Risk Tolerance	Moderate to intermediate term
	Low to long-term
	Losses not to exceed 11% per year
	With a 90% confidence level

Asset Allocation	Cash equivalents	3%
	U.S. fixed	37
	Int'l fixed	5
	U.S. large cap	24
	U.S. small cap	11
	International	15
	Real estate	5

Allocation Variance Limit	Quarterly	10%
Broad Classes	Yearly	5%

Representative	Cash equivalent	–Donoghue Tax MMA
Evaluation Benchmarks	Fixed income	–Salomon 3 to 7yr Treas.
		–Value Line Short Muni
		–Lehman 5yr G.O.
		–Lehman Aggregate
	Equity	–S&P 500
		–Morningstar Growth & Inc.
		–Morningstar Equity Inc.
		–Morningstar Growth
		–Morningstar Small Co.
		–Morningstar Int'l
		–EAFE

OVERVIEW

This section is customized to reflect the client's needs. For example, many of our clients do not need current income. In that case, the first sentence would not include the words "current and." We also begin the investment policy with a strong statement reflecting our commitment to diversification and a reminder that the client's goals direct our recommendation.

> Building capital to generate current and future income is a primary objective of your investment policy. Our strategy for accomplishing this objective is based on the concept of diversification, which we call asset allocation. It is a long-term strategy, designed to suit your individual aspirations and circumstances, which provides a durable framework within which to make specific investment decisions.
>
> In designing your personal investment strategy we began by reviewing your objectives and constraints. We then developed recommendations appropriate for you.

INVESTMENT OBJECTIVES

As the following examples (from many different client policies) illustrate, we attempt to describe our understanding of their goals with as much specificity as possible.

> - Before retirement, provide for supplemental income during your preretirement years in the amount of approximately $7,200 per year, after taxes.
> - You wish to retire in three years and maintain your standard of living during your retirement. You estimate this to be $62,000 (after tax and in today's dollars) and $16,400 annually for 13 years for your mortgage payment. In addition, your families are long-lived and you believe that it is appropriate to plan for an income need for approximately 30 years.
> - Factor in part-time income of $50,000 per year until Harold reaches 70.
> - Provide for a wedding in two years. You estimate this to be approximately $30,000. You have reserved funds for this purpose.
> - Provide for the purchase of a second home in Maine in approximately 2+ years. You estimate this goal to require $100,000 (in today's dollars).

- Provide for the purchase of a second home in Maine in approximately 2+ years. You estimate this goal to require $100,000 (in today's dollars).

- Provide for a portfolio that will be diversified and managed such that you can take an extended sailing trip through the Pacific and Australia without having to be concerned about your investments.

- Provide for gifting of approximately $30,000 per year for the balance of your life.

- Provide for at least half of the cost of a four-year college education at a major private university for your two grandchildren, ages 4 and 7. We estimate this to be approximately $12,000 per year, per child, in today's dollars.

- For the next three years, plan for the investing of future savings, particularly your $52,000 annual pension contributions.

- Preserve principal. Reasonable efforts should be made to preserve principal, but preservation of principal shall not be imposed on each individual investment.

- Reduce risk by diversifying markets, managers, and maturity dates.

INVESTMENT TIME HORIZON

This is a formal reiteration of the EB&K five-year mantra. The time horizon in the plan is always at least 5 years and usually 10 years.

The investment guidelines are based upon an investment horizon of more than five years, so that interim fluctuations should be viewed with appropriate perspective. Similarly, your strategic asset allocation is based on this long-term perspective.

RISK TOLERANCE

This section continues our efforts to educate our clients regarding risk; it serves to remind them that markets are volatile and uncertain. It also reminds them that they have living-standard goals that cannot be achieved by short-term, "safe" investing (e.g.,CDs). The concluding paragraph, based on question #7 in the risk-tolerance questionnaire, is a reminder that they are loss averse, not risk averse. They are prepared to take risk (i.e., volatility) in order to avoid the loss of their standard of living. The following are examples:

- Building capital to generate future income is a primary objective of your investment policy. Our strategy for accomplishing this objective is based on the concept of diversification, which we call asset allocation. It is a long-term strategy, designed to suit your individual aspirations and circumstances, which provides a durable framework within which to make specific investment decisions. I know that you said you didn't want to hear, "You have to be patient, you're in it for the long haul." Unfortunately, it's true. Building your capital in order to protect your purchasing power from the erosion of inflation requires investments in the equity markets. Equity markets rise and fall with the business cycle. In simple terms, that means you need to have substantial investments in the stock market and those investments WILL lose money when the whole market goes down—and it WILL! The good news is that your current allocation to stock is more than adequate!

- In establishing your risk tolerance, we have considered your ability to withstand short- and intermediate-term volatility. Based on our discussions and your answers to our risk-tolerance questionnaire, we understand that you can accept a moderate volatility portfolio. However, based on your current portfolio and our capital needs analysis, we believe that you can comfortably accomplish your goals with a low-volatility portfolio and our recommendations are governed by your retirement goals. Note, however, that due to the significant nonrepositionable Life Annuity, our recommendation for your repositionable assets (referred to as the "managed portfolio") is growth oriented.

- Your strategic asset allocation is based on this long-term perspective. Short-term liquidity requirements are anticipated to be nonexistent, or at least should be covered by your earnings before retirement.

- Your personal income prior to retirement cannot be projected with any assurance. However, your expectations are that your new consulting venture will provide you with adequate income to cover your living expenses. In addition, between your personal cash reserves and your personal stock and bond holdings, you have adequate emergency reserves. Based on these assumptions, the policy for your 401K assets does not include any "emergency reserve."

- In establishing your risk tolerance, we have considered your ability to withstand short- and intermediate-term volatility. The results of our analysis of your risk-tolerance questionnaire and your current portfolio were somewhat contradictory. The answers to a number of our questions suggest that you have a very low tolerance for short-term volatility. Other answers, however, indicated a willingness to accept moderate volatility and your current portfolio is allocated almost 75 percent in the equity market. Finally, our analysis indicates that in order to approach your retirement goals, you must invest for growth. We have balanced these issues in our recommendations.

- In order to develop an investment policy for your nonsheltered investment assets, we have taken into consideration your IRA and pension accounts and the relative inflexibility of many of your investments.

- In establishing your risk tolerance, we have considered your ability to withstand short- and intermediate-term volatility. Based on our discussions and the composition of your current portfolio, we understand that you can accept, in the intermediate term, a moderate volatility portfolio. Although you indicated a strong preference for a low-volatility portfolio, your investments are currently almost 70 percent in stock. This includes your Exxon holdings for which you are taking significant, unrewarded, unsystematic risk. Your Exxon stock comprises over 40 percent of your current portfolio.

- Note that our recommendation is for a portfolio somewhat more volatile than that indicated by your answers to our risk-tolerance questionnaire. The decision to make this recommendation was influenced by our attempt to balance your clearly defined objective to maintain your current living standard, your acknowledged willingness to accept volatility in order not to lose your standard of living, a recognition that this investment portfolio does not include a significant investment in emergency reserves (i.e., the $50,000) and the fact that the recommendation will reduce your current exposure to the equity market and significantly reduce the unsystematic risk. If, in spite of these considerations, you are uncomfortable with our recommendations, we will revise the allocation and discuss with you the projected impact on your cash flow.

EXPECTED RETURN

Although we quantify the portfolio performance expectations in terms of real ROR, we continually remind the client not to expect these returns to be achieved in a smooth pattern. To further manage our client's expectations, we continually invite him to consider the underlying assumptions we make regarding financial markets (See Table 10–2 in the Chapter 10 Appendix.). During the delivery of the policy to the client, a process we refer to as *plan presentation*, we discuss our assumptions and relate them to both long-term and recent-term historical real returns (See Table 10–3 in the Chapter 10 Appendix.). We warn the client that if he does not find our underlying assumptions credible, he should not accept our policy recommendations. If a client has radically different market expectations, we will revise the policy to reflect his assumptions. However, the revised policy will include a caveat noting that the conclusions are based on the client's assumptions. Also, we will not assume the responsibility of implementing a modified policy, as we do not feel competent to manage what we believe to be unrealistic expectations.

Our recommended portfolio allocation is for a moderate-growth portfolio of 45 percent fixed income and 55 percent equities. A reasonable expectation for the long-term rate of return of the recommended portfolio is 4.5 percent greater than the rate of inflation as measured by the Consumer Price Index (CPI). This expectation is based on the assumption that future real returns will approximate the historic, relative long-run rates of return experienced for each asset class in your Investment Policy. You realize that market performance varies and that a 4.5 percent rate of return may not be meaningful during some periods. The financial assumptions that provided the basis for our analysis may be found in the Appendix (Table 10–2).

ASSET ALLOCATION

This sets forth the bias of our firm. As a standard policy, we consider only six major asset classes. We reject high-yield bonds because we believe that our clients will rapidly forget all of the technical arguments in their favor should their prices drop and the media headlines begin using the pejorative term "junk bonds." An element of our investment selection criteria is measured by how well an investment helps our clients sleep during bad markets. High-yield bonds fail this criterion. For the same reason, we do not consider short sales or margin trades. Metals and natural resources are generally eliminated from consideration due to our inability to find appropriate investment vehicles. Commodities fail both the "sleep" and availability criteria.

- We believe that your portfolio's risk and liquidity are, in large part, a function of asset-class mix. We have reviewed the long-term performance characteristics of various asset classes, focusing on balancing the risks and rewards of market behavior. The asset classes selected reflect your risk tolerance and the unique circumstances of your current investments. Six major asset classes were considered:

*Cash equivalents	*Domestic equities
*Domestic bonds	*International equities
*International bonds	*Real estate

  The following securities and transactions were not considered: high-yield bonds, metals, natural resources, commodities or commodity contracts, short sales, or margin trades.

INVESTMENT RECOMMENDATIONS

Allocation Table

This is a detailed numerical description of the client's existing portfolio and our recommended reallocation. We refer to our recommendations as "generic but specific." They are generic in that we do not recommend the purchase of named investments (e.g., IBM or Sogen International); however, they are specific in that we make allocations to very narrow investment classes and styles.

Table 10–1 is a simplified example. Column #1 describes the broad asset classes; Column #3 further divides these classes into subclasses and styles. Column #4 identifies the client's current investments in terms of these subclasses and styles; Column #2 is used if there are multiple accounts (e.g., IRAs, individual and joint, etc.). We treat the entire portfolio as a single unit. Column #5 quantifies the current investment in terms of both dollar and asset-class percentages. Column #6 is the quantification of our policy recommendation. As a client rarely comes to us with all cash, the recommended reallocation may be constrained by existing investments. Column #7 is our recommendation for reallocation reflecting these constraints.

Observations on the example:

- **Short Corporate/Government.** Although the policy calls for a 6 percent allocation, the recommendation is to maintain the client's current 9 percent. The transaction cost of selling the short treasuries and moving to short municipals does not justify making the change. The 3 percent excess allocation will be moved to the short municipal allocation as the T-bills and CDs mature.

- **Short/Intermediate Corporate/Government.** Having analyzed the "ABC" fund, we concluded that it was well managed and had an appropriately low expense ratio. The recommendation is to sell $100,000 of the fund to bring the investment in line with the policy.

- **Short Municipal.** The recommendation is to gradually fund this allocation with the proceeds of maturing treasuries and CDs.

- **Short/Intermediate and Intermediate Municipals.** We determined that both funds were acceptable. The $50,000 recommended sale of "GHI" is simply to bring the allocation down to meet the policy.

- **International Bonds.** Using the proceeds from "GHI," purchase $50,000 of foreign bonds (or funds).

- **Index, Tactical Large-Capitalization Value, Small-Cap Value, Emerging Markets, and REITs.** Invest in diversified portfolios of stocks or appropriate mutual funds to match the policy allocations.

- **Growth.** "JKL" is well managed and style consistent. The sale of a portion is simply to bring the fund allocation into alignment with the policy. The liquidation of IBM is recommended due to lack of diversification. The liquidation of "MNO" fund is recommended due to excessive expenses, style drift, and new management.

- **International Developed.** "STU" fund is inconsistently managed and, as a consequence, exhibits significant style drift. It should be sold and replaced with new stocks or funds.

- **Ownership.** To the extent possible, we use sheltered accounts to improve after-tax returns. In this case, the short-term, fixed-income and municipal bond investments are concentrated in the joint account. Due to the relative tax efficiency, the market index and tactical equity funds have also been placed in the joint account.

T A B L E   10-1

Investment Policy Allocation

Policy	Owner	Style	Description	Current		Policy		Proposed	
MMA	Joint		MMA	$30,000	3.0%	$ 30,000	3.0%	$30,000	3.0%
	MRIRA		MMA	40,000	4.0			0	
U.S. Fixed Income	Joint	SH Corp/Govt	T-Bills and Notes	60,000	6.0	60,000	6.0	60,000	6.0
	MRIRA		CD (6-Month Maturity)	30,000	3.0			30,000	3.0
	MSIRA	S/I Corp/Govt	"ABC" Short-Term Gov't Fund	170,000	17.0	70,000	7.0	70,000	7.0
		SH Muni				30,000	3.0	0	
	Joint	S/I Muni	"DEF" Short/Inter Muni Fund	110,000	11.0	110,000	11.0	110,000	11.0
	Joint	Inter. Muni	"GHI" Intermediate Muni Fund	150,000	15.0	100,000	10.0	100,000	10.0
International BO	MSIRA	International	New International Bonds			50,000	5.0	50,000	5.0
			Fixed Income	**590,000**	**59.0**	**450,000**	**45.0**	**450,000**	**45.0**
U.S. Large Cap	Joint	Core	New Index Fund			50,000	5.0	50,000	5.0
	Joint	Tactical	New Tactical			40,000	4.0	40,000	4.0
	MS	Value	New L.C. Value			90,000	9.0	90,000	9.0
	Joint	Growth	"JKL" L.C. Growth Fund	130,000	13.0	60,000	6.0	60,000	6.0
	MS		IBM (Recently Inherited)	90,000	9.0			0	
	Joint		"MNO" L.C. Growth Fund	120,000	12.0			0	
U.S. Small Cap	Joint	Value	New S.C. Value	0		70,000	7.0	70,000	7.0
	Joint	Growth	"PQR" S.C. Growth Fund	30,000	3.0	40,000	4.0	40,000	4.0
International	Joint	Developed	New International			110,000	11.0	110,000	11.0
	Joint		"STU" International Fund	40,000	4.0			0	
	MRIRA	Emerging	New Emerging Mkt			40,000	4.0	40,000	4.0
Real Estate	MSIRA		New REITs			50,000	5.0	50,000	5.0
			Equity	**410,000**	**41.0**	**550,000**	**55.0**	**550,000**	**55.0**
			Total	**$1,000,000**	**100.0%**	**$1,000,000**	**100.0%**	**$1,000,000**	**100.0%**

Pie Charts

Table 10–1 provides significant detail. Unfortunately, many clients find this level of detail overwhelming. In an effort to simplify the recommendations and convey a feeling for the broad allocation changes, we include the two pie charts shown in Figures 10–1 and 10–2. In the actual policy, they are in color.

Current Portfolio

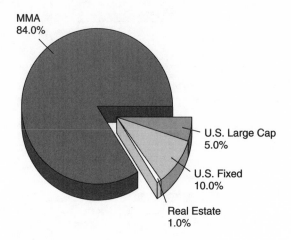

Proposed Portfolio

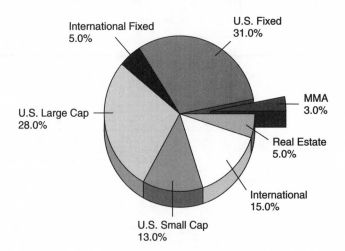

Your Personal Investment Policy

These are the same recommendations presented in Table 10–1 and the pie charts. It is just an alternative way of communicating the information. We have learned by experience to err on the side of redundancy when presenting information to clients. Throughout our continuing client relationship we present data and concepts in repetitive but differing formats. (Another example of our conscious use of redundancy is our risk-tolerance questionnaire, discussed in Chapter 4, Data Gathering.)

YOUR PERSONAL INVESTMENT PORTFOLIO

Establishing the Fixed Income Category—Proposed Allocation

Invest in the following fixed-income investments:

Money Market	$ 3,000
Short-Term Government/Corporate Bonds	67,000
Short-Intermediate-Term Government/Corporate Bonds	78,000
Short-Term Municipal Bonds	35,000
Short/Intermediate Municipal Bonds	122,000
Intermediate Municipal Bonds	111,000
International Bonds	56,000

Establishing the Equity Category—Proposed Allocation

Invest in the following equity investments:

Large Capitalization U.S. Core	$ 55,000
Large-Cap U.S. Tactical	45,000
Large-Cap U.S. Value	100,000
Large-Cap U.S. Growth	67,000
Small-Cap U.S. Value	78,000
Small-Cap U.S. Growth	45,000
International Developed Equities	122,000
International Emerging Equities	44,000
Real Estate Index	56,000

YOUR RETIREMENT PORTFOLIO

Although this policy does not cover your retirement funds, we recommend the following:

Your TIAA is invested in fixed income. We suggest that you move this to the CREF, which is invested in equities. The time horizon for these funds is at least 20 years. Your current IRA investments are also fixed income. We suggest that you place these funds in a U.S. Large-Cap Index fund (e.g., the Schwab 1000 or the Vanguard S&P 500). Again, the time horizon for these funds is at least 20 years.

MANAGER PORTFOLIO GUIDELINES

This is an example of the specific guidelines we recommend for each broad asset class.

Domestic Equities:

- Equity holdings in any one company should not usually exceed more than 5 percent of the market value of the manager's portfolio. The industry sector weightings should not generally exceed 3 times that of the S&P 500.

- Equity managers shall have the discretion to invest a portion of the assets in cash reserves when they deem appropriate. However, the managers should, in accordance with AIMR standards, be evaluated against their peers on the performance of the total funds under their direct management.

- Equity mutual funds, if well diversified, should generally have moderate Betas and long-term positive Alphas, and less well-diversified funds should have favorable Sharpe ratios as compared to comparable style managers. Funds should have no loads and expense ratios less than 1.2 percent. The managers should have at least a five-year operating history and a consistent management record.

CAPITAL NEEDS ANALYSIS

This section is only included in those cases that require a capital needs analysis. It spells out the basic assumptions made in the analysis and a brief summary of the conclusions.

In conjunction with your investment policy, you have asked us to address the issues of Capital Needs Planning to ensure that each income source is utilized in proper balance to create an adequate stream of income, including adjustments for inflation, throughout the balance of your life. Your investment policy is driven by this analysis and we incorporate projections based on our investment recommendations. However, the total return assumptions vary from the investment policy as noted in our assumptions for retirement.

Capital Needs Assumptions:

Inflation Projection	4.0%
Social Security Annual Increase	3.0
Taxes—Marginal	28

Capital Accumulation:

There are no projected savings.

Income Sources (in addition to capital):

Social Security while both boys are in school	$24,800
Social Security when William is 16 until he is 18	8,200
Pension from Exxon (no COLA)	4,056
Insurance Annuity (after tax)	14,800
Social Security after the "blackout" period	10,000

Income Needs:

Your expenses are classified, as necessary, into two categories:

    Inflatable-Basic—Nondiscretionary living expense

    Fixed Terminable—Home mortgage

CAPITAL NEEDS PLANNING CONCLUSIONS

The capital needs projections we've prepared are at best a very rough projection of the future. Your life expectancy and uncertainty regarding future income, growth of investments, and expenses are major question marks in the analytical process.

Based on the assumptions noted, we believe that you will fall short of your stated goals. However, you should keep in mind that these are long-term projections and incorporate many variables. We believe that the more short- and intermediate-term volatility you can tolerate, the more likely you are to improve your overall financial picture. We also note that returning to work and moving to a less expensive home will also add favorably to your financial future. We will discuss this with you, in detail, during our meeting.

FINANCIAL PLANNING OBSERVATIONS

These are client unique noninvestment issues that we believe need the client's attention. (These are issues that although not a formal part of the investment planning process, have come to our attention.)

EMERGENCY RESERVES

As we have discussed, your emergency reserves are far in excess of any recommendation we might make for this purpose; however, we understand your desire to maintain a substantial cash reserve for your personal comfort and the investment recommendations reflect this.

As we have discussed, the recommended cash flow reserves are far in excess of any recommendation we might make solely for emergency reserves; however, we believe that maintaining a liquid cash reserve for your supplementary cash flow needs over the next few years is an effective way to manage your short-term needs.

RISK MANAGEMENT

We suggest that you review your disability coverage, as well as property/casualty (renter's) insurance. You do not have an umbrella liability policy. You should discuss these issues with Mr. Brown, your insurance agent.

Based on our review, your health coverage with Exxon seems to be adequate. Your property and casualty umbrella is appropriate; however, the coverage on your antique furniture is inadequate. You should immediately have the furniture appraised and obtain a rider from your insurance company. It would be appropriate to take the opportunity to completely review your property and casualty coverage with your agent.

Given the substantial size of your estate, have your property and casualty insurance professionally reviewed, especially your liability coverage on your real estate, auto, and boat as well as your personal umbrella coverage.

We also believe that you should consider the purchase of individual long-term care policies, which meet the guidelines outlined in the attached.

You do not currently have adequate disability coverage. It is imperative that you obtain coverage. You should address this need as your first priority.

TAX CONSIDERATIONS

The income from your pension, annuity, and the taxes generated by your significant investment portfolio are likely to keep you in the 28 percent marginal bracket. Our investment recommendations reflect this. If, after reviewing your taxes with your accountant, we find that your marginal bracket drops to 15 percent, we will work with you to adjust the investment portfolio accordingly.

As we have discussed, we recommend the sale of the Exxon in spite of the significant capital gains that will be due upon sale. As we noted, the only ways to ultimately avoid the taxes are to die holding the stock, to wait until the market price drops to the basis price, or gift the stock to charity. The first two choices are clearly unacceptable, and, with the exception of minor gifting to Big Brothers/Big Sisters, charitable strategies are not a viable alternative. By delaying the sale, taxes are not avoided but merely deferred. The savings are the present value of the possible earnings on the deferred taxes. This is not an adequate reward for accepting the unsystematic risk associated with holding one unmanaged stock position.

ESTATE PLANNING

Your current estate planning documents incorporate guardianship and trusts for your sons. We suggest that you also consider the possibility of establishing a living (revocable) trust. Although a living trust is frequently recommended for the purpose of probate avoidance, we do not consider that, in and of itself, an adequate justification. The primary reason we recommend consideration of such a trust is to prearrange for the management of your affairs in the event of your incapacity. We also strongly recommend that you consider the preparation of a durable power of attorney, a health care power, and a "living" will.

We will be happy to discuss these issues with your other advisors (with your permission) and/or refer you to knowledgeable professionals should you request any assistance in these matters.

APPENDIX TO CHAPTER 10

This includes the firm's current financial market projections and tables of historical returns, as shown in Tables 10–2 and 10–3.

T A B L E   10–2

Financial Market Projection

Fixed-Income Investments	ROR	Std Dev
Money Market	5.0%	3.4%
Govt Short	5.3	6.3
Corp Short	5.5	7.0
Municipal Short	5.5	6.6
Govt Short/Intermediate	6.3	9.0
Corp Short/Intermediate	6.6	9.2
Municipal Short/Intermediate	7.0	9.4
Govt Intermediate	7.2	12.6
Corp Intermediate	7.6	13.5
Municipal Intermediate	8.0	13.5
Int'l Bonds	8.0	17.0
Growth Investments		
Index	10.7%	19.6%
Tactical	9.0	16.0
Yield	9.8	16.0
Value	10.0	16.0
Growth	10.8	19.9
Small Cap - Value	11.5	23.0
Small Cap - Growth	12.2	26.0
International Developed	11.0	22.0
International - Emerging	12.5	40.0
Real Estate	9.5	17.0
Metals	9.0	36.5

T A B L E   10–3

Historical Returns

Asset Class	1926–1994		1985–1994	
	ROR	**Real RO**	**ROR**	**Real ROR**
U.S. T-Bills	3.7%	0.6%	5.8%	2.2%
Intermediate Govt Bonds	5.1	2.0	9.4	5.8
Long-Term Govt Bonds	4.8	1.7	11.9	8.3
Long-Term Corp Bonds	5.4	2.3	11.6	8.0
Common Stock	10.2	7.1	14.4	10.8
Small Company Stock	12.2	9.1	11.1	7.5
Inflation	3.1		3.6	

Source: Ibbotson

Manager Selection and Evaluation—Basics

Mutual funds are like a box of chocolates.
You never know what you're going to get.

—Worth Magazine

Chapters 11, 12, and 13 all address the issues of manager selection and evaluation. Let me confess, up front, that the titles of these three chapters are a tad biased. As the reader will soon learn, the discussion to follow is almost entirely focused on mutual funds. However, since I believe that, with rare exception, the wealth manager should use fund managers as his money managers, I consider the terms interchangeable. If you disapprove, don't despair. Although the focus is on funds, the concepts and criteria are useful for any management type.

Chapter 11 discusses many of the basic issues necessary to form the framework for a manager selection and evaluation process. It begins with a description of the various types of management available to the wealth manager and then discusses the many ways managers may be classified. Because of their importance, classifications related to "active," "passive," and "style" will be treated separately in Chapter 12. As practitioners are generally familiar with various data sources, the section on information sources will only be a brief review of information available from the managers and independent data suppliers. Also, as Chapter 6, Mathematics of Investing, covered much of the subject in detail, the section on measurements will only recap the most significant measurements used in manager evaluation. Because of its popularity, the measurement technique of style analysis is accorded its own section in Chapter 12. Chapter 13 provides a structured framework for selecting and evaluating managers.

MANAGER TYPES

The wealth manager has two broad options for implementing the investments in each asset class—individual management and pooled (or comingled) management. The second option, pooled management, is the universe of mutual funds. Individual management may be further divided into two forms.

INDIVIDUAL MANAGEMENT

Personal Management— Would You Play High-Stakes Poker with the World's Best Players?

In this form of individual management, the wealth manager changes hats and becomes a money manager. He personally makes the specific individual security buy and sell decisions. A wealth manager considering this alternative should apply the same standards of evaluation to his role as money manager as he would any independent money manager. This would include an unbiased evaluation of his investment management experience and credentials (e.g., CFA), his performance record (AIMR standards), his peer performance, trading costs, technology, research facilities, time devoted to money management, etc. Setting aside the inherent conflict of interest in judging himself (and the possible fiduciary breach), a competent wealth manager is unlikely to pass the screen as a money manager—if for no other reason than both wealth management and money management are full-time professions. It is difficult (if not impossible) to maintain competence in both. Any wealth manager considering wearing two hats should ask himself if he knows of any competent— not exceptional, just competent—part-time money managers.

Private Money Manager

This professional is usually referred to as a *money manager*. Once again, we need to subdivide this category:

Individually Managed Account

This is a form of management uniquely customized and professionally managed for the client. From the client's perspective, primary attributes of this form of management are:

- The account is in the client's name.
- The securities are in the client's name.
- The process is based on a relationship between the client and the manager.
- The portfolio is specifically tailored and managed for the unique requirements of the client.
- The portfolio goals can be changed significantly without changing managers.

From the manager's perspective, individually managed accounts
- Require substantial minimum investments, typically ranging from $10 to $50 million or more.
- Require the attention of the most experienced, successful, and highly compensated of the management team.
- Limit the number of clients the firm can accept.
- Require individual attention to each security in each portfolio.
- Require a direct relationship between the client and the manager.

Separately Managed Accounts

This is a packaged form of private money management. Its name, *separately managed,* is derived from its similarity with an individually managed account:

- The account is in the client's name.
- The securities are in the client's name (i.e., separate from others).

Hypothetical Example—Unlike individually managed accounts, customization of a separate account is based on computer screening and arbitrary reallocation. A separate account is based on a model portfolio. Each separate account will own a pro rata share of the model portfolio's securities. The actual client portfolio construction is determined by computer. It is a result of this mechanical process that separate accounts often seem to have such odd lot positions. For example, consider Ms. Boone with $100,000 placed with manager "Hot":

Manager Hot's Model Portfolio Allocation		Stock Price	Ms. Boone's Portfolio Allocation		
Stock A	25%	$20	$25,000	1,250 Shares	25%
Stock B	25	30	25,000	833 Shares	25
Stock C	25	40	25,000	625 Shares	25
Stock D	25	50	25,000	500 Shares	25

Suppose that after the client reviews her portfolio, Ms. Boone discovers that Stock A is in a company that she believes is harming the environment. Unlike a mutual fund, she may request that Stock A be eliminated from the portfolio. In an individually managed account, the manager might search for a replacement for Stock A. In a separate account, the customization simply requires a programmer to instruct the computer to reallocate the client's funds against the model while setting the allocation to Stock A equal to zero.

Ms. Boone's new customized portfolio is as follows:

Ms. Boone's Customized Portfolio			
Stock B	$33,333	1,111 shares	33%
Stock C	33,333	833 shares	33
Stock D	33,333	667 shares	33

Actual Example—I recently had an opportunity to review a client's separately managed account. The portfolio held 42 positions. The following is representative of the size of those positions:*

Quantity	Description
30	American General
5	Citicorp SR 13 Pr
45	Ford Motor Corp.
2,000	Pennzoil 6.5% 1/15/03

---

*Did the manager *really* decide that the client needed 30 shares of American General and not 35 shares, or 5 of Citicorp, not 10? I believe that a computer, not the manager, made the decision.

From the manager's perspective, separate accounts have the following characteristics:

- They provide for significant leveraging of management talent. Senior management can design model portfolios, and junior managers, following the model and using computer allocations, can manage hundreds of accounts.
- Client contact can be managed by sales staff and third-party representatives (e.g., brokers or RIAs).

Private Money Management—Summary

For the wealth manager, the only form of private money management realistically available is the separate account. Even if the minimum for truly customized private management was as low as $500,000 or $1,000,000, it would be impossible to adequately diversify most portfolios. A wealth manager using minimal asset-class allocations would still need five or more managers (e.g., large-cap growth and value, small-cap growth and value, international, short- and intermediate-term bonds, and taxable and municipal bonds).

In considering separate account management, the wealth manager must determine the pros and cons vis-à-vis a pooled management alternative. The issues most frequently considered are:

- Customization. Separate accounts offer limited and mechanical customization. However, on the rare occasion that a client has a very specific need (e.g., "I refuse to own any company whose name begins with the letter C"), a separate account may be the only choice. Such unique needs are rare.

Of course, the ability to restrict certain positions from a portfolio is only one form of customization. For the wealth manager, the ability to customize by a diversification is far more important. With thousands of fund managers to choose from in every conceivable asset class and style, the ability to customize with funds dwarfs the limited choices available in separate accounts.

- Tax advantages. One argument in favor of separate account management is that the account can be 'tax managed.' As demonstrated in Chapter 3, Taxes, this is a good story but without substance. At best, the value of separate account tax management is 10 basis points and there is no research to indicate that, in practice, separated accounts have even achieved this minimal advantage.

Another tax-related argument is that long-term investors in funds will suffer when less patient fund investors sell in panic during a bear market. This assumes a number of unsubstantiated "facts." First, that well-managed mutual funds (wealth managers do not pick funds at random) have a significant percent of naive investors. Second, that the funds selected by wealth managers will not have adequate liquidity to meet redemptions. Finally, the argument assumes that in a bear market, the forced sales, if any, will generate gains, not losses. None of these assumptions have been substantiated.

- Access to Exceptional Managers. Managers of separate accounts are rarely the most talented of a firm's management team. Extraordinary talent is drawn to larger portfolios—they provide more challenge and more compensation. Mutual fund portfolios are commonly multibillion-dollar portfolios. In addition, their performance commands significant, immediate, and continual public scrutiny. Basic economic logic (and greed) suggests that large and/or visible portfolios are where firms are going to devote their top resources. In addition, it is the rare successful separate account manager that a wealth manager cannot access either through a public or institutional mutual fund.

- Costs. Occasionally, the argument is made that separate account management is more cost effective. Pooled accounts have the advantage of institutional commissions but separate accounts have narrower spreads. So where is the cost benefit of the separate account? Usually, the argument for cost efficiency relates to a strategy of implementing separate account management known as the *wrap account*.

Wrap accounts derive their name from the packaging of the fees, commissions, and other expenses. In effect, they are wrapped into a single one-charge-covers-all. Wrap accounts offer the advantage of eliminating any concerns regarding excess trading and other potentially excessive fees. Typically, a wrap account also includes the services of an independent advisor who assists the client in selecting and maintaining the specific money manager.

The cost advantage projected when marketing wrap accounts is usually based on adding "average" independent advisor fees to "average" mutual fund fees. Unfortunately, the fee comparisons are grossly misleading. As an example, the "average" mutual fund fee is typically based only on equity funds and include funds with 12b-1 fees. The average of the expense ratio for funds used by a wealth manager is likely to be 1/2 (or less) of the fees shown in wrap account marketing material.

On the other hand, the independent fee advisor, marketing against wrap accounts, tends to present equally misleading information. The standard wrap account fee is represented as 3 percent, although the average actual is much lower. The independent advisor also frequently ignores the expense ratio of the funds used to implement the policy and almost always ignores the fund manager's commission costs. A fair comparison is likely to find that the total costs for separate account, wrap account, and wealth manager "mutual fund management" are fairly close.

■ Reporting. Separate account proponents argue that ownership of individual securities results in greater accountability by the manager. To some extent, that is true. Fund managers frequently drift in their management style and, as they only have to report positions semiannually, there are potential gaps in accountability. The danger, however, is small and mutual fund accountability is increasing.

The wealth manager's primary insurance against this risk is his original due diligence, i.e., hire managers who are prepared to be accountable. In addition, new technology, including factor analysis, provides additional tools to warn of drift. Finally, as the presence, prestige, and economic clout of wealth managers grow, fund companies will find it to their advantage to become more accountable. Many already voluntarily provide positions quarterly and a few are beginning to provide information monthly, on a 30-day delayed basis.

With little lost regarding accountability, a great deal is gained regarding independent performance and portfolio data. With resources such as Morningstar, Value Line, CDA, Wilson, and others, there is an almost endless stream of independent, substantive data available to the wealth manager to use in monitoring his selected fund managers. By comparison, the independent reporting on separate accounts is nonexistent.

Manager Types—My Conclusion

Before proceeding to select a money manager, a wealth manager must determine the type of management he will consider. The two basic choices are separate account management and pooled account management. I recommend pooled account management (i.e., mutual funds).

CLASSIFICATIONS

Today there are more mutual funds than there are stocks on the New York Stock Exchange. There are more than one trillion dollars invested in mutual funds and one-quarter of all households own a mutual fund. As a result, a fund exists to meet almost every investment objective. However, with thousands of funds it is difficult to select the appropriate fund to meet individual needs. An initial step in the selection process is to classify funds by objective, style, strategy, and asset class.

OBJECTIVE

The most common classification system, and the one most familiar to the public, is the fund's objective as reflected in its prospectus. Ostensibly, this is a statement of the objective the fund is trying to achieve. Although there are many variations, the most common objectives are reflected in Tables 11–1 and 11–2 and discussed below.

Equity Funds

Balanced Funds   A balanced fund invests in a combination of stocks and bonds. In general, many balanced funds will keep at least 25 percent of the portfolio's assets in stocks and bonds at all times. Balanced funds can be flexible in response to economic change by shifting their mix of stocks and fixed income securities.

Growth and Income Funds   Growth and income funds seek both long-term capital growth and current income by investing primarily in equity securities. Growth and income are usually considered equal objectives, although many funds classified as "Growth & Income" specifically state that income is secondary (e.g., Vanguard Windsor and Mutual Shares). These funds tend to invest in well-established companies that have a stable and reliable dividend history. When compared to growth and aggressive growth funds, these funds tend to have less volatility, lower expenses, lower turnover, and lower market value (price/earnings and price/book) ratios.

Equity Income Funds   Equity income funds have as their prime objective current income, with capital appreciation being secondary. As a result, these funds emphasize companies that pay above-average

T A B L E   11-1

Equity Fund Objective—Statistics

	Number of Funds	% Bonds	% Stocks	% Small Cap	% Foreign	Standard Deviation	Sharpe Ratio	R Squared	Turnover
Balanced	259	35.2	53.3	12.7	6.9	6.4	0.8		103.0
Equity Income	132	4.0	77.9	11.7	5.4	7.0	1.0	71.0	79.0
Growth	812	0.8	91.3	22.5	5.5	9.9	1.0	65.0	88.0
Aggressive Growth	93	0.5	44.5	68.0	6.7	13.4	1.1	42.0	150.0

Source: Morningstar

dividends. Since dividend yield is the less volatile component of total return (compared to price appreciation), these funds are generally less volatile than growth and growth & income funds.

Growth Funds   Growth funds invest for capital appreciation rather than current income. Their focus is on companies whose long-term-earnings growth may exceed that of the market. Current income is either a secondary objective or not an objective at all.

Aggressive Growth Funds   Aggressive growth funds seek maximum capital gains. Towards this objective they may take high risks, buy volatile stocks, and trade them actively. Techniques such as options, short selling, and leverage may be employed.

Fixed-Income Funds

Corporate Bond (General)   Funds that seek income by investing in fixed-income securities, particularly investment grade bonds. They may be further defined by the quality of bonds in the portfolio. Subclasses include:

   Corporate Bond (High Quality)—Primarily invested in bonds with ratings of A or better. Generally maintain an average rating of AA.

   Corporate Bond (High Yield)—Primarily invested in bonds with ratings below BBB.

   Convertible Bond—Invested in convertible bonds and preferred stock.

T A B L E   11-2

Fixed Income Fund Objective—Statistics

	Number of Funds	Average Maturity	Average Quality	Average Expenses	Standard Deviation	Sharpe Ratio
Corporate Bond	390	10.9	AA	0.9	4.4	0.5
Government Bond	375	7.3	AAA	1.1	4.0	0.2
Municipal Bond	504	14.2	AA	0.9	5.3	0.5

Source: Morningstar

Government Bond (General) Funds that seek income by investing in Treasuries, agencies, and government-guaranteed-mortgage-backed securities. Subclasses include:

Government (Treasury)—Largely restricted to Treasury issues.

Government (Mortgage)—Primarily invested in GNMAs, FNMAs, and FHLMCs.

Municipal Bond Funds that seek income in fixed-income securities exempt from federal income taxes.

Unfortunately, the fund's stated objective is often misleading. For example:

- Heartland U.S. Government's prospectus allows investments of up to 25 percent of the portfolio in bonds rated BB or B and up to 25 percent in futures contracts.

- MFS Intermediate Income may invest up to 50 percent of its assets out of the United States.

- In mid-1995, Fidelity Balanced had almost 50 percent of its portfolio in foreign stock and Fidelity Blue Chip had almost a quarter of the portfolio in small cap, 11 percent in foreign stock, and a median market cap only about 25 percent of the S&P 500.

The point of these examples is not to single out particular funds or managers, but rather to emphasize how worthless the traditional classification by "objective" is, in terms of providing useful and dependable information. The wealth manager must be familiar with the various fund objectives, as they are the classifications clients will normally use (at least until they have been reeducated by the wealth manager). However, for selecting and evaluating managers, the wealth manager must use a more fundamentally sound classification system. In this regard a number of different classification alternatives should be considered.

ASSET CLASS*

Small Cap   Mutual funds that invest in companies with low market capitalizations are considered small-cap mutual funds. Although there is no precise definition of small-cap, evaluation services such as Morningstar often define a small company as one with a market capitalization of below $1 billion.

Mid Cap   Mutual funds that emphasize medium-size companies are considered mid-cap. A mid-cap company usually has a market capitalization ranging from $1 billion to $5 billion.

Large Cap   Mutual funds that emphasize companies with market capitalizations above $5 billion are considered large-cap funds.

International   International mutual funds invest in markets outside the United States. Global funds mix asset classes and generally invest in any country in the world, including the United States. Most international managers focus on the 20 major markets that represent the principal economies of the developed world.

Emerging Markets   Emerging market funds focus on smaller, less efficient markets (not necessarily smaller companies), which, despite the diminutive size of the individual markets, in aggregate are estimated to account for a significant percentage of the world's total economic output. Although investments in these funds tend to be very volatile, they offer the potential for high returns. During the past decade economies of developing countries grew 55 percent faster than those of industrialized countries. For the next five years, World Bank economists estimate that developing markets will grow at an annual rate of more than twice that of developed markets.

---

*For a more detailed discussion, refer to "Asset Classes" Chapter 4, Data Gathering.

Sector   Not true asset classes, specialty, or sector funds represent various undiversified funds that emphasize a specific market sector. This could include financial services, health care, technology, and utilities. Many specialty funds have high expenses, high portfolio turnover, and high manager turnover.

Metals   Precious metal funds are undiversified and direct their investment dollars to companies that derive the majority of their profits from precious metals. As a result, in concentration, they present considerable risk. However, the underlying investment is a tangible asset that tends to be poorly correlated to the stock market. Therefore, in the context of an overall portfolio, metal funds may add diversification to a portfolio. One caveat is that it is important to determine the correlation of the fund with the asset-class assumptions (e.g., metals prices). A significant risk in utilizing an optimization program is to assume that a specific fund will perform in a manner similar to the asset-class assumptions. Metals funds are frequently a good example of the failure of this assumption.

Real Estate   Real estate funds direct their investment dollars to companies that derive the majority of their profits from real estate (primarily REITs). As with metals funds, it is important to verify the correlation of the selected fund(s) with the asset class assumptions.

INFORMATION SOURCES

THE FUND

All too frequently, when evaluating managers, the wealth manager turns to independent data providers. Although the independent provider is an indispensable source, the wealth manager must also carefully analyze the information available from the fund.

Prospectus

■ **Summary of Expenses**—The summary includes the various types of expenses that the fund will incur, such as management fees, 12 B-1 fees, audit, legal, shareholders' services, transfer agent, and custodian expenditures. It will also provide information regarding items such as sales charges and deferred sales charges.

Warning: One common technique used by fund companies is to absorb a portion of the expenses. If so, the agreement will be described in this portion of the prospectus. The agreement to absorb expenses is at the option of the fund and may be terminated without shareholder action. The wealth manager needs to carefully monitor such funds. If not monitored, a wealth manager may naively maintain a fund that subsequently eliminated its subsidy, effectively raising the expenses to the investor beyond an acceptable level.

- **Financial Highlights**—Includes information regarding income and capital charges. In addition, the ratio/supplemental data table includes historical data on the fund's net assets, expense ratio, and portfolio turnover.

- **Objective, Policy, and Risk Considerations**—This details how the fund will be invested and limitations regarding the types of securities it can invest in. It also details such things as the ratings on bonds, the various countries it is allowed to invest in, and limitations regarding the investments in any one security or type of securities. Another limitation may stipulate its limitation on investing in restricted securities. Requested changes in a prospectus should be a caution flag for an advisor. For example, the request of a domestic equity manager to increase foreign holdings or a fixed income manager's request to increase its holdings in illiquid private placement securities should be a trigger for further investigation.

This section also discusses to what extent a fund may borrow or lend its portfolio securities; whether or not it can write options on securities, indexes, or currencies; to what degree the fund will use futures; and its hedging ability if it invests in foreign securities. Other areas that may be covered are the ability of the fund to invest in closed-end funds or use repurchase agreements. Unfortunately, the trend has been for funds to request, from their shareholders, the authority to do practically anything they wish; hence, there is less value in monitoring these restrictions.

- **Purchasing Shares of the Fund**—Covers the sales charge break points and minimums. Also, there may be provisions in this section by which an advisor can acquire a load fund at a net asset value purchase.

- **Management of the Fund**—Discusses the management of the fund. Unfortunately, there is limited information in this section. Rarely will the name of the individual(s) be disclosed; at most it will alert the advisor to the existence of a submanager. The advisor must use other sources to adequately evaluate the management.

Statement of Additional Information

The Statement of Additional Information in most cases provides significantly more detailed information about the practices of the mutual fund.
The statement will be provided by the fund upon request.

▪ **Investment Limitations**—Included are the restrictions imposed
upon the fund manager, the types of securities, and investment techniques
that they are allowed to use.

▪ **Trustees and/or Board Members and 5 Percent Shareholders**—In addition, the Statement provides a more detailed view of the
Board of Directors which oversees the fund. If a single shareholder owns
too much of the fund and decides to liquidate his ownership, it may adversely affect the market value of the fund. This is a particular risk in
funds that invest in limited market securities such as small stocks, real estate investment trusts, municipal bonds, or any other low-trading-volume
security.

▪ **Detailed Financials**—In addition to a detailed listing of investment positions, the Payable section under Liabilities provides information
regarding the dollars being redeemed versus the amount being invested.
This allows the advisor to review the degree of in-flows and out-flows of
funds under management on a net basis that occur over a period of time. If
too much cash in relation to the fund's asset base is flowing into or out of
the fund, it may have too much cash, which may cause the fund manager
to deviate from his management style. Too much cash outflow may force
the manager to sell illiquid securities. The next items to review are the
fund's investment income and expenses. In the case of some high-
expense funds, the investment income may actually be negative. The next
and last section to review are the statement footnotes. The footnotes many
times provide substantial detail on what occurred in the fund, as well as
the history behind its operations.

Annual and Quarterly Reports

Included in the quarterly or annual report, of course, are the financial
statements. These statements provide the same type of financial data discussed earlier. Semiannually, the funds are required to provide their current holdings. As many of the independent data providers have
agreements with many funds to receive more current updates, the independent is a better source for position information.

A significant part of the Annual and Quarterly Reports is the letter written by the fund management. The letter may provide valuable insight as to the ongoing business and investment philosophy that the fund will use over time. A management that pens a letter providing little insight may in fact be providing important information regarding their "concern" for the fund's investors.

INDEPENDENT PUBLISHERS, ANALYSTS, AND DATABASES

There are a number of independent firms that provide data services regarding fund managers to the practitioner. As the major players are so well known and heavily marketed, I will simply share with the reader my biases and recommendations.

Primary Independent Sources

I use the expression *primary independent* to describe those firms that are in the business of obtaining and distributing information regarding funds. Typically, the criteria recommended for selecting these sources include:

- Is a rating system used?
- How is risk measured?

I believe that these kinds of criteria are irrelevant for the wealth manager. Each of the providers has his own proprietary systems. They vary in their definition of *peer group,* in their use of time periods, and in their definition of risk. All are so simplistic as to be useless.* Gary Greenbaum, a respected New Jersey wealth manager, shared Table 11–3 with me.

It is the responsibility of the wealth manager to evaluate a fund's style, performance, and risk in a far more detailed, sophisticated, and professional manner. A more useful list of criteria for selecting data providers would include:

---

*For example, Morningstar equity ratings do not account for capitalization, country, or style, and the fixed-income rating ignores maturity, credit, and currency exposure.

T A B L E   11-3

Garry Greenbaum's Rating of the Raters

Publication	Issue	Fidelity Select Technology	Mutual Shares	Vanguard World International Growth
Business Week[1]	Feb 93	↓↓↓	↑↑↑	↓↓↓
Financial World	Feb 93	A+	C+	B+
Morningstar[2]	Jun 93	☆☆	☆☆☆☆☆	☆☆☆☆
Money	Feb 93	C	B	D
Wall Street Journal	Jun 93	A	D	D

1. 3 up arrows is highest, 3 down arrows is lowest.
2. 5 stars is highest, 1 star is lowest.

Hard Copy and Software:

- **Extent of coverage**—How many funds are covered by the service?

- **Frequency of Updates**—How frequently are the data updated and how current are the data in the updates?

Software:

- **Technology**—Is the software Windows™-based? Windows 95™? Networkable? CD Rom?

- **Search Capabilities**—What fields are available for screening? Can specific search criteria be saved for future reference? Can the results be ranked?

- **Customization**—Does database allow customized comparisons (e.g., one fund versus another) or tracking of customized portfolios? Does it allow you to display only those data fields of interest?

- **Hypotheticals**—Does the program allow you to design hypothetical portfolios? Does it provide for comparisons between benchmarks and/or funds? Will it handle variable cash flows? Taxes?

- **Graphics**—Can the data be graphically displayed? In color? Printed? Printed in color?
- **Technical Support**—What kind of technical support is available?

Based on these criteria, we have purchased the following for our practice:

- Morningstar

225 West Wacker Drive
Chicago, Illinois 60606
800/876-5005

The Rolls Royce of data vendors; in fact, the "Rolls Royce™" of wealth manager support systems. Rather than rave endlessly about Morningstar and its staff, suffice it to say that no one can call himself a wealth manager if he does not at least have Morningstar on his shelf.

Morningstar has a number of products available. Currently the primary ones are the hard copy mutual fund reports and the mutual fund CD Rom. One of the unique benefits of Morningstar reports is not only that there is an independent commentary on the fund by a Morningstar analyst, but the name of the analyst is disclosed and she is available by phone should the wealth manager have specific questions regarding the fund.

A more recent addition is Morningstar's Principia. In addition, the firm has similar reporting services for closed-end funds and variable annuities. We currently use the mutual fund hard copy, CD Rom, and Principia. Don Phillips has indicated that Morningstar is working on major enhancements that will allow the wealth manager not only access to the extensive Morningstar database but powerful new analytical tools to be used in analyzing the data. These enhancements will be delivered through new versions of Principia. We have a standing order to receive any new product as it becomes available.

- Wilson Associates International

21300 Victory Boulevard
Suite 920
Woodland Hills, California 91367
818/999-0015

Phil Wilson is, along with Don Phillips, a member of a small group of vendors to wealth managers who never seem to tire of volunteering their time to assist us in becoming better professionals. As with Morningstar products, Wilson software is constantly being updated and improved. Unlike current Morningstar software, the Wilson Power Center provides the wealth manager the ability to perform detailed analytics on the fund and benchmark database. This includes the ability to calculate correlations, standard deviations, and Sharpe ratios for time periods of the wealth manager's choosing.

- CDA/Weisenberger

CDA Investment Technologies, Inc.
1355 Piccard Drive
Rockville, Maryland 20850
800/232-2285

Similar in many ways to the Morningstar CD Rom, the HYSALES windows-based software still provides enough additional information and presentation graphics to be included in our practice. One unique feature of this product is the ability to easily create an effective scatter gram comparing funds and indexes. It also has a powerful hypothetical module with excellent presentation graphics.

- Ibbotson Associates

P.O. Box 97837
Chicago, Illinois 60678–7837
312/616-1620

Currently, Ibbotson's Style Analyzer is the most effective style analyzer available for the wealth manager. As noted earlier, the downside is the limited number of funds and the inability to manipulate data. Ibbotson's Fund Analyst provides the ability to calculate correlations, standard deviations, and Sharpe ratios for time periods of the wealth manager's choosing. Although priced at relatively high institutional levels, the complete series of Ibbotson software is a valuable addition to the wealth manager's software library.

- Overlap

8000 Savage Drive
Kansas City, Kansas 66109
800/693-7527

A simple but powerful program that allows the wealth manager to compare two or more funds for investment overlap. The software provides for an overlap analysis by either individual positions or by industry sector. The downside is that the vendor is dependent on the fund's reporting of his positions. As there is currently little accountability on the part of funds (they are only required to report positions semiannually), the data may be outdated as well as based on different dates from different funds. Still, the software provides an important screen to alert the wealth manager regarding possible excessive overlapping investments by managers selected for their complementary styles.

- DFA

1299 Ocean Avenue
11th Floor
Santa Monica, California 90401
310/576-1127

DFA provides, to its clients monthly reporting for their asset-class-based passive funds along with an extensive database of benchmarks. This is particularly useful when evaluating value style managers.

- Value Line

P.O. Box 3988
Church Street Station
New York, New York 10008-3988
800/634-3583

We currently subscribe to Value Line Mutual Fund Reports. Although a seeming clone of the Morningstar reports, it includes an analysis of many funds by a Value Line analyst, which may provide a different perspective than Morningstar's. A major downside is that the analyst is neither disclosed nor available to the wealth manager by phone.

RISK MEASURES AND RETURNS

A manager's performance record must be viewed in light of the risk the manager took to achieve that record. A manager who assumes a higher level of risk *should* earn higher returns; if he does not, the investor would be taking a degree of risk for which he or she is not fully compensated. An advisor who recommends a manager operating at a high risk level because of that manager's attractive returns must realize that his client is more vulnerable to losing money in the future.

Risk Measures   The following is a recap of a number of the major measures discussed in Chapter 6, Mathematics of Investing. Remember, the advisor must determine what level of R^2 he considers significant. As noted earlier, we use a standard of 75.

  ▪ **Standard Deviation**—Total Portfolio Risks (a measure in isolation), Average Variability of Returns. Standard deviation is occasionally provided for monthly variations. These can be converted to yearly by multiplying by 3.464.

  ▪ **Sharpe Ratio**—Single Manager, Total Portfolio Risks. Portfolio Excess Return (Portfolio Sharpe Ratio = (Portfolio Return—T-bill)/Standard Deviation.

  ▪ **Beta**—Systematic Risk, Diversified Equity Market Volatility Relative to the Market. Note that the Beta measures the relationship between a fund's excess return *over T-bills* and the excess return of the benchmark index. Accordingly, a fund with a 1.10 beta is expected to perform 10 percent better, *after deducting the T-bill rate,* than the index in up markets and 10 percent worse in down markets. A low beta *does not* imply that the fund has a low level of volatility, only that the fund's market-related risk is low. As noted above, the significance of the market-related risk is measured by the R^2.

  ▪ **Alpha (Jensen Index)**—Systematic Risk-Adjusted Return, Diversified Equity Market Alpha = (Fund Return − T-bill) − [Beta × (Benchmark − T-bill)]. As noted above, the significance of the Alpha is dependent on the diversification of the fund relative to the benchmark (i.e., R^2) and it is also subject to significant statistical error.

- **Time Horizon**—The time horizon of the investment portfolio.
- **Duration/Convexity**
- **Quality**—S&P, Value Line, Moodys.
- **Rate of Return (ROR)**

Dollar-Weighted Return (Internal Rate of Return—IRR, discounted cash flow)— This is simply the return per unit of asset. This measure, incorporating the amount and timing of cash flows, is also referred to as the internal rate of return. This method weights each time period by the dollars invested. This was the standard used for the measure of manager performance until 1968 when the Bank Administration Institute developed a measure known as *time weighted* return. Because money managers do not control the inflows into and out of the funds, a dollar-weighted return calculation measure may give misleading results. Time-weighted return eliminates the impact of cash flows.

Time-Weighted Return (Standard Mutual Fund Method, AIMR Standards)— This measure neutralizes the timing and size of cash flow and provides a more appropriate measure of an individual money manager's performance.

AIMR Standards*— Based on time weighted returns and developed by the Association for Management and Research, these standards are designed to provide uniform reporting of composite numbers by money managers. Currently only mandated for members of AIMR, the standards are expected to become de facto required standards for all major money managers. Although useful for evaluating independent money managers, the standards are not an appropriate criterion for the measurement of a wealth manager's performance. The most significant reason is that time-weighted return measurements are frequently inappropriate for wealth manager portfolios. Time-weighted measurements neutralize the impact of the timing and size of cash flows on the premise that the money manager does not control these cash flows. Wealth managers, however, frequently advise clients regarding both the timing and the magnitude of cash flows (a prime example is the use of dollar cost averaging). Hence, the time-weighted-based AIMR performance standards are fundamentally inappropriate as a measurement standard for wealth manager portfolios.

---

*AIMR standards are available from the Association for Management and Research, 5 Boar's Head Lane, P.O. Box 3668, Charlottesville, Virginia 22903, 804/977-6600. For an excellent discussion of the differences between time (i.e., AIMR) and dollar-weighted returns, refer to "Performance Reporting: The Basics and Beyond, Part I," *Journal of Financial Planning,* July 1995.

CHAPTER 12

Manager Selection and Evaluation— Special Issues

On April 22, 1982, Daryl Short, of Grubb, Oklahoma, hit a long drive toward the first hole at Broken Springs golf course. The ball grazed a caddie's head, bounced off a ballwasher, hit a large woodchuck, and ricocheted over a water hazard, onto the green and into the cup for a hole in one.

There are a number of issues associated with the selection and evaluation of managers that deserve detailed consideration but that do not conveniently fit any particular niche in the flow of the discussion. As a very clever solution to this problem, I've elected to simply add this chapter, titled "Special Issues."

STRATEGY—ACTIVE VERSUS PASSIVE

The debate between proponents of active and passive management has a long and acrimonious history. Some of the conflict results from a confusing use of terminology. In order to remove one element of confusion from the discussion, I will first define my use of a few terms:

▪ **Active management** is the art and science of security selection based on a belief in a manager's ability to consistently and accurately evaluate current and/or future events better than other investors. The core philosophical basis is that by brains, hard work, and/or technology the active manager can, over time and net of costs, beat the system. As selecting one asset class in lieu of another is an "active" decision, market timing and active asset allocation are subsets of active management.

▪ **Passive management** is the antithesis of active management. Its core philosophical tenet is that by brains, hard work, and technology, a manager cannot, over time and net of costs, beat the system; he can, however, beat most active managers. Passive management is often assumed to be the equivalent of index management. It is not. **Index management** is a special subset of passive management. A passive manager may make active trading decisions. His decisions, however, are based on information currently available to all investors, not on an ability to read between the lines or predict future trends and events. Index management is passive management with the added constraint that the manager does not make active trading decisions.

The notion that active managers cannot beat the market dates back to the 1950s and the rediscovery of the concept of market randomness. It was propelled by the work of Gene Fama in the late 60s. The first index fund was started in July 1971 with an initial investment of $6 million for the Samsonite luggage company's pension account. In 1976, Wells Fargo Bank established a comingled S&P 500 fund open to any bank trust client.*

▪ The **efficient market** is a subject covered in some depth in Chapter 7, Investment Theory. For purposes of this discussion, I will use the version of the concept accepted by most proponents of passive management. They do not argue that markets are perfectly efficient. In fact, most readily acknowledge market inefficiencies and anomalies. Efficient market proponents do argue, however, that net of transaction costs and management fees, markets are "functionally" efficient. In other words, active management proponents win no points arguing that markets are "obviously" inefficient. Many passive managers agree.

CURRENT STATUS

As measured by investment dollars, active managers are currently winning the debate. It is estimated that today, although more than $1 trillion dollars is invested in passive portfolios, this impressive figure represents only a small percentage of the investment market. On the other hand, passive investing is a relatively new concept (only about 25 years old) and its growth has been extraordinary. In 1973 only $50 million was passively

---

*This information is from Peter Bernstein's *Capital Ideas*, and this footnote is just another pitch to encourage you to buy and read his fascinating book.

managed. Today, it is estimated that 30 percent of the funds in the nation's largest pension plans are passively managed.

The strategy decision whether to use passive management is too important to be ignored or to be rejected by default. It is the responsibility of the wealth manager to become familiar with the pros and cons of passive management and to decide if it should be incorporated into his practice.

IN FAVOR OF ACTIVE MANAGEMENT

> History doesn't repeat itself but it rhymes.
>
> *—Mark Twain*

It is unnecessary to defend active management. As almost all investment management is active, it seems the value added must be obvious. Given that, I will simply recap the way in which active managers might add value.

Fundamental Research

Graham and Dodd subscribe to this philosophy. They advised the intelligent investor to "devote his attention to the field of undervalued securities . . . which are selling well below the levels apparently justified by a careful analysis of the relevant facts." Another famous proponent of this form of value added is Warren Buffett, who as a disciple of Graham, has made many long-term investors in Berkshire Hathaway quite wealthy.

Other managers attempt to add value through fundamental research, but rather than focus on current financials such as assets and capital structure, these growth managers make educated guesses about the future. They attempt to add value by purchasing securities they believe to be undervalued as a result of other investors underestimating the company's future prospects. By any standards, adding value is a tough hurdle. Whenever the debate over passive and active management is encountered, the active proponents martial the few same names: Buffett and Lynch (and occasionally Neff and Templeton).

Market Timing

By market timing, I am referring to the traditional strategy of moving the portfolio allocation between equities and cash equivalents (e.g., T-bills) based on technical indicators. There have been innumerable studies of market timing and the vast majority conclude that the strategy cannot add value. I have mentioned, on numerous occasions, my belief that market timing does not work. Chapter 5, Client Education, included a number of tables, designed for client presentation, addressing the difficulties with market timing. As a last attempt to persuade any lingering timer to mend his ways, I will briefly discuss two interesting studies:

> Wells Fargo Study[1]–This study illustrates the patience needed to reap the benefits of even perfect foresight; a patience not in keeping with classic market timing. Using a crystal ball model with perfect accuracy, the study allocated investment funds to either bonds or stocks depending on the model's prediction of the asset class with the best expected five-year return. The model had perfect foresight, as the study used actual long-term future returns (i.e., the study was done in hindsight and used actual returns).
>
> The analyst found that over a 10-year period (1970 to 1979) the crystal ball portfolio outperformed the bond benchmark by 70 percent and the stock benchmark by 30 percent. However, for the first two years, the portfolio only matched the bond returns and underperformed stocks by 30 percent.
>
> SEI Study[2]–This study addresses a major conceptual failure of market timing. The consequences of a timing decision are not analogous to the flip of a coin. It results in 4, not 2, possible outcomes:

Actual Forecast	Success of the Forecast	Return Earned
Bull	Correct	Bull stock market return
Bull	Incorrect	Bull year with T-bill return
Bear	Correct	Bear year with T-bill return
Bear	Incorrect	Bear year with stock market return

In addition, there is much more room for error on the upside (i.e., a bull market) than in a bear market, as Table 12–1 demonstrates.

Missing the bull markets has such a significant impact that in order to match the buy-and-hold return of 9.4 percent, a market timer would have to correctly call the bull and bear markets 69 percent of the time, not 50.1 percent of the time. Factoring in a one-quarter delay for implementation (after all, it takes even the best timer some time to confirm a trend), the timer's accuracy would have to increase to an incredible 91 percent in order to match a buy-and-hold. The SEI analyst noted that timers frequently defend their strategy not on the basis of beating the market but rather as a "defensive strategy." Using this hypothesis, SEI found that if the timer accurately called 100 percent

T A B L E   12-1

Range of Returns

	1901–1990	
Asset Class	**57 Bull Years**	**33 Bear Years**
Stock	23.1%	−11.0%
T-Bills	3.6	4.2
Spread	19.5	15.2

of the bear markets and 50 percent of the bull markets, his return would have been 9.1 percent versus the buy-and-hold return of 9.4 percent!

I have completed my say on timing. But, for the reader who still wishes to beat the system, do not despair; there still may be a viable option, so read on about active asset allocation.

Active Asset Allocation

This is a strategy that adds value by managing the weights of investments relative to the normal policy. Active asset allocation may be further divided into three substrategies.

Policy Tilt   This is a strategy designed to add value by overweighting an investment class or style in order to take advantage of a perceived market anomaly. An example would be the overweighting of small-cap stocks in January to take advantage of the January effect. A more general example would be the permanent overweighting of the portfolio with low price/book stock. At this stage, strategies get fuzzy, as passive managers also use similar portfolio tilts. The difference is that active managers see themselves as taking advantage of a market anomaly overlooked by others and passive managers see themselves as accepting additional risk in order to take advantage of a different factor of market returns.

One quasi strategy that straddles market timing and portfolio tilt is sector rotation, i.e., the technique of tilting the portfolio in favor of market sectors that are expected to benefit most from the next economic wave.

Dynamic Asset Allocation*[3]   Dynamic asset allocation (DAA) is a term that evolved from the work on portfolio insurance by professors Leland and Rubenstein in 1976. The term itself was introduced as a service mark in 1981 for a firm they established to market the strategy. Based on arbitrage concepts, DAA is a mechanistic strategy designed to respond to market movements. The portfolio asset mix is constantly shifted between risky (e.g., stocks) and riskless (e.g., T-bills) assets. Unlike other active management strategies that attempt to increase returns, the value added by DAA is to "insure" the portfolio from declines below a floor value. A later version, known as Constant Proportion Portfolio Insurance (CPPI), was developed in 1986. CPPI has the advantage, compared to traditional portfolio insurance, of being simpler to implement and non-time-dependent.

Tactical Asset Allocation*[4]   Tactical asset allocation (TAA) is similar to DAA in that it requires periodic rebalancing. However, while DAA rebalances in order to avoid losses, TAA rebalances in order to enhance returns by shifting from relatively overvalued asset classes to relatively undervalued classes. DAA is thus reactive and TAA is proactive. As tactical allocators are typically move assets from overvalued areas (i.e., hot investment classes) to undervalued (i.e., underperforming) areas, the strategy is inherently contrarian.

Most TAA is based on the theoretical assumption that asset-class returns are mean reverting, i.e., their returns will fluctuate around equilibrium values. As a result, TAA requires only the limited forecasting ability that enables an allocator to determine if the current pricing is above or below equilibrium. Mean reversion will then generate the profits. A simple example of a TAA is the model shown in Table 12–2, designed by Kidder Peabody for a totally discretionary account.[5]

The model uses the following definitions:

Equity Risk Premium
   = Market Expected Return—Yield on 1-year T-bills
Bond Risk Premium
   = Spread between the yield on 5-year T-notes and 1-year T-bills

It assumes that markets over- and underreact to trading noise but that risk premiums will revert to their long-term means.

T A B L E   12–2

Kidder Tactical Asset Allocation Model

Equity Risk Premium	Stock Allocation	Fixed-Income Allocation	Bond Risk Premium	Bond Allocation	T-Bill Allocation
>5.5%	100%	0%			
5–5.5	75	25	>0.5%	100%	
4.5–5	50	50			
4–4.5	25	75	<0.5		100%
<4.0	0	100			

SUMMARY—IN FAVOR OF ACTIVE MANAGEMENT

The advantages of active management are:

▪ **Adding Returns and Minimizing Downside Risks**—These are the most frequently offered reasons for selecting active management. In a thoughtful article published by *Financial Planning Magazine* titled "Devising an Investment Philosophy," Lou Stanosolouvich wrote that he rejects passive management because it lacks the potential downside protection offered by active management and the ability to invest in the best portfolio managers who have outperformed their corresponding indexes over time.

▪ **Psychological Rewards**—Active management offers a number of psychological benefits.

1. The investor is a player. For example, an understated boast to a friend: "Oh yea, I made a little on my technology play."

2. The investor can get rich. For example: "Look at the 10-year record. If you invest now and compound at that rate, you will have a zillion dollars by the time you retire."

3. The investor is likely to feel brilliant or abused but never stupid. For example: "I have quite a record of selecting successful money managers." Or "I lost a bundle. That manager was a disappointment but I've replaced him with a real winner."

IN FAVOR OF PASSIVE MANAGEMENT

Proponents of passive management have no quarrel with the benefits proposed by active management. They simply do not believe that active management can deliver these benefits. Unquestionably, the most passionate (and most fun) critic of active management and defender of passive management is Rex Sinquefield, of DFA. In his well-known, understated way, he staked out his position in an address to participants at the 1995 Schwab National Conference:

> Active management does not make sense theoretically, isn't justified empirically, and doesn't work for your clients. Passive management stands on solid theoretical ground, has enormous empirical support, and works very well for your client.

Lest that seem a little strong, I will add the observation of Charles Ellis, a less fiery commentator, but no less eloquent:

> The investment management business . . . is built upon a simple and basic belief: professional money managers can beat the market. The premise appears to be false.[6]

The argument in support of passive management is based on three premises:

- Active management can best be described as "that dog don't hunt."*
- Passive management works. It does not result in average returns; it is analogous to shooting par in golf.**,***
- Investing is second only to health where you want life to be boring.

Specifically:

Efficient Markets

As noted earlier, passive management supporters point out that the question is not whether the market is totally efficient but is there a systematic

---

*My thanks to Cy Hornsby for this useful colloquialism.
**And my golfing friends tell me that par is *VERY* good.
***Goldman Sachs reported in their October 1995 *The Coming Evolution of the Investment
     Management Industry* that for 1, 3, and 5 year periods, equity managers outperformed the
     S&P 500 Index only 28.3% of the time (based on Plan Sponsor data).

way to find, after costs, a better security and/or portfolio. The answer is "no." On the average, Fama suggests, information moves so fast that the market knows more than any individual.[7]

Historical Returns

The active manager's use of historical returns and market anomalies assumes unusual behavior will repeat. Research suggests it does not. As many observers have suggested, active management based on historical returns is akin to driving forward by looking in a rear view mirror.

Gurus

Basic economics suggests that profitable quantitative investment analysis will not be commercialized. Successful research requires consistent detection of opportunities that others do not see. It is more profitable to take advantage of the research than to market the results.[8] Paul Samuelson acknowledges that some market gurus may exist but they are hard to find and expensive to rent.[9] And, if they exist, it's unlikely they will hire out to manage wrap accounts, or "small" (i.e., multimillion-dollar) portfolios. Active management supporters always reply with their mantra of Buffett and Lynch. Passive management defenders point out that there are tens of thousands of managers and the laws of probability predict that some will demonstrate outstanding performance due to chance. Statistically, no manager has a long enough track record to rule out luck as the basis for his success. Even if one was proven to be exceptional, how does the investor find the next Buffett or Lynch (in each asset class)?

Costs

The major hurdle active managers must leap is not beating a benchmark return but beating the cost of getting there. Charles Ellis provides a simple formula for calculating this threshold:[10]

> The Required Break-Even Return Relative to the Benchmark for Active Management
> = [(Turnover × Cost) + Management Fee + Target Return]/Market Return

> Using his example, assume:

Equities earn a historical rate of 10 percent.

Target return = market return.

Turnover equals a modest 30 percent.

The average cost of transaction (commission and spread) = 3 percent.

A modest management fee of 0.5 percent.

Break-Even Return = [(0.3 × 6) + 0.5 + 10]/10 = 12.3 = 123% of the benchmark

This is a useful calculation for the wealth manager to use when comparing active and passive management. However, keep in mind that as the formula ignores taxes, it is biased in favor of active management. An appropriate tax adjustment would be to add 25 to 75 basis points to the numerator.

Why has this active premium cost hurdle received so little attention? The answer is that investors (and investment professionals) have short memories and recent market returns have been historically high. During the last 10 years or so, market returns have compounded at around 15 percent. At this rate the hurdle drops by almost 40 percent. John Bogel of Vanguard, making a similar observation in a Vanguard publication,[11] notes that assuming an active management cost of 2 percent, it "eats up" only 1/8 of the returns of the 1980s and 1990s, but almost 20 percent of the long-term historical equity returns.*

Policy Drift

Actively managed funds often exhibit style, asset class and/or size drift, and active asset allocation result in asset class drift. The result of either form of drift is a portfolio that does not maintain a strategic balance.

In a paper titled "Diversification Returns and Asset Combination," published in the May/June 1992 issue of *Financial Analyst Journal,* Booth and Fama investigated the value of a passive, strategically balanced portfolio. Their conclusion should be considered by the wealth manager when making decisions regarding the use of active management (particularly active asset allocation) and when making decisions regarding a rebalancing policy:

---

*According to Ibbotson's *SBBI 1995 Year Book,* the return on Large-Company Stocks from 1926 to 1994 was 10.2 percent. A 2 percent management fee would represent 19.6 percent at that return.

Investors need a large premium to be willing to incur the additional uncertainty of active management. Recent studies indicate that investors cannot
expect such a premium.

Active management introduces so much uncertainty that we cannot document a premium return over benchmark returns. By contrast, fully diversified portfolios reliably increase portfolio compound returns through the
diversification process and eliminate 'benchmark risk.'

Loser's Game

Charles Ellis subtitled his book *Investment Policy, "How to Win the
Loser's Game."** He argues that investing, once a "winner's game," has
now become a "loser's game." In a winner's game, victory goes to the
participant winning more than others. In a loser's game, the outcome is
determined by the actions of the losers. A participant "wins" a loser's
game not by winning more; the system makes that impossible. He wins by
avoiding mistakes and letting other participants blunder. Examples of
"losers' games" other than professional investing include:

- War—Patton said, "Let the other poor dumb bastard lose his life
  for his country."
- Tennis—"The way to win is by making fewer bad shots."

Investing has become a loser's game because money managers are
no longer competing with amateurs; they are competing with themselves—they are the market. Since the old common sense rules do not apply, Ellis recommends the following guidelines for wealth managers:

- Stop searching for winners. "Only a sucker backs a 'winner' in
  the loser's game."
- "the real opportunity to achieve superior results is not in
  scrambling to outperform the market, but in establishing and
  adhering to appropriate investment policies over the long term."

RESEARCH–ACTIVE VERSUS PASSIVE

So much for the debate; what does the research on this issue conclude? I
will begin this section with the answer.

---

*Remember, this book is not only a "must-read"; it is a "must read frequently."

▪ The research concludes that both sides of the debate are right, that both sides are wrong, and that "it depends" or "it's impossible to reach a conclusion." In other words, there is a research study with a conclusion that will match any bias you may have.

The following synopsis of the research on active versus passive is included for two purposes:

▪ To alert the wealth manager, whatever his current bias, that neither active nor passive proponents have managed to "bury" their opponents based on practice or research. In spite of Rex's passion, there are academics and academically sound practitioners who beg to differ. And Buffett, Neff, Lynch, and the popular media notwithstanding, there are sophisticated real world practitioners who support the arguments in favor of passive investing.

▪ To provide the wealth manager with a background on the research available and the sources, so that he can complete his own due diligence on this important subject.

Academic and Quasi-Academic Research

The most comprehensive summary I have found of the academic research was included in "Does Historical Performance Predict Future Performance," by Ronald Kahn and Andrew Rudd, published in the November/December 1995 *Financial Analyst Journal* and the BARRA Newsletter.[12]

Studies in favor of the persistence of winners (i.e., the efficacy of active management) include:

Greenblatt and Titman—based on 157 mutual funds during the period 1975–1984.

Lehman and Modest—130 funds from 1968 to 1982.

Brown and Draper (United Kingdom)—530 pension managers from 1981 to 1990.

Hendricks, Patel, and Zeckhauser—165 funds from 1974 to 1988.

Goetzman and Ibbotson—728 funds from 1976 to 1988. This recent study, reported in *Financial Planning Magazine,* [13] concluded that performance ranking was important and that winners repeated with frequency when analyzed for three-year periods. However, their caveats noted that superior performance was relative to other active managers. The superior performers might not "beat the market." Also, the study did not consider risk (volatility).

Studies demonstrating that performance does not persist include: **Jensen**—115 funds, from 1945 to 1964. This was the seminal study that led to the familiar disclaimer "past performance is no guarantee of future performance," which every prospectus includes but few practitioners believe. Ibbotson and Goetzman referred to this as "the most influential article on the topic."[14]

Kutzman—10-year study of 32 fixed-income managers employed by the AT&T pension plan.

Dunn and Theisen—201 institutional portfolios, from 1973 to 1982.

Elton, Gruber, and Rentzler—51 commodity funds, from 1980 to 1987.

Kahn and Rudd found many potential problems with the earlier research—incomplete accounting for fund expenses and fees, survivorship bias, period-specific conclusions, and style variations. Their analysis adjusted for each of these factors. Their conclusions were encouraging for the passive camp. They wrote:

> For equity funds, the implications are simple. With no persistence of selection returns, unless you have another basis for choosing future winners (i.e., your selection criterion includes information other than historical performance), the solution is to index perhaps to a set of style indexes weighted to match your investment objectives.
>
> For fixed-income funds they found significant evidence of persistence. The appropriate use of historical performance information provided strong odds for beating the median. Unfortunately, fear and transaction costs reared their ugly heads, and the median had a negative selection return. They concluded, "The investment implications for fixed income funds, surprisingly, are similar to those for equity funds. Once again, index funds are a very attractive strategy."

Not referenced by Kahn and Rudd, but frequently reported, was a study by **Lakenishok, Schleifer, and Vishny** (LSV), titled "The Structure and Performance of the Money Management Industry."[15] Their results generally supported Kahn and Rudd. After almost 30 years, the research comes back to echo Jensen's conclusion: past performance is no guarantee of future performance.

Practitioner Research

Just like their academic brethren, the practitioner's results seem to support any conclusion one could wish. In the fall of 1995 Mobius revisited LSV, and after adjusting for problems they found with the earlier study, reevaluated the data and concluded that, both on a risk-adjusted and style basis, superior performance persisted.[16] Callan concluded that active management added a 135 basis point risk-adjusted premium for non-U.S. equity managers versus EAFE. However, they did acknowledge a significant variation among managers.[17] Frank Russell, on the other hand, reported that: "Given the wide range of previous statistical attempts to find persistence, it should come as no surprise that our data, likewise, support no such hypothesis."

John Bogle developed a number of tables demonstrating over various holding periods the failure of funds to maintain their superior rankings.* One of his more fun (and marketing-oriented) comparisons was *Bogle Tests the Forbes Honor Roll*. He found the following:

For the Period 1973–1990**

Honor Roll	12.2%
S&P 500	12.2%
Wilshire	12.4%

Dimensional Fund Advisors, having a bit of similar fun with their active manager competitions, provide me the following comparisons through the end of 1995:

Worth Magazine's "Best Mutual Funds," Selected November 1994

"Best Global Equity Fund"	Performance 12/31/94–12/31/95	Value Added
Worth: Warburg Pincus Int'l Equity	9.85	–2.42
DFA Large-Company International	13.05	
DFA International Value	11.49	

(continued)

---

*These tables are included in his book.
**This assumed a purchase of an equal amount of each honor roll fund each year with no fees or transaction costs.

Worth Magazine's "Best Mutual Funds," Selected November 1994—concluded

"Best Large-Cap Growth Fund"		
Worth: Fidelity Disciplined Equity	29.01	−8.07
DFA U.S. Large Cap	37.03	
"Best Large-Cap Value Fund"		
Worth: Mutual Beacon	25.89	−12.47
DFA U.S. Large-Cap Value	38.36	
"Best Small-Cap Growth Fund"		
Worth: Wasatch Aggressive Equity	28.12	−6.34
DFA U.S. 9-10	34.46	
"Best Small-Cap Value Fund"		
Worth: Heartland Value	29.80	+0.51
DFA U.S. Small-Cap Value	29.27	

Of all the practical research, the most interesting is from SEI.[18] They note that many of the more recent studies, when adjusted for style, reached not one but two conclusions. First, when using the S&P 500 as a benchmark, selection ability was statistically insignificant. Second, where performance was measured relative to each manager's appropriate style, selection ability was both positive and statistically significant. SEI's independent research confirmed these findings.

OK, once again, what's a poor, confused wealth manager to do? By now, you know I have an opinion.

My Opinion

On the one hand, the arguments in favor of passive management seem far too compelling to ignore. On the other hand, there are a number of problems associated with passive management (at least from the perspective of the wealth manager) that academics and institutional research do not address.

- There are a very limited number of passive funds available to the wealth manager and these are for a limited number of asset classes.
- Passive funds are designed to track a specific benchmark. The selection and management of that benchmark may be based on the vendor's intuition and may change (e.g., DFA Real Estate

Index originally included land development companies but was changed to include only REITS). Passive funds are not all science; there is plenty of room for art.

- Similar benchmark descriptions may mask fundamental differences in composition (e.g., whose definition of value).

- Many passive funds have moderate to high turnover and may not be especially tax efficient. For example:

Fund	Turnover
DFA Large-Cap Value	39%
Dreyfus-Wilshire Small Company Growth	110
Fidelity U.S. Bond Index	73
Schwab Small-Cap Index	24
Vanguard Total Bond Index	33
Vanguard Index Value	32

- Wealth managers deal with real retail clients. One of our responsibilities is to make our clients comfortable with their investment portfolio. At least today, many clients are incapable of being comfortable with an all-passive portfolio.

- Wealth managers are human. The research in favor of passive management is compelling but not overwhelming. Many of us are as attached to passionate money managers as is Don Phillips. We are unprepared to reject their possible contribution to our clients' well-being.

- Financial theory is not the only academic input of interest to the wealth manager. With our roots in financial planning, the contributions of behavioral psychology are important to us. For example, risk-adjusted performance is certainly important, but for some of our clients, so are bragging rights. We may be able to provide our clients performance with passive management, but not bragging rights. As an early commentator noted, "Each investment professional is responsible for his or her client's expectations."* Roger Gibson constantly reminds us to first manage our clients' expectations and then their portfolio.

---

*Fred Spence at the 1988 Institute of Chartered Financial Analysts Seminar "Serving the Individual Investor."

Balancing these conflicting issues is more of the art of wealth management. Too often the choice is presented as either/or. In fact, there is a third choice. We use both active and passive managers. In those asset classes and styles where we believe the passive manager has an advantage, we select him, in cases where the advantage is less clear and/or where we find an active manager with a persuasive philosophy and a passion, we select him.

Currently, our portfolios are approximately one-third passive and two-thirds active. In fixed income we use passive management at the low end of the maturity range and active managers at the intermediate end where the manager has more opportunity for implementing active strategies. In our equity allocations we use passive management for a core domestic equity position and for our value style allocations (more on that in the next section). We use active managers for our growth style and emerging market allocations. Our international-developed country allocation is two-thirds active and one-third passive value. Our real estate is split 50/50 active and passive.

STYLE—GROWTH VERSUS VALUE

HISTORY

On the surface, the issue of growth versus value style seems simple. Until recently it was not much of a discussion. If the client wanted growth, he was advised to look for high Beta (i.e., growth) managers and close his eyes to short-term volatility. If he couldn't sleep with volatility, then he should seek out stodgy, low Beta (i.e., value) managers and accept lower returns.

The investment world has changed and the old paradigm has been shattered. In order to understand how and why, it is important to know investment history. Graham and Dodd's *Security Analysis,* published in 1934, was the seminal event regarding the concept of intrinsic value in security pricing. As noted in Chapter 7, Investment Theory, Graham and Dodd emphasized balance sheet analysis and financial ratios as the technique for determining a firm's intrinsic worth.

Subsequently, researchers have investigated variations based on earnings projections rather than dividends, and the Price to Earnings (P/E) ratio has become a measure of prominence. For the 20-odd years following the publication of *Security Analysis,* investment professionals meandered along, many following the tenets of Graham and Dodd, others searching for market secrets in mystical chart patterns, and many simply using judgmental intuition (along with good sales skills). Then along came Harry Markowitz with MPT and William Sharpe with CAPM and Beta. The new market paradigm was "higher Beta=higher growth=higher returns." The once-sleeping giant of academia had awakened. Investment research, once a field only for academic dilettantes,* became a legitimate calling. One of the areas of interest to this new crop of investment theory academics was the study of market returns. Gene Fama and Ken French were two academics who joined forces to consider this question.

Fama and French

These two University of Chicago professors posed the following questions:

- Which of the many variables claiming to have some value in explaining market return, really did have value?
- Of those variables that had value, what subset provided the most information if they were all combined?

Their research was first released as a white paper, titled "Size and Book-to-Market Equity: Returns and Economic Fundamentals."[19] It was finalized and published as "Cross-Section of Variation in Expected Stock Returns," *Journal of Finance,* June 1992. Their conclusions, summarized in Tables 12–3 and 12–4, stimulated a debate that continues today.

The Fama/French research has become known as the three-factor model after the three factors (market risk, company size, and BtM ratio) that collectively explain 95 percent of the variability of expected market returns. By now you may be wondering what all of this has to do with the subject at hand—growth versus value. To paraphrase two of my favorite TV characters, Perry Mason and Ben Matlock, when they addressed the bench, "Just a minute, dear reader, I'm about to get to the point."

Implications for Portfolio Construction

Much to the dismay of many money managers, Fama and French concluded that Beta is a useless measure for explaining the variation of equity

---

*Remember Milton Friedman's comments regarding Markowitz's dissertation quoted in Chapter 7, "It's not math, it's not economics, it's not even business administration."

T A B L E   12-3

Summary of Fama and French Results
July 1963–December 1990

Factor(s)	Result
Beta	Not meaningful.
Size	Size is significant. Small stocks have higher standard deviations than large stocks.
Beta and size	Size is significant. Not only is Beta not meaningful, but it works in the wrong direction. Adjusted for size, low-Beta stocks have higher returns than high-Beta stocks.
Book value	Book value is significant. Stocks with high book-to-market (BtM) ratios have higher returns than stocks with low BtM ratios.
Leverage	Adjusted for book value assets, the smaller the company and the greater the book value of equity assets, the greater the stock return. Leverage is significant.
Earnings	Earnings are significant. Stocks with high-earnings yields (E/P) have higher returns than stocks with low-earnings yields.
Size and BtM	Both factors are significant, and in the same way as when each factor is considered separately.
Size, BtM, and earnings yield	Only size and BtM are significant when the three factors are taken together. Earnings yield is not meaningful.

returns. In other words, the statement, "Higher Beta portfolios are expected to have higher returns," is wrong. This conclusion led to an almost cottage industry of articles discussing, "Is Beta Dead?"* What is a poor wealth manager to do for higher returns if he can't search for high Beta managers? The answer is, concentrate on the Fama/French factors.

The first two factors are easy to accept. The market factor simply suggests that the higher the equity market commitment, the higher the returns. The second factor suggests that the higher the small-company

---

*The answer to that is it depends on whom you ask. The debate continues.

T A B L E   12-4

**Three Factors Determine the Majority
of an Equity Portfolio's Expected Return**
1964–1994

Market Factor	Size Factor	Style Factor
4.78%	4.03%	5.66%
All-Equity Universe	Small Stocks	High BtM
minus	minus	minus
T-bills	Large Stock	Low BtM

allocation in the equity portfolio, the higher the return. Also, as shown in Table 12–5, the higher return for the size factor is associated with higher standard deviation. This is consistent with the tenet of CAPM that higher returns are associated with higher systematic risk. The surprise in the Fama/French research was the third return factor—higher BtM. This is a measure typically associated with value, not growth investing. Also, the higher returns associated with the BtM factor were not associated with higher levels of systematic risk. Much of the debate regarding this high BtM factor (i.e., the value factor) centers on its lack of a theoretical underpinning.*

Whatever the cause, the conclusion remains the same. If the wealth manager wishes to invest his client's money for higher returns, he should seek value managers, not growth managers. Although the original research was based on domestic equities, subsequent research suggests that the value factor is universal.**

Harold's High-Tech Analysis

Perhaps the most persuasive argument in favor of investing in value for returns is simply to look at the historical return series. What got

---

*Fama and French argue that the higher returns must either be related to rewards for taking risks or inefficient pricing. Their tentative conclusion is that returns are risk related; however the specific risks are as yet unproven. In the journals, the debate continues.

**For example, a number of articles in *Financial Analyst Journal,* including "Car Fundamentals Predict Japanese Stock Returns," July/August 1993; "International Value and Stock Returns," January/February 1993; and "Value versus Growth Stocks: Book-to-Market-Growth and Beta," September/October 1994.

T A B L E   12–5

Investment Dimensions
1964–1994

	Large-Value Strategy	S&P 500 Index	Large-Growth Strategy	Small-Value Strategy	CRSP 6–10 Index	Small-Growth Strategy
Annualized Compounded Return	13.9%	10.2%	9.2%	17.4%	12.7%	11.7%
Annual Standard Deviation	16.9%	15.4%	16.9%	25.0%	26.1%	28.2%

my attention was comparing growth versus value returns over long periods and many cycles. You might try for yourself the technique I have named "Harold's High-Tech Analysis." It requires a piece of heavy paper, scissors, and DFA's "Investment Dimensions" matrix charts that provide historical return series for large and small, growth and value styles. With the charts in hand, make a template from the sheet of paper to lay at an angle over the chart and scan down the return matrix for similar series (e.g., large-cap growth and large-cap value) and different cycles (e.g., 1-year, 3-year, and 5-year). Figure 12–1 demonstrates the concept behind "Harold's High-Tech Analysis."

Figure 12–1 (Cycle Template Overlay) visually extracts the 3-year cycle performance for value stocks. Preparing a similar template for growth stock returns, makes it easy to compare returns.

After using the template to compare a number of the return series for growth and value, the constant dominance of the performance of value style over growth may not make you a total convert to Fama/French but it will certainly disabuse you of the notion that high returns and growth style are synonymous.

Although the Fama/French research (and the empirical comparisons I have suggested) make a strong case for investing solely in value securities, agreement on this conclusion is not unanimous, either in academia or in practice.

F I G U R E   12–1

| Value Stock Returns | Value Stock Returns with 3-Year Cycle Template Overlay |

Beginning of 19xx

Value Stock Returns — Beginning of 19xx

End of 19xx	50	51	52	53	54	55	56	57	58	59	60	61	62	63	64	65	66	67
50	2	3	1	4	3	2	3	3	1	2	4	3	3	4	1	3	2	3
51	1	4	3	2	3	3	1	2	4	3	3	4	1	3	2	3	4	3
52	2	4	3	4	4	5	2	3	4	4	3	1	2	5	3	4	2	1
53	3	5	6	4	3	2	3	3	1	2	4	2	3	4	1	3	2	3
54	1	2	3	4	4	2	4	2	2	4	4	2	1	4	3	2	3	3
55	1	3	4	5	9	1	4	3	3	6	4	3	2	5	2	4	2	2
56	3	6	5	4	3	3	2	3	2	3	4	4	2	3	1	4	3	3
57	2	4	4	3	2	3	3	1	2	4	5	9	1	4	3	2	3	4
58	2	2	3	1	4	3	2	3	3	5	4	3	3	4	2	6	6	5
59	3	4	1	4	3	1	3	3	4	4	3	2	3	5	3	1	4	4
60	1	4	3	2	3	2	3	5	5	3	1	4	3	2	3	4	3	2
61	2	5	2	4	4	4	3	2	3	1	4	3	1	3	4	5	2	4
62	2	3	1	2	2	5	2	4	2	3	2	3	2	4	3	2	4	3
63	1	4	3	4	2	3	1	4	3	3	4	2	4	3	2	1	3	3
64	2	4	2	5	1	4	3	2	3	2	3	2	4	3	3	5	3	4
65	3	5	3	3	2	4	2	6	4	3	2	1	4	2	1	2	3	2
66	1	2	3	2	3	5	3	1	4	5	1	3	2	1	3	3	4	3
67	1	3	4	4	1	2	3	4	4	2	4	2	6	2	3	5	5	2

Value Stock Returns with 3-Year Cycle Template Overlay — Beginning of 19xx

End of 19xx	50	51	52	53	54	55	56	57	58	59	60	61	62	63	64	65	66	67
50							3	3	1	2	4	3	3	4	1	3	2	3
51							1	2	4	3	3	4	1	3	2	3	4	3
52	2							3	4	4	3	1	2	5	3	4	2	1
53		5							1	2	4	2	3	4	1	3	2	3
54			3							4	4	2	1	4	3	2	3	3
55				5							4	3	2	5	2	4	2	2
56					3							4	2	3	1	4	3	3
57						3							1	4	3	2	3	4
58							2							4	2	6	6	5
59	3	4						3							3	1	4	4
60	1	4	3						5							4	3	2
61	2	5	2	4						1							2	4
62	2	3	1	2	2						2							3
63	1	4	3	4	2	5						2						
64	2	4	2	5	1	4	3						4					
65	3	5	3	3	2	4	2	6						2				
66	1	2	3	2	3	5	3	1	4						3			
67	1	3	4	4	1	2	3	4	4	2						5		

Issues to Consider

Inadequate Definition of Value

Even if a wealth manager accepts the concept of a value factor, there remains the problem of describing *value*. Value seems to be a classic case of, "in the eyes of the beholder." This reminds me of Peter Bernstein's story about the three baseball umpires describing how they define balls and strikes:

> The first umpire says, "I call them as I see them."
> The second umpire says, "I call them as they are."
> The third umpire says, "They ain't nothing 'til I call them."[20]

Fama and French used the simple BtM ratio as their measure. However, it is not the only choice. SEI research suggests a number of additional subclassifications of value:

- Relative dividend yield, i.e., yields > historical average.
- Low expectations—multifactors, e.g., price-to-book, price-to-earnings, dividends, "fallen angels."

T A B L E   12–6

Large-Cap Value Portfolios
Portfolio Statistics

	DFA Large-Cap Value Portfolio	SEI Large-Cap Value Index
Median Market Cap	1.8	2.9
Book-to-Market	0.8	1.8
Price-to-Earnings	11.0	20.1

These differences in definition can result in significantly different portfolio structures. As an example, study Table 12–6 and compare the statistics for DFA Large-Cap Value Portfolio with SEI Large-Cap Value Index.

Valuable Companies versus Valuable Stock

Another issue related to the definition of value is distinguishing between valuable companies and valuable securities. It is the stock that is priced by the market. Thus, the stock of a valuable company may be priced so high relative to the company's value, that there is no value in the stock (i.e., it is overpriced). Or a lousy company's stock may be so underpriced that even relative to its poor prospects, the stock may have value.

An interesting study that illustrated the see-saw relationship between a company's value and the value of its stock was based on the performance of two portfolios. Using the criteria in Tom Peters's bestseller *In Search of Excellence* as a standard for excellent companies, two portfolios were constructed, one of "excellent companies" and the other of "unexcellent companies" (e.g., poor earnings, negative net worth). The study compared the performance of a portfolio made up of the stock in "excellent" companies and a portfolio consisting of stock in "unexcellent" companies. During the period of the original study, 1981–1985, the unexcellent portfolio outperformed both the portfolio of excellent companies and the S&P 500. The conclusions were touted as a strong argument in favor of value investing. Unfortunately, the conclusions of the original study did not go unchallenged for very long. An update of the empirical work, by the same author, for the period 1987–1992, found that the excellent companies outperformed the unexcellent by 6 percent. So much for consistency of results.

Lack of Theory

Fama and French readily admit that the fundamentals driving the BtM effect are not well understood. Many academics argue that without a definite theory, the empirical results are interesting, but may simply be a chance blip in the data. Fisher Black, famous for the Black/Scholes option pricing formula, warns that the availability of market data provides a false sense of security and a temptation to data mine (i.e., search historical data for a period during which the data will "confirm" the researcher's conclusions). Black suggests that "Fama and French do not seem to believe much in theory."

Inadvertent Sector Concentration

Selecting securities solely with a value criterion might result in a portfolio overweighted in a few industries and underweighted in others.

Psychological

Value stocks are not very "pretty." Don Phillips quotes value managers, recalling, "the stocks that made a difference were the ones that make you want to hold your nose."[21] Gene Fama says that a value manager does not manage a portfolio, he manages a kennel, a kennel of "dogs." Hence, value investing runs afoul of the client's heuristics (e.g., fear of regret). If he buys a value stock and it goes down, what a dummy. If, however, he buys a stock in a good company that all the experts like (i.e., a growth stock) and it declines in price, it's either bad management or bad luck; no blame on him.

REAL WORLD PERFORMANCE–VALUE VERSUS GROWTH

The strongest argument against value investing is the history of real world returns. Growth managers achieve higher returns than value managers. What's the use of theory if it does not work in practice?

My first inkling of an answer came when I saw an analysis of style attribution for a large universe of value managers. All the managers clustered tightly around a neutral growth/value axis but about one-third showed a growth weighting exceeding their value weighting. In other words, they called themselves value managers but they either behaved like core-market managers or growth managers. It seems that even professional managers have trouble with their heuristics.

> Value managers attempt to add their value by carefully picking and choosing among the available pool of value stocks, selecting the best and rejecting the dead dogs. The result of their process seems to be that much of the value in value stocks gets screened out. The premium for the Fama/French high BtM factor seems to be largely attributable from those dead dogs that don't die. Evan Simonoff, editor of *Financial Planning,* wrote of one manager's avoidance of value stock.[22] "By definition they are highly speculative . . . That's the kind of investment a Saudi prince should make."

Morningstar

For me, the most important study concerning the failure of value managers to live up to the promise of extra returns attributable to the Fama/French value factor was John Rekenthaler's article, "Where Have All the Top Value Funds Gone?"* in the April 1995, *5-Star Investor Newsletter.* In the article, Rekenthaler notes that many academics and practitioners claim that the way to great returns is to buy value. He adds:

> There's only one catch: It doesn't work that way in the mutual-fund industry. Value investing may dominate the academic studies, but it sure doesn't dominate the fund performance charts.

Based on 5-, 10-, and 15-year periods, Morningstar studies concluded that growth funds outperformed value funds. Rekenthaler then asks, "Who is to blame?"

> If growth funds have performed unexpectedly well relative to value funds given the academic evidence, then either growth funds have been especially well-run or value fund managers have failed in some fashion.

Morningstar addressed this question by preparing Tables 12–7 and 12–8, reproduced on the next page. The tables compared the performance of growth and value-style funds with that of similarly labeled Wilshire stock indexes for various periods through February 28, 1995. A negative number indicates that the funds trailed the indexes by that amount.

---

*The *5-Star Investor* is one of two newsletters I regularly read. Although I consider the fund statistics of little value, the commentary alone is worth the price of admission.

T A B L E   12–7

Growth-Style Funds versus the Indexes: A Draw?

	5-Year Excess Total Return	10-Year Excess Total Return	15-Year Excess Total Return
Large Growth	−1.31%	−1.37%	−0.54%
Mid Growth	−2.73	−0.78	−0.44
Small Growth	−1.26	−1.10	−1.19

T A B L E   12–8

Value versus the Indexes: Not Even Close

	5-Year Excess Total Return	10-Year Excess Total Return	15-Year Excess Total Return
Large Value	−0.3%	−2.87%	−3.75%
Mid Value	−3.90	−3.26	−4.99
Small Value	−2.41	−4.19	−7.86

The failure of growth managers to match their index benchmark is in line with what one might expect for average, after-expense performance. The magnitude of the failure of value managers is staggering. Rekenthaler concludes by suggesting that the tables demonstrate that investors seeking the most profitable funds over the long haul may need to attempt something more complex than simply seeking those funds with the cheapest, ugliest portfolios.

To supplement his conclusion, Rekenthaler includes examples of underperforming managers he assumes to be value managers (specifically the AAII's shadow stock and DFA's 9-10 Small Cap). The assumption, however, is incorrect. These funds were not designed to be "value" funds as defined by Fama, French, and others. The AAII Shadow Stock uses criteria other than BtM (e.g., institutional holdings) and the DFA 9-10 is solely based on a size criterion. I found the statistics in the Morningstar article compelling, but the conclusions misleading.

I believe that the underperformance of the active value managers is due to two factors:

T A B L E   12–9

DFA Value Funds
Value versus the Indexes: Passive Wins

	5-Year Excess Total Return	10-Year Excess Total Return	15-Year Excess Total Return
DFA Large Value	1.75%	0.82%	–0.19%
DFA Small Value	0.87	–0.90	–2.43

- Their efforts to add value by eliminating the "dogs," in fact, subtracts value by eliminating the real value stocks.
- By their very nature, value stocks, particularly small-cap value stocks, have relatively large trading spreads; therefore, active management of a value portfolio generates significant trading costs.

Contrary to Rekenthaler's conclusion, the solution to participating in the benefits of value investing is not to search for more complexity. It is just the opposite. Search for greater simplicity. Eliminate the active management, thereby avoiding the errors of active value management as well as saving the management fee and the transaction costs. Morningstar's analysis, extended to include the DFA value funds, supports this conclusion. Table 12–9 shows that the DFA funds, in almost all cases, nearly matches or exceeded the index returns.

DFA

Weston Wellington, director of research financial advisor service, for DFA, provided another excellent example of the efficacy of this solution in his commentary on an article from *The Wall Street Journal* which quoted Scott Lummer's (managing director of Ibbotson) suggestions for 5 small cap value managers. Wellington's response was to compare the performance of these active managers to DFA's value portfolios. Tables 12–10 and 12–11 compare the returns of each of the active managers, since inception and for 1995:*

---

*The DFA return series includes simulated data for periods prior to the live DFA portfolio. As the simulated return series is adjusted for transaction costs and based on a passive, not actively managed portfolio, I believe it to be a credible benchmark.

T A B L E   12-10

Active Management:
Amount of Value Added from Inception

Name	Fund Inception	Begin Date	End Date	Annualized Return	DFA Small Cap	Value Added
FAM Value	1/1/87	1/87	12/95	13.1%	14.6%	−1.5%
Lazard Special Equity	1/16/86	2/86	12/95	11.9	14.7	−2.8
Pennsylvania Mutual	12/12/62	1/76*	12/95	17.7	21.6	−3.9
Royce Value	12/31/82	1/83	12/95	12.7	17.5	−4.8
T. Rowe Price (SCV)	6/30/88	1/88	12/95	13.4	15.2	−1.8

*Due to data availability

T A B L E   12-11

Active Management:
Amount of Value Added for 1995 (all live data)

FAM Value	19.7%	29.3%	− 9.6%
Lazard Special Equity	16.3	29.3	−13.0
Pennsylvania Mutual	18.7	29.3	−10.6
Royce Value	18.7	29.3	−10.6
T. Rowe Price (SCV)	29.3	29.3	0.0

MY CONCLUSIONS AND RECOMMENDATIONS

I find the argument in favor of value so compelling that, as reflected in our optimization constraints, we weight our domestic equity style allocations two-thirds value and one-third growth. Our international allocations explicitly call for one-third value.

Regarding the implementation of value investing, the wealth manager should consider passive management. After reading Rekenthaler's Morningstar *5 Star* article on the value fund performance/underperformance "mystery," I wondered how our active value managers would fare in a similar comparison. I went through an exercise very much like Wellington prepared for his response to the *Journal* article. However, instead of comparing DFA value funds to the Lummer's recommendations, I compared DFA's value portfolio performance to that of the active value managers we selected for our clients' portfolios.

My analysis considered "inception to date," numerous cycles, and risk-adjusted returns. Much to my astonishment, the results looked very much like Wellington's. DFA won hands down and across the board. Add to DFA's performance premium the inherent tax advantage of passive management and the elimination of style drift risk and it was an easy decision for our investment committee to conclude that our value allocations would largely be passive. I recommend that every wealth manager make a similar analysis of his value allocations and compare the performance of his active value managers to passive value managers.

STYLE ANALYSIS/FACTOR ANALYSIS

Don't blame me if, once again, you get confused because the same terms are used to describe different concepts. I didn't start the problem, so all I can do is help the wealth manager move through the shifting vocabulary so he can understand the substance of the concepts. Having said my piece, let's start with Table 12–12. It attempts to make some sense out of this mish-mash and it is followed by my definitions of these confusing terms. The superscripts are included to distinguish between different concepts described by the same name (e.g., factor analysis) or terms that include many concepts (e.g., style analysis).

Having defined my terms in Table 12–12, I will narrow the discussion of style analysis to style analysis^G, i.e., return-based style analysis. In order to minimize the confusion, for the balance of the discussion I will use the phrase *return analysis* to describe style analysis^G. When most commentators use the expression *style analysis,* they are referring to return analysis. This is a growth industry, one the wealth manager must understand.

BENEFITS

One obvious question is, why bother? The benefits attributed to return analysis are many. In fact, according to some proponents, they almost approach guaranteeing wealth. The following are some benefits of return analysis:

- Helps analyze the size and location of a manager's selection/style bets.

T A B L E   12-12

The Universe of Style Analysis[A]

Philosophy	Name	Sub-Class	Also Known As	Example
Open the hood and look inside at the Portfolio.	Portfolio[B]	Positions	Fundamental Qualitative[C]	Wealth manager with a green eyeshade
		Mathematical	Fundamental Factor[D]	Morningstar Style Box
If it walks like a duck, quacks like a duck, it is a duck.	Statistical Factor[E]	Style-Style[F]		DFA
		Style Analysis[G]	Returns Analysis[G]	Sharpe/Ibbotson

Style Analysis[A] This is the generic use of the term *style analysis*. It describes all of the techniques used for determining the nature of a portfolio. Includes those terms with superscripts B–F.

Portfolio Style Analysis[B] Techniques of style analysis based on an evaluation of the actual portfolio. Includes fundamental qualitative and fundamental factor analysis. Includes terms with superscripts C and D.

Fundamental Qualitative Analysis[C] A detailed review of the portfolio's actual positions, position by position.

Factor Analysis.[D, E, F, and G] Techniques of style analysis that attempt to relate risk and return in terms of one or more financial or economic characteristics. Includes those terms with superscripts D–G.

Fundamental Factor Analysis[D] A mathematical form of portfolio style analysis. Unlike other forms of factor analysis, it does not depend on time series data but rather statistical measurements of stock attributes that are deemed related to performance (e.g., size, BtM). Similar to balance sheet analysis, fundamental factor analysis reviews snapshots of portfolio composition. It has an intuitive appeal, the advantage of simplicity, and the disadvantage of lack of discrimination (i.e., many blend portfolios). This is the basis for the Morningstar style boxes.

Statistical Factor[E] Based on a time series regression. Includes terms wth superscripts F and G.

Style-Style[F] A form of statistical factor analysis employed by DFA and SEI based on time series analysis that defines a manager's orientation relative to size and value factors.

Style Analysis[G] A returns-based statistical factor analysis developed by William Sharpe.

- Sees beyond the obvious (i.e., what the manager owns) to the hidden economic exposure of the portfolio (e.g., the interest rate risk of a utility stock).
- Provides insight regarding the contribution of a manager's security selection and asset allocation skills.
- Helps monitor style drift.
- Distinguishes between good and lucky managers. Avoids hiring bad lucky managers or firing unlucky good managers.
- Assists in coordinating multimanager portfolios by exposing gaps and overlaps in asset-allocation mixes.

CONCEPT

Return analysis, as popularized by Sharpe, analyzes the pattern and consistency of a manager's returns, over time, compared to various style benchmarks. The analysis provides measures of the portfolio's exposure to economic influences. The result is not the snapshot of fundamental factor analysis but rather a watercolor picture (i.e., having fuzzy shading) of the portfolio's shifting exposure to economic currents. Returns-based analysis assumes that the economic effect of an investment is no less important than the investment itself;[23] hence, it is concerned with how a fund behaves economically.

Unlike other techniques, it distinguishes between the contribution of the style and the contribution of the manager. As explained by Sharpe:

> Once you're in a fund you want to look at performance. It [return analysis] may not predict the future but you sure as hell want to know what you've been getting and why you've been getting it. So it's very important to know if a manager has done badly for you whether it's because it was his style (which is your fault because you picked him knowing his style) or whether he's done badly, given his style (in which case it's his fault).[24]

PROCESS

Return analysis begins with the selection of a set of style-specific benchmarks. The benchmarks should represent all possible aspects of the portfolio to be analyzed. As an example, Sharpe uses a palette of 12 benchmarks.

William Sharpe's Style Benchmarks[25]

Large-Cap Value	T-bills
Large-Cap Growth	Intermediate Government
Medium Cap	Long-Term Government
Small Cap	Corporate
European Stock	Mortgage Related
Japanese Stock	Non-U.S. Bonds

The next step is to develop an adequate historical time series of returns for each benchmark and for the portfolio to be analyzed. The period should cover an economic cycle. Sharpe's calculations include 60 monthly returns. With data in hand, the Sharpe model utilizes a modified multiple-regression algorithm. The modifications of the regression equation are intended to eliminate a number of potential problems.[26]

▪ Unconstrained, the solution will not add to 100. As the goal is to determine the portfolio's total exposure to all style benchmarks, a constraint to 100 is consistent with 100 percent portfolio allocation. Therefore, the Sharpe model constrains the sum of all the factors to 100 percent.

▪ Adding only the constraint that all factors must sum to 100 still leaves open the possibility of a portfolio allocation in excess of 100 percent due to the possibility of short positions. As Sharpe believes that short positions are inconsistent with most portfolios, he adds a second constraint that each style factor must be ≤100 percent. According to Sharpe, his modified constrained quadratic program algorithm loses little in explanatory value.

RESULTS

Sharpe very pointedly warns users of his algorithm (and by extension, users of any form of return analysis) that the conclusions are tentative and the user should "proceed at his own peril."

The following are a few examples of observations Sharpe makes from style analysis results:

▪ Trustees Co-mingled U.S. Fund—Compared to the S&P it underperformed by 10 percent. Compared to its benchmark, it only underperformed by 3 percent. The manager favored small cap and value. Most of his underperformance was attributed to the underperformance of the asset classes (i.e., investors' responsibility).

▪ Utility Funds

Selection	Style
41%	59%

Asset Class	Factor
Intermediate Bonds	18%
Long Bonds	32
Mortgage Backed	5
Value Stock	42

- Utilities funds tend to concentrate in one industry. As a result there is relatively little style influence. Although utility funds largely hold equities, their return behavior reflects a significant exposure to the economic factors influencing bond returns.

SOURCES OF STYLE ANALYSIS

There are numerous sources for style analysis and many vendors indicate they are working on offerings. Today, the most economically available to the wealth manager are:

William Sharpe via Internet http://gsb-www-stanprd.edu/ ~wfsharpe/ls100.htm

Although there are a limited number of managers covered, for browsing, the price is right. The site also includes a great deal of informative background information.

Advisor Software http://www.advisorsw.com

Individual fund investment style analysis (based on the work of Sharpe) is available, free of charge, on the net. The firm's Style Data software, providing style analysis for over 4000 funds can be ordered on the net.

CDA Technologies

The style analysis, provided by Optima, is for a single point in time; however, it is part of CDA's Hysales program and is a useful supplement.

Ibbotson Style Analysis

Beautiful "watercolor," CD-ROM-based graphics. Downside is cost, limited coverage, and lack of flexibility (you cannot do your own analysis) but still, a disk that belongs in every wealth manager's office. Other more powerful, but less affordable systems include those developed by BARRA and Mobius.

OBJECTIONS TO STYLE ANALYSIS

One of the more interesting aspects of wealth management is that for every colorful pro there is an equally colorful con. In this case, if William Sharpe is cast as the champion of style analysis, John Rekenthaler and Don Phillips are the champions of the critics.

Lowering his lance and charging full tilt, Rekenthaler says:

Style analysis is fun, easy to use, colorful and miscast. Too often, it's being billed as the lead action of fund analysis, a 'revolutionary' technique using 'sophisticated' software . . . In reality, it's Jack Palance, not Jack Nicholson. Like a good character actor style analysis can enrich the show, but it can't drive the plot.

More specifically, the objections to style analysis include:

- It is intuitively uncomfortable. Style analysis only looks at the shell. It does not look 'under the hood.' Basically, it is a black box.
- There are no standards for benchmarks.
- There are some asset classes for which there is either limited or no historical data.
- It is only an estimation of reality. Morningstar argues that if fund portfolio data were available monthly, style analysis would no longer be needed.
- It measures past exposures, not necessarily current ones.
- It is blind to style dynamics. It fails to capture the true style of eclectic and flexible style managers (e.g., momentum managers).

MY CONCLUSIONS AND RECOMMENDATIONS

Although I agree with Rekenthaler and Phillips that style analysis is not the gold at the end of the rainbow, I disagree with their general rejection of the technology. Style analysis supplements portfolio analysis; it is neither a replacement nor an alternative. Contrary to Rekenthaler's contention that style analysis "assumes that the blend pretty much depicts the fund's holdings," it assumes that the blend reflects the economic exposure of the portfolio, a quite different but nevertheless useful body of information. The fact that technology is uncomfortable does not necessarily mean that it is useless. It reminds me of Harry Warner's (Warner Brothers) quote: "Who the hell wants to hear actors talk?"

Using the "looking under the hood" analogy, I do not have to be a mechanic or know the differences between fuel injection systems, gas mixes, piston ratios, and so on to reach some valid conclusions regarding race cars and drivers if I have an extensive historical record of their success in past races. That there are no standards for benchmarks is a challenge, not a barrier. Look back to the discussion on optimizer input and Ibbotson's efforts at dealing with just such issues for examples of intelligent and artful solutions.

Style analysis is an estimate of a form of reality. Even if wealth managers have monthly position reports, style analysis can provide value. For example, how much is a domestic stock portfolio likely to be influenced by the foreign equity market as a result of the domestic firms' international business ventures? Style analysis supplements; it doesn't replace. The fact that returns analysis fails to capture useful information regarding eclectic and flexible style managers is only a problem when the wealth manager has an interest in evaluating such a manager. As most funds are selected to implement investments in style-specific asset classes, the wealth manager will rarely hire an eclectic manager.*

I believe that a wealth manager must use all the tools and techniques available to him in order to both select and monitor managers to implement his clients' policy. Those techniques include portfolio position analysis, portfolio mathematical analysis, style-style analysis, and return analysis (i.e., Sharpe style analysis). As with optimization, the caveat is that the wealth manager should not employ style analysis as a 'black box' solution. He must understand the concept of the mathematics and dynamics driving the style analysis before incorporating its results into his selection process.

Now, having had such fun picking on Phillips and Rekenthaler regarding factor analysis, I have to 'fess up. For serious manager evaluation, portfolio style analysis should be the primary analytical tool; return style analysis is secondary. The same recommendation holds true for the ongoing evaluation of a wealth manager's approved managers. In addition, return style analysis should never be the sole criterion for firing a manager. It should only serve as an additional tool for monitoring style consistency. Any significant deviations need to be further investigated by portfolio analysis. Our most common use for return analysis is to review the style consistency of managers we do not follow but who may be part of a prospect's portfolio.

---

*Of course there are exceptions. We did make up a whole special "asset class" just to be able to include Jean-Marie of Sogen.

ENDNOTES

1. Janice L. Deringer and Lawrence G. Tint, "Development and Implementation of a Tactical Asset Allocation Model at Wells Fargo," *Global Asset Allocation,* John Wiley & Sons, Inc., 1994, 234–236.

2. SEI Capital Resources, *Position Paper: The Asset Allocation Decision,* April 1992.

3. Mark Kritzman, *Asset Allocation for Institutional Portfolios,* Business One Irwin, 1990, 92–104; Robert Arnott and Frank Fabozzi, editors, *Asset Allocation A Handbook of Portfolio Policies, Strategies and Tactics,* Probus, 1988; J. S. Parsons, "Incorporating Options Technology into Asset Allocation", Scott L. Lummer, PhD, CFA and Mark W. Riepe, "Introduction: The Role of Asset Allocation in Portfolio Management," p. 3, *Global Asset Allocation,* John Wiley & Sons, Inc., 1994, 97–100; Charles DuBois, "Tactical A.A.: A Review of Current Techniques," *Citicorp Investment Management,* 283–336.

4. Mark Kritzman, *Asset Allocation for Institutional Portfolios,* Business One Irwin, 1990, 48–59; Arnott and Fabozzi, Probus, 1988; Scott L. Lummer, PhD, CFA and Mark W. Riepe, *Global Asset Allocation,* 3–4; E. K. Easton Ragsdale and Gita Rao, "Tactical Asset Allocation at Kidder, Peabody," *Global Asset Allocation,* 208–225; James D. Macbeth and David C. Emanuel, "Tactical Asset Allocation: Pros and Cons," *Financial Analysts Journal* (November/December) 1993, 30–43; DuBois, "Tactical A. A.," 283–336.

5. E. K. Easton Ragsdale and Gita R. Rao, "Tactical Asset Allocation at Kidder, Peabody," *Global Asset Allocation,* 208–225.

6. Charles D. Ellis, "The Loser's Game," *Classics An Investor's Anthology,* 524–535.

7. Peter Bernstein, *Capital Ideas,* Free Press, 1992, 136.

8. H. Russell Fogler, "Investment Analysis and New Quantitative Tools," *Journal of Portfolio Management* (Summer) 1995, 39–47.

9. Bernstein, *Capital Ideas,* 143

10. Ellis, "The Loser's Game," *Classics An Investor's Anthology,* 532–533.

11. The Vanguard Group, *Selecting Equity Mutual Funds Conference Paper* (Chicago: June 14, 1991), 1–14.

12. Ronald Kahn and Andrew Rudd, "Does Historical Performance Predict Future Performance?" *BARRA Newsletter.*

13. Roger Ibbotson & William Goetzmann, "History Does Repeat Itself," *Financial Planning* (February 1995), 95–96.

14. Ibid.

15. Josef Lakonishok, Andrei Shleifer, Robert W. Vishny, *The Structure and Performance of the Money Management Industry,* Brookings Papers: Microeconomics, 1992, 339–391.

16. Mobius Group, Inc., *Mobius Strip,* Vol. 2, No. 5 (Fall) 1995, 1–12.

17. Callan Letter. (Spring) 1995, 4–9, 13–14.

18. SEI Corporation, *SEI Equity Portfolio Structure: Large Captitalization Value,* 1994, 1–19.

19. Eugene F. Fama and Kenneth R. French, "Size and Book-to-Market Equity: Returns and Economic Fundamentals," *Draft Paper,* 1992, 1–33.

20. Peter Bernstein, *Capital Ideas,* 117.

21. Evan Simonoff, "Value. Why Funds Can't Find It," *Financial Planning,* (July) 1995, 38–44.

22. Ibid.

23. *Fee Advisor,* "Returns-Based Style Analysis" (September/October) 1995, 43–44.

24. *Investment Advisor,* "A Matter of Cost and Style" (October) 1994, 83–89. *Financial Planning Journal,* "Measuring Risk" (September) 1995, 56–68.

25. William F. Sharpe, "Asset Allocation Management Style and Performance Measurement," *The Journal of Portfolio Management,* 18, No. 2 (Winter 1992), 7–19.

26. Ibid.

CHAPTER 13

Manager Selection and Evaluation— Selection Process

Stars tend to twinkle a lot.

—Gary Helms

Asset allocation and the optimization process build a multiasset class portfolio based on specific assumptions regarding an asset class's expected return, standard deviation, and correlations. It is critical, in the selection of individual managers, that the fund's MPT characteristics match the assumptions made for its asset class. It is not enough to rely on the nomenclature of the mutual funds themselves. As noted earlier, fund descriptions such as "aggressive growth" and "growth & income" may have little meaning when selecting managers to implement an optimized portfolio. Once the wealth manager has determined which asset class and strategies he will use in his practice, he can begin the manager selection process. The following discusses the process we use in determining those managers to include in our approved list.

EVENSKY'S MANAGER SIEVE*

This technique for selecting a manager is a variation of the Evensky Sieve method described earlier for selecting capital needs software. In this case,

---

*The following screens are general guidelines. If an exceptional manager comes to our attention and he does not pass Screens #1 and #2, we will still pass him on to be tested by Screen #3.

the sieve is designed to screen out inappropriate and unsuitable managers. Because there are thousands of managers to select from, the Manager Sieve requires multiple screens. A brief description of these screens is illustrated and followed by recommendations for specific criteria to be used in each screen.

▪ Screen #1

This first pass eliminates thousands of inappropriate managers. The process requires that the wealth manager screen the available list of managers against his selected asset classes. For example, if he restricts his choice of managers to those participating in the Charles Schwab One Source program, he would overlay the One Source list with his selected asset classes. The funds passing that screen would include only One Source funds that matched the asset classes used in his firm's allocations. If, for example, he did not use sector funds, their past performance, risk profile, and expense structure would be irrelevant and they would not pass his screen.

▪ Screen #2

Like Screen #1, this is a global screen, i.e., it is applied across the board to all of the managers remaining in the selection pool after having passed Screen #1. The criteria in Screen #2 are what I call fatal flaws. Screen #1 eliminated inappropriate but possibly "good" funds. Screen #2 is intended to eliminate generically "bad" funds. Naturally, the criteria for generically bad is the responsibility of the wealth manager. An example of such a criterion is a maximum expense ratio.

▪ Screen #3

This screen is applied to each group of funds, asset class by asset class. It is based on a manager selection model suggested by Robert Ludwig of SEI, which I call "Ludwig's 3 Ps."[1] The premise of the model is that manager performance is an "output." Manager evaluation should not focus on performance but on the critical "input factors" that result in the performance output. These factors are Philosophy, Process, and People. Screen #3 filters out managers based on these 3 Ps.

▪ Screen #4

Now, after the universe of available managers has been whittled down to the relatively few remaining after passing through Screens #1 to #3, I apply the test of performance. It is applied asset class by asset class.

SCREEN #1

As noted earlier, the screening process begins with the universe of available funds. At our firm, we generally begin with the no-load funds available through Charles Schwab. This includes the Schwab retail and advisor, regular and One Source funds, as well as those load funds offered to the clients of advisors at net asset value.

Selecting Funds by Asset Class

This is our first filter. Using our asset class taxonomy as detailed in Chapter 4, Data Gathering, we eliminate thousands of managers from consideration. For example, our criteria eliminates all long-term and low-quality fixed-income funds, global fixed-income and equity funds, specialty funds, convertible funds, and aggressive growth funds.

Selecting Funds by Capitalization Class

This criterion narrows down the pool of appropriate managers by eliminating those funds that do not meet our required capitalization criteria. Table 13–1 shows how capitalizations relate to market decile (it is worth noting that a $1 billion cap would place a company in the fourth decile).

A significant decision required of the wealth manager is to determine whether the criteria he chooses to select a manager's capitalization class will be average capitalization or median capitalization.* For example, Morningstar uses median and Value Line uses average. I recommend that the wealth manager use the median. We eliminate from consideration any manager who purports to be a small-cap manager but has a portfolio median capitalization in excess of $1 billion.

Selecting Funds by Style

At this stage of the process, we use a style screen based on the portfolio style analysis used by Morningstar. This standard will pass a number of managers who have a weak style orientation and/or managers who do not remain consistent to their style. I am not concerned, as Screen #3 will later eliminate any managers I may consider wishy-washy. In the early

---

*The median for the stock on the NYSE is under $700 million; the average is closer to $9 billion.

T A B L E   13-1

Size as Defined by NYSE Market
Capitalization Deciles

	Market Capitalization Deciles	Size ($MM)	NYSE Largest Company	Number of Companies		
				NYSE	AMEX	Natl NASDAQ
Large	1	75730	Exxon Corporation	204	4	17
	2	5088	Tenneco Inc.	204	5	31
	3	2271	Westvaco Corporation	204	9	53
	4	1160	Perkin Elmer Corp.	204	15	76
	5	721	Micron Technology Inc.	204	20	112
Small	6	438	Rollins Truck Leasing	204	25	172
	7	270	Unifirst Corp.	204	40	244
	8	172	Zenith Electronics Corp.	204	80	386
	9	98	Offshore Pipelines Inc.	204	97	453
	10	56	General Housewares Co.	204	507	1234

DFA Data 12/31/92

stage of the analysis, I would rather err on the side of passing an unacceptable manager through the screen than inadvertently rejecting a good manager.

SCREEN #2

These are the criteria that a wealth manager considers mandatory. For example, we apply the following criteria:

Concentration

We do not believe in the use of sector funds. We are concerned with excessive sector concentration. In order to avoid such managers, we screen out funds with sector weightings in excess of three and one-half times that of the S&P 500. For international equity funds we screen for weightings in excess of 35 percent for any country ex-Japan. The fund is eliminated in Screen #2 if the allocation to Japan exceeds 150 percent of Japan's weighting in the EAFE index.

T A B L E   13–2

Expenses and Returns

	Expense Ratios All Funds	<$500 Mil.	>$500 Mil.	5-year Total Return through 5-30-92
Pure No-Load	1.19	1.27	0.80	8.34%
No-Load w/12b-1	1.80	1.83	1.37	8.39
Front Load	1.48	1.57	0.97	8.49
Back Load	2.26	2.34	1.79	7.31

Quality

In keeping with our focus on high-quality, fixed-income investments, Screen #2 eliminates those funds with less than an average bond quality rating of A.

Foreign Equities

As we believe that the asset class allocation is a critical factor in the long-term performance of the portfolio, we are hypersensitive regarding managers who drift from their style. At the stage of Screen #2 we eliminate domestic equity managers who have allocations in excess of 20 percent in foreign equities.

Expenses

If future returns revert back to the mean of long-term historical returns, as we believe likely, then a fund's expenses will be one of the primary determinants of its performance for the next decade. Funds that are able to control costs and manage expenses will, all else being equal, outperform their peers that are burdened by higher expenses. A 1.5 percent expense ratio on an equity fund that earns 10 percent means that 15 percent of the return is lost to expenses. Table 13–2 shows the impact of expenses on performance.

Based on our belief that even the best of managers cannot overcome the hurdle of excessive expenses, we generally eliminate all fixed-income funds with expense ratios in excess of 0.8 percent, domestic equity funds with expense ratios in excess of 1.2 percent, and international equity (developed countries) funds with expense ratios in excess of 1.5 percent, and emerging market funds in excess of 2 percent.*

Performance Record

In spite of all of the research and the traditional warning that "past performance is no guarantee of future performance," most investors begin the manager selection process by starting with the manager's past performance. Evensky's Manager Sieve, with one exception, does not seriously consider performance until after Screen #3. The exception is the elimination of poor performers at this stage. The traditional warning actually misstates the results of many studies.

A more accurate statement describing the results of the research would be that past superior performance does not guarantee future superior performance; however, past poor performance may predict future poor performance.** As a result, we screen out those funds that have performed in the bottom half of their asset class for the last 5 years and/or the bottom third for the last 3 years.

"Soft Sieves"

The following criteria do not automatically eliminate funds in Screen #2. They are applied to each of the funds passing the screen. The decision to eliminate a fund based on these soft criteria is made by the investment committee case by case.

Fund Capitalization

There are different schools of thought about the ideal size of a mutual fund. One says that "bigger is better"—the more assets, the more a fund can benefit from economies of scale, in administration and other expenses, brokerage costs, etc. Also, a small fund may lack the buying power necessary to command a large enough share of the choicest stock issues, especially IPOs. (This has occurred among real estate mutual

---

*I consider these generous standards; however, at this stage I would still rather err on the side of passing through a manager I might later reject than reject a manager I should have considered.
**The consistency of poor performance seems to be related primarily to excessive fund expenses, not incompetent management skills.

funds, where the smaller funds may not be able to obtain positions in new REITs.) On the other hand, some studies (including a Morningstar 1992 analysis) have indicated that the promised economies of scale often never materialize.

As funds increase assets, the manager may find it difficult to find stocks meeting his investment criteria. This may cause the manager to purchase equities outside his guidelines, or to hold large sums of cash. Both problems can negatively impact performance. However, the stupendous growth of some successful funds, such as Fidelity's Magellan Fund, belie this belief.

In addition to the absolute size of the fund capitalization, it is important to study the history of a fund's growth in assets. Has the fund lost assets over the past few years? Why? Has the fund grown too rapidly over the past few years? Many funds solve the problem of rapid growth and large influxes of cash by closing to new investors. Part of the art of fund selection is to evaluate the credibility (or lack thereof)* of fund closings. We rarely eliminate funds from consideration solely due to the size of assets; however, we do eliminate funds at this stage due to rapid growth.

Manager Tenure

When analyzing a fund's historical performance, it is obviously important to determine whether the person(s), or at least the philosophy and process, responsible for the past performance is still there. At Screen #2, we typically eliminate funds with new managers if their management style seems to be significantly different from the prior managers. In effect, hiring such a manager would be to accept the famous "pig in a poke." As funds rarely report this information, we rely on our manager interviews and the observations of Morningstar and Value Line analysts to alert us to these changes.

Turnover

A fund's total expenses are not completely revealed by an examination of its expense ratio. Brokerage commissions, trading costs, including bid-to-ask spreads *are on top of* the disclosed expense ratio. A fund's turnover rate is often the best indicator of trading costs. Hence, we will occasionally eliminate a fund due to what we consider excessive turnover.

---

*For example, was the closing enacted well in advance of the effective date as a marketing strategy to generate new investments?

SCREEN #3

We consider Screen #3 the heart of our selection process. By the time we have completed Screens #1 and #2, there are relatively few funds in each asset class remaining. With a reasonable number of candidates to consider, we can devote significant resources to evaluate each manager.

Philosophy

We ask the manager why we should give him some of our clients' funds to manage. We expect a clearly defined, credible, and consistent statement of the manager's strategic view of his investment markets. We want to know how he will provide our client's excess risk-adjusted returns on the funds under his care.

In order to evaluate a fund's philosophy (and process and people), we employ the following steps:

- First, we review the fund's prospectus, most recent quarterly reports, annual reports, and marketing materials.
- With that as background, we then review the comments of the Value Line and Morningstar analysts. We save all our Value Line reports; thus we can and do read back over the old reviews. Morningstar's CD Rom includes a library of past commentaries so it is easy to find and read the full series of past reviews.
- We then query our Alpha Group friends for any information or thoughts they may have regarding the manager.
- We then request that the manager complete a questionnaire developed by the Alpha Group. An example of a completed Alpha questionnaire (from a responsive manager) is included in Appendix C.
- Finally, with all this information at our disposal, we interview the manager. On occasion the meeting is in person, but it is usually by phone. The interview allows the manager to elaborate on his answers to the questionnaire. It is also an opportunity for us to obtain a gut feeling as to the manager's competency and a comfort level with his style and personality. Although it may not be scientifically sound, we have rejected managers based on our interview. We hire commitment, brains, and passion, and we reject pomposity, simplicity, and marketing hype.

Process

By process, I am referring to the manager's daily implementation of his philosophy. As with the philosophy, we are looking for a clearly defined, consistent, and verifiable process. Examples of process would include:

- Who makes the decisions (e.g., research, allocations, purchases, and sales)?
- How are new investment ideas generated?
- What resources are devoted to research?
- What is the manager's trading discipline?
- What is the manager's buy and sell discipline?
- What is the firm's compensation policy? We are not concerned with the amount anyone is paid. We want to know if the manager is paid based on long-term or short-term performance. We want to know if the compensation structure encourages teamwork or star performance.

People

Generally, we are concerned with the background and experience of all the members of the fund's management team. Also important are the capabilities of the staff support and the process for managing professional growth. Naturally, we are particularly concerned with the lead decision maker(s). It may be of little value to know that the fund passed the philosophy and process test if the manager is new and plans on implementing a new philosophy and a new process. A new manager may have a fabulous track record, but if his investment style is different from that of his predecessor, his portfolio repositioning may generate portfolio turnover. This could mean increased trading costs and increased capital gains distributions, as well as style drift. However, just because a fund has a new manager does not automatically eliminate a fund from consideration. We review a new manager's investment philosophy/discipline by examining his record. If it is consistent with the fund's historical philosophy and process, the fund may still be an acceptable choice (e.g., Selected American Shares when Shelby Davis replaced Don Yacktman).

Philosophy, Process, and People— An Example

Not long ago I received a marketing piece from the Alger Fund Group. I was so impressed that I saved it for future reference. When writing this section I realized that although the 3 Ps describe the core of our selection process, it may not be meaningful without an example. So, I pulled out the brochure in order to quote a few sections to provide an excellent example of a marketing piece that reflects the substance of the 3 Ps instead of marketing hype.

OUR INVESTMENT PHILOSOPHY

Over the years we have been guided by the philosophy that the most profitable investment opportunities are found in companies experiencing periods of rapid change. We believe these dynamic companies fall into one of two categories:

High Unit Volume Growth: includes both established and emerging firms, offering new or improved products.

Positive Life Cycles: companies experiencing major change— change as varied as new management, products, or technologies.

THE RESEARCH STAFF

Most analysts have gone through the Alger in-house training process. As a further aid to staffing, in 1980 we established Analysts Resources, Inc., to track the careers of thousands of practicing securities analysts.

STREAMLINED DECISION MAKING

Purchase Decisions—Our "bottom up" approach to stock selection places primary emphasis on individual security selection. Analysts present investment ideas directly to senior management. If senior management agrees with the case made for a stock, a buy program is implemented immediately. For optimum liquidity, we never own more than eight days average trading volume of any stock across all accounts (four days for NASDAQ stocks).

PORTFOLIO MANAGEMENT

A performance run is done twice daily to give us a sense of overall performance. Additional computer tabulations show how each stock is performing in absolute terms and relative to the market for 5, 10, 15, and 20 days, and for the year-to-date.

The top-down component links the Alger database to each portfolio. Portfolio managers can evaluate overall portfolio characteristics such as weighted growth of earnings per share, as well as each portfolio's reaction to different stimuli from the economy.

Only after a fund has passed through Screen #3 do we begin to seriously consider its performance record.

SCREEN #4

> If the only reason you give someone to buy your fund is because you are No. 1, then you should expect people to sell when you are No. 2.
>
> —*William Guilfoyle, president of G.T. Global*

As this screen is performance-based, I think it is worthwhile to once again place the importance of performance in perspective. Having already mentioned numerous studies that suggest how worthless past performance is as a predictor of future performance, I thought it would be interesting to hear from the "real world." The following are the comments of three of the best of today's wealth managers:[2]

> Ross Levin*—"Past performance has been a very poor indicator of future performance."
>
> Roger Gibson—"Trying to identify funds which will beat the market represents a triumph of hope over experience."
>
> Lynn Hopewell—"Picking individual mutual funds is the last thing a financial advisor should get paid to do."
>
> Wrapping it all up, my favorite curmudgeon-journalist, Bob Veres wrote, "Put another way, all of the time and research spent evaluating track records may be just as ineffective as consulting an astrologer, relying on a Ouija board, or using Tarot cards to select mutual funds."

---

*This is a surprise for Ross. He didn't think I would ever publicly admit that he's "one of the best."

With those sobering reminders regarding the "importance" of performance (and the admission that I keep a Ouija board in my office), I'll continue my description of the EB&K performance screen.

Total Return—Relative

Historical returns should not be viewed in a vacuum, but must be viewed *relative* to appropriate benchmarks. The selection of appropriate benchmarks is another piece of the wealth manager's art.* Once the benchmarks have been selected, it is necessary to compare the fund's performance over a wide variety of periods. The following are suggested cycles for domestic equities.

By Cycles (for example)

Domestic equity bear markets	S&P
11/29/68–5/26/70	–36%
1/11/73–10/3/74	–48
9/21/76–3/6/78	–19
11/28/80–8/12/82	–27
8/25/87–12/4/87	–34
7/16/90–10/11/90	–20

Domestic equity bull markets	S&P
5/26/70–1/11/73	74%
10/3/74–9/21/76	73
3/6/78–11/28/80	62
8/12/82–8/25/87'	229
12/4/87–7/16/90	65

Similar cycle comparisons should be made for other asset classes.

By Year, Quarter, and Month

An examination of a fund's total return on a rolling year-by-year, and even a quarter-to-quarter or monthly basis is advisable. Did a fund "get

*An indispensable source of benchmark data is Investmentview, the software provided by Chase
   Global Data and Research, 76 Junction Square, Concord, Massachusetts 01742
   (508/371-9100).

lucky" in only one year, which has boosted its historical 3-year or 5-year returns, but has never repeated that superior performance before or since?

"Exceptional Returns"

Did the fund achieve returns that were "too good"? That is, did the fund's performance far exceed the returns of other funds in its asset class? Such exceptional returns can be a warning that the manager is either investing outside his asset class and/or implementing aggressive strategies. How about the *bad* returns? If a fund had a quarter or an entire year where it showed a substantial loss relative to its benchmark, can your clients stand a similar loss in the future? Both Morningstar and Wilson software have easily prepared monthly return tables that can be quickly scanned for exceptional returns.

MONITORING THE MANAGER—EB&K POLICY

What gets measured gets managed.

Once the wealth manager has selected his universe of approved managers, he must constantly monitor their performance. The primary focus of the process should be to monitor the managers' adherence to their stated philosophy and process; presumably that's why they were hired. We are very patient with poor performance and very impatient with changes in philosophy or process.

Performance

- **Relative to the S&P 500**—Unless the manager is a core domestic manager we consider his performance relative to the broad domestic market irrelevant and it is our policy to ignore the underperformance. This seems like an obvious policy. Unfortunately, the media loudly and consistently trumpet "market" returns (i.e., the DOW or S&P 500) as if they represent the only real measure of performance. The normalization of this policy is part of our continuing effort to manage our clients' expectations. By discussing our policy, early on, with new clients, we reduce their discomfort during those periods when our asset class managers underperform the broad market.

- **Relative to Other Peer Group Managers**—Although we track our managers' performance compared to other managers with similar asset class/style orientations, we do not use a divergence in performance as a specific criterion for manager evaluation. We use the comparison of a manager's performance to his peer group as an early warning signal for style drift. For example, extraordinary short-term performance vis-à-vis a peer group raises a red flag. We then investigate the cause of the superior performance. If it is attributable to the successful implementation of his stated philosophy, we smile and call the managers to say "Great job." If it is attributable to a successful, but out-of-style bet, we frown and call and say, "What's up?" Our primary standard for relative performance is comparison to an appropriate benchmark.

▪ **Relative to Their Benchmark**—If the manager has remained consistent to his philosophy and process, we are patient with underperformance. For approximately three quarters, we take no action. If the underperformance continues through the fourth quarter, we place the manager "under review."

> *Under review*—At this stage, we neither fire the manager nor do we remove him from the approved list. We do, however, significantly increase our monitoring efforts. This includes a personal interview with the manager to discuss the underperformance, contact with the Morningstar analyst who monitors the manager, and queries of Alpha Group friends for any observations they may have. We also carefully review the changes in the fund's portfolio positions as well as a detailed historical review of its MPT statistics. The goal of this process is to confirm our preliminary conclusion that the manager has remained consistent to his philosophy and process and is just suffering from the endemic market malady of being at the wrong place at the wrong time. If we are comfortable with the manager's response to our concerns and we believe that he is remaining consistent in his style, we make no changes. However, we notify our clients that the fund is on our watch list and, as a precaution, we also begin the process of searching for a possible replacement manager.

▪ If the manager's performance continues to be subpar for an additional three to four quarters, we either place him on the "watch list" or replace him with a new manager.

> *Watch List*—This describes a list of funds that are no longer on our approved list but in which we maintain positions. Although we are patient, there comes a time that the pain of underperformance becomes so strong as to require action. For our practice, that is about two years. By then, even if we cannot account for the underperformance, we consider firing the manager. The problem we frequently face is that firing a manager may generate a

significant taxable event for our taxable clients. As I made clear in Chapter 3, Taxes, we do not let taxes dominate our investment management, but we do not ignore their potential impact. Once again relying on our intelligent application of the art of wealth management, we attempt to balance the tax consequences of firing the manager with the market risk of keeping the manager. If he has remained consistent to his style, if his underperformance is relatively modest, if we believe that his performance is likely to improve, and if our clients have significant capital gains exposure, we will keep our positions in the fund for our taxable clients. For sheltered accounts and new clients, we will use a new manager in that asset class. The old manager is placed on our watch list.

Consistency

Someone might ask: "Did they turn stupid overnight?" The answer is no. We underperformed, but we stuck to our philosophy.

—David Minella, president, LST asset management

For managers on our approved list, our monitoring of consistency is based on fundamental qualitative portfolio analysis and mathematical fundamental factor analysis, not statistical factor analysis. That's a fancy way of saying we look at the portfolio and talk to the manager. We look at, but do not rely on the style analysis charts.

- **Portfolio**

In spite of my belief in the value of return analysis, fundamentally I agree with Don Phillips. When it all shakes out, it's what's in the portfolio that counts. What is the manager doing with my client's money? We review the positions, name by name, to see if they seem consistent with the manager's philosophy. We do not expect to see "go-go" firms in our value manager's portfolio or "dogs" in our growth manager's portfolio. The process is unquestionably subjective but we consider it our first line of defense.

- **Fundamental Factors—Primary**

The four primary factors we track are Management, BtM, Capitalization, and Standard Deviation. If there are any significant changes in any of these factors, the result is in an immediate and detailed review of the portfolio.

- **Fundamental Factors—Secondary**

These are secondary in that variations do not necessarily trigger an immediate full-scale review but often trigger a call to the manager for an explanation. These factors include:

Cash positions—We look for variations from the manager's normal cash allocation range.

Turnover—A 50 percent plus increase in turnover. For example, if the normal turnover is 40 percent, we become concerned if it exceeds 60 percent; if the normal turnover is 80 percent, we are unlikely to become concerned unless it exceeds 120 percent.

Maturity/Duration—We look for movements toward either end of the fund's policy range.

Quality—Any change in the average quality rating.

Expenses—Any change in excess of 5bp gets our attention.

Sector Allocations—Any changes that result in the portfolio's allocations exceeding the standards described in Chapter 10, Policy, result in a call to the manager.

- **Statistical Factors**

Although our primary criteria for monitoring our approved managers are fundamental factors, we see little reason to ignore the possible benefits of statistical factors, so we regularly review the fund's style analysis charts.

- **External Factors**

This includes any source of independent information. Examples include:

Morningstar and Value Line Analysis

No-Load Fund Newsletter—The only newsletter we subscribe to for the purpose of learning about our managers. Ken Gregory and Craig Litman's manager interview and comments are always worth reading. Add their newsletter to your "must subscribe" list.

Information provided directly from the fund—This includes the fund's marketing material.

- We can't count on information being available on every manager. We use what we can find.

Interviews, Commentary, and Analysis in the Media—For example, *Forbes, Barrons, AAII Journal, Fee Advisor, Financial Planning Magazine.*

Manager Interviews—Conference calls: Schwab, Fund sponsored, Alpha; Meetings: Morningstar, IAFP, ICFP.

Networking—Alpha, Financial Planning On-Line (http://www.tisny.com/fponline), Professional Conferences.

Conclusion

Once a manager has been approved, it is critical to continually monitor the manager's adherence to his investment philosophy and how consistently he follows his investment process. A fund manager should not change his stripes as market cycles come and go. Otherwise, all of the effort expended in the selection process will be worthless. Although we may not be able to guarantee the manager's performance, we should be able to guarantee our diligence.

E N D N O T E S

1. Robert Ludwig, "The Role of Performance in the Mutual Fund Selection Process," SEI Research 1994; Ludwig, "Mutual Fund Performance: Predictive or Deceptive," IAFP 1994 Convention & Exposition, September 1994.
2. Robert N. Veres, "Rest in Peace?" *Investment Advisor,* September 1994, 54–67.

CHAPTER 14

The Business of Wealth Management

Uncared for wealth is one risk you can't afford.

—Unknown

. . . the area second only to health where you want life to be boring. Easy to do, inherently interesting and makes a whole lot of difference.

—Charles Ellis

This chapter is an odd duck. Unlike the others, it considers issues related to the business aspects of wealth management. When developing an outline for this book, this chapter was included and deleted on numerous drafts. I finally decided that *Wealth Management* was such an eclectic book, with or without this chapter, I might as well include it. As with other subjects, I have not attempted to provide a comprehensive guide to the business side of a wealth management practice. Instead, I have included items and issues that I believe are particularly unique to wealth management.

The chapter discusses the organization, process, and technology of a wealth manager's office. The discussion is based on my firm. I do not suggest that our system is the best; it is simply what I know best. The reader is encouraged to pick and choose those ideas that are useful and reject the rest. After all, that's how we built our practice—borrowing and adapting everyone else's good ideas. The chapter also discusses our primary institutional and professional relationships and provides basic information on other types of relationships that the wealth manager may wish to investigate. It concludes with a brief discussion of my perception of the market for wealth management.

EB&K—HISTORY

Evensky and Brown was founded by Peter Brown and me in 1985. The practice was fee-based (i.e., fee and commission) comprehensive financial planning. Soon after its inception, we also established our own broker-dealer in order to have complete flexibility in product offerings. In 1990 Deena Katz joined the firm as a one-third owner and president. Her first order of business was a comprehensive reappraisal of our practice. Based on her work we came to a few conclusions:

- We enjoyed our relationships with clients, assisting them in achieving their goals through the financial planning process.
- We did not enjoy managing other planners (when Deena joined the firm, we had 10 planners and 15 registered representatives licensed with our broker-dealer).
- We were frustrated that we had only limited involvement in much of the final implementation of our plans. The more complex, the more control that was transferred to the CPA, attorney, life, property, and casualty insurance specialists.
- We were frustrated at our inability to keep current, at the level we wished, in all the disciplines involved in comprehensive planning. Each of us typically earned between 50 and 100 hours per year of continuing education; yet we still could not begin to keep up.
- We agreed that investment issues were our primary interest.
- We recognized that we could not concentrate on investments and maintain the flexibility and independence we considered necessary, by continuing to use commission products.

The result of this reappraisal was a major restructuring of our practice. We sold the broker-dealer, significantly reduced the number of professional associates, eliminated commission sales, and began to evolve into a wealth management practice. By May 1992, we had completely eliminated our commission business and had $15 million under fee management.

Today, our practice consists of five planners (including Deena, Peter, and myself), all CFPs (that is a requirement of the firm). The staff is comprised of an office manager/comptroller, two associate advisors, two secretaries, and two clerical staff.

Although the firm specializes in wealth management, one planner specializes in comprehensive planning. As we believe that a planner can only serve between 50 and 100 clients, we manage the firm's growth by controlling for client size. The current firm minimum is $500,000. As of July 1996, the firm advises clients regarding approximately $200 million in assets.

ORGANIZATION AND OPERATIONS

EB&K is totally focused on client service. Each staff person is trained to work directly with our clients and although some of us are more responsible for the external communication, we are all in the business of client service.

We have three principals. We elected to have a partnership* arrangement for three reasons:

- It's lonely working alone.
- It's limiting working alone. There is so much material that we need to consider daily, that spreading the responsibilities allows us to have better leverage and to be away from the office without being in constant contact.
- We each have different skills to bring to the relationship that make us more well-rounded in our approach.

It is necessary in this type of arrangement for one partner to accept the responsibility of managing partner. This is the person responsible for running the business. Duties of the managing partner include establishing operations and personnel policy, staffing, and operations. It is important to assign this task to someone with good management and business skills and allow that partner absolute control over the day-to-day operations of the business. As our legal form is a corporation, our managing partner is assigned the role of president.

---

*Legally we are structured as a corporation; however, we think of ourselves as partners.

OPERATIONS POLICY

There are two fundamental aspects of the firm's operations policy:

- A system of checks and balances. This system has been established in order to assure accuracy and to maintain a high level of fiduciary responsibility.

- Delegation of significant authority and responsibility to staff. We view each employee as a professional in his or her own area of responsibility.

STAFF

• *ASSOCIATE ADVISORS*—The associate advisors (AAs) support the practitioners. Aside from three partners, we have two additional CFP practitioners. Because we operate on a team basis with our clients, each new client is assigned his own personal AA, even though he also meets with one of the practitioners on a regular basis. The AA sits in on the initial meeting with the practitioner and new client, and assists in the data gathering and the preparation of the investment policy. After the plan has been delivered and new accounts need transferring and opening, the AA coordinates a meeting between the operations manager (OM) and the new client in order to complete and execute the necessary documents. The AA is the liaison between the practitioner, the client, and operations. When the client has a problem with an account or requests funds, he calls the AA–not the practitioner. In turn, the AA coordinates operational activities and initiates the trade requests with the OM (at the direction of the practitioner). All trading is implemented by the OM. The associate advisor's additional duties include mailing material of interest to clients, calling clients periodically to nurture the relationship, and preparing articles of interest for the monthly newsletter.

• *OPERATIONS MANAGER*—In addition to opening accounts, facilitating transfers, and implementing all trading requests, the operations manager maintains our client database and produces our monthly reviews. (As part of the cross-checking requirements, the AA is responsible for validating the accuracy of those reviews.)

• *COMPTROLLER/OFFICE MANAGER*—Reporting directly to the president, our comptroller also serves as office manager. She is responsible for our company books, as well as daily staff supervision, ordering and approving supplies, payroll, and designing and maintaining our job description book. She approves staff vacations and sick days according to company policy. She, in effect, implements the company policy established by our president. Our comptroller/office manager (CM) also maintains our SEC registration and any state licensing required. Schwab provides a monthly compliance newsletter and our Schwab regional office frequently initiates compliance conference calls. Also, as we have access to National Regulatory Services through Schwab Link, it is easy for her to keep up with changes that we may need to make for compliance reasons.

Another example of checks and balances is our comptroller's management of our client account data download and client account posting. This provides an independent review of the OM and AA activities. Based on the interchange among the CM, the AAs, and the OM, the staff is authorized, within a broad latitude, to adjust operational activities as they deem appropriate. The AAs and OM appreciate the opportunity to share ideas, resolve problems, and modify operations with the CM instead of always having to take them to the president. This reflects the firm's policy of delegation.

▪ *SECRETARIAL/CLERICAL*—Each contact with the client requires copious notes detailing the discussion. Initially we left out information that we thought might be unnecessary or extraneous, but we have discovered that nothing the client tells us is unimportant. Therefore, we will include names of grandchildren, hobbies, recent trips made, the fact that one daughter works for a lawyer and one is a CPA. All these items may influence our relationship with the client and we want each person who works with this client to be aware of his unique story. Because we maintain our notes on the network database, anyone speaking to the client has instant access to this information. Our secretarial support is fairly typical of a small office, with one secretary giving support to more than one practitioner. One secretary is assigned to handle AA mailings as well. An overlap, but with different responsibilities are our receptionist, our high-touch tech, and our binding and mailing clerk.

▪ *PRACTITIONERS*—The practitioners have the primary relationship with the clients and make individual decisions with regard to their client base within the guidelines established by company policy.

STAFF DEVELOPMENT

It is our policy to promote from within where possible. Therefore, each associate advisor must have or be working on his CFP designation with the intent to become a practitioner. AAs are encouraged to attend professional functions, join the local chamber of commerce, etc. The company pays for this involvement. The company pays for the first CFP course for AAs who do not have the CFP and reimburses for the balance after they have attained the CFP designation.

Staff members have attended time management and administrative assistant courses and several even attended Dale Carnegie courses at company expense. These courses are in addition to those designed for specific software such as Word, Excel, Centerpiece, or Schwab Link.

Staff is encouraged to maintain professional relationships with our external support systems. As an example, our office manager arranged for our operations staff and AAs to spend a few days in Orlando to meet with the Schwab institutional staff. As a result of this meeting, working relationships blossomed between the two offices and business runs smoother.

Retreat

Once a year we hold our annual retreat. We schedule a full day away from the office, usually at a nearby resort. All staff, including advisors, participate. We use role playing to explore our various responsibilities, to demonstrate how important each of us is to the success of the company, and to figure out how we can do a better job collectively. A sample agenda is in Appendix D.

One year, our support staff played the role of the advisors, Deena and I took the place of the receptionists, and Peter and our comptroller were clients. We walked our phantom clients through our entire process, from prospect through their first review. Then we critiqued the process from our new perspectives, as well as our conventional roles.

We also used the day to vent. We got this idea from Eleanor Blayney. Each person was provided a post-it notes pad. Using as many post-it notes as we wished, we finished the sentence, "The thing that drives me crazy is . . ." These notes were posted, unsigned, on the wall. We then focused on those that seemed to be the most frequently repeated.

Later in the day we paired off, 15 minutes with each person, to discuss situations and ideas, then we all returned as a group to relate our personal goals and the company vision. Our retreats force us to evaluate what we're doing and why we're doing it. No one walks away from the retreat without a renewed sense of self-worth and value to the company.

INTERNAL COMMUNICATIONS

Each Friday, office staff members meet to discuss problems and issues. Practitioners are not invited, although the president presides along with the comptroller/manager. The agenda is set by staff and decisions are made by staff. See Appendix D for examples of issues discussed. As noted earlier, the goal is to delegate the responsibility for organizational changes to staff. They tackle organizational issues and make decisions to implement new systems or techniques.

At the end of the meeting, staff nominate each other for the "TUR-KEY OF THE WEEK." This award is given weekly to the person who completed the dumbest work-related activity of the week. This award is an attempt to decrease embarrassing mistakes and find a healthy way of correcting unnecessary errors. Instead of focusing on the person, we focus on the problem. The TURKEY recipient gets the stuffed turkey perched on his desk for the week. Each year the TURKEY OF THE YEAR award is given and staff members vote on the past year's entries. The activities related to some turkeys resulted in fundamental changes in our office procedures; others just gave us a good laugh. For example, past turkeys have been given for lopping off a tie in the paper cutter or confusing two clients with similar names while talking with one of them on the phone. The client confusion caused us to institute a system of keeping more detailed and copious client notes and more effectively using our networked computer system.

Deena instituted the turkey when she joined us six years ago and everyone was included. However, after I received the turkey nearly each week for two years, I was placed permanently in the hall of fame and am excluded from further awards.

Because the turkey has been such a success, four years ago we initiated the "STAR OF THE WEEK." This gives staff an opportunity to thank each other for exceptional assistance. It promotes teamwork and is a nice balance to the turkey. I am somehow exempt from this award, too (I have never been told why). As an example, a star was given to a staff person who, upon discovering that an associate was having trouble completing a project on time, stayed overtime to assist in completing the work. During a week of total frustration with clients and support services, a star was awarded to someone who spontaneously brought in a surprise box of donuts and cookies.

Once a month we have an advisors' meeting, which includes practitioners, operations, and associate advisors. This meeting is designed to present policy set by the investment committee and to discuss other policy issues that involve the practitioners' support system. Practitioners report on their marketing efforts and share ideas. Intermittently we set aside additional time for special education and training-related issues. Examples include a detailed presentation of the educational material we use with new clients and an analysis of a sample case with unique issues (e.g., the tax consequences of the sale of low basis stock). The agenda is constructed in advance with input from the attendees. The inclusion of the operations manager and the associate advisors in these meetings insures a seamless integration of our policy decisions with our operations. For example, the decision to add a new manager to our approved list requires changes to our computer system as well as a number of internal reference manuals.

INVESTMENT COMMITTEE

The investment committee is composed of my two partners and me. I serve as chair of the committee. The committee meets formally at least once every month and the minutes are recorded. I am responsible for the preliminary development of the strategic policy. Peter is primarily responsible for the ongoing monitoring of the managers. The committee members only make recommendations to the committee, as all decisions regarding changes to the policy and selection or firing of managers are made by the entire committee. Examples of the agenda are included in Appendix D.

OPERATIONS PROCESS

INTERNAL

Client relationships formally begin with the preparation of our investment policy. Before its preparation, the client signs a contract agreeing to provide us with material to complete this plan, and agreeing to a fee for this plan. Practitioners, along with the associate advisors, gather the data necessary to complete the plan. When the associate advisor and the practitioner review the material, they determine what accounts must be opened, which assets must be transferred, and who must transfer them—either the client or the firm. For example, if we see proprietary funds, we know they cannot be transferred in kind and must be liquidated. Certain limited partnerships may not be able to be moved at all. Some stock issues may be more efficiently sold at the sending broker.

When the plan is delivered, the operations department has already prepared the necessary documents for the client to complete to effect the transfers and open the accounts. If the client wishes to continue a relationship, he then signs our Investment Advisory agreement. This provides for our assuming the responsibility for managing a specific pool of assets in accordance with the previously prepared investment policy. There is neither a charge to the client for beginning the relationship nor a charge for terminating the relationship. We receive no compensation other than our fees. These are based on a percent of assets that we are managing. At this stage, we have the client execute the required new account and transfer forms. We also offer the client a proxy voting rights form for the funds. This is a document that allows us to vote our clients' proxies as a block.

Fees for assets under management are, for the most part, deducted from the client accounts on a quarterly basis. We do not just use calendar quarters in order to spread the work and make our cash flow consistent from month to month. Each client is assigned his own quarterly review and billing cycle. The billing can be designed to the client's specification, i.e., one master account can be billed for the fees attributable to all the clients' related accounts. The exception is that we do not use IRA and pension accounts to pay for other accounts.

Because of SEC rules, we are hypersensitive about taking checks or securities at our office. The SEC considers this taking custody. If a client walks in with a check or securities, since our local Schwab office is literally down the street from our office, we offer them transportation to deliver the material. Alternatively, we provide them with preaddressed Schwab envelopes. If there is significant business to transact, we will contact the Schwab office most convenient for our client and make an appointment for the client with the branch manager.

We take our fiduciary responsibility seriously so each pension account is bonded. This is a minimal cost and a wonderful marketing position, as a bonded investment advisor is one of the necessary elements to provide a safe harbor for our ERISA fiduciary clients.

Also, as we maintain our own database, we can provide specialized tax reports at the request of the client or the client's accountant. We used to mail them out to every client, but this caused more questions and discussions than we expected, so we now just send them by request.

As described in Chapter 1, Client Goals and Constraints, if a client requires cash flow, we set up a separate "cash flow" account, for which we do not bill. Initially we fund it with an 18- to 30-month cash reserve, usually a combination of money market and short-term bond funds. When we rebalance the investment portfolio, we continue to fund the client's cash account to maintain this 18- to 30-month reserve.

On an annual basis, or upon the request of the client, we prepare an updated capital needs analysis to ensure that the client is continuing to meet his goals and objectives.

CLIENT RELATIONSHIP

Although the client relationship process begins with our marketing efforts, I will jump ahead and assume that a motivated prospect is in my office.

Prospect Interview

There is nothing particularly unique in our approach to prospect interviews. They begin with a welcome and "What brings you here?" Our mission is to listen, listen, and listen. Our goal is to determine what the prospect's needs are and to decide if we can be of assistance, so we generally request that they bring along all their investment statements, wills, trusts, pension, social security, and tax documents, as well as any other items about which they have questions. This portion of the interview process may take as little as 20 minutes or as long as several hours. At the end of this meeting, we have usually reached one of four conclusions:

▪ The client's primary needs are not ones we can assist in resolving. In these cases we make professional referrals. Typical examples would be referrals to estate planning attorneys, elder law attorneys, disability, life, and property and casualty specialists. We will usually provide two or three referrals. However, if we deem it appropriate, we will refer to a single professional. We encourage the prospect to let us know if his problem is resolved, or to return for a future appointment if it is not resolved. We neither charge for this service nor receive referral fees.

▪ The client, in our opinion, requires broad-based (i.e., planning beyond wealth management) or comprehensive planning. In this case we will bring in our firm's specialist in comprehensive planning. With the prospect's permission, we complete a preliminary but detailed data-gathering questionnaire. This enables us to evaluate the nature of the work and to develop a proposal. The proposal is typically presented at a subsequent meeting.

• Although it is a rare occurrence, as our marketing material clearly describes the firm's minimum account size, occasionally the client needs guidance regarding his investment assets, and does not meet our minimum. If we believe it to be appropriate under the circumstances (e.g., a small IRA account), we will recommend an allocation model using Vanguard index funds. We explain the basis for the allocations and describe the funds. We provide the prospect with Morningstar sheets on the funds and encourage him to call us should he have any questions in the future. We also keep on hand copies of *The Fidelity Guide to Mutual Funds* or *A Commonsense Guide to Mutual Funds* by Mary Rowland and *The Wall Street Journal Guide to Financial Planning*. We give these to the prospect. We do not charge the prospect for this advice or the materials given.

• The client is a candidate for a wealth management investment policy. For these qualified prospects, we explain how we believe we may be of assistance. We describe, in detail, our services and fees. If not previously provided, we will give the prospect our ADV Part II, a copy of our Investment Planning Agreement, our firm's philosophy (see Chapter 16), our preliminary data-gathering questionnaire, and instructions on what missing or supplemental documentation to bring to the next meeting. We schedule a future appointment.

Data Gathering

The data-gathering meeting begins with the education program described in Chapter 5, Client Education. Depending on the client, the time devoted to the education varies from ½ to 2½ hours. After completion of the education program, we complete the risk-tolerance questionnaire (Chapter 4, Data Gathering).

The balance of the data-gathering sessions is typical of any planning practice. The goal is to gather accurate and detailed information regarding the client's fiscal life (and related personal issues).

Plan Preparation

With the information obtained from the client during the data-gathering process, the planner will analyze the data, develop the necessary tables (e.g., allocations), and perform the necessary analyses (e.g., cash flows, capital needs) to determine the appropriate recommendations. Based on these analyses, a customized investment policy is developed. An example is described in detail in Chapter 10, Policy.

Before being submitted to a client, the investment policy is reviewed by at least one other practitioner. The reviewer checks for any obvious errors, for the logic of the recommendations based on the supporting documentation, and for consistency of the recommendations with the firm's overall policy guidelines.

Plan Presentation

Before meeting with the client, the practitioner marks with a highlighter those aspects of the policy he believes are most pertinent and important to the client. This highlighting serves a number of purposes. It gives focus to the presentation, and it makes the document seem more of a working tool than a manuscript to be filed. The client is encouraged to make notes on the plan as it is discussed. We find them much more willing to do so if we have already marked up the paper.

The plan presentation typically takes between one and two hours. Although this completes the commitment of the firm under the Investment Policy Agreement, the client is invited to schedule a follow-up appointment in order to discuss any questions that may arise after he has had an opportunity to reread and think about the policy. We do not charge for this additional meeting.

Plan Presentation—Implementation

Our plans are generic but specific. For those Investment Policy clients who, after receiving their plans say, "It makes sense, let's do it," the next step is to translate the generic to the specific. In these cases, after the completion of the plan presentation, we schedule a follow-up appointment to present our fund manager specific recommendations, which we present in the form of an action plan.

At the subsequent meeting, we discuss in detail the allocations we propose to make and the managers we have selected to implement the investments in each asset class. At this meeting, we also have the client complete all the paperwork necessary to establish a new account to be managed by EB&K,* including account transfer documents and our investment advisory agreement.

The new account forms typically provide for the client authorizations noted below:

A. Release of Information Authorization. I authorize the custodian to send duplicate copies of my trade confirmations and account statements to the advisor.

B. Trading Authorization. I authorize the advisor to direct the custodian to execute trades in my account.

C. Disbursement Authorization. I authorize the advisor to direct disbursal of funds for investment purposes or to me personally. I authorize the custodian to remit checks, wire funds, and otherwise make disbursements of funds held in the account (1) to banks, broker-dealers, investment companies, or other financial institutions to an account of identical registration, or (2) to me at my address of record.

D. Fee Payment Authorization. I authorize the custodian to pay management fees, as invoiced by the advisor, from my account.

We require clients to complete A and B and encourage them to complete C and D. Authorization A is necessary if we are to monitor our clients' accounts. Although we rarely initiate trades without our clients' prior authorization, experience has taught us that the flexibility of obtaining discretionary trading authorization outweighs any potential disadvantage. As we cannot churn the account in order to generate commissions for our benefit, we have never had a client object to providing authorization B.

Although Authorization C is not necessary for us to manage, frequently clients will call and ask us to send them funds from their managed account. Without Authorization C, we cannot do so. No client has ever objected to Authorization C.

---

*We have the client send to us, in advance, copies of all the current statements necessary to transfer accounts to the custodian we have mutually selected to handle the client's account.

Authorization D, the authority to bill our fees to the account, is the only one we occasionally leave blank. From our firm's standpoint it is convenient to bill the account directly. On the other hand, we have never had a client fail to pay our fee, so the issue is not critical. For the clients, if we bill the accounts, their statements will reflect our performance net of all fees and our performance reports can be presented net of fees. On rare occasions, a client will request that we not bill the account. Occasionally, we will recommend not billing the account (e.g., IRA or pensions when there is no mandatory distribution required). In these cases, Authorization D is left blank.

Postimplementation Meeting

Once a client has executed an Investment Advisory Agreement and becomes a wealth management client of the firm, our regular reporting format is the quarterly report. For new clients, however, there is one extra meeting, i.e., one scheduled shortly after the initial implementation. Although we have, during the plan presentation/implementation meeting, discussed in detail the actions we will be taking, we believe that our clients appreciate seeing where their money is once the transfers are completed and the purchases have been made. That is the purpose of the postimplementation meeting. It is scheduled for one to two weeks after implementation has been completed.

Quarterly Reports

We generally report to our clients, on a formal basis, quarterly. We do not use calendar quarters for all our clients. Rather, we attempt to balance our reviews evenly over the year. Based on discussions with our Alpha friends, our staggered quarterly policy seems to be the exception. However, I encourage wealth managers to consider staggering quarterlies. This not only results in a much more efficient work flow; it may also, for clients not on a calendar quarter cycle, help break the client's focus on short-term performance. If his quarter does not match that of the media's quarterly manager performance rankings, it is harder to play the performance game.

Many years ago we "required" our clients to visit us each quarter. After a number of years, many began to tell us, "You're nice people, but we trust you and we're comfortable with what you're doing so why do we have to schlep down here every quarter?" Having no good answers, we have since modified our policy. We now send out a post card at the end of the month preceding the reviews, which provides the client four choices:

- Please call our office and schedule an appointment to visit and review your quarterly.

- Please call our office and schedule a telephone appointment to review your quarterly. We will send you the quarterly in advance of the call.

- Please call and request your quarterly. Upon your instructions, we will mail the quarterly to you and you may call with any questions.

- This is a default option, i.e., it is unwritten. If we get no response, the quarterly is automatically mailed at the end of the following month, with a quarterly review letter prepared by my partner and our president, Deena Katz. Examples are in Appendix E.

Quarterly Report Format

The format for our quarterly report is constantly evolving. The following version is the current manifestation. The actual quarterly is printed in blue with a few multicolored pages; however, it is our goal to add multicolor to most, if not all pages. All illustrations are in color.

Page 1 is a summary of market highlights from the last three months. It is prepared internally by my partner, Peter Brown. Examples are included in Appendix E.

Page 2 (Table 14–1) is internally referred to as the "performance" report. Until a client has been with the firm for a full 12-month cycle, this is not included in the bound report. For the first three years, the report is titled "Volatility Report." Only after three years is it called "Performance Report." Also, for the first three years, a target return line is not included.

In discussing this page with clients, we emphasize that returns for periods less than an economic cycle are not meaningful for long-term projections. If, as was so frequently the case during the last decade, our clients' returns were well in excess of our projected returns, we reminded them that our policy sets targets, not caps. When the world gets rich, so do our clients. We warned them, however, not to spend the difference between our target and their actual returns. We believe that one day they will need the nest egg constructed from those excess returns to replace bear market losses.

T A B L E   14–1

Volatility Analysis					Month-Year
	Current Quarter xx/30/199x xx/31/199x	YTD 12/31/199x	1 YR xx/30/199x xx/31/199x	2 YR xx/30/199x xx/31/199x	From Inception xx/30/199x
Beginning Portfolio Value					
Contributions					
Withdrawals					
Ending Portfolio Value					
Net Earnings					
Time-Weighted Return					
Dollar-Weighted Return					
Risk Tolerance =					
Cumulative Return (Net of Fees)					
CPI (Inflation)					

We also include a color graph plotting cumulative returns versus CPI and target returns.

Page 3 (Table 14–2) is a table similar to one in our investment policy. This one, however, lists in detail our client's current positions (including the ownership, e.g., spouse's IRA) listed by asset class, subclass, and style. The columns reflect current value (i.e., quarter end), last quarter's ending value, and the original investment. With this format it is easy for the client to see where his investments are, how much is committed to each, and how well (or poorly) each has performed since the original purchase and during the last quarter.

When reviewing the quarterly with a client, we use this page to review the concept of maturity laddering, various asset classes (e.g., large-cap versus small-cap and developed international versus emerging markets), and style (growth versus value); we also use it as a reference to discuss each of the managers.

For the first few reviews, we typically discuss each of these items in detail, including a brief description of the philosophy of each manager. Subsequent reviews tend to go faster and we focus only on new managers and respond to client questions.

T A B L E   14-2

Current Positions   Month-Year

Policy	Owner	Style	Description	Original Investment		Last Quarter		Current	
Reserve			MMA - Cash Flow Reserves						
MMA			MMA						
U.S. Fixed Income		Sh Corp/Govt	Federated S\I Govt						
			DFA 1 year						
		S/I Corp/Govt	Federated Int Govt						
			PIMCo Low Duration						
			Solon 3 Year Govt						
		Intr. Corp/Govt	Blackrock Core						
			PIMCo Total						
		Sh Muni	Calvert Ltd MUNI						
			Vanguard Short MUNI						
		S/I Muni	Schwab S/I MUNI Index						
			Thornburg Ltd MUNI						
		Inter. Muni	Dreyfus Inter MUNI						
			Vanguard Inter MUNI						
International Bond		International	PIMCo Foreign						
			Lazard Frere						
			TR Price Int'l Bond						
			FIXED INCOME	$0	0.0%	$0	0.0%	$0	0.0%
U.S. Large Cap		Core	Schwab 1000						
			Vanguard S&P 500						
			J.P. Morgan						
		Tactical	Sogen						
		Value	DFA Large-Cap Value						
			Montgomery Eq. Inc						
		Growth	Yacktman						
			Harbor Capital Appn						
			SEI Capital Appn						
			SEI Large-Cap Growth						
U.S. Small Cap		Growth	Meridian						
			Warburg Emer Growth						
		Value	DFA S.C. Value						
International		Developed	Warburg Pincus						
			TR Price Int'l						
			DFA Int'l Value						
			Schwab Int'l Index						
		Emerging	Montgomery Emer MKT						
			PIMCo Adv Inst Blair						
			Matthews Pacific Tiger						
Real Estate			DFA R.E.						
			Cohen & Steers						
			EQUITY	$0	0.0%	$0	0.0%	$0	0.0%
			Total	**$0**	**0.0%**	**$0**	**0.0%**	**$0**	**0.0%**

F I G U R E   14–1

Mr. & Mrs. Client
Proposed Portfolio

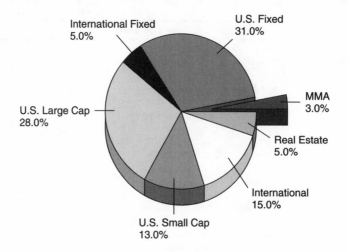

Page 4 (Table 14–3) is the tabular presentation of our clients' current allocations compared to the policy allocations. We use this page to discuss the basis for any rebalancing we may be recommending.

Page 5 (Figure 14–1) is a pie chart of the client's policy and current allocation.

The last pages are our manager review section. We explain to our clients that we subscribe to numerous data services (e.g., Morningstar) as well as regularly interview our managers. In order to provide the client with some background about the current activities of the manager, Peter keeps a running commentary on all our managers. For the quarterly we copy the most recent reviews. Also included are a number of statistical tables, exported from Morningstar, including what we believe to be some of the more important statistics regarding our selected managers. We do not usually review the summaries but invite our clients to read them at their leisure. We do, however, at least for the first few reviews, review the tables, explaining the meaning and significance of such items as R^2, standard deviation, and expense ratio. For subsequent reviews we use the statistical table to discuss the activities of managers whom we believe deserve special attention.

T A B L E   14–3

Rebalance   Month-Year

Policy	Owner	Style	Description	Current		Policy		Proposed	
Reserve			MMA - Cash Flow Reserves						
MMA			MMA						
U.S. Fixed Income		Sh Corp/Govt	Federated S\I Govt						
			DFA 1 Year						
		S/I Corp/Govt	Federated Int Govt						
			PIMCo Low Duration						
			Solon 3 Year Govt						
		Intr. Corp/Govt	Blackrock Core						
			PIMCo Total						
		Sh Muni	Calvert Ltd MUNI						
			Vanguard Short MUNI						
		S/I Muni	Schwab S/I MUNI Index						
			Thornburg Ltd MUNI						
		Inter. Muni	Dreyfus Inter MUNI						
			Vanguard Inter MUNI						
International Bond		International	PIMCo Foreign						
			Lazard Frere						
			TR Price Int'l Bond						
			FIXED INCOME	$0	0.0%	$0	0.0%	$0	0.0%
U.S. Large Cap		Core	Schwab 1000						
			Vanguard S&P 500						
			J.P. Morgan						
		Tactical	Sogen						
		Value	DFA Large-Cap Value						
			Montgomery Eq. Inc						
		Growth	Yacktman						
			Harbor Capital Appn						
			SEI Capital Appn						
			SEI Large-Cap Growth						
U.S. Small Cap		Growth	Meridian						
			Warburg Emer Growth						
		Value	DFA S.C. Value						
International		Developed	Warburg Pincus						
			TR Price Int'l						
			DFA Int'l Value						
			Schwab Int'l Index						
		Emerging	Montgomery Emer MKT						
			PIMCo Adv Inst Blair						
			Matthews Pacific Tiger						
Real Estate			DFA R.E.						
			Cohen & Steers						
			EQUITY	$0	0.0%	$0	0.0%	$0	0.0%
			Total	$0	0.0%	$0	0.0%	$0	0.0%

EXAMPLES FROM THE MANAGER REVIEW SECTION

COMPASS CAPITAL/BLACKROCK
CORE FIXED INCOME

This fund seeks to realize a total return that exceeds the return of the Lehman Brothers Aggregate Index. The portfolio invests in a broad range of investment grade, fixed-income securities, including U.S. Government, mortgage-backed, asset-backed, and corporate debt securities.

Recently, EB&K met with key personnel at Blackrock's New York headquarters. In discussing the fund's philosophy, Karen Sabath, the managing director, reiterated that Blackrock is a duration-controlled manager and adds value primarily through sector rotation and security selection. This means that market timing and frequent significant adjustments are not part of Blackrock's modus operandi. Currently, the fund's duration stands at a moderate 4.42 years.

For the first nine months of 1995, the fund returned 12.9 percent. Management has maintained a neutral posture towards the corporate sector, decreasing its allocation to these securities as a relatively light new issuance calendar caused corporate spreads to tighten relative to alternatives in the short and intermediate duration sectors. The portfolio allocation is currently 44 percent mortgage-backed securities, 10 percent asset-backed, 17 percent corporates, and 29 percent Treasuries and cash.

DFA VALUE PORTFOLIOS

DFA's value strategies are based upon studies conducted by professors Eugene Fama and Kenneth French, of the University of Chicago, that concluded the three economic factors—size, book to market, and the performance of the equity market as a whole—explain most of the variation of equity portfolio average returns. The firm's value strategies incorporate the Fama/French research in multifactor portfolios designed to capture the return premiums associated with high book-to-market (BtM) ratios for both large and small-cap stocks.

The small-cap value strategy uses a highly disciplined approach to stock selection. The fund invests in companies whose market capitalization is in the size range of deciles 6.5 through 10 of the New York Stock Exchange (NYSE), currently $500 million or less, and have BtM ratios in the upper 30 percent of publicly traded companies on the NYSE. Stocks on the AMEX and NASDAQ with similar size and BtM characteristics are also eligible. Book value is reconstructed for each eligible issue based on management's interpretation of how accounting charges affect "real" book value.

MATTHEWS PACIFIC TIGER

This fund, managed by Paul Matthews and Carol Chuang, invests exclusively in the equity markets of the developing Asian region (excluding Japan, Australia, and New Zealand). Currently, investments are held in Hong Kong, Singapore, Taiwan, Korea, Malaysia, Thailand, Indonesia, the Philippines, and China. The managers utilize a long-term investment approach that seeks to participate in the growth of Asian companies and exploit the market inefficiencies found in less developed markets. While top-down considerations are an important part of the investment process, bottom-up company research is the driving force in portfolio construction.

Tiger mid-caps ($200 million to $1 billion) form an integral part of the portfolio due to an attractive combination of above-average growth potential, sufficient track record, and market inefficiencies. Regular company visits by fund personnel, as a means of assessing a company's potential and management quality, is also a vital part of the investment process. The fund is diversified across a number of markets and industries throughout the region as an important means of risk reduction.

In a recent visit to Matthews's office, EB&K met with Matthews and Chuang to discuss their outlook for the Asian markets and their current investment strategy. Because of political uncertainties, the team has recently reduced portfolio weightings in Taiwan and South Korea. On the plus side, positions have been added in Thailand in anticipation of monetary easing by the end of the second quarter and Hong Kong, where CPI has dropped unexpectedly and the economy is improving as interest rates fall. Another area in which the team is finding good values is Indonesia, where p/e ratios are fairly low for an emerging market.

MONTGOMERY EQUITY INCOME FUND

Although this fund is relatively new, John Brown and his team of analysts had previously worked for six years at Merus Capital (manager of the SEI Equity Income Fund) as a vice president and senior portfolio manager. He had been responsible for the management of over $1.4 billion in assets.

The discipline Brown employs in the management of the Equity Income Fund is called "relative dividend yield." It is a process in which the universe of domestic stocks with market capitalization in excess of $500 million (currently only one issue has a cap under $1 billion) and a dividend yield of at least 1.3 times the market yield (S&P 500) are examined. To qualify for inclusion in the portfolio, the companies must have a 30-year dividend history and be priced at the high end of the historical yield range. To insure diversification, Brown requires that the maximum position in any one company does not exceed 5 percent of assets, and for industries other than telephone and other utilities the limits are 10 percent. For the latter two segments, a 20 percent cap is imposed. What ultimately comes from the process is a diversified portfolio of 50 to 60 high-quality, undervalued stocks with high dividend yields. For 1995 this fund had a total return of 35.2 percent.

During the course of two recent dinners, John Brown discussed with EBK the attributes of the relative yield approach and how he has positioned the portfolio for 1996. Among the strengths of "relative yield" are its low volatility, good upside, high dividend yield, repeatable disciplined process, and low portfolio turnover. Its weaknesses include an investable universe limited to large established companies with long dividend-paying histories, buying too soon, and selling too soon. In the current environment, Brown is emphasizing quality, owning A to A− companies versus a B+ average for the S&P 500. He has a defensive overweight in energy, utilities, and noncyclicals (more predictable earnings); an underweight in cyclicals; and no technology.

TECHNOLOGY

Although this is a moving target, technology is such an important issue that I felt it imperative to address it at least briefly.

HARDWARE

We have learned from experience that the advice of computer gurus is true—always buy more than you need. Tomorrow, you'll need it. In fact, you probably need it today and just do not know it.

▪ **Computer** In terms of CPU, this means always buying the faster chip commonly available (i.e., not the newest cutting edge, but last cycle's cutting edge). Today that would be at least a Pentium® 133 MHz. Computers with 386 chips and below should be replaced now. Those with 486 chips should be replaced soon.

The box housing the mother board and CPU should be a mini-tower model with at least 250 w power and dual cooling fans. The hard disk should be a minimum of 1 gigabyte. The system should also include, at a minimum, a 4x CD and preferably one holding 4+ disks and a graphics accelerator board.

The internal memory must be at least 16 MB and more is better. The screen should be at least 15″, preferably 17″ with super VGA.

Our office currently has 12 desktop systems, three laptops, a network server (we use Novell®), and two printer servers. All are Pentiums and most have 32 megs of memory.

- **Modem** 28.8 Kbps Fax/Modem. We are planning on adding ISDN.

- **Backup** An adequate backup is critical. Develop a backup schedule and an off-site archive plan. At a minimum, maintain off-site (e.g., in a bank vault) a five-day, four-week, three-month, and one-year backup. We maintain daily for a week, weekly for a month, and monthly for a year and yearly. Develop a scheduled routine to verify that the backup is, in fact, working. The use of a DAT is recommended.

- **Power Backup** An emergency power supply and surge protector is mandatory.

- **Printers** It is impossible to function today without a fast, dependable laser printer. We have had long-term success with Hewlett–Packard® LaserJet® printers. Because I believe that color will become a mandatory aspect of presentations, I would also include a color printer in the minimum office configuration. We have also been pleased with our H–P® color printers (855 and 1600).

- **Scanner** We have just begun to experiment with scanners. Although we believe they will play an important role in our practice in the future, our experience is too limited for me to comment further.

SOFTWARE

Office Management

For our basic infrastructure software, about a year ago we decided to stop fighting and join the multitudes—we traded in WordPerfect® for Word™,

Lotus® for Excel®, and installed Microsoft® Office.™ Although it was tough leaving our old and trusted friends (i.e., WP and Lotus) the transition was incredibly easy and the integration of Microsoft products a pleasure. All in all, one of our better technology decisions.

The office has been Windows®-based for years and we are currently transitioning to 95. We are switching reluctantly, but we find Windows increasingly unstable as we place more demands on our system. Windows 95™ has proven to be much more stable. Our longer-term goal is to move the entire office to Windows NT.®

At the heart of our daily management system is a software package called Day-Timer.® It combines scheduling, calendar, task, and notes capabilities. Day-Timer is an evolution of an earlier system called Instant Recall. Our office has a love/hate relation with Day-Timer. When it is working, it is wonderful. Unfortunately, we seem to consistently have problems with it on our Novell network. We are currently reviewing other alternatives in case we are unable to resolve our network problems. Other particularly handy (and inexpensive) programs include:

E-Note™   A simple and inexpensive pop-up messaging system for Windows, which we use constantly for internal e-mail. For information contact E Ware, 212/564-7791.

Eclipse Find™   A simple but powerful program for searching through files (word processing, spreadsheets, graphics, database, etc.) to locate documents based on contents rather than file name or location. If you are like me, you frequently lose documents on the hard drive. As an example, it took approximately two minutes to completely index the text of this book and less than two seconds to search the text and locate this entry, after requesting a search on the word "phoenix." For information contact Phoenix Technologies, 312/541-0260.

ClickBook®   Allows you to convert documents to "books" and brochures of many sizes. For information contact BookMaker Corporation, 415/354-8166, Fax 415/856-4734.

Day-Timer and References   As I noted earlier, there are numerous magazines and journals that a wealth manager should be reading on a regular basis as well as seminars and symposiums he should be attending. In addition, as a financial planner, he also needs to stay abreast of issues in the related fields of insurance, taxes, and estate planning. The problem is how to save pertinent articles, notes, and outlines for future reference. For many years I collected information and filed by subject (e.g., mutual funds). Unfortunately, I ended with a large body of reference material that, for the most part, was worthless. For example, if I wanted to find any references on the issue of taxation of mutual funds, I didn't know whether to look under taxes, mutual funds, variable annuities, tax strategies, etc. Even if I knew the tax-related articles were filed under "mutual funds," I would still have to wade through hundreds of unrelated articles to find the ones I wanted. Day-Timer notes solved my problem. Basically, Day-Timer is a random database. I now assign any item I wish to save a reference number (I'm now in the thousands) and key-word the article. Key-wording simply means listing any possible word that I might think of relating to the article. At a minimum, I include author, title, publication, and date. I type the assigned number and key words onto a single note file in Day-Timer. If I now want to search for tax/mutual fund articles, I would go to Day-Timer and search for any documents with the words *tax* and *mutual fund.* If I were specifically interested in the impact of turnover on taxes and mutual funds, I would add "and turnover." If I have documents on the subject in my file, my search would return their reference numbers. The articles are filed numerically and are easily retrieved. I have been using this system for a few years and it is extremely efficient. For information contact Day-Timer Technologies, 800/362-9927.

Analysis
The following are the analytical programs we currently use in our practice.

Portfolio Management   We have been using Centerpiece® as our portfolio management software for many years. However, as our practice has grown, we have pushed the limits of the software and find it increasingly difficult to use. Still, we are reluctant to switch to our alternate choice, Advent. Although Advent provides undeniably fine software, my impression has been that the company's commitment is to the institutional market. This is reflected in the pricing and the inflexibility of the product structure. It is our intention to continue to work with Centerpiece with the expectation that they will soon expand the capabilities of the system to serve the larger wealth manager. If they do so successfully, I would recommend that any wealth manager consider moving to Centerpiece, as we are their primary target market. For information contact Performance Technologies, Inc. 800/528-9595, Fax 919/876-2187.

Schwab Link   This is an integral part of our system. Although not without problems, it has been improving at a geometric rate and is supported by a responsive technical staff that cares about our practice.

INTERNET

We are still trying to figure out what this is all about. I am sure we devote more time and resources to it than can be justified by its contribution to our business. However, we are convinced that it is not a short-lived story but rather technology of profound significance and we want to participate. Because one of our associate advisors is a dedicated semiprofessional hacker, we were one of the earliest wealth managers with a home page. In fact, we had a home page before I knew what that meant or how to find it.

Today we primarily use Internet for e-mail with professional friends around the country, a few clients, and family. Although it is not our intention to use our home page for prospecting new clients, we do publish our newsletter on the Web. From a marketing standpoint, we would expect to use Internet increasingly for client communications and for establishing relationships with other professionals (e.g., CPAs and attorneys).

On a daily basis, we use the Web as a way to keep up with business information, economic forecasts, and business-related issues. Intermittently, we use the Web to research specific stocks (e.g., positions a client may already hold), legal issues (e.g., fiduciary investing), tax law changes, investment issues, and technology reviews (e.g., if we are searching for new hardware or software).

The following is a selection of a few of the sites I've found particularly useful or interesting:

SELECTED INTERNET SITES

Investment-Related Sites

Investments

Resources in Finance = http://www.cob.ohio-state.edu/dept/fin/research.htm#Link4

Java Applet—Stock Trace http://www.cs.virginia.edu/~cd4v/graph/Stock-Graph.html (Impressive resource for information on individual equities.)

Woodrow: Federal Reserve Bank of Minneapolis = http://woodrow.mpls.frb.fed.us/

WallStreetWeb Features = http://www.bulletproof.com/wallstreetweb/features.htm

Investors Library = http://www.investools.com/cgi-bin/Library/library.pl

Wall Street Research = http://www.wsrn.com/

Journals

Journal of Finance Home Page = http://www.cob.ohio-state.edu/dept/fin/journal/jof.htm

The Journal of Financial Economics = http://www.ssb.rochester.edu/fac/jfe/jfe.htm

The Journal of Financial Abstracts = http://www.ssep.com/ssep/ssep310.html

Search

Yahoo—Business and Economy: Markets and Investments = http://www.yahoo.com/Economy/Markets_and_Investments//

The Financial Data Finder = http://www.cob.ohio-state.edu/dept/fin/osuda-ta.htm

Home Pages

William F. Sharpe = http://gsb-www.stanford.edu/~wfsharpe/home.html (Lots of interesting stuff on the home page of this Nobel laureate.)

FINWeb Home Page = http://www.finweb.com/

BARRA = http://www.barra.com/

EB&K = http://www.evensky.com/(Welcome to our homemade home page.)

AIMR = http://global.village.virginia.edu/aimr/

Conscious Investing Home Page = http://www.conscious.investing.com/ (Michael Corning provides guidance to cutting-edge issues for wealth managers [as well as an example of a VERY sophisticated home page]. Be sure to check out the audio business card.)

SEI = http://www.seic.com/irg

News

Financial Planning News = http://www.tisny.com:80/fponline/news/index.html (I check this out almost every morning.)

PointCast = http://www.pointcast.com (This is a last-minute addition but one of the first you should try.)

Reuters Headlines = http://www.yahoo.com/headlines/

Reuters Headlines—Current = http://www.yahoo.com/headlines/current/news

Nation = http://www2.nando.net/nt/nation/

Financial Times Group = http://www.ft.com/

USA TODAY = http://www.usatoday.com/

U.S. News Online = http://www2.USNews.com/usnews/main.htm

Bloomberg News = http://www.bloomberg.com/cgibin/tdisp.sh?bbn/index.html

RealAudio = http://www.realaudio.com/ (This is REALLY neat!)

Search

Alta Vista = http://altavista.digital.com/ (If you're looking for a general search engine, try this one first.)

Federal Register/Congressional Record = http://ssdc.ucsd.edu/gpo/

Code of Federal Regulations = http://www.pls.com:8001/his/cfr.html

Library of Congress = gopher://marvel.loc.gov/

LawLinks—The Attorney Center = http://lawlinks.com/lawatty.html

Starting Point—Magazines = http://www.stpt.com/magazine.html (A direct connection to dozens and dozens of internet magazines. Includes technical, business, and general publications.)

PC Magazine Online—Search = http://www.zdnet.com/pcmag/search.htm (An example of a magazine located in "Starting Point." Useful in researching for reviews on computer hardware and software.)

Reference—Fun and Useful

AT&T 800s = http://att.net/dir800

Thesaurus—Roget = http://humanities.uchicagoedu/forms_unrest/ROGET.html

Bartlett's Familiar Quotations = http://www.columbia.edu/acis/bartleby/bartlett/

Legal References = http://www.netaxs.com/people/evansdb/

U.S. Govt. Printing Office = http://ssdc.ucsd.edu/gpo/

U.S. Census Bureau = http://www.census.gov/

Amusement and Diversion— Fun but Not Very Useful

The T.W.I.N.K.I.E. Project = http://www.rice.edu/~gouge.twinkies.html

CUSTODIAL RELATIONSHIPS

To function as a wealth manager, a practitioner must establish a relationship with one or more broker-dealers or trust companies. These organizations provide a process for a wealth manager to direct trades for his client's benefit and/or as a custodian for the client's assets. At a minimum, the organization should provide access to appropriate managers, duplicate copies of all client communications (including statements and trade confirmations), and security for the client's assets (e.g., SIPC insurance). Although there are numerous service providers offering services to the wealth manager, many are structured to support the fee and commission advisor. Only a few are committed primarily to the independent, fee-only wealth manager.

CHARLES SCHWAB

Although we continue to monitor the offerings of the other organizations, we use Charles Schwab as our primary service provider. Our selection was based on the following criteria:

- People. For a number of years, I had been privileged to serve on the Schwab advisory board and council. That involvement provided me an excellent opportunity to meet Schwab staff from all areas of the organization. I was (and continue to be) impressed with their concern for my practice.

- Commitment to technology. Schwab believes, as I do, that technology is the lifeblood of our business. They have committed significant resources to continuing to improve their systems. The results are impressive.

- Reputation and availability. The Charles Schwab name is one comfortable to our clients and the availability of a retail office in almost every community is a comfort to our out-of-state clients.

Having now dealt with Schwab for many years, we find that the high point of our relationship continues to be the people we work with. We receive significant support from our regional marketing representative, continual attention from our dedicated operations group, and, when requested, responsive and professional assistance from local offices and departments such as compliance, technology, and trading.

Concerns that we continue to monitor include:

- Their commitment to the wealth manager as a *primary* client.
- Schwab's original success was a result of providing service to the retail market. The needs of the retail market may occasionally differ from those of the wealth manager. We are concerned that there seems to be an institutional difficulty in recognizing that, as wealth managers, we expect to be considered a primary client.
- Schwab's rate of growth and ability to staff accordingly.
- Transaction costs.
- Improvements in Schwab Link and Centerpiece.

SEI

As with Schwab, our relationship with SEI dates back many years. SEI offers wealth managers the unique opportunity to access their universe of institutional funds without transaction costs, while providing the technology for the structuring of easy modeling and rebalancing. Added to this is a refocused commitment on the part of SEI to support the serious wealth manager.

DFA

Actually, DFA does not belong in this particular list, as it does not provide the wealth manager the services of either a broker-dealer or a trust company. Still, we have been so strongly influenced by Rex Sinquefield and educated by Dan Wheeler and others at DFA, that we consider them part of our support team. I believe that any serious wealth manager must consider establishing a relationship with DFA.

EVENSKY'S ADVISOR SUPPORT SIEVE

My knowledge of other relationships is largely limited to the comments of friends (e.g., Lou Stanasolovich has been a consistent advocate of Jack White). The following is my recommendation regarding a systematic process for selecting a provider along with a list of the primary providers.

This technique is the same recommended earlier for selecting capital needs software and money managers. In this case, the sieve is designed to screen out inappropriate and unsuitable support organizations. **The criteria marked with an asterisk (*) are ones we consider mandatory.**

*Funds Available

Does the advisor support group offer an adequate number of no-load funds in all of the asset classes utilized by the wealth manager (including passive funds)? Are load funds available at NAV?

*Transaction Costs

Are there funds available at no transaction cost? Are transaction costs lowered as the advisor has more money under management? Are the estimated transaction costs per client, based on your practice, acceptable?

Electronic Support

- *Downloading Capabilities—Can transactions be downloaded via modem to the wealth manager's portfolio software, such as Centerpiece, Advent, dbCAMS, CAPTOOLS, or Axys? It is imperative for a wealth manager to have current information available at any time. Is the software regularly updated? Is it Windows based? Is it networkable?
- *Electronic Trading—Can trades be placed electronically via modem? Telephone trading can be time consuming and expensive. Electronic trading offers more flexibility. Is bulk trading available?
- *Technical Support—Is there adequate and capable technical support for the interface system? When errors occur, it is important to have access to a technical support staff familiar with various portfolio management software as well as their own reporting software. What are their hours? What is their response time? Is there an 800 number?
- *Automatic Fee Deductions—Can fees be automatically deducted from clients' accounts? Is it possible to electronically enter fee

schedules and have the fees deducted from the various accounts? Is consolidated billing of clients' accounts available?

- Electronic Applications/Transfers—Can applications and transfer forms be entered via modem? It is often important to open accounts and assign an account number while the client is still in the office.

- Electronic Financial Data Delivery—Does the advisor support group have indexes or other financial data such as Bloomberg or Morningstar available via modem? Is there a cost?

Operations

- *Operations Department—Is there a dedicated operations department for advisors? Is the staff competent, efficient, and prompt? Are there enough staff to comfortably handle transfers, withdrawals, and other operations requests in a timely manner?

- Trading Department—Is there a dedicated trading department available or will the advisor have to use a general trading desk?

- Trust Services—Are trust services available?

Advisor Benefits

- *Consolidated Statements—Does the advisor support group provide consolidated statements to clients and copies to advisors? Can they be electronically transferred to the advisor? Can they be customized for the advisor?

- Minimums—Does the advisor support company request minimum assets under management? Are there benefits as new asset levels are attained, such as lower transaction costs or additional services provided to advisor at no cost?

- Insurance—Is low-cost liability insurance available through the support company?

- Compliance—Is there a dedicated compliance department providing information and access to their expertise at little or no cost?

- Referral Program—Is there a referral program that a qualified advisor may participate in? If so, what are the qualifications and company participation requirements?
- Conferences—Are there networking and educational opportunities available for the advisor? Do they provide continuing education credits?
- Teleconferencing with Managers—Does the support company provide access to portfolio managers by sponsoring teleconferencing experiences?
- Marketing Material—Does the support group provide generic marketing material, graphs, or charts on disk for advisor's use?

Unique Client Needs

- *Custodial Accounts—Can advisor support IRAs, pension accounts, 401k accounts, etc.? Additional charges?
- Cash Management Programs—Are there cash management accounts available? Additional charges?
- *Specialized Tax Reporting—Does the firm provide year-end tax summaries, gain and loss reports, or other reports that enhance the service to the client?
- Systematic Instructions—Can advisor set up systematic withdrawal or distribution instructions? Additional charges?
- Unique Assets—Will support company hold unique assets such as limited partnerships or variable annuities? Are there additional charges for any of these?

ADVISOR SUPPORT ORGANIZATIONS

Charles Schwab Co., Inc.
Schwab Institutional
101 Montgomery Street
San Francisco, CA 94104
800/648-6021

Jack White & Company
Financial Advisor Division
9191 Towne Centre Drive, Second Floor
San Diego, CA 92122
800/895-0777

First Trust Corporation
717 17th Street, No. 2600
Denver, CO 80202
800/525-2124

Fidelity Brokerage Services, Inc.
Fidelity Investments Advisor Group
82 Devonshire Street, A6A
Boston, MA 02109
800/854-4772

ORGANIZATIONS AND PUBLICATIONS

Although there are innumerable fine organizations and publications that a
wealth manager might consider joining or subscribing to, there are a few I
would recommend for all wealth managers:

PROFESSIONAL ORGANIZATIONS

The International Association for Financial Planning
5775 Glendridge Drive, NE
Suite B-3003
Atlanta, GA 30328–5364
404/845-0011

Institute of Certified Financial Planners (for CFPs)
3801 East Florida Avenue, Suite 708
Denver, CO 80210
303/759-4900

Association for Investment Management & Research*
5 Boar's Head Lane
Charlottesville, VA 22903
800/247-8132

Academy of Financial Services
C/O Dr. Robert McLeod
University of Alabama

---

*AIMR accepts for regular membership individuals who have either passed CFA Level 1 and have 3
    years work experience, or who have 6 years of qualifying experience and successfully
    complete a self-administered standards and professional practice exam.

Dept. of Economic Finance & Legal Studies
P.O. Box 870224
Tuscaloosa, AL 35487–0224
205/348-8993

PROFESSIONAL PUBLICATIONS

Financial Analyst Journal
Association for Investment Management and Research
P.O. Box 3668
Charlottesville, VA 22903
804/980-3668

The Journal of Investing
488 Madison Avenue, 16th Floor
New York, NY 10022
212/224-3599

The Journal of Portfolio Management
488 Madison Avenue, 16th Floor
New York, NY 10022
212/224-3185

Journal of Financial Planning
3801 E. Florida Avenue, #708
Denver, CO 80210
303/759-4900

Financial Services Review
55 Old Post Road, No. 2
P.O. Box 1678
Greenwich, CT 06836–1678
203/661-7602

TRADE PUBLICATIONS

Financial Planning Magazine
40 West 57th Street, 11th Floor
New York, NY 10019
212/765-5311

Investment Advisor
179 Avenue at the Commons, 2nd Floor
Shrewsbury, NJ 07702
908/389-8700

Fee Advisor
179 Avenue at the Commons, 2nd Floor
Shrewsbury, NJ 07702
908/389-8700

Morningstar Investors
225 W. Wacker Drive, Suite 400
Chicago, IL 60606–9630
312/696-6000

No-Load Fund Analyst
L/G Research
4 Orinda Way
Suite 230-D
Orinda, CA 94563
510/254-9017

Inside Information
2087 Shillingwood Drive
Kennesaw, GA 30152
770/424-8755

RETAIL PUBLICATIONS

These are publications that wealth management clients are likely to be
reading. It is important to be familiar with their coverage.

Money Magazine
Rockefeller Center
1271 6th Avenue
New York, NY 10020
212/522-6710

Smart Money
1790 Broadway
New York, NY 10019
212/492-1300

Worth
575 Lexington Avenue, 35th floor
New York, NY 10022
212/223-3100

Kiplinger Personal Finance
1729 H Street NW
Washington, DC 20006
202/876-6489

Financial World
1328 Broadway, 3rd floor
New York, NY 10001
212/594-5030

ALPHA

Originally, I intended to put this discussion about the Alpha Group in an Appendix; however, my partner Deena persuaded me that it belonged in the discussion of the development and management of a wealth management practice. The Alpha Group has had a significant positive influence on our practice and I believe that similar professional networking groups will be equally beneficial for other wealth managers. So, hoping it helps stimulate the reader to consider forming his own network, here's our story.

THE ALPHA GROUP

In September 1990 my partner Deena Katz and three friends, Eleanor Blayney, Lou Stanasolvich, and Greg Sullivan, and I were sitting in a coffee shop at the New Orleans IAFP National Convention, bemoaning the fact that it was difficult to maintain our professional edge. Although we were active in our professional organizations (the IAFP and ICFP) and regularly attended their national conventions, we realized that the highlight of the conventions was the opportunity to visit and chat with each other. The result of our ruminations was an informal meeting of a few like-minded planners at the Crystal City Hilton during the 1991 IAFP Conference for Advanced Planning. In spite of having no plans, no agenda, no goals, and no idea of what we wished to accomplish other than to meet and chat about professional issues of mutual concern, the meeting was such a success that we decided to get together on a regular basis. As three of the original members were on the national IAFP board, we agreed to meet at the IAFP National Convention and the IAFP Conference for Advanced Planning. Still missing was an identity—who were we? Everyone contributed their thoughts and Deena's idea of value added won the day. The Alpha Group was born.

Today, Alpha is comprised of 15 members representing nine firms and operates (usually) according to the bylaws adopted in May 1994 (Appendix F). We meet in person twice a year for two days and once or twice per month by conference call. The two-day meetings allocate a half day for presentations about technical subjects by invited guests (e.g., currency hedging by PIMCo, factor analysis by SEI, and fund evaluation by Morningstar), one day for technical presentations by Alpha members (e.g., tactical allocation by Stanasolovich, risk tolerance by Deena, and an update on the Fama/French three-factor model by Dongieux and Chambers) and a half day for miscellaneous discussions. As Jim Budros is our designated gourmet chef, he is responsible for ensuring two terrific dinners. The regular monthly conference call includes "hired and fired" (i.e., what managers have been hired and what managers have been fired), a technical discussion (e.g., portfolio tax management), and anything else that members find interesting. The other monthly call is our manager interview. The members take turns selecting a manager to invite for the call. Once an invitation has been accepted, the manager is provided a detailed questionnaire with the request that it be completed and a copy provided to each Alpha member before the call. The call is scheduled for 60 minutes. The first 30 to 40 minutes are allotted to the manager to expand on the questionnaire and the balance is for Q&A.

Now for full disclosure. The synopsis above described yesterday but is unlikely to accurately describe tomorrow. One of the exciting things about Alpha is that it is composed of 15 VERY independent entrepreneurs. Nothing stays the same. In fact, when deciding on a potential change or a new idea, we usually start off with 15 to 20 different ideas.

With the exception of our bylaws, Alpha is "rigorously" informal. Our goals are to improve our professional expertise and our practice quality. There is no "official" policy and no spokesperson. Alpha members represent themselves and their firm, not Alpha. The membership size has been determined by the constraints of efficient conference calls and convenient meeting rooms. Operational responsibilities (e.g., coordinating phone calls, minutes, and meetings) are determined by self-selection—i.e., who volunteers first. The Alpha Group members are:

Members

Mark Balasa
Burton Investment Management, Inc.
Schaumburg, IL

Don Chambers
Gene Dongieux
Mercer
Santa Barbara, CA

Eleanor Blayney
Greg Sullivan
Sullivan Bruyette Speros
& Blayney
McLean, VA

Harold Evensky
Deena Katz
Evensky, Brown & Katz
Coral Gables, FL

Jim Budros
Peggy Ruhlin
Budros & Ruhlin
Columbus, OH

David Bugen
Ram Kolluri
Individual Asset Planning
Morristown, NJ

Ross Levin
Accredited Investors
Minneapolis, MN

Lou Stanasolovich
Legend Financial Advisors, Inc.
Pittsburgh, PA

John Uleke
Bob Winfield
Middle South Advisors
Memphis, TN

MARKETING

When a professional elects to specialize, it behooves him to have a good idea of who is likely to need his specialized services. A cardiologist is unlikely to expect demand for his services from a patient with a broken arm. A real estate lawyer will not market his services to clients needing securities advice. Who, then, is the market for the wealth manager?

During the early stages of practice development, the answer may be "anyone who fogs a mirror." Many years ago when I started my practice, I was accused of accepting clients even if they did not "fog a mirror"; after all, they might miraculously recover. An established practice, however, needs to focus on those clients who will most benefit from the firm's services.

CLIENT SIZE

The number of clients a wealth manager can service is dependent upon many factors, particularly the quality and depth of the firm's support staff. The general range is from 30 to 100 clients per advisor with an average of about 50 relationships. Using 50 as a standard, Table 14–4 shows the projected revenue (or various median account sizes assuming an average fee of 1 percent of assets).

Based on this relationship and my own experience, I believe that in order to provide the service of wealth management, a wealth manager should consider an account minimum of $300,000 to $500,000.

T A B L E   14-4

Gross Revenue/Wealth Manager

Average Account	Gross Revenue
$ 100,000	$ 50,000
300,000	150,000
500,000	250,000
1,000,000	500,000

CLIENT PROFILE

- As a result of having to meet the minimum account size, the client has already acquired wealth, i.e., clients with little wealth and high incomes are not likely to be wealth management clients.

- They are likely to perceive themselves as conservative investors and/or believe that their fiduciary duty requires a conservative approach to investing.

- They are passive investors. If they have or have had brokerage accounts, they are most likely to be wrap accounts. More often, their funds are invested in bonds, CDs, or are being managed by a trust company. They are not particularly interested in 'bragging' rights.

- They are not knowledgeable regarding investments and they freely admit their ignorance.

- They seek comfort and security, not performance.

- They do not expect to get rich in the market; they already feel rich. They do not want to get poor.

- They expect high-quality personal and confidential service.

- Their source of wealth typically comes from selling a business, inheritance, or divorce, or is the corpus of a fiduciary account (e.g., pension or trust).

Using the profiles described in *Cultivating the Affluent,** the wealth management client is not likely to be a:

Mogul—An investor who sees investing as a way of keeping score.

---

*Russ Alan Prince and Karen Maru File, *Cultivating the Affluent,* pp. 21–25, Private Asset Management on *Institutional Investor Newsletter,* 1995. Another "must-read."

VIP—One looking for bragging rights.

Gambler—Someone who sees investing as a hobby.

Innovator—An investor who wants to be in the newest and latest.

The wealth manager's primary client is likely to be a:

Family steward—A client for whom the investing goal is to provide for the needs of his/her family.

Independent—One who participates in investment decisions reluctantly in order to provide for his/her financial independence.

I am often kidded when I describe for professional friends the profile of our clients as those "with significant assets and no problems." Certainly the description is intended to garner a chuckle but it's not far off the mark. If we see a prospect with multiple and complex issues (e.g., a closely held business owner with complex tax and insurance problems), we may be able to assist him as a specialist in comprehensive planning but we would not consider him a wealth management client, at least not initially. Once we have resolved his other (and usually more pressing) problems, he may be a candidate for wealth management.

Our typical client is retired, has a standard of living modest compared to his wealth, and desires to maintain his standard of living during his lifetime and pass on some estate to his children and grandchildren. Our clients typically have no need for disability insurance or life insurance for risk management. Their other risk management needs are related to the relatively simple issues of Medicare supplement, long-term care, and property and casualty. Income tax management is largely an investment issue (e.g., municipals versus taxable bonds). Their retirement plan design days are over. The only financial planning complexities other than investments might be estate planning issues, an area of expertise for the wealth manager. As I said, "Significant assets and no problems."

CLIENT NEEDS

If the client is not looking for our expertise in risk management, tax planning, or pension design, and if he is not driven by investment performance, what does he want from the wealth manager?

- Expertise. He wants an advisor who is expert in the issues discussed in this book.

- Someone who will focus on his total welfare, not just his portfolio (i.e., a financial planner specializing in wealth management, not a money manager). As David Biehl of BBK has noted, "a counselor not just a money manager." Someone who offers his judgment, not just advice.

- Someone with an expertise in important related areas (e.g., estate planning, fiduciary responsibilities).

- Portfolio reporting, not portfolio accounting. Brokerage firms and money managers account for their clients' positions and returns. Wealth managers report on how well the client is succeeding in meeting his life's goals.

Accredited Investors Wealth Management Index

The difficulty has been how to measure this success. The good news is that help is on the way. Ross Levin is currently completing his book, *Wealth Management Index,* soon to be issued by Irwin. Levin has developed the concept of a "wealth management index"—a tool to quantify a client's annual success toward reaching his stated ends. In Levin's words, the index "can be used by financial planners to regularly measure their clients' progress through the myriad of financial goals and decisions they make and *do not make.* It evolves every year and is communicated to the client. The index helps us manage expectations by continuing to focus the relationship on all of the clients' stated goals and objectives." I had the privilege of reviewing some of Levin's preliminary work and I believe that he has created a real breakthrough concept for all financial planners. I anxiously await the opportunity to have his book in hand and utilize his Wealth Management Index for the benefit of my clients.

CLIENT RECAP

Table 14–5 includes selections from *Cultivating the Affluent.* They compare the responses of wealth management profile clients (i.e., family stewards and independents) to that of moguls and VIPs. These statistics reflect much of the criteria described above.

T A B L E   14–5

Client Responses*

Percent of the Sample**	Family Stewards 21%	Independents 13%	Moguls 10%	VIPs 8%	Weighted Total 100%
Percent Rating Criteria as Very Important					
Selection criteria					
Overall manager expertise	90%	90%	92%	85%	91%
Care manager takes to identify needs	86	89	80	93	89
Investment performance record	1	19	16	23	27
Expertise in other financial services	37	33	0	27	26
Financial planning and estate planning expertise	16	22	1	14	16
Assets under management	3	17	23	78	13
Cost of services	0	0	9	14	9
Detail of report	1	1	3	0	5
Services					
Asset allocation	66	82	88	46	57
Financial and estate planning	72	24	3	20	41
Tax planning	30	5	11	14	24
Percent Reporting High Familiarity with Products					
Money market accounts	73	78	73	92	69
U.S. equity	13	9	7	50	18
U.S. municipal bonds	10	6	9	53	16
Wrap accounts	14	16	10	31	15
Int'l bonds (developed countries)	6	6	3	45	12
Int'l equities (developed countries)	7	6	3	41	11
Percent very interested in learning more about products					
Money market accounts	0	0	0	0	0
U.S. equity	13	11	9	4	8
U.S. municipal bonds	14	13	11	3	8
Wrap accounts	49	39	38	57	34
Int'l bonds (developed countries)	9	4	7	7	6
Int'l equities (developed countries)	9	11	8	5	6

*The data are based on a cluster of sampling surveys of 879 affluent investors (i.e., those with at least $400,000 in investable assets). The excerpts in Table 14–6 are just a small sampling of the valuable data included in *Cultivating the Affluent.*
**Rounded to the nearest percent. The survey data are to one decimal place.

THE MARKET*

Traditionally, the financial planner's market has been the retail client. These individuals represent a significant market. Estimates vary; however, the core market is about 5 million households.**

If from this we eliminate those with more than $10,000,000 in investable assets,*** the remaining market is still more than 4 million households. To recap, I believe the wealth manager's natural market is the individual investor with $500,000 to $10 million in investable assets, with "no problems," and the needs described earlier.

Although that is a significant market, I believe that there is an exciting new market on the horizon—namely, the fiduciary investor. The law moves at a glacial pace but it does evolve. In terms of fiduciary investing, the evolution is at the stage that I believe the law will soon effectively mandate that an investment fiduciary employ the services of a wealth manager. For the "retail level" fiduciary (i.e., a portfolio with less than $20 million), there is no professional better positioned to integrate the theory and technology of institutional investing, the lessons of modern portfolio theory, and the knowledge and skills of financial planning for the benefit of the funds' beneficiaries than the wealth manager.

I believe that this legal evolution is so important to the future of wealth management that I have elected to devote the next chapter to the issue of fiduciary investing.

---

*The following studies included research related to the wealth manager's market:
  Bernstein Research, *The Future of Money Management in America, 1995 Edition*
  Goldman Sachs, Investment Management Group, *The Coming Evolution of the Investment Management Industry: Opportunities and Strategies,* October 1995
  KPMG Investment Companies Practice, *State of the Investment Company Industry,* Winter 1996
  U.S. Trust, *Survey of Affluent Americans,* July 1995
**Bernstein Research reported in its *The Future of Money Management in America, 1995 Edition,* that there were 5.27 million households with discretionary financial assets in excess of $500 million.
***Although the superwealthy (i.e., over $10 million investable assets) are candidates for wealth management, they are a less opportune market than those with .5 to 10 million. The superwealthy often have many complex issues unrelated to investments, frequently invest in less traditional asset classes (e.g., hedge funds and venture capital), and are often surrounded by an almost impenetrable shield of advisors. These advisors, unlike their clients, are often VIP or mogul profiles.

CHAPTER 15

Fiduciary Investing

The most treasured asset in investment
management is a steady hand at the tiller.

—Robert Arnott

Any intelligent person assuming the responsibility of a fiduciary best
mind his p's and q's regarding his actions. The level of personal liability a
fiduciary assumes is significant. Investing as a fiduciary was once a rather
simple process of defaulting to a "conservative" portfolio of high-quality
bonds with an occasional sprinkling of blue chip stocks. Today, for most
fiduciaries, this simple investment solution no longer suffices. Beginning
with ERISA (1974) and followed by the Restatement of Trust 3rd (1992)
and the Uniform Prudent Investor Act (1994), there has been a shift in the
standards applied to investing as a fiduciary. For anyone serving as an investment fiduciary, or advising clients who are fiduciaries, a knowledge
of these changes is imperative. With a primary focus on the requirements
for private fiduciaries, the following discussion provides a history of the
law, concluding with its current status. The section concludes with recommendations for investment actions necessary to meet the standards today.

EARLY HISTORY

The concept of trusts dates back to 12th-century England and was frequently related to endowments of land. In the simple world of those early
trusts, land rents provided a consistent and increasing income stream and

the land itself provided for capital preservation and growth. As society progressed and the economy became more complex, there was an evolutionary development leading to the creation of securities such as bonds and a shifting of trust investments from real property to financial securities. Whereas the earlier focus had been the preservation of real wealth, the focus now became the preservation of capital. Based on the premise that the only security appropriately safe for trust investments was government bonds (and, as some commentators suggest, the government's desire to assure a market for government bonds), English law mandated government bonds as the sole investment acceptable for most trusts. This was the legal heritage in the United States until *Harvard College* v. *Amory* in 1830.

HARVARD COLLEGE V. *AMORY,*
26 MASS.(9 PICK.) 446(1830).

Francis Amory had been appointed the trustee of his friend John McLean's estate upon McLean's death. The estate consisted of approximately $50,000 in bank, insurance, and industrial stock. Mrs. McLean was the income beneficiary until her death, and Harvard College one of the remainderman beneficiaries. At the time of Mrs. McLean's death the estate corpus had shrunk to $40,000, and Harvard sued Amory claiming that he, as trustee, should make up the $10,000 shortfall as a result of his improper investments, i.e., equities. Under existing English common law it seemed clear that Harvard would succeed in its claim.

The final ruling of the Massachusetts court, however, was a relaxing of the English common law standard regarding investments. In what has been called the single most profound state court decision, the court developed what has become known as *the prudent man* standard, a clear and flexible guideline for fiduciaries based on conduct and not results.

In rejecting the claim of Harvard College, the court recognized that all investments have risk—"Do what you will, the capital is at hazard." The court also specifically addressed the myth of the safety of government bonds. The court queried "What becomes of the capital when the credit of the government shall be so much impaired as it was at the close of the last war?"

In what has become a well-known statement of prudence, the court ruled that trustees should "observe how men of prudence, discretion, and intelligence manage **their own** affairs, not in regard to **speculation,** but in regard to the **permanent disposition** of their funds, considering the *probable income* as well as the probable *safety of the capital* to be invested." As the balance of this article will discuss, the words in italics highlight the major issues that have plagued fiduciaries and the courts ever since.*

It is important to note that the decision did not explicitly approve of common stocks as appropriate investments for fiduciaries. Rather, as noted earlier, it established the prudent man rule with two definitive but flexible standards:[1]

- A process standard based on "how men of prudence . . . manage their own affairs."

The court recognized that investing funds is a continual and implicitly risky process. They also recognized that there is no rational basis for setting strict and arbitrary standards for fiduciary investing. Decisions must constantly be made, the results monitored, and, if appropriate, revised. Their solution for establishing a viable and living standard against which to measure the actions of a trustee was the prudent man standard.[2]

- A standard for judging the appropriateness of a fiduciary investment, namely, one appropriate for the "permanent disposition" of the trustee's "own funds." The court also recognized that generally the funds placed under the control of a trustee have a long investment horizon. In the terminology familiar to modern financial planners, permanent disposition equates to "long term." They also recognized that beneficiaries of trusts do not become a unique form of humanity by act of law. Beneficiaries are likely to have the same general goals as the balance of humanity. No unique constraints on the trustee's investment authority was appropriate; hence, the reference to "own funds."

AFTER *HARVARD COLLEGE* V. *AMORY*— THE NEXT 120 YEARS

The new freedom provided by the flexible prudent man standard of *Harvard College* v. *Amory* was short-lived (in fact, for the next 110 years only eight other states adopted the rule). The next seminal case was *King* v. *Talbot* (1869). From the perspective of today's financial planner, this case threw trustees back into the stone ages. However, in fairness, the

---

*The italics and bold notation in this paragraph and throughout are the author's.

New York court that ruled was living in a far different investment world than today's.

KING V. *TALBOT,* 40 N.Y. 76(1869)

During the 1800s, purchasing power risk was not an issue. Deflation was as probable as inflation and the price level in 1916 was the same as 1776. The Tontine Coffee House (precursor of the New York Stock Exchange) had only been founded a little over 70 years earlier, and by 1892 more than 75 percent of the trading was still in bonds. Bondholders were promised a return on their principal and a return *of* their principal. If the company failed to pay, the bondholders had powers to enforce their claims. Stockholders had only expectations of gains. Bondholders generally had liquidity and could expect to sell "in the market," whereas for many stocks there was no market. Further, for the most part, stocks represented ownership in venture businesses in fledgling industries. With this background in mind, is it little wonder that the court ruled:

"The moment the fund is invested in . . . stock, it has left the control of the trustees, its safety is no longer dependent upon their skill, care or discretion, in its custody or management, and the terms of the investment do not contemplate that it will ever be returned to the trustee."

The real wonder is that the *Harvard College* v. *Amory* justices were so enlightened in their view.

Unfortunately, the result of the ruling in *King* v. *Talbot* was a shift from the *prudent man* to a *prudent trustee.* King did not accept the standard of safety as "how men of prudence . . . manage their own affairs." Instead, the court ruled:

> not according to its nature, nor within any just idea of prudence to place the principal of the fund in a condition, in which, it is necessarily exposed to the hazard of loss or gain, according to the success or failure of the enterprise in which it is embarked.
>
> It, therefore, does not follow that, because prudent men may, and often do, conduct their own affairs with the hope of growing rich, and therein take the hazard of adventures which they deem hopeful, trustees may do the same; the preservation of the fund, and the procurement of a just income therefrom are primary objects of the creation of the trust itself.

Following the lead of King, in 1889 the New York legislature passed a statute limiting trust investments to bonds and mortgages unless otherwise provided for in the trust documents. Led by New York's action, by 1900 most states had enacted *legal list* laws and Massachusetts was almost alone in adhering to the original prudent man standard.

AFTER WORLD WAR I

During the first 40 years of the 20th century, the United States rapidly grew as an industrial nation. Industries matured, corporate stock investments evolved from venture capital to blue chips, and economic regulation flourished. Following the Great Depression, along with the enactment of the Securities Act of 1933 and the Securities Exchange Act of 1934, the nation began an almost uninterrupted period of continual inflation.

SCOTT (1935)

Still, little change came to the law of fiduciary investing until 1935 with the issuing of the *Restatement of Trusts** and the first publication of *The Law of Trusts,* by Professor Austin Wakeman Scott, the father of American trust law. The *Restatement,* for which Scott was the reporter, and *The Law* formulated the drafter's interpretation of the *Harvard College* v. *Amory* prudent man rule. Unfortunately, the result was a constrained prudent man standard. The three constraints were:

▪ A standard of safety described as "having primarily in view *the preservation of the estate*" versus *Harvard College* v. *Amory*'s "*permanent disposition* of their funds." In this difference you will recognize the conflict between the preservation of principal and the preservation of real value. Although today the term *preservation* might include the concept of purchasing power, at the time of the ruling it clearly referred to the original corpus. This constraint severely restricted a trustee from considering any form of equity investment. As the court in *King* v. *Talbot* noted, there are no guarantees with stock. Permanent disposition, however, is a less restrictive criterion. As noted above, it suggests a long-term investment horizon. Under these circumstances, the preservation of purchasing power is a legitimate factor to be considered.

▪ Support for the prudent trustee standard over the prudent man rule as reflected in Scott's commentary in *The Law,* "men who are safeguarding property for others."

---

*See Appendix to this chapter—The American Law Institute

- An attempt to separate speculation from prudence by setting specific rules that had the effect of significantly limiting investment flexibility as investment knowledge grew and as new investment vehicles and strategies were developed.

TRUST DIVISION OF THE AMERICAN BANKERS ASSOCIATION (1942)

Whether in response to the changes in the economy noted previously (particularly inflation) or, as has been suggested, in response to the migration of trust business to Massachusetts (where trust company portfolios operating under the Massachusetts prudent man rule were outperforming legal list-governed trust companies by 100 percent), the ABA developed a model prudent investor act modeled after *Harvard College v. Amory.*

The bad news was that the influence of Scott and the old paradigm remained, as reflected in the following description of "speculative" investments by one of the central participants in the development of the ABA model:

> all purchases of even high-grade securities for the purpose of resale at a profit . . . and . . . all programs not mandated by the trust instrument that are undertaken to increase the number of dollars to compensate for loss of purchasing power.

The good news was that by 1950, following the release of the ABA model, most states had adopted some form of the prudent man standard eliminating the legal list* and allowing at least some allocation to common stock. By 1990 only three states had any form of legal list.

RESTATEMENT OF TRUSTS 2ND (1959)

Scott was also the reporter for the *Second Restatement* and there was little substantive change, as reflected by the following comment from the *Second Restatement:*

"Where, however, the **risk is not out of proportion [to return],** a man of intelligence may make a disposition which is speculative in character with a view to *increasing his property instead of merely preserving it.* Such a disposition *is not a proper trust investment.*"

---

*A legal list was an actual published list of legally approved forms of investments.

The description of improper (i.e., speculative) investments above reads as today's definition of an efficient investment, i.e., an investment where the risk is appropriate for the return. Further, such an investment is acknowledged as appropriate for a man of intelligence and in fact is appropriate for an investor desirous of preserving real value. Even so, such investments were deemed inappropriate for trust property.

THE LAW AND ENDOWMENT FUNDS (1969)

Following World War II, public institutions (e.g., college and universities) were having trouble balancing the demands of beneficiaries with their resources, which were invested largely in fixed-income securities. These institutions were truly "between a rock and a hard place." By the late 1960s, few institutions had adopted a total return policy and little was invested in common stock. Inflation ravaged the real value of their endowment bond portfolios. Funding from major foundations became a critical source of income. This dependence was of concern to the foundations and the largest, the Ford Foundation, commissioned a study of the investment practices of endowments. Known as the *Barber Report,* after its chief author, and published in 1969, the study found that endowment returns were poor compared to large general growth funds. The reason for the poor performance was attributed to the institutions' erroneous adherence to what the report considered an outdated investment paradigm.

Institutions, for the most part, managed their investments under the belief that they were governed by trust law. As such, they felt constrained by the legal standard that capital gains belonged to corpus and only interest income and dividends could be spent. The result was a traditional trust policy of preserving capital and maximizing current income.

The *Barber Report* concluded that endowments did not have beneficiaries as construed under trust law. Hence, there were no parties with conflicting interests. In fact, endowments were not subject to trust law but were subject to corporate law. As such, institutions could consider total return and long-term real growth.

UNIFORM MANAGEMENT OF INSTITUTIONAL FUNDS ACT (1972)

Although there was no immediate rush by institutions to test the new nontrust theory, the report led, in 1972, to the adoption by the National Conference of

Commissioners on Uniform State Laws of the Uniform Management of Institutional Funds Act (UMIFA). Concerned with the long- as well as short-term needs of institutions, the Act explicitly provides for:

- The prudent use of appreciation (a total return policy).
- Investment authority to invest in stock.
- The board's right to delegate investment authority.

Compared to the restrictions faced by those controlled by traditional trust law, this was an extraordinary change. By September 1995, 38 states had adopted, in whole or in part, the UMIFA. Still, many institutions continue to manage their assets under the old paradigm. As late as 1993, the Council on Foundations lamented, "The sad truth is that too many foundation endowments (of whatever kind) are currently managed in a way that is woefully behind the times."[3]

ERISA—A SPECIAL CASE

The most significant act regarding fiduciary investing since *Harvard College* v. *Amory* was the enactment of ERISA, more formally known as the Employee Retirement Security Act of 1974. It would be difficult to overemphasize the fundamental changes that ERISA brings to legal mandates regarding investment fiduciary responsibility. Suffice it to say that ERISA, at least in the realm of its influence, was the first act to bring fiduciary investment law into the 20th century. While the subsequent work of the Restatement of Trust Third and the Uniform Prudent Investor Act may ultimately prove more important due to their wider influence, ERISA in a real sense paved the way for their acceptance.

Some commentators have suggested that the ERISA standard is that of a "prudent expert." Although I believe that this overstates the intention of the law, ERISA clearly introduces the requirement that fiduciaries consider the concepts of modern investment theory and manage in accordance with the unique nature of the plan:

> Section 404(a)(1)B requires a fiduciary to act "with the care, skill, prudence, and diligence *under the circumstances then prevailing* that a prudent man acting in a like capacity and *familiar with such matters* would use in the conduct of *an enterprise of a like character and with like aims.*" [My emphasis.]

RESTATEMENT OF TRUSTS THIRD (1990/1992)*

In the early 1980s, Columbia, Harvard, Princeton, and Stanford commissioned a study of fiduciary investing. The universities selected Bevis Longstreath, a former SEC Commissioner, to lead the project. The results of Longstreath's work were published in 1986 as *Modern Investment Management and the Prudent Man Rule*. In his conclusions, Longstreath recommended that the American Law Institute (ALI) undertake a new Restatement of Trusts (see the Appendix). Whether or not a direct result of this recommendation, on May 18, 1990, the ALI adopted *The Restatement of the Law Third, Trusts, Prudent Investor*. It was published in 1992. The Restatement reflects statutory trends (e.g., ERISA and UMIFA) as well as the efficacy of the significant empirical and theoretical research in investment management. It provides for a dynamic model of trust investment management, unique to the needs of the trust. For experienced financial planners, it is a familiar and comfortable model.

The Foreword, by Geoffrey Hazard, Director of the American Law Institute, places the Third Restatement in perspective:

- ". . . the revised *rule focuses on the trust's portfolio as a whole* and the investment strategy on which it is based, rather than viewing a specific investment in isolation."

- "Reflecting modern investment concepts and practices, the prudent investor rule *recognizes that return on investment is related to risk, that risk includes deterioration of real return owing to inflation, and that the relationship between risk and return may be taken into account* in managing the trust assets. Correlatively, the formulation *requires the trustee to take account of the relationship between return and risk in light of the purposes and circumstances of the trust."*

In the Introduction, Professor Edward C. Halbach, Jr., the Reporter, concisely and specifically summarizes the heart of the Restatement in terms of "Principles of Prudence":

---

*I must begin this section with a personal aside. For anyone remotely interested in the subject of intelligent investing, I can suggest no better text than the Third Restatement. When I put the book down, my first feeling was awe at the clarity with which the author had discussed so many issues dear to my heart. My second thought was that I would never be able to understand the structure of the Restatement. Restatements are composed of three components—statements of principle, explanatory comments, and reporters' notes. I am sure that to attorneys the structure and endless footnoting is no more difficult than reading the comics. For me, it was a shade more difficult. My final thought was to be doubly impressed with an author who had me raving about the clarity of a document I had to wade through with highlighters and multicolored pens. It really is that good of a book.

In addition to the fundamental proposition that no investments or techniques are imprudent per se, there are a few principles of prudence set out in the sections that follow. These principles instruct trustees and the courts that:

1. *Sound diversification is fundamental* to risk management and is therefore ordinarily required of trustees.

2. Risk and return are so directly related *that trustees have a duty to analyze and make conscious decisions concerning the levels of risk appropriate to the* purposes, distribution requirements, and other *circumstances of the trusts* they administer.

3. Trustees have a *duty to avoid* fees, transaction costs, and other *expenses that are not justified by needs and realistic objectives* of the trust's investment program.

4. The fiduciary duty of *impartiality requires a balancing of* the elements between production of *current income* and the *protection of purchasing power.*

5. Trustees *may have a duty as well as having the authority to delegate,* as prudent investors would.

UNIFORM PRUDENT INVESTOR ACT—UPIA (1994)

Although the Third Restatement is a very influential document, by the date of its publication only six states (California, Delaware, Georgia, Minnesota, Tennessee, and Washington) had modified their rules regarding prudent investing to allow much of the flexibility reflected in the Restatement. Illinois, having developed a new law based on a draft of the work of the ALI, was noted in the Restatement as the first "prudent investor" statute based on the Restatement. Still, at the time, most states had "constrained" prudent investor legislation dating back to the 1950s. The next step in this now rapidly moving evolutionary process was the introduction of the Uniform Prudent Investor Act (UPIA) in 1994.

The UPIA was approved and recommended for enactment in all states in August 1994 and approved by the American Bar Association in February 1995. As discussed in the Appendix, the UPIA was not just an academic exercise, but a draft of specific legislation issued by Commissioners representing all 50 states. Finally, U.S. fiduciaries, after a history dating back more than 90 years, will have the opportunity (as well as the obligation) to invest in a flexible and intelligent manner, based on objective standards. Since the UPIA is likely to serve as the framework for most state prudent investor legislation in the future, the most significant changes enacted by the Act are set forth below.

The UPIA recognizes the significant changes in investment practice in the last 30+ years and the development of modern portfolio theory. It draws heavily on the Restatement of Trusts Third. The sections of the Act generally mandate the same kinds of actions noted earlier in the discussion of the Restatement. The primary objective of the act is to make fundamental changes in five criteria for prudent investing. As noted in the Act's prefatory note:

- The standard of prudence is applied to any investment as part of the total portfolio, rather than to individual investments. In the trust, setting the term *portfolio* embraces all the trust's assets.

- The trade-off in all investing between risk and return is identified as the fiduciary's central consideration.

- All categorical restrictions on types of investments have been abrogated; the trustee can invest in anything that plays an appropriate role in achieving the risk/return objective of the trust and that meets the other requirements of prudent investing.

- The long familiar requirement that fiduciaries diversify their investments has been integrated into the definition of prudent investing.

- The much criticized former rule of trust law forbidding the trustee to delegate investment and management functions has been reversed. Delegation is now permitted, subject to safeguards.

ACTIONS REQUIRED OF A FIDUCIARY

In the real world, what does this all mean in terms of prudent investing? What specific actions are required of a fiduciary under the Third Restatement and UPIA?

The following discussion relates my interpretation of the actions required of an investment fiduciary to meet the mandates of the Restatement and the UPIA. Quotations from the Restatement and the UPIA are italicized.

FOLLOW THE INVESTMENT PLANNING PROCESS

Throughout this book, wealth management has been referred to as a specialty of financial planning. Both the Restatement and the UPIA reflect this in numerous ways. In almost identical language, they remind the trustee that he must adhere to the cardinal rule of financial planning—attention to the unique goals of the client:

- *a trustee shall invest and manage trust assets . . . by considering the purposes, terms, distribution requirements, and other circumstances of the trust.*
- The danger of ignoring this requirement is illustrated in the following hypothetical illustration from the Restatement. *T is trustee of a trust that pays its income to L for life, with remainder thereafter to pass to R or R's issue. T has adopted a continuous long-term strategy of investing the trust estate in short-term bank and federal obligations. Although in a sense cautious, this investment program would ordinarily be viewed as failing to take adequate account of the fiduciary duty of caution as it applies to safeguarding the real value of capital.*[R]
- The UPIA and the Restatement constantly reiterate that the measure of prudence is adherence to a prudent process (i.e., the financial planning process). *The test of prudence is one of conduct, not one of performance.*[R, UPIA]

DEVELOP AN INVESTMENT POLICY (STRATEGY)

Most wealth managers are familiar with ERISA's requirement of an investment policy. This same standard is now mandated for all fiduciaries.

- *The trustee must give reasonably careful consideration to both the formulation and the implementation of an investment strategy, with investments to be selected and reviewed in a manner reasonably appropriate to that strategy.*[R]
- *A trustee's investment and management decisions . . . must be evaluated as part of an overall investment strategy.*[UPIA]

DESIGN THE POLICY FOR TOTAL RETURN

The archaic concept of separating income and capital appreciation has been discarded. Fiduciaries are now required to use the more rational criterion of total return.

- *Among circumstances that a trustee shall consider in investing and managing trust . . . expected total return.*[UPIA]
- *In the absence of contrary provisions in the terms of the trust, this requirement of caution requires the trustee to invest with a view both to safety of the capital and to securing a reasonable return.*[R]
- The Restatement continues in its commentary . . . *Reasonable 'return' refers to total return, including capital appreciation and gain as*

well as trust accounting income . . . The capital growth element of these
return objectives, however, is not necessarily confined to the preservation
of purchasing power, but may extend to growth in the real value of princi-
pal in appropriate cases.[R]

- Included in the discussion of total return is a more modern concept
of "safety" that includes purchasing power, interest rate, and reinvestment
risk, as well as market risk. Particular attention is devoted to the preservation of real value.

   'Safety' of capital includes not only the objective of protecting the
trust property from the risk of loss of nominal value but, ordinarily, also a
goal of preserving its real value—that is, seeking to avoid or reduce loss
of the trust estate's purchasing power as a result of inflation . . . The
trustee is also under a duty to the remainder beneficiaries to exercise rea-
sonable care in an effort to preserve the trust property, and this duty ordi-
narily includes a goal of protecting the property's purchasing power . . .
Thus, a trustee has a duty to seek to balance the income and principal el-
ements of total investment return.[R]

MANAGE RISK

Modern fiduciary law now recognizes the seminal work of Harry
Markowitz. Risk management, rather than risk avoidance, is the standard.

- *These changes have occurred under the influence of a large and*
broadly accepted body of empirical and theoretical knowledge about the
behavior of capital markets, often described as 'modern portfolio theory'
. . . Subsection (b) also sounds the theme of modern investment practice,
sensitivity to the risk/return curve . . . The Act impliedly disavows the
emphasis in older law on avoiding 'speculative' or 'risky' investments.
Low levels of risk may be appropriate in some trust settings but inappro-
priate in others. It is the trustee's task to invest at a risk that is suitable to
the purpose of the trust.[UPIA]

- *. . . the duty of caution does not call for avoidance of risk by*
trustees but for their prudent management of risk. For these purposes,
risk management is concerned with more than failure of collection and
loss of dollar value. It takes account of all hazards that may follow from
inflation, volatility of price and yield, lack of liquidity, and the like."[R]

Should there be any lingering doubt that risk management no longer
suggests implementing a traditionally conservative portfolio, the notes to

the Restatement warn that . . . *Beneficiaries can be disserved by undue conservatism as well as by excessive risk taking.*[R]

MINIMIZE DIVERSIFIABLE RISK

The conclusion of Sharpe and others, that unsystematic risk is unrewarded risk, is an integral part of the investment mandates required by the Restatement and the UPIA. Unsystematic risk (i.e., diversifiable risk) is referred to as uncompensated risk. For fiduciaries, unwarranted acceptance of diversifiable risk is irresponsible. This serves as a strong warning to any trustee who contemplates concentrating the trust investment portfolio.

   ▪ *In the absence of contrary statute or trust provision, the requirements of caution ordinarily impose a duty to use reasonable care and skill in an effort to minimize or at least reduce diversifiable risks . . . minimization of the latter [diversifiable risk] becomes a significant goal of prudent investing.*[R]

   ▪ The UPIA clearly delineates between these risks. *Modern portfolio theory divides risk into the categories of 'compensated' and 'uncompensated' risk . . . compensated risk—the firm pays the investor for bearing the risk. By contrast, nobody pays the investor for owning [uncompensated risk] . . . Risk that can be eliminated by adding different stocks (or bonds) is uncompensated risk. The object of diversification is to minimize this uncompensated risk . . .* [UPIA]

DETERMINE THE RISK TOLERANCE OF THE TRUST

Investment fiduciaries must not only *consider the purposes, terms, distribution requirements, and other circumstances of the trust; they must consider the risk tolerance of their client* (i.e., the trust). Thus, an investment fiduciary must be able to not only manage risk; he must have an understanding of cognitive psychology and know how to evaluate risk tolerance.

   ▪ *. . . risk management by a trustee requires that careful attention be given to the particular trust's risk tolerance, that is to its tolerance for volatility.*[R]

   ▪ *. . . the trustee can invest in anything that plays an appropriate role in achieving the risk/return objectives of the trust . . . Returns correlate strongly with risk, but tolerance for risk varies greatly with the financial and other circumstances of the investor, or in this case of a trust . . . It is the trustee's task to invest at a risk that is suitable to the purpose of the trust.* [UPIA]

DIVERSIFY ACROSS POORLY
CORRELATED ASSET CLASSES

Although the courts have long recognized the importance of diversification, until the Second Restatement the legal mandate for diversification was limited. The Second Restatement provided for "reasonable diversification." However, without an awareness of the concept of correlation, diversification simply referred to the number of investments. Harry Markowitz's seminal work, *Portfolio Selection: Efficient Diversification of Investments,* was not published until 1959. Now that Dr. Markowitz has been awarded the Nobel Prize for his work in this area and 37 years of new portfolio theory has accumulated, fiduciary investment law incorporates this concept in the definition of diversification.

■ *These changes have occurred under the influence of a large and broadly accepted body of empirical and theoretical knowledge about the behavior of capital markets, often described as 'modern portfolio theory.'* [UPIA]

■ Should a fiduciary contemplate falling back on the traditional default of government bonds, the Restatement's Reporter's notes include an ERISA case example:

The court does not question that United States Treasury bonds are among the most liquid of all investments and that they carry essentially no risk of default. However, the issue is not whether government bonds are, as a general rule, a sound investment; nor is the issue whether the court approves of Trevor Stewart's [the defendant] philosophy of investing heavily in long-term United States government bonds . . . Trevor Stewart in essence argues that the risk of loss through default is the only risk of loss contemplated by ERISA . . . This argument is without merit.

■ The Restatement provides clear guidelines for asset classes to be considered.

Basic asset classifications might begin with cash equivalents, bonds, asset-backed securities, real estate, and corporate stocks, with both debt and equity categories further divided by their general risk-reward or income/growth characteristics, by the domestic, foreign, tax-exempt, or other characteristics of the issuers, and the like.

■ I am sure that it will come as a surprise to many "sophisticated" fiduciaries; however, the commentary goes even further on this subject. *Foreign Investments. The amount of assets held in trust in the United States and looking for favorable investment and diversification opportunities is so large today as to make a rule proscribing or even looking askance at off-shore investments both unworkable and unwise.*[R]

DEVELOP AN ASSET ALLOCATION POLICY

Expanding beyond the broader definition of diversification, the Third Restatement unequivocally adopts the concept of asset allocation as an integral part of the prudent investment process:

- *Asset allocation decisions are a fundamental aspect of an investment strategy and a starting point in formulating a plan of diversification.*

CONSIDER THE USE OF MUTUAL FUNDS

In order to assist in diversification and control costs, the modern investment fiduciary may consider mutual funds as a vehicle for diversification.

- *". . . for a trust of moderate size . . . the alternative of purchasing suitable mutual funds might be more inviting to the trustee because it offers a means of obtaining much greater diversification for what will usually be a lower cost."*[R]
- *Trusts can also achieve diversification by investing in mutual funds.*[UPIA]

LIQUIDATE INAPPROPRIATE INVESTMENTS ORIGINALLY TRANSFERRED INTO THE TRUST

In the past, trustees have frequently maintained positions transferred into the trust. Often little or no thought was given to the appropriateness of the assets in light of the needs of the trust beneficiaries. Frequently, the trustee took comfort in the language of the trust document. Standard "boilerplate" frequently had a clause allowing the trustee to maintain "inherited" assets. In the future, such a naive defense will no longer serve as a safe harbor for fiduciaries. Modern trust standards mandate that, in all circumstances:

- *In making and implementing investment decisions, the trustee has a duty to diversify the investments of the trust unless, under the circumstances, it is prudent not to do so.*[UPIA]
- Regarding inherited assets, the Restatement and UPIA make it clear that unsuitable "inherited" assets remain unsuitable, even if the assets were suitable when purchased and even if the trustee is given authority to continue to hold inherited assets.

- The UPIA requires that . . . *within a reasonable time after accepting a trusteeship or receiving assets, a trustee shall review the trust assets and make and implement decisions concerning the retention and disposition of assets, in order to bring the trust portfolio into compliance with the purposes, terms, distribution requirements, and other circumstances of the trust and . . . to dispose of unsuitable assets within a reasonable time . . . [and that] extends as well to investments that were proper when purchased but subsequently became improper.*

- The Restatement echoes this requirement. If by the terms of the trust or an applicable statute the trustee is permitted but not directed . . . *to retain investments originally transferred to the trust, the trustee is not liable for retaining them when there is no abuse of discretion in doing so. The authorization to retain, however, ordinarily does not justify the trustee in retaining such assets if, under the circumstances, retention would be imprudent.*

- *This may require the trustee to convert investments received as part of the trust estate even though those assets are not otherwise either improper investments for the trustee or of a type unsuitable to the trust's investment objective. Thus, if the trustee receives a testator's residuary estate in trust and half of the trust estate consists of the shares of a particular corporation, the trustee is ordinarily under a duty to sell some or all of the shares to invest the proceeds in other assets so that the trust portfolio will not, without some special justification, include an excessive amount of the securities of a single corporation or carry an unwarranted degree of uncompensated risk.*

DELEGATE INVESTMENT MANAGEMENT RESPONSIBILITY AS APPROPRIATE

As noted earlier, one of the most significant changes is the authority to delegate active investment responsibility. Because the issues of modern investment management are varied and complex, there is a recognition that the trustee may not have the requisite knowledge and that professional advice will be in the best interest of the trust. In addition, for trustees who intelligently select competent and qualified advisors, the law provides a safe harbor that will insulate the trustee from the actions of the advisor.

- *As a start, it is important that a trustee be reasonably knowledgeable or have professional advice in order to achieve the informed diversification normally required of trustees.*[R]

▪ A trustee who meets the duties of care, skill, and caution in the selection of an investment advisor . . . *is not liable to the beneficiaries or
the trust for the decisions or actions of the agent to whom the function
was delegated.* ᵁᴾᴵᴬ

CONSIDER THE USE OF BOTH PASSIVE AND ACTIVE MANAGERS

Both the Restatement and the UPIA emphasize the trustee's responsibility
to control costs. This mandate requires the trustee to consider the cost ef-
ficiencies of passive investing and mutual funds. Trustees should be able
to justify the additional costs incurred for active management.

▪ *Current assessments of the degree of efficiency support the adoption of various forms of passive strategies by trustees . . . On the other
hand, these assessments do not bar the prudent inclusion of active management strategies as well in the investment programs of trustees . . .
The greater the trustee's departure from one of the passive strategies, the
greater is likely to be the burden of justification and also of continuous
monitoring.*ᴿ

CHARITABLE TRUSTS

Although both the Restatement and the UPIA apply to private trusts, they
make abundantly clear that the standards are expected to apply to all fiduciaries, including those of charitable trusts.

▪ *The Uniform Prudent Investor Act regulates the investment responsibilities of trustees. Other fiduciaries—such as executors, conserva-
tors, and guardians of the property—sometimes have responsibilities
over assets that are governed by the standards of prudent investment. It
will often be appropriate for states to adapt the law governing investment
by trustees under this Act to these other fiduciary regimes . . .*

*Although the Uniform Prudent Investor Act by its terms applies to
trusts and not charitable corporations, the standards of the Act can be expected to inform the investment responsibilities of directors and officers
of charitable corporations . . . In making decisions and taking actions
with respect to the investment of trust funds, the trustee of a charitable
trust is under a duty similar to that of a private trust.*ᵁᴾᴵᴬ

LESSONS FOR THE WEALTH MANAGER—SUMMARY

In addition to these new laws, there are numerous other circumstances that will serve to increase the potential liability of fiduciaries:[4]

■ The expectations of beneficiaries, molded by the historically extraordinary returns of the last decade, are frequently unrealistic. During periods of more "realistic" returns, beneficiaries are likely to become disappointed and angry. This may well provide fertile ground for litigation.

■ Popularization of investment issues by the public media (e.g., *Money, Worth, and Kiplinger*) means a more knowledgeable beneficiary. If the beneficiaries' own evaluation of the markets contradicts the investment results of the fiduciary, the beneficiary may no longer meekly accept the benefits offered.

■ Increased government enforcement at both state and national levels to protect beneficiaries.

■ If a portfolio has been managed by an independent fiduciary, the significant transfer of wealth over the next decade will, in many cases, trigger a review by the children of the past investment management of their parents' funds.

■ Boards and participants of charitable trusts are demanding a higher level of accountability than in the past.

This complexity of investment markets, the overwhelming influence of institutional investors, the continuing evolution in investment theory, and the enforcement of the new laws governing investment fiduciaries provide wealth managers both an opportunity and a responsibility. The opportunity is to become a professional advisor to nonprofessional fiduciaries and the responsibility is to provide competent and legally defensible advice to those fiduciaries.

THE AMERICAN LAW INSTITUTE

In the early 20th century, in prominent legal circles, there was a growing discomfort with some aspects of the legal system. To address these concerns, a group of eminent judges, lawyers, and academics formed The Committee on the Establishment of a Permanent Organization for the Improvement of the Law. The recommendation of this committee was the creation of a nonprofit organization to be known as the American Law Institute (ALI). The ALI, incorporated in 1923, is composed of leading legal scholars, judges, and distinguished lawyers. The original membership included the then Chief Justice of the United States Supreme Court and the future Chief Justice Charles Evans Hughes. Early leaders included legal icons Justices Benjamin Cardoza and Leonard Hand.

The founding committee recommended that the first undertaking of the new ALI should be to address areas of uncertainty in the law through a thorough restatement of the relevant legal issues. The ALI adopted this recommendation as a mandate to summarize and define (restate) major legal doctrines. Today the ALI is composed of 2,500 elected and ex officio members.

Restatements of the Law

Restatements cover 10 specific fields of law including trusts. The restatements are composed of:

Principles of Law—These are in **boldface** and are known, as a result of the heavy weight of the boldface, as black-letter principles (or rules).

Explanatory Comments—These are discussions designed to elucidate the Principles and may include one or more illustrations in the form of hypothetical applications.

Reporter's Notes—Background information on the development of the related section with references both in support and in opposition to the Principle.

While restatements attempt to "restate" the basic principles of ever changing common law, they are not law and do not represent either legislative or judicial authority. The authority of the restatement comes from the credibility and expertise of the author (reporter), committee, and members of the ALI.

Restatements are not without their critics. One major criticism is that some restatements move ahead of the law, i.e., stating what the law should be rather than restating what the law actually is. Another quasi criticism is that because restatements implicitly claim to set forth clear rules properly derived from case law and need only be applied, they are much more restrictive for the court than a line of precedent where the earlier case may have unique features. However, authoritative commentary is useful for the courts as it crystallizes cases into clear legal rules and provides precision to rulings. As a result of their credibility and efficacy, over the last 60+ years, restatements have become some of the most important commentaries and most frequently cited secondary sources in judicial America.

NATIONAL CONFERENCE ON COMMISSIONS ON UNIFORM STATE LAWS

The original idea for a group to meet regarding uniform state laws is attributed to the Alabama Bar's recommendation at the American Bar Association's 12th annual meeting in 1889. This work led to the establishment of the Conference, initiated by the New York legislature, in 1892. Seven states attended the first meeting. By 1912, all states were represented. The Conference, a nonprofit association, is composed of practicing lawyers, judges, academic scholars, and government officials. Each member must be a member of the bar in their jurisdiction. The approximately 300 current members (commissioners) represent all 50 states, District of Columbia, Puerto Rico, and the Virgin Islands. The primary mission of the Commission is to publish Uniform Acts and Codes and Model Acts. Uniform Acts are intended to be adopted by the states exactly as written. Model acts are designed to serve as guidelines.

As no laws may be imposed by the Commission, all legislation must be adopted on a state-by-state basis. The goal of the commission, through its development of Uniform and Model Acts, is to create uniformity among state laws.

ENDNOTES

1. Jeffrey N. Gordon, "The Puzzling Persistence of the Constrained Prudent Man Rule," *New York University Law Review,* 1987, 1–52.
2. Paul G. Haskell, "The Prudent Person Rule for Trustee Investment and Modern Portfolio Theory," *North Carolina Law Review,* 1995, 1–24.
3. John A. Edie and Lowell S. Smith, "Investing: What Every Foundation Trustee Should Know," *Foundation News,* November/December 1993.
4. Donald B. Trone, "Fiduciary Responsibility," *IAFP,* 1995 Success Forum. Donald B. Trone, "Fiduciary Responsibility: The Third Restatement of Trusts and The Prudent Man Rule," *Track VI/Special Issues,* Monday, September 11, 1995, 407–418.

CHAPTER 16

Philosophy

Find Your Niche   *Listen Closely*   *Reward Substance*

Insist on Value   *Recognize Quality*   *Demand Quality*

Question Basic   *Encourage Simplicity*   *Question Certainties*
Assumptions

Imagine the Future   *Become Better Informed*   *Give the Most*

In Chapter 13, Manager Selection and Evaluation, I suggested that the criteria for selecting a money manager should be philosophy, process, and people. I believe that wealth managers should be judged by the same standards. Of these three, the most important consideration is the wealth manager's philosophy. Without a clearly defined philosophy, the process is irrelevant and the people rudderless.

This concluding chapter is about philosophy—the philosophy of Evensky, Brown & Katz. As with all of the opinion pieces in *Wealth Management,* the following is not intended as a recommendation or model for everyone's practice. It is offered as a framework for the reader to stimulate him to develop his own philosophy. It is important that the wealth manager have a philosophy, not that he adopt ours.

The first portion of *Wealth Management* focused on the client. This was followed by discussions on theory and process. The latter sections discussed the business aspects of wealth management and the markets for wealth management services. As our philosophy is integral to my selection and treatment of these aspects, this chapter will also serve as a summary of *Wealth Management.*

Having set the scene for this chapter, the following is a formal statement of the philosophy that defines our firm's practice. The entire staff of Evensky, Brown & Katz participates, at different levels, in the development of our philosophy. All members of the firm are committed to its consistent implementation.

FINANCIAL PLANNING

We believe that ours is a financial planning practice, albeit one specializing in what we call wealth management. We are solely concerned with assisting our clients in meeting their life goals through the proper management of their financial resources. Our success is not measured by performance statistics but rather by our clients' success in achieving their goals.

Our practice begins and ends with the needs of the client. It is client-driven. Solutions can be developed only after appropriate data (both quantitative and qualitative) have been gathered and evaluated. Related issues should be identified and clients should be directed to other appropriate professionals for their resolution. Implementation, continuous monitoring, and, as necessary, modification, is an integral part of the process.

The firm's advisors are expected to become CFP licensees, and associate advisors are encouraged to become CFP licensees. All of the advisors are expected to be active participants in the IAFP, ICFP, and other professional organizations.

Continuing education is mandatory and the expectation is that the hours earned will far exceed the minimum required by the CFP Board of Standards. Advisors are expected to maintain basic competence in all areas of comprehensive planning as well as particular expertise in the specialties of estate, retirement, and investment planning.

FINANCIAL PLANNING ISSUES

Goal Setting

We believe that our clients must set their goals. It is our responsibility to educate them in the process and to assist them to define, quantify, and prioritize their goals. It is also our responsibility to assist them to recognize that there may be "hidden goals" (e.g., risk management issues) that may take priority over investment issues.

Rule of Thumb Planning

We believe that 'rule of thumb' planning is an incompetent and unprofessional way for a wealth manager to plan for a client's financial independence. Examples of rule of thumb planning include simplifying assumptions for capital needs analysis, life cycle investing, packaged asset allocation models, and black box optimization.

Cash Flow

We believe that clients need total return, not dividends or interest. The traditional concept of an 'income' portfolio is archaic and places unnecessary and inappropriate restrictions on portfolio design. Plans structured to match dividends and interest with cash flow, in the long run, are likely to fail to meet the clients' inflation-adjusted cash flow needs.

Capital Needs Analysis Assumptions

We believe that conservative assumptions are a dangerous myth. A conservative assumption (e.g., ignoring social security) will result in a need for a higher return, greater volatility portfolio. Capital needs analysis return requirements should be based on real rate of return estimates. Time horizons (i.e., mortality) should be based on the client's unique family health history, not standard mortality tables. Plans should not be prepared based on a client's unrealistic expectations; if necessary, we will refuse the engagement.

THE CLIENT

As noted many times, wealth management is a specialty of financial planning and, as such, the wealth manager's primary concern and allegiance is to the client. However, we cannot successfully assist a client without his full cooperation. The planning process must be at least as important to the client as it is to us. If this commitment on the part of the client is not forthcoming, we will not agree to an engagement.

The client need not be an individual. It might be a trust, endowment, or pension plan. However, as a financial planner, we will treat the client as we would an individual, following the financial planning process as it applies to that client. For example, with a trust client, we will not simply focus on the investment portfolio. We will carefully balance the unique needs of each of the income and remainderman beneficiaries (e.g., current cash flow requirements, inflation, taxes, risk tolerance, and legal constraints).

Risk Tolerance

We believe that a client's risk tolerance is a significant constraint in the wealth management process. Our success can be measured by our clients' ability to sleep well during turbulent markets. Clients have a fuzzy understanding of risk. Their tolerance for risk is dynamic, changing with markets and personal circumstances. It is our responsibility, to be sure, before proceeding with the development of recommendations, that we share with the client, the same concept of risk. This can be accomplished by client education and appropriate risk-tolerance questionnaires. We believe that we must make an effort to continually improve our knowledge of cognitive psychology as it applies to these issues.

Tax Constraints

We believe that tax issues must be considered, much like the need for liquidity. However, the goal of tax planning should be to maximize after-tax returns, not to minimize taxes. Investment decisions should be made based on this criterion. For example, generally, pensions subject to the excise tax should not be liquidated early in order to avoid the tax, and the plan's funds should be invested in equities. Investment issues (e.g., risk exposure) should take priority over taxes. For example, nondiversified low-basis stock should be sold, and the quality of asset management should take precedence over portfolio tax management. Neither reported turnover nor holding period calculated from reported turnover is a useful measure of tax efficiency. Variable annuities should only be considered when asset protection is an issue (in those states where the law protects annuity assets), or when the tax savings can demonstrably overcome the costs associated with the annuity and provide a premium adequate to offset the annuity's relative inflexibility.

INVESTMENT THEORY

Risk and Return Measures

We believe in the use of appropriate mathematical measures of risk and return. The primary measure of risk should be standard deviation. The concept of semivariance is intellectually appealing but not yet a useful measure for the wealth manager. Total return should be the basic criterion for the measurement of return. This includes real time and dollar-weighted returns.

The primary measure of risk-adjusted return is the Sharpe ratio. We no longer use Alpha and Beta as measures. Duration, not maturity, is the appropriate measure of a bond's exposure to interest rate risk (within narrow rate changes). Convexity is an important measure of a bond's sensitivity to large changes in rates.

Mathematical Tools and Techniques

We believe that wealth managers should stay abreast of useful mathematical tools and techniques and utilize them in their practices as they become useful. Current examples of useful tools include Monte Carlo Simulation and Regression Analysis (e.g., factor analysis). Examples of the techniques that wealth management should be following include semivariance, neural networks and tactical asset allocation.

Efficient Market Hypothesis (EMH)

We believe in the weak form of the EMH. We reject the use of classic technical analysis and market timing.

Growth versus Value

We believe in the conclusions of the Fama/French research that, over time, value portfolios will provide superior returns. However, we also believe that eliminating growth allocations will result in interim divergence from the broad markets that our clients would find unacceptable. We believe a two-thirds weighting for value and one-third for growth is the most appropriate weighting to balance these conflicting issues.

Active versus Passive

We believe that the choice between active and passive management is not either/or. We use both. Passive management offers lower transaction costs and minimal asset class drift, frequently a more tax-efficient portfolio, and there is significant academic research suggesting long-term superior investment performance. Active management offers the opportunity for superior returns, controlled volatility, and bragging rights. We believe that our value portfolios should generally be passively managed and our growth portfolios actively managed.

Asset Allocation

We believe that the portfolio policy is the primary determinant of long-term portfolio performance. Implementation of concentrated portfolios, either in economic sectors or with specific managers, is risky and inappropriate for wealth management clients. Multiasset class and multimanager portfolios are more appropriate.* The major asset classes are cash equivalents, fixed income, and equity. We consider taxable and tax-free domestic and foreign bonds all to be important fixed-income classes. We divide maturities into short (1 to 3 years), short/intermediate (3 to 5 years), and intermediate (5 to 10 years). We do not consider long-term or low-quality fixed income. Equity allocations are divided between domestic and foreign. We also use REITs as we believe they represent real estate investments. Domestic stock allocations are divided between large and small cap; with the break point at $1 billion. We do not recognize mid-cap as a class. We further divide the domestic allocations between growth and value styles. We believe that international equity allocations, including commitments to emerging markets, belong in all portfolios. We do not believe that the performance of metals and natural resource stocks or funds are correlated with either metals or natural resource prices; hence, we do not usually use them.

Because we believe in the overriding importance of the strategic allocation, we reject managers who do not have clearly defined, asset class/ style philosophies or who diverge from their stated policies. Because we do not believe in market timing, we reject sector managers.

We believe in maintaining a strategic allocation and only infrequently revise that allocation. Although we believe in rebalancing to the strategic allocation, the influence of taxes and transaction costs leads us to conclude that contingent rebalancing with fairly wide bands is the most appropriate solution. We do not currently implement a tactical allocation overlay; however, we believe it is an appropriate strategy.

Optimization

We believe that mathematical optimization is the appropriate method for designing a strategic asset allocation model. However, we also believe that an optimizer is simply a tool to be used by a knowledgeable wealth manager. The primary controls over the optimizer are the development of logical input data (expected returns should not be historical projections), an awareness of the optimizers' sensitivities to the input and other appropriate constraints. The final recommendations should not be based on the

---

*To repeat an earlier footnote, the nation's largest pension plans use an average of 33 managers per plan.

optimizers' unconstrained optimal solutions but rather the optimal suboptimal solution (OP_{SOP}).

Arithmetic versus Geometric Returns

We believe in using geometric returns for historical analysis and future estimates.

Time Diversification

We believe that the concept of time diversification is appropriate in its conclusion that the relative risk of increasing equity exposure decreases as the time horizon of the goal increases. As a related issue, we do not believe that any investment should be made for a goal with less than a five-year time horizon. Funds required in less than five years should be placed in money markets or fixed-income securities (e.g., CDs, Treasuries) with maturity dates equal to or less than the goal's time horizons.

IMPLEMENTATION

Policy

We believe that an investment policy should be written and should be customized to the needs of the client. It should describe the client's goals and discuss his risk tolerance. The policy should describe the strategic model and the parameters for rebalancing. Any special constraints should be specified. Criteria for manager selection and evaluation should be included.

The policy should include a measure of expected real return and a discussion of expected volatility. It should include pertinent assumptions used in the development of the strategic allocation.

Managers

We believe that professional money managers will provide results far superior to a client's or wealth manager's direct security selection and management. With rare exception, separate account management (including wrap accounts) is inefficient and expensive. The universe of public and institutional funds offers the best alternative for the superior management of multiple-asset-class portfolios.

We believe that managers should be selected and evaluated based on their philosophies, processes, and people. Once selected, a manager should be allowed periods of poor performance if he remains consistent to his philosophy and process. He should be replaced immediately if he strays significantly from his stated philosophy or process.

Evaluation of managers should entail a detailed review of all available pertinent information including both fundamental qualitative and return factor analysis. However, the ultimate decision to hire or fire should be based on fundamental data. Performance measurement should be against appropriate benchmarks, not broad market indexes.

Ongoing Management

We believe that there should be a regular review of a client's situation to determine if he is continuing to move in the direction of achieving his goals. This includes revisions in strategic allocations as a result of revised assumptions or changing client circumstances or goals. We should continue to educate our clients, always remaining sensitive to the volatility of each one's expectations. Our responsibility is to assure that our client stays the course and does so with a minimum of emotional pain. The focus should always be the client and the achievement of his goals, not the performance of the portfolio.

THE PRACTICE OF WEALTH MANAGERS

We believe that we are uniquely qualified to integrate the skills and talents of financial planning with investment skills, knowledge, and technology previously available only to large institutional clients, for the benefit of the retail client. In effect, we are the institutional advisor for the retail client.

The primary market for our services are clients (including trusts, pensions, and other fiduciary accounts) with investment portfolios between $500,000 and $20,000,000.

We believe that, in general, we serve as a fiduciary, and that we are particularly qualified to serve as advisor to investment fiduciaries.

We've come full circle now. Our philosophy is the description of how we put the previous 15 chapters into practice. Now it's your turn to determine and define what sets you apart. My best wishes for a successful practice.

Marginal Tax Rates for Three Investor Types

Year	Low Tax Rate		Middle Tax Rate		High Tax Rate	
	Income	K Gains	Income	K Gains	Income	K Gains
1963	20	10	26	13	59	25
1964	17.5	8.75	27	13.5	53.5	25
1965	16	8	25	12.5	50	25
1966	17	8.5	25	12.5	50	25
1967	17	8.5	25	12.5	53	25
1968	18.275	9.1375	26.875	13.4375	56.975	25
1969	18.7	9.35	30.8	15.4	58.3	25
1970	19.475	9.7375	28.7	14.35	56.375	25
1971	17	8.5	28	14	55	25
1972	19	9.5	28	14	55	25
1973	19	9.5	28	14	58	25
1974	19	9.5	32	16	58	25
1975	19	9.5	32	16	58	25
1976	19	9.5	32	16	60	25
1977	19	9.5	36	18	60	25
1978	19	**	36	**	62	**
1979	18	7.2	37	14.8	64	25
1980	18	7.2	43	17.2	64	25
1981	17.775	7.11	42.4625	16.985	63.2	20
1982	16	6.4	39	15.6	50	20
1983	15	6	35	14	50	19
1984	16	6.4	33	13.2	49	19.6
1985	16	6.4	33	13.2	49	19.6
1986	16	6.4	33	13.2	49	28
1987	15	15	28	28	38.5	28
1988	15	15	28	28	33	28
1989	15	15	28	28	33	28
1990	15	15	28	28	33	28
1991	15	15	28	28	31	28
1992	15	15	28	28	31	28

**The marginal tax rate on long-term capital gain realizations in 1978 is the lesser of 50% of the income rate or 25% for realizations made from January through October. For November and December capital gains realizations, the marginal rate is the lesser of 40% of the income rate or 25%.

Source: Pechman, Federal Tax Policy, 5th edition and Internal Revenue Service, Statistics of Income (SOI), various years.

Taxable income for the low tax rate individual is compared as the median adjusted gross income (AGI) (computed from SOI) less the standard deduction for married couples and less three exemptions. Taxable incomes for the middle and high tax rate individuals are comparably calculated using three times median AGI and ten times median AGI respectively. Median AGI for 1990–1992 is held constant (in real terms) at the 1989 level.

Tax Management Research

As this is such an important issue for the wealth manager, the following is my summary and interpretation of the critical assumptions, conclusions, and observations of the most important research to date on the subject of investment portfolio tax management.

The first of these papers makes the case for some form of active tax management. The *No Load Fund Analyst* argues against active tax management. The last paper, by Randolph, discusses related and important issues.

The items in quotes are directly out of the research. The interpretations and observations are mine.

GEORGE M. CONSTANTINIDES: CAPITAL MARKET EQUILIBRIUM WITH PERSONAL TAX[1]

Assumptions

- ". . . the investor has a high probability of bypassing this regulation [wash sale] by waiting at least thirty days before repurchasing the stock. Alternatively, the investor may purchase a different stock with similar risk and return characteristics." I believe that the assumption that stocks are fungible is questionable.

- " . . . the investor may satisfy the routine needs of consumption and portfolio rebalancing without realizing capital gains." "The investor may oftentimes avoid the realization of a capital gain by satisfying routine consumption needs with cash income." Now that's an astute observation!

Conclusions

- "We prove the optimal liquidation policy is to realize losses immediately and defer gains until the event of a forced liquidation, i.e., until the investor's death, or until an exogenous event beyond his control forces him to sell the asset." Of course, this recommendation ignores the importance of rebalancing for purposes of maintaining a strategic balance or the need to replace managers.

JEFFREY AND ARNOTT: IS YOUR ALPHA BIG ENOUGH TO COVER ITS TAXES?[2]

Data
Based on the 72 funds in the Morningstar database labeled "Growth" or "Growth & Income," with at least $100 million in ending net assets throughout the 1982–1991 study period.

Assumptions
- The study is ". . . concerned primarily with taxes on realized capital gains, not on dividends and interest, because these are the taxes that are precipitated by trading activity."

  "Conservative" Combined Marginal Tax
  for Capital Gains   = 35%
  for Ordinary Income   = 35%
  Holding period   = 10 years

Conclusions
- ". . . the tax consequences of trading are a function not of turnover, but of holding period." Prior to the work of Jeffrey and Arnott, most advisors considered turnover a direct measure of tax efficiency, i.e., a portfolio with a turnover of 20 percent was twice as tax efficient as one with a 40 percent turnover and four times as efficient as one with an 80 percent turnover. This research concluded that tax efficiency is related to holding period, not turnover. Subsequent research has suggested that both holding period and turnover are inadequate measures. See Dickson, Shoven, and Gregory.
- Because closed-end funds are not subject to "redemption gains," they are more tax efficient than open-end funds.
- The study concluded that there was a significant change in the pre- and post-tax rankings. I do not agree with this conclusion. My analysis of the data presented in the report does not support this conclusion. See Table B–1.
- Regarding the wash sale rule— ". . . given any reasonable assumption about the difficulty of predicting short-term market prices, calculable 'cash value' of realizing a loss would seem to outweigh the risk of 'being out of the stock'—especially if the replacement investment were another equity." It doesn't "seem" so to me.

T A B L E   B-1

Number of Funds Outperforming the Index*

Total Return	"Closed-End Index 500"	Vanguard Index 500
Pretax	15	15
After all taxes	10	13

*10-year holding period

• "Common sense dictates that . . . no economically realizable losses be left unharvested." I would remind the reader that common sense may not be good sense.

JOEL M. DICKSON AND JOHN B. SHOVEN: RANKING MUTUAL FUNDS ON AN AFTER-TAX BASIS[3]

Data
Based on the largest 150 funds in the Morningstar database labeled "Growth" or "Growth & Income," with at least a 10-year history.

Assumptions
"Low-tax" individual: Income = (1992 median AGI—standard deduction for married and 3 dependents)

"Middle-tax" individual: Income = 3 × "low tax"

"High-tax" individual: Income = 10 × "low tax"

• "Post-tax" return assumes a step-up in basis at the end of the accumulation period.

• "Liquidation value" assumes full taxable liquidation at the end of the accumulation period.

• Taxes were those applicable during the year of taxable event.

• Holding periods of 10 and 30 years.

T A B L E   B-2

Differences in Ranking—Before and After Taxes

Study Period	Median Change in Rank	Number of Funds in the Sample	Number of Levels Changed
1963–1972			
Low-Tax Rate	0.80	62	0
Mid-Tax Rate	1.60	62	1
High-Tax Rate	3.60	62	2
1973–1982			
Low-Tax Rate	0.80	126	1
Mid-Tax Rate	1.60	126	2
High-Tax Rate	3.60	126	4½
1983–1992			
Low-Tax Rate	0.0	147	0
Mid-Tax Rate	0.80	147	1
High-Tax Rate	1.20	147	1¾

Conclusions

- "The differences in actual return over the thirty-year period to a taxable investor is immediately evident." A strong statement in favor of active portfolio tax management.

- " . . . the differences between the various after-tax rankings and the published pre-tax rankings are large over a thirty-year horizon, particularly for middle and high income investors. A question that this information raises is whether it takes a thirty-year period for this to become important." I would agree that this is a good question. I believe that the answer is yes.

- " Our conclusion is that the ranking differences are still considerable for ten-year intervals." Refer to Table B–2 to determine if you concur in this conclusion.

- " . . . there seems to be no significant correlation between the amount a fund turns over its portfolio and the percentage of its pre-tax value that must be paid in taxes." This recognizes that a portfolio turnover of 100 percent may represent a 10 times turnover of the positions with losses.

- ". . . funds with higher turnover may still be good investments for the tax conscious investor." A reiteration of the conclusion that turnover and tax efficiency are not related.

JOEL M. DICKSON AND JOHN B. SHOVEN: A STOCK INDEX MUTUAL FUND WITHOUT NET CAPITAL GAINS REALIZATIONS[4]

Following up on the work of Jeffrey, Arnott, and their own earlier work, Dickson and Shoven propose the development of stock index funds that, they believe, will significantly outperform traditional open-end index funds such as the Vanguard S&P 500.

Assumptions
Same as prior study.

Conclusions
- Contrary to the conclusions of Jeffrey and Arnott, Dickson and Shoven conclude that for taxable investors, open-end funds outperform their closed-end equivalents. The ability to invest significant amounts of new investment dollars flowing into an open-end fund results, over time, in open-end funds outperforming closed-end counterparts. Constant flow of new funds results in separate tax lots that can be effectively used with the identified shares method of sales. The result is that a lower percentage of capital gains will be realized than for a closed-end alternative. The authors estimate the net advantage of the open-end fund is 20–40 basis points for mid- and high-tax investors.
- An S&P 500 open-end stock index fund, managed for tax consequences, can greatly enhance the investor's after-tax performance.
- Most of the benefits of tax management can be attributed to the strategy of implementing lot basis accounting (i.e., HIFO).
- The results of the studies of two hypothetical portfolios are noted in Table B–3. The portfolios are referred to as the SURGE (Strategies Using Realized Gains Elimination) funds. The strategy solely using HIFO accounting is noted as "HIFO Only" and the strategy combining both HIFO accounting and annually offsetting gains and losses is called "HIFO, 75%."

T A B L E   B-3

Annualized Returns—Pre-Tax and After-Tax (Mid- and High-Tax Brackets)

Study Period	Pre-Tax Returns	After-Tax Returns	
		Mid-Tax Bracket	High-Tax Bracket
1987–1991			
Vanguard S&P 500	15.0%	13.6%	13.4%
SURGE HIFO Only	14.9	13.9	13.7
SURGE HIFO, 75%	14.9	14.0	13.8
1982–1991			
Vanguard S&P 500	17.1	15.2	14.6
SURGE HIFO Only	17.1	15.8	15.4
SURGE HIFO, 75%	17.0	15.9	15.5
1977–1991			
Vanguard S&P 500	13.8	11.8	10.9
SURGE HIFO Only	13.8	12.5	11.8
SURGE HIFO, 75%	13.8	12.5	11.9

My Observations

The use of HIFO accounting provided significant return benefits (e.g., a 90-basis point improvement for the 1977–1991 period). Offsetting gains and losses provide insignificant gains in returns.

KEN GREGORY AND CRAIG LITMAN[5]

Based on their own independent research, Gregory and Litman reached a radically different conclusion from the research previously reviewed. They claim that many researchers, by using unrealistic models and/or assumptions, ". . . assumed their conclusions."

Data

Screened the equity mutual fund database of funds with 10-year records under the same manager. The 10-year holding period sample included 75 funds, the 3- and 5-year sample included 91 funds. Their conclusions are reflected in Table B–4.

T A B L E   B–4

Changes in Rank from Before to After Tax

	10-Year Holding Period		5-Year Holding Period		3-Year Holding Period	
	# Funds	% Funds	# Funds	% Funds	# Funds	% Funds
No Change	8	11	18	20	33	36
Down 1–5 Places	46	61	57	63	53	58
Down 6–10 Places	17	23	15	16	5	6
Up or Down 10 Places	4	5	1	1	0	0

Conclusions

- The difference in fund rankings before and after taxes is relatively minor.
- At the margin, high dividend-paying funds are more likely to slip in after-tax rankings.
- The Vanguard Index 500 fund does not rank significantly better on an after-tax basis compared to a pre-tax basis for holding periods of 10 years or less.

My Observations

For 10-year holding periods, Vanguard S&P 500 ranked 26th out of 79 funds both before and after taxes. For 3-year holding periods, the Vanguard S&P 500 moves only from #60 to #59.

WILLIAM LEWIS RANDOLPH[6]

Data

From the 1993 AAII Mutual Fund Guide, five-year data regarding 12 aggressive growth funds, 25 growth funds, 9 growth funds, and 12 balanced funds:

Assumptions

- 35% aggregate capital gains tax rate.
- 35% aggregate ordinary income tax rate.

Conclusions

- Repeated turnover has a low correlation with computed after-tax returns. The correlation between the reported turnover and return lost to taxes for the aggressive growth and growth funds was only about 0.25.

- Average tax drag (i.e., the loss of potential return due to taxes) is relatively consistent across fund categories.

- Low tax drag funds are in the growth category.

- "Effective turnover," a measure based on the percentage of accumulated unrealized capital gains that are realized at year-end and distributed on an annual basis, is a superior indicator of a fund's tax drag. For the growth funds sample, the correlation between return lost to taxes and reported turnover is less than 0.28; for "effective turnover" the correlation was 0.68.

GLOBAL ASSET ALLOCATION STRUCTURED TO MAXIMIZE AFTER-TAX RETURNS, SEI, 1996[7]

I was privileged that SEI shared with me this wide-ranging research study.

One major conclusion of their research was confirmation of Gregory, Litman, Dickson, Shoven, and Randolph's conclusion that turnover is not a good indicator of tax efficiency.

As measured by Randolph's "effective turnover," the percent of annual capital gains realization, not the simple annual rate of turnover, is the best measure of the impact of trading on after-tax returns. SEI's analysis demonstrated that most actively managed equity funds, independent of their turnover, have realization rates of about 50 percent, and index funds have realization rates of 15 percent. Table B–5 shows that relationship.

T A B L E   B–5

SEI
Turnover and Realized Capital Gain*

Category	Annual Asset Growth	Annual Portfolio Turnover	Realized Capital Gains as a Percent of Total Return	Total Return
All funds	25.1%	81.9%	52.0%	25.1%
Large blend	25.0	73.3	56.8	25.0
Large growth	24.4	83.8	56.8	24.4
Large value	22.2	82.5	46.2	22.2
Small growth	34.6	117.4	53.1	34.6
Small value	22.8	51.1	49.3	22.8
Large	24.1	78.0	54.0	24.1
Small	24.9	86.7	49.8	24.9
Mid	24.8	85.4	50.1	24.8
Growth	26.1	98.7	49.1	26.1
Value	23.3	69.6	50.6	23.3
Blend	25.6	78.6	55.0	25.6
Vanguard Index				
Large	47.3	15.0	15.1	15.0
Small†	45.6	31.3	16.3	13.7

*Data for 10-year period ending 12/31/93—Morningstar Diversified U.S. Equity Funds.
†Data from 1990–1993

E N D N O T E S

1. George M. Constantinides, "Capital Market Equilibrium with Personal Tax," Econometricia, Vol. 51, No. 3 (May 1983), pp. 611–637.
2. Robert H. Jeffrey and Robert D. Arnott, "Is Your Alpha Big Enough to Cover Its Taxes?" *The Journal of Portfolio Management,* Spring 1993, 15–23.
3. National Bureau of Economics Research, Inc., Working Paper No. 4393, July 1993.
4. National Bureau of Economics Research, Inc., Working Paper No. 4717, April 1994.
5. Ken Gregory and Craig Litman, *No-Load Fund Analyst,* November 1995, "Evaluating Stock Funds: How Important Are Taxes?" 1, 5–11.
6. William Randolph, "Impact of Mutual Fund Distributions on After-Tax Returns," *Financial Services Review,* 3(2) 1994, 127–141.
7. *Asset Allocation for Taxable Investors: Maximizing After-Tax Returns,* SEI, 1996, 19.

Alpha Domestic Equity Manager Questionnaire

What is your investment philosophy? The Micro Cap philosophy is to participate in the long-term growth of the equity markets by constructing fully invested portfolios of stocks selling at reasonable relative valuations in relation to the relative fundamental prospects of the underlying companies.

Is your investment style more value oriented or growth oriented?
Our investment style is classified as "Growth at a Price."

What size capitalization stocks do you normally buy?
The portfolio focuses on stocks below $100 million in market capitalization.

Will you increase the capitalization size of stocks that you own as you manage more money?
No, size is clearly a limitation to growth, and this was the driving force behind our decision to limit the size of our small cap service. Similarly, we feel liquidity can affect the Micro Cap fund. As a consequence, we have established a dollar limit of $100 million contributed capital for this fund.

If the assets exceed the amount, what will you do?
The fund will be closed to new investors when it reaches $100 million in contributed assets.

How many stocks are currently in the portfolio?
As of March 31, 1994, the fund held 75 issues.

Do you expect this number to materially change in the next five years?
The number of stocks in the portfolio should range between 75 and 100.

What is your investment decision making process?
Portfolios are managed using a systematic stock selection process developed in the mid 1970s. The selection process begins with a universe of over 4,000 large/mid, and small/micro cap stocks. Each stock is ranked using five computerized models, each of which contains a growth-oriented component and an offsetting valuation component:

Positive Fundamentals	Reasonable Valuations
Expected EPS Growth	Prospective P/E
Return on Equity	Price-to-Book Value
Reinvestment Rates	Dividend Yield

| Earnings Momentum | Current P/E |
| Positive Earnings Revisions | Avoid negative surprises |

Our "value-added" comes from identifying those securities having the most favorable combinations of growth and price. These stocks—about 10 percent of the beginning universe—form our Focus List of potential buy candidates. Focus List stocks are then subjected to qualitative in-house research prior to purchase to identify the key factors driving the stock. The universe is rescreened twice each month, ensuring a favorable composition of value and growth characteristics for the entire portfolio.

Of equal importance in the Micro Cap process is monitoring our portfolios daily to identify potential "losers" early—then selling. Sell candidates include companies that have a worse-than-median screen rank, rapidly declining earnings expectations, or negative earnings surprises and poor relative price performance.

Who is involved?

Micro Cap's three managing directors have overall business development, client relationship, and investment management responsibilities. The five portfolio manager/analysts have investment research and client relationship responsibilities. Each portfolio manager/analyst follows specific sector and industry groups, which consumes the majority of his or her time. In addition, each has portfolio management responsibilities for up to 12 client relationships. Our traders are responsible for all aspects of the trading function. All key investment professionals participate in a profit-sharing plan, which provides the same incentives as an equity interest in the business.

How are your allocations or weightings set?

Sector and industry weights are mostly a by-product of our investment process. However, we limit the weighting in any one of five broad macro economic sectors—consumer cyclical, consumer noncyclical, interest sensitive, capital spending, and inflation sensitive—to a maximum of 40 percent of the portfolio.

We ensure compliance with this policy by daily review of holdings in each broad investment strategy. We have developed reports that show individual holdings across all portfolios in each product category. This enables us to identify individual holdings or industry weightings that may differ from policy.

How do you control risk?

We control risk by (1) limiting our exposure to any one of the five broad macroeconomic factors (Consumer Cyclical, Consumer nonCyclical, Interest Sensitive, Capital Spending, and Nation to a maximum of 40 percent of the portfolio, (2) by structuring broad portfolios of 75 to 100 stocks, any one of which is less than 2 percent of the portfolio, and (3) adhering to our disciplines by stocks that do not meet expectations and trimming back our most successful holdings so that selling any one stock cannot materially impact performance.

To what extent do you use cash?

Micro Cap remains essentially fully invested at all times, and makes no attempt to add value by the tactical use of cash. Cash levels range from roughly 3 percent to a maximum level of around 9 to 10 percent. Normal levels are below 5 percent.

What other types of securities do you hold? None—U.S. domestic equities only.

Do you buy foreign securities? If so, to what extent and what types?

Micro Cap invests in domestic equities.

Does your firm use leverage?

Micro Cap does not use any form of leverage for the Micro Cap Portfolio.

What types of markets will you outperform and underperform?

We expect to outperform the market in most up market cycles and to keep pace with or slightly underperform the market in most down market cycles. Micro Cap typically underperforms the market during periods of narrow market leadership.

How do you obtain your research?

Micro Cap utilizes a team approach to research and security analysis. Each portfolio manager has specific industry responsibilities for research and is responsible for day-to-day review of his or her accounts. All investment ideas are internally generated. We try to capitalize on the research provided by Wall Street analysts, rather than building earnings models or preparing earnings estimates for the companies we follow. We control the agenda by speaking to analysts about the companies we discover, rather than reacting to the latest recommendations by the Street. We discourage calls from brokers, unless they are about stocks in which we have an interest.

How do you add value?

We add value by generating ideas internally, through an objective screening process, through explicit sell disciplines, and focused qualitative research efforts.

What is different or unique about your firm or fund?

Our competitive advantage comes from both our size and our disciplined investment process. Clearly the bigger the firm, the more difficult it becomes to buy and sell stocks. We like to say that we can fit into some pretty small holes that much bigger managers cannot get near. Our investment process is unique in how we evaluate and rank the growth oriented and offsetting value attributes. The process levels the playing field for all stocks, from oil companies to software firms, and eliminates the biases that both pure growth and pure value approaches experience.

How long have the current decision makers been in place?

Our decision makers have been together since the inception of the firm in 1988. Some investment professionals have worked together since 1977.

Do you provide the same advice on a separately managed basis?

Because of the Micro Cap's limited size and a restriction on maximum investments per client, the Micro Cap will not be offered as separately managed accounts, but as a mutual fund only.

Are the decision makers responsible for other accounts and funds?

Micro Cap employs a team approach, which means that everyone at Micro Cap is working on every product and for every client.

EB&K–Internal Agendas

STAFF MEETING AGENDA–EXAMPLES

July
Client reviews as of July
ADV—Do you know what it is?
CP/word billing, being consistent
Cross training, writing down
    what we do
Notes: Vacations, Turkey, & Star

August
Client reviews as of August
Organizing the file room
New trading order list
Notes

September
Client reviews September
401K plan
Visit ISG
EBK picnic
Notes

October
Client reviews October
Newsletter
Prospect files (how long to
    keep?)
Intern
Notes

November
Client reviews as of November
New centerpiece
End-of-year planning
Odds and ends
Notes

December
Office policy update
Managers' performance report
Keeping wall calendar update
Schwab tickets

January
How do we spend our time?
Let's talk quarterlies
Transfers
Leaving early
Investment Committee report

March
Appointments
Review final quarterly
Trades on Schwablink
Schwab—how to review
    statements
Advanced Word

INVESTMENT COMMITTEE AGENDA—EXAMPLES

May

New allocations; proposed changes to model

Large-cap value, DFA, and passive story

Scudder International Bond

Wealth Management real estate allocation

Tactical models

December

Funds: JP Morgan, Russell, Turner

Variable Annuities: Providian

Montgomery Institutional Funds

Beginning-of-year trading

Allocation modifications

February

Market volatility: Options

Investing schedule
   Modified dollar cost averaging

New manager prospects

Projections

March

Funds: DFA new equity strategy, Federated bond index, Greenspring

EB&K Policies
Rebalancing
Account size

FIRM RETREAT

Time	Activity
8:30–8:45	Introduction: Taking it to the next level—Deena Katz
8:45–9:15	Getting to know you—Peter Brown
9:15–9:30	Break
9:30–11:30	Case Studies (The Associate Advisors played the role of Advisor and the other staff members played the roles of clients and receptionist)

Mr. & Mrs. Client—Prospect & Data Gathering
   Clients—Advisor & Officer Manager
   Receptionist—Deena Katz

Mr. & Mrs. Client—Plan Delivery &
   Opening Accounts
   Clients—Peter Brown & Receptionist
   Receptionist—Harold Evensky

Mr. & Mrs. Client—Prospect & Data Gathering
Clients—Advisor & Secretary
Receptionist—Advisor

11:30–12:00	Case critiques: What can we take back to the office?
12:00–1:00	Lunch and general discussion
1:00–1:30	Encounter group: "The thing that drives me crazy is . . ."
1:00–3:00	Team building: How do we interact and how can we do better?
3:00–3:15	Break
3:15–4:30	Brainstorming: Standardization versus Customization
4:30–5:00	Business/Personal goals for next year

EB&K Client Communications

QUARTERLY LETTERS

August 30, 1995

Enclosed is your review through July 31, 1995. Another three months of record performances. Since the beginning of 1995, some sectors of the domestic market have seemingly ignored fundamentals and enjoyed a spectacular binge. With the Dow surging over 800 points in seven months, it is a little difficult to keep long-term portfolio performance in perspective. Because your portfolio is not 100 percent invested in the few hot sectors, it might be appropriate to step back and look at the returns of all the major asset classes. It is also a good time to reconsider the risk of buying into the hot class of the current cycle. Towards that end, let's look back at past performance for the end of the second quarter from 1992 through 1995:

Ranking By Asset Class

	6/95	6/94	6/93	6/92
Donoghue MMA	7	4	8	4
Salomon 1–3 Yr	6	5	4	3
Lipper Gen'l Muni	8	6	1	2
Merrill Global Bond	5	2	6	1
S&P W/Div	2	8	7	7
Lipper Equity Income	3	7	3	6
S&P Barra Value	4	9	2	5
Russell 2000	1	10	5	8
EAFE	9	3	9	9
MS Far East	10	1	10	10

You'll notice that in June 95, small-cap and large-cap domestic ranked 1 and 2 while municipals and foreign stock ranked 8, 9, and 10. All lost money, and the emerging markets were off over 4 percent. Does that mean everyone should jump from bonds and foreign stock to domestic equities? Not unless you like to sell low and buy high. Look back one year. Small cap was ranked last (and lost money) while emerging markets ranked 1.

A year before that emerging markets ranked last, small cap is a middling 5th place, and municipals lead the pack. The moral is, markets go up and down in different cycles. Asset allocation may mean that you'll never have all of your funds in the hot sector but you'll never have them all in the worst sector either. Unless you believe in market timing (we don't), enjoy your more modest gains and don't get jealous of short-term market lottery winners. Your house is built of bricks, theirs of straw.

October 31, 1995

Enclosed is your review for September 30, 1995. The domestic market is still enjoying extraordinary performance. We, once again, remind you to enjoy the ride but remain realistic. Are we telling you to prepare for a market correction? Financial experts every day say we are due for a correction. My car's due for a wash, too. So what? We've had at least 29 corrections of 10 percent or more since World War II. And, after a bitter winter, the sun breaks through and buds appear on the trees. And, long-term investors keep making money because they are not trying to time the market.

Speaking of seasons, as September fades and everyone is back from vacation, it's a good time to step back and look at your other financial planning issues. When was the last time you reviewed your property/casualty insurance coverage? Is your umbrella liability coverage appropriate? How current is your will and do you have durable powers and health care powers?

Remember, as your advisors, we encourage you to bring your questions and discuss your financial planning needs with us.

December 4, 1995

Sometimes things just aren't what they seem. Last month many investors were confused to find that their portfolios were down slightly. How could that be when the media kept hyping the market's record-breaking returns? The answer is—markets are volatile, especially in the short term, and the Dow is not "the market." In fact it's not even the U.S. market.

As you'll see from the table and graph attached, October was not such a terrific month; all major equity markets were down. Even the Dow was not much to write home about. The moral is don't watch and worry about the market's short-term volatility. Remember five years, five years, five years and go about enjoying your life.

Cordially yours,
Deena Katz, CFP
President

HIGHLIGHTS OF THE   AUGUST 1995
ECONOMY AND THE MARKETS

During the first eight months of 1995, you couldn't have asked any more from the U.S. equity markets without seeming greedy. Good news, bad news, the markets just kept on rising. Bonds didn't do so badly either. Only the international markets stayed away from the party, with the outlook for the Japanese economy still looking reasonably grim. Well, summer came and even the internationals perked up a little.

If you thought the Dow Jones Industrials were in nosebleed territory when they hit 4100 in March, look again. They were sitting at 4556 by the end of June and after breaking through 4700 in July, they settled at 4611 at the end of August. The S&P 500 gained 8.8 percent in the second quarter, while the small-cap Russell 2000 Index, though appreciably lagging its larger brethren for the year, rose 8.75 percent over the April–June period. Even the Dow Transports and Utilities attended the party. The latter performed well in anticipation of lower interest rates. Of course, if you really wanted to be where the action was, semiconductors were the answer, sprinting ahead over 45 percent in just 90 days. So where was the gloom? Japan with the world's second largest stock market, seems to be heading for a recession after four years of economic stagnation. Its Nikkei stock average, which had fallen 62 percent since 1989, and thought to be still too high, has recently rallied. Some estimates put the overvaluation of Japan's assets at $7.7 trillion. In addition to Japan's dismal economic outlook, performance in other world markets has been nothing to write home about.

Because the economy looked like it was slowing down, the Fed actually lowered interest rates. Bonds, until late spring, had been behaving like stocks, with prices rising as rates fell. By the end of the second quarter, the 30-year Treasury yield had fallen to 6.62 percent, from 7.87 percent at the end of 1994. During the same stretch, the 5-year and 2-year paper rates fell from 7.84 percent and 7.69 percent to 5.96 percent and 5.79 percent, respectively.

Although everything has gone right for the U.S. markets recently, there are some clouds on the horizon. The excess supply of dollars in the world is growing by $12 billion a month and the trade deficit isn't getting any better. Additionally, the slowdown in the domestic economy seems to be accelerating. The leading economic indicators have been falling and consumer confidence is not upbeat. Somewhere down the road we must pay for all the fun we are having now.

HIGHLIGHTS OF THE   NOVEMBER 1995
ECONOMY AND THE MARKETS

For the first three quarters of 1995, the U.S. stock markets went from one new peak to another, with most of the popular averages ending September within hailing distance of their all-time highs. October brought some bad days and much churning, but there were only small losses by month end. It seemed the euphoria was about to end. Well, along came November and unless you were a semiconductor, life was wonderful. The Dow broke 5000 and managed to end the month at 5074.

Overseas, market performance has been quite lackluster this year. The broad-based EAFE Index has risen a mere 5.5 percent through three quarters .Meanwhile, returns in the emerging markets have been negative on balance. As far as Japan is concerned, depending on the day and who you're talking to, the market is either poised for a major recovery from its multiyear depression or just taking a breather before tumbling to new lows. There are good arguments on both sides.

The bond markets have turned in solid performances so far in 1995. After being hammered in 1994, long-term government bonds have rallied and yields are at their lowest point in almost two years. Muni bonds, while recovering nicely, have lagged governments and corporates because of fears related to the possibility of a "flat income tax," and the resulting loss of the advantages of muni paper.

Looking at the economy, we are now four and a half years into this expansion and a slowdown may not be far off. Corporate investment is strong, but consumer spending is diminishing while the level of debt is at a record high. Bankruptcies and loan delinquencies continue to climb. One of the remaining bright spots is the continuing low inflation. It appears that once again this figure will come in under 3 percent for the year. Furthermore, the government is studying a proposal to revise the CPI calculation, which would knock about a percentage point a year off the index. Such a move would reduce cost of living increases on such items as Social Security payments and other inflation-adjusted federal programs—a slick way to reduce the budget deficit. Well, we can at least enjoy the good times while they last.

HIGHLIGHTS OF THE   FEBRUARY 1996
ECONOMY AND THE MARKETS

It was quite a party the domestic stock and bond markets threw in 1995. Everyone, except for possibly a few short-sellers, had a wonderful time. Stocks soared as interest rates fell, which in turn led to a dynamic bond market. In the meantime, the economy went nowhere and the year ended with Congress and the President fighting over how and when to balance the budget. Everyone said 1996 would be different. While the Dow continues to make new highs, ending February just below 5500, the balance of the indexes has started to flag. Small caps haven't been robust and the techies have gotten slammed. Even bonds have weakened over the last few weeks.

There is hardly a person alive who doesn't know that the Dow, the S&P 500, and the NASDAQ soared from one new peak to the next in 1995. Each of these indexes gained over 30 percent during the year. It was the year Wall Street met and fell in love with the Internet and any stock related to this phenomenon. Among the other top market performers were technology, biotechnology, oil drilling, and banking stocks.

Overseas results were a mixed bag. Europe was generally up, Asia was flat, and the emerging markets, down. The Japanese stock market, the largest outside the United States, plunged during the first half of 1995 and rallied in the second half, finishing the year up less than 1 percent. Elsewhere, our neighbor Mexico had another disastrous year, with the Bolsa falling 27 percent in U.S. dollars. The rest of Latin America performed almost as poorly.

Alan Greenspan said the economy was going to have a soft landing and so far, so good. After raising interest rates early in 1995, the Fed cut them twice at year's end. As a result, long-term government rates topped out at 7.9 percent in January and finished the year at 5.94 percent, producing significant capital gains for bondholders. Munis fared well, but were not in the same ballpark as their taxable brethren. The cloud of a flat-tax and its ramifications kept a lid on this market.

Looking at the economy, we are seeing evidence of a slowdown. Retail sales in 1995 were poor, with an especially dismal holiday season. There has been continued pressure on industrial output and employment, as businesses adjust their inventories to more desirable levels. Consumer confidence is not buoyant and inflation was 2.5 percent for the year. All things considered, it does not appear that the economy is about to bloom. In this environment, why are stock prices so high?

Alpha Bylaws (5/2/94)

ARTICLE I. MISSION

The Alpha Group is a membership of nationally recognized and respected fee-based investment consultants who believe that the financial planning process and perspective is a fundamental part of prudent investment management. Alpha Group members are dedicated to learning, sharing and expanding, at the very highest level, technical and professional knowledge regarding all aspects of individual portfolio management. Members support each other individually and collectively in areas of investment research, practice management and practice development, in order to further each member's professional and financial success.

ARTICLE II. GOALS

To be on the technical and intellectual forefront of planning oriented professional investment advisors in order to provide superior service to the members' clients and to advance the knowledge and the overall quality of the profession.

To increase the public recognition and acceptance of each member and his or her firm.

To work with and motivate vendors, suppliers and others to develop and/or modify vehicles to better serve the members, clients of members and other professionals.

To share with non-member professionals, professional associations and the professional and public media, the expertise of the members for the benefit of the members, the profession and the public.

ARTICLE III. POLICIES

Membership
Membership in Alpha is open to principals of fee based, financial planning oriented investment advisory firms. Specific admission requirements are determined by unanimous agreement of all Alpha members.

Membership is individual.

There shall be no more than two members per firm.

No member shall be admitted to membership or remain a member if they have, or expect to develop, a significant practice in the marketing area of any existing member.

Admission of new members shall require a unanimous vote of all members.

Revocation of membership without specific cause requires a unanimous vote of all members except the member(s) under consideration. Revocation of membership for failure to abide by the by-laws shall require a 2/3 vote of all members except the member(s) under consideration.

All balloting regarding membership shall be by secret ballot.

Member Obligations

Commitments proposed during a regularly scheduled phone conference to any project requiring over $1,000 or a time commitment in excess of one day/firm shall require a 3/4 vote of all member firms voting. However, similar commitments proposed during a regularly scheduled "out of office" meeting will require a 3/4 vote of all member firms voting but no less than five member firms voting affirmatively.

Commitment for any project requiring less than $1,000 or a time commitment less than one day/firm shall require a majority vote of all member firms participating in a regularly scheduled meeting or phone conferences.

Once an Alpha commitment has been made, all members and member firms are expected to participate equally, unless an exception is voted by 3/4 of all member firms (except the member appealing).

Individual members are expected to attend at least 2 out of every 3 regularly scheduled "out of office" meetings and attend at least 2 out of every 3 regularly scheduled phone meetings.

Alpha assignments shall be equally apportioned. Each member shall faithfully and punctually complete all designated Alpha assignments.

Expenses proportionate to the participation of firms shall be apportioned by firms. Expenses proportionate to individuals shall be apportioned by individuals.

All members agree to abide by the Code of Ethics of the CFP Board of Standards and to maintain the confidentiality of all information shared by other Alpha members and their firms. All members agree to sign a confidentiality agreement.

ARTICLE IV. MEETINGS

There will be at least two regularly scheduled meetings annually.

There will be regular monthly one-hour telephone conference business calls. The calls will be scheduled by majority agreement of the members.

There will be regular monthly one-hour telephone conference manager calls. The calls will be scheduled by the member responsible for that call.

ARTICLE VI. AMENDMENTS

Amendments shall be by 3/4 vote of the members.

INDEX